The Conseque͟ ͟ ͟ ͟ ͟ ͟ Honour:

Bonaparte, Britain and the Peace of Amiens

By Mark Grenville Lucas

Published by Lulu

Copyright © Mark Grenville Lucas 2013

ISBN: 978-1-304-11603-1

2013.07.13

In memory of my father Edward Lucas (1929–1980), a diplomat, and my friend Bruno Derrick (1961–2012), an archivist.

Cover Illustrations

Front Cover:

Jules Claude Ziegler (1804 – 1856) "La Paix d'Amiens", 1853, collection du Musée de Picardie (photo Irwin Leullier / Musée de Picardie), no inv. M.P.D.55.

Scene depicting the signing of the Treaty of Amiens in the city town hall. Joseph Bonaparte and Cornwallis are shaking hands in the centre. The Dutchman Schimmelpenninck on the left is signing the Treaty and the Spanish Chevalier d'Azara on the right is putting his seal to it.

Back Cover:

James Gillray (1756 – 1815) "Armed Heroes", 1803, Bohn Edition of 1849 – 1851, author's private collection.

Bonaparte:

"Ah! Ha. Sacre Dieu! Vat do I see yonder? Dat looks invitingly red & de vite? Oh by gar! I see 'tis de Roast Beef of Londres vich I vill chop up, at von letel bite!"

Addington (standing over the roast beef of old England):

"Who's afraid? Dam'me! (O Lord, O Lord. What a firey fellow he is!) Who's afraid? Dam'me! (O Dear! What will become of ye Roast Beef?) Dam'me! Who's afraid?"

Table of Contents

Acknowledgements

I would like to thank my partner Beata, who has patiently tolerated my obsession to finish this book and has constantly encouraged me to continue. I am also grateful to my sister Jocelyn, who kindly agreed to design my book cover, my brother Gavin and Diana Ingrey for providing last-minute criticism and advice.

I would like to thank my editor, Christopher Summerville, who kindly agreed to provide a service tailored to the tight constraints of my self-publishing budget. As a consequence of his help and advice, I have corrected and revised a significant portion of my text. Any mistakes that remain must be considered as purely my own. I am grateful for the staff at the French Diplomatic archives and Gauthier Gillman of the Musée de Picardie: the former for helping me how to view and copy documents from microfiche, the latter for providing the image for the book cover and them all for tolerating my poor French. I would also like to thank Laurence Hepworth at Look and Learn for licensing most of the illustrations inside this book and Yale University Art Gallery for the picture of Louis Guillaume Otto.

My thanks are also due for Palgrave Macmillan for allowing me to reproduce an English translation of dialogue quotes from Lucien Bonaparte's memoirs used in the book, *Napoleon and the Rebel*, By Simonetta and Arikha.

I would like to mention my appreciation for those organisations that provide access to old books on the internet, especially Google Books and Archive.org. I recognise Google's book scanning project has generated significant controversy, but I believe I have only been able to access complete copies of those works out of copyright. Without this mode of research, and because I work full-time in a completely unrelated sphere, I am not sure I could ever have contemplated writing this book by relying on traditional resources. Nevertheless, the traditional resources played a vital part, so I would also like to thank the staff of those traditional institutions, notably those of the British Library and the National Archives in Kew. At Kew I had the help of my friend Bruno Derrick, whose opinion I valued as much as his friendship, but whose recent tragic death in December 2012 deprived me of both, and whom I can now only thank posthumously.

Maps

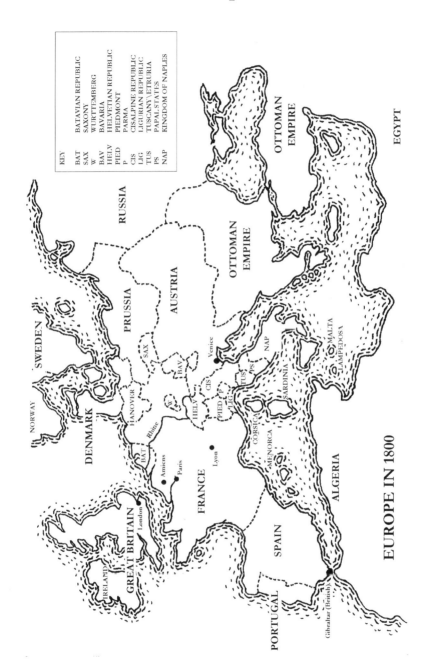

EUROPE IN 1800

KEY	
BAT	BATAVIAN REPUBLIC
SAX	SAXONY
W	WURTTEMBERG
BAV	BAVARIA
HELV	HELVETIAN REPUBLIC
PIED	PIEDMONT
P	PARMA
CIS	CISALPINE REPUBLIC
LIG	LIGURIAN REPUBLIC
TUS	TUSCANY/ETRURIA
PS	PAPAL STATES
NAP	KINGDOM OF NAPLES

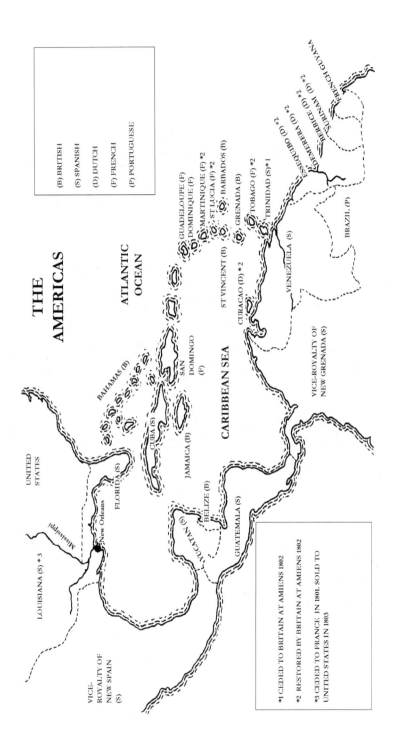

THE AMERICAS

ATLANTIC OCEAN

CARIBBEAN SEA

(B) BRITISH
(S) SPANISH
(D) DUTCH
(F) FRENCH
(P) PORTUGUESE

UNITED STATES

Mississippi

New Orleans

LOUISIANA (S) * 3

VICE-ROYALTY OF NEW SPAIN (S)

FLORIDA (S)

BAHAMAS (B)

CUBA (S)

JAMAICA (B)

SAN DOMINGO (F)

BELIZE (B)

YUCATAN (S)

GUATEMALA (S)

GUADELOUPE (F)
DOMINIQUE (F)
MARTINIQUE (F) *2
ST LUCIA (F) *2
BARBADOS (B)

ST VINCENT (B)

GRENADA (B)

CURACAO (D) * 2

TOBAGO (F) *2

TRINIDAD (S)* 1

VENEZUELA (S)

VICE-ROYALTY OF NEW GRENADA (S)

ESSEQUIBO (D) (D)* 2
DEMERERA (D) * 2
BERBICE (D) (D) * 2
SURINAM (D)
FRENCH GUYANA

BRAZIL (P)

*1 CEDED TO BRITAIN AT AMIENS 1802

*2 RESTORED BY BRITAIN AT AMIENS 1802

*3 CEDED TO FRANCE IN 1801. SOLD TO UNITED STATES IN 1803

THE EAST INDIES

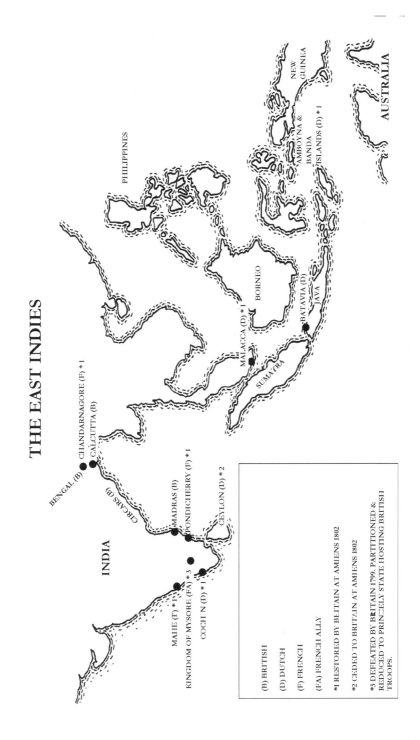

PHILIPPINES

NEW GUINEA

AMBOYNA &
BANDA
ISLANDS (D) * 1

BORNEO

BATAVIA (D)

JAVA

MALACCA (D) * 1

SUMATRA

AUSTRALIA

CHANDARNAGORE (F) * 1

CALCUTTA (B)

BENGAL (B)

CIRCARS (D)

INDIA

MADRAS (B)

PONDICHERRY (F) * 1

CEYLON (D) * 2

MAHE (F) * 1

KINGDOM OF MYSORE (FA) * 3

COCHIN (D) * 1

(B) BRITISH

(D) DUTCH

(F) FRENCH

(FA) FRENCH ALLY

*1 RESTORED BY BRITAIN AT AMIENS 1802

*2 CEDED TO BRITAIN AT AMIENS 1802

*3 DEFEATED BY BRITAIN 1799. PARTITIONED &
REDUCED TO PRINCELY STATE HOSTING BRITISH
TROOPS.

11

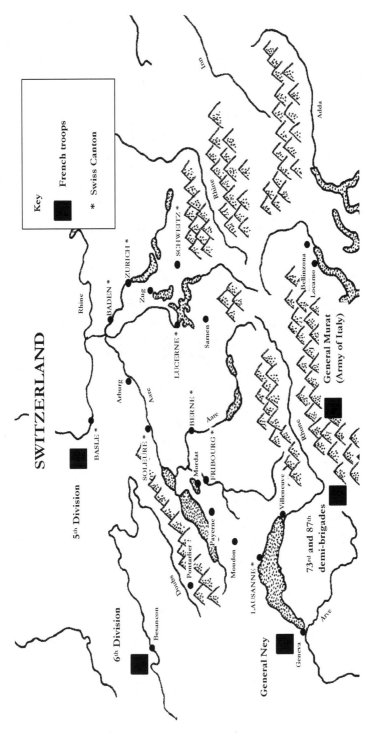

SWITZERLAND

Key

French troops

* Swiss Canton

5th Division

6th Division

General Ney

General Murat
(Army of Italy)

73rd and 87th demi-brigades

Rhine

Inn

Adda

BASLE *

BADEN *

ZURICH *

SCHWEITZ *

Zug

LUCERNE *

Samen

Arburg

Aare

BERNE *

SOLEURE *

FRIBOURG *

Mordat

Payerne

Moudon

Pontardier

Doubs

Besancon

LAUSANNE *

Villeneuve

Rhone

Geneva

Arve

Bellinzona

Locarno

Rhine

Illustrations

PROLOGUE

The English artillery officer, Captain Mercer, found it difficult to sleep doubled up on the footboard of a gun carriage. He decided to get up and walk around. It was cold and damp, and in the pale moonlight he could see the thousands of corpses that surrounded him. Scattered among the dead were soldiers still clinging to life: some seeking to stem the flow of blood from seeping wounds, some struggling to rise, some staggering a few steps only to collapse from exhaustion. The human misery was mirrored by that of many horses, some trying to get up, but unable to move, some with their entrails out, one with both its hind legs shot off neighing pitifully as if exhorting for help. Mercer realised that killing the poor animal would have been a mercy, but could not find the courage even to give the order, sickened at the thought of spilling yet more blood.

A little further away, Prussian soldiers were plundering the dead and the helpless – enemies and allies were both fair game. A young English ensign, his legs crushed by a gun-carriage, was killed by one of them after refusing to give up a trinket. Another wounded English officer, lying nearby, would have suffered the same fate, but the marauding Prussian was shot by two English soldiers who then stripped him. They apologised for not helping the cold and thirsty officer with the excuse that had they done so, their absence from their regiment would have been noted. Another English officer, Colonel Ponsonby, suffering from a lance wound in the back was luckier. When he was found by a man in an English uniform he had already been pillaged by a French skirmisher and roughly searched by a disappointed Prussian. The weight of a noisy, dying soldier with air issuing from a side-wound lay across his legs. His rescuer moved the soldier and then stood guard over Ponsonby with a sword until the morning when a cart arrived, conveying him to the village of Waterloo.

When Major Harry Smith of the 95th Rifles awoke, the whole field from left to right was a mass of dead bodies: eight square miles of tens of thousands of dead, dying and wounded soldiers. One of the highest heaps was to the right of the La Haye Sainte farmhouse. Here French cavalrymen, breast-plated cuirassiers, lay piled on top of each other, some still alive and trapped by their horses. All around were officers and soldiers weeping over dead or dying comrades. Many of those Captain Mercer had seen struggling to survive the night were now motionless. He endeavoured to get his troop of artillery ready to move on. They rounded up stray horses and scavenged for equipment to replace what they had lost the day before, in which Mercer estimated that his battery had fired 700 rounds per gun. Despite his military responsibilities, he could not ignore the misery that still surrounded him. He tried to calm two Irish light infantrymen who were lying in a hollow, howling and swearing profusely. One had a leg shot off, the other his thigh smashed by cannon shot. When he failed and walked away, they shouted abuse after him, making him feel like a hard-hearted wretch leaving two poor fellows to die like dogs. There were simply too many to help.

Thirst often dominated a wounded man's thoughts. A grenadier of the French Guards, his bowels hanging out, begged to drink from the bowl of water just used to wash the wounds of a hussar. All Mercer could do was order his men to fill their canteens with water from a well in the nearby chateau of Hougoumont and disperse it among as many of the wounded as they could. Hougoumont was a pitiful sight, its trees smashed and splintered, its buildings ravaged by a fire that had spread from a large barn, which now contained the charred remains of those caught inside. Among the ruins survivors were bandaging their own wounds.

The greatest fear of the French wounded was to be plundered and murdered by the numerous groups of Belgian peasants that were picking their way through them. Unlike the Prussian soldiers who wanted small valuables, the peasants were prepared to take everything, including the clothes, and many of them were indifferent to whether their prey was alive or dead. If they were alive and resisted, they might be killed. The peasants staggered away with as much clothing their arms could carry, many of them overtly enjoying their good fortune. When Mercer offered water to the French wounded, they were particularly grateful, but when he tried to leave them they pleaded with him to stay, fearing they would be murdered by the peasants as soon as Mercer and his troops had left. Mercer tried to assure them that carts would be sent to pick them up, but to no avail. "Ah, Monsieur, tuez moi donc! Tuez moi, pour l'amour de Dieu!" They would rather die a soldier's death, be killed by an enemy soldier, than be murdered by a villainous peasant. Only one Frenchman was ungrateful, an angry lancer who refused Mercer's water with an emphatic "Non!"

The wounded that survived the cold nights, the dehydration and the pillaging soldiers and peasants would eventually be carted to makeshift hospitals in Brussels nine miles away, although many would remain in churches around Waterloo for weeks. The unclaimed dead were buried in their hundreds in long lines of pits, from which, before they were covered, an appalling stink poisoned the air. Even with all the bodies gone, the fields remained cluttered with debris: caps, shoes, gloves, belts, scabbards, bits of cloth, fur or leather, playing cards and books (including a volume of *Candide* and numerous German bibles), French military papers, sheets of martial music, private letters ...[1]

What triggered this slaughter? The battle of Waterloo in 1815 was the conclusion of a sequence of events starting a hundred days earlier when Napoleon Bonaparte escaped from the island of Elba, marched on Paris and restored himself as Emperor of the French. Waterloo happened because the European powers that had obliged him to abdicate the previous year feared that a France ruled by Bonaparte would always be a threat. This fear was founded on his record of ten years of bloody campaigning throughout Europe, extending his power and the influence of France at the expense of their own.

Britain was the first country to be threatened with invasion by Napoleon, but avoided this fate when Admiral Nelson destroyed the Franco-Spanish fleet at Trafalgar. Austria was the first to suffer. After the battle of Austerlitz in 1805, Austria lost Venice and Tyrol and paid France an indemnity of forty million Francs. An attempt to re-assert itself in 1809 by invading Bavaria was thwarted at Wagram, costing the Austrian empire another indemnity, its Balkan provinces of Croatia, Dalmatia, Slovenia and Trieste and its Polish lands of West and East Galicia.

Prussia was crushed at Jena in 1806 and Russia defeated at Friedland in 1807. The Treaty of Tilsit created the Grand Duchy of Warsaw from Prussian Poland and obliged the vanquished powers to recognise Bonaparte's brothers as Kings of Westphalia, Naples and Holland. Sixteen German states formed the Confederation of the Rhine under the presidency of Napoleon.

In 1808 Napoleon deposed the Spanish Bourbons and imposed his brother Joseph on the throne of Spain, provoking an insurrection which forced Joseph out of Madrid and defeated the French at Baylen. Napoleon led an army into the peninsular, forcing out a British expedition from Corunna in 1809. In Portugal, the French failed to dislodge another British force under the Duke of Wellington, who took the fight into Spain

---

[1] Herold pp.141-142, Naylor pp.174-185

The Consequences of Honour

in 1811. After beating the French at Salamanca and Vitoria, the Duke chased the French across the Pyrenees before defeating them on their own soil at Toulouse in 1814.

The success of the British in Portugal and Spain was complemented by their economic blockade of the rest of the continent. After his plans for invading Britain had been dashed by Trafalgar, Napoleon could only strike at Britain through its commerce. In 1803 he had occupied Hanover and closed the Elbe and Weser rivers to British trade. His Berlin and Milan decrees in 1806 forbade French satellites, then neutral countries, from trading with Britain. In response the British Royal Navy, its domination of the seas secured by Trafalgar, blockaded ports from Brest to the Elbe, causing severe economic hardship. In his determination to destroy England, Napoleon obliged the European powers he had defeated to enforce controls on their trade, encouraging a resentment that manifested into resistance when an opportunity arose.

When in 1810 the Tsar relaxed the enforcement of Napoleon's Continental System, he provoked the French Emperor into a disastrous invasion of Russia in 1812. Although Napoleon forced the Russians to give up Moscow at the battle of Borodino, he decided on a withdrawal that tumbled into a retreat through the merciless winter-stricken steppes. By 1813, both Austria and Prussia had re-joined Russia and Britain in a new coalition against France. They defeated Bonaparte at Leipzig in 1813 and by 1814 were fighting him in France. In April that year, Napoleon abdicated and was exiled to the island of Elba. The allies restored the French Bourbons, whose unpopularity made Bonaparte's brief return to power in 1815 so easy.

Waterloo was not just the conclusion of a hundred days of drama, but the end to a conflict that had raged since 1803. Throughout this time, Britain alone remained a constant enemy, and it was with Britain that the struggle began. In 1803 Britain declared war on France, ending a short peace concluded at Amiens only the year before, a peace that had ended the French Revolutionary Wars. Although this peace divides the latter conflict from the Napoleonic Wars, they are often seen as two epochs of a wider conflict, with the peace just a truce, the eye of great storm. The peace did not resolve the tensions straining beneath the changes in Europe that the Revolution had wrought.

Despite the immense literature on Napoleonic history, there is very little dedicated to telling the story of the Peace of Amiens, yet it deserves as much attention as the great military events like Trafalgar,

Austerlitz, the Retreat from Moscow and Waterloo. It is often told in books with a wide scope, such as Charles Esdaile's *Napoleon's Wars*, which devotes a whole chapter to it, but rarely as a topic in its own right. The only contemporary book on the Peace in English is John Grainger's *The Amiens Truce*. This is a thorough examination, but a high density of facts and analysis make it a serious read, while it admits to being told mainly from the British perspective. A French perspective can be gleaned from *La Paix Amiens*, but this is a compilation of articles by French academics and not available in English. The Peace and British politics at the time is well covered by Charles Fedorak's *Henry Addington*, but this is more of a biography focusing on Addington's ministry. The kind of book I wanted to read about the Peace was nearly satisfied by *The Terror before Trafalgar* by Tom Pocock, but its emphasis was on Nelson and the naval war.

The following is my attempt to address this gap in contemporary Napoleonic literature. It is a narrative of this period of calm, of how it came about, of what it allowed, and of how it broke down. Although the main theme is the diplomatic story, the book also covers the internal politics and personalities of the two countries at the time. To take a break from the politics I also explore the experiences of visitors to Paris during the Peace and focus on Napoleon's private life, as I feel this is just as much a story about him as anything else. It is a narrative rather than analytic history, so I try to keep my own commentary to a minimum. I have consciously tried to make it an interesting read, so have used a wide range of sources. As some of these sources are considered unreliable by some historians, I have included some comments on these in an appendix to avoid interrupting the narrative flow.

PART 1: THE PURSUIT OF PEACE

1 King George III

Illustration from Cassell's *History of the United States* by Edward Ollier (c 1900). (Look and Learn collections)

1. A Christmas Message

Windsor Castle, perched on a hill on the south bank of the river Thames, twenty miles west of London, was the favourite residence of King George III of England. It was here that he and his family spent the Christmas of 1799. The King was in a good mood, as the youngest of his many daughters, the sixteen year-old Princess Amelia, had just recovered from an illness. On Christmas day, he enjoyed the solemnity and propriety with which the Archbishop of Canterbury administered Holy Communion in St George's Chapel. He was also so delighted with the sermon delivered by the Bishop of St David's that he later promised to find the prelate a more lucrative bishopric when the appropriate opportunity arose. He particularly appreciated that the Bishop's sermons were on Christianity, not on mere moral subjects.[1] A few days later, a reminder came of perhaps the greatest moral subject of the day. He received an unexpected letter from France addressed to him personally. It had been enclosed in a diplomatic despatch to the British Foreign Secretary, Lord Grenville, from the enemy Foreign Minister, Talleyrand.

The writer, after introducing himself as the ruler of France, got to the point. Was the war they had been fighting for eight years to last forever? Were there no means of coming to an understanding? How could their two nations, with more power than they needed for their own security, continue to sacrifice their resources and people to "ideas of vain glory"? Why did they not feel that peace was their first priority and bring them both the greater glory? The author proposed a "general pacification" to end the war that had engulfed the whole world. The letter was signed: "Bonaparte".[2]

Napoleon Bonaparte had come to power in France a month earlier in a military coup which overthrew the previous revolutionary government known as the Directory. It was now over ten years since the Revolution had erupted and for most of this time the French had been at

---

[1] Jesse vol. IV pp.447-450

[2] OPRP p.2

war with much of Europe, including England. In 1789 France had been ruled by the Bourbon King Louis XVI. He was an absolute monarch, but considered himself merely the steward of the nation's finances, which were in crisis. Louis had spent a great deal supporting the American colonies' fight for their independence from England and had been unable to meet the consequent deficit with his usual revenues. To raise new taxes the King summoned representatives of the people in the form of an ancient institution called the Estates General in the hope they would oblige. Unfortunately for him, the delegates of the common people, the Third Estate, had their own agenda. Supported by the Paris mob, they transformed themselves into a national legislative assembly intent on reform. They abolished feudalism, created an elective judiciary and curtailed the power and independence of the Catholic Church by appropriating its land, dissolving its ecclesiastical orders and requiring the clergy to be publicly elected. By 1791 the King's political power was limited to a temporary veto, while his personal freedom, and that of his family, was threatened by increasingly violent citizens of Paris. Disaffected nobles had fled the country and formed a counter-revolutionary army of émigrés in the Rhineland. An attempt by the King to join them was thwarted, resulting in his eventual imprisonment. Alarmed at this turn of events, Austria and Prussia made a joint declaration at Pilnitz. They invited other countries to join them to attack France unless it restored Louis to his throne with full powers. Angered by this, the French declared war against Austria, beginning in 1792 the conflict that was still raging in 1799.

Initially the war went badly for France, which had the effect of bringing to power the radical mob-rousing Jacobins. In the autumn of 1792, the monarchy was abolished and a republic declared. The new assembly, called the National Convention, was elected by universal suffrage. It introduced a national education system, abolished slavery in French colonies and repealed the law of primogeniture. In December it tried the King for treason and in January 1793, executed him. The Jacobins, under their leader Robespierre, ruled France from April via the Committee of Public Safety. Faced with uprisings within France, as well foreign foes, the Committee encouraged its citizens to defend and promote the Revolution by guillotining its suspected opponents, including the late King's wife, Queen Marie-Antoinette. This coincided with a reversal in the fortunes of war in France's favour. An anti-Jacobin uprising in the southern port of Toulon (supported by the British Royal Navy) was crushed, mainly due to the efforts of the Corsican-born commander of siege artillery, Napoleon Bonaparte. By the summer of 1794 the allied powers had been driven out of France and Belgium while

Holland, Prussia and Spain had withdrawn from the conflict. However, as the Terror Robespierre inflicted on France began to run out of real counter-revolutionaries, aristocrats and priests, it turned on anyone who questioned the Jacobins, and then any Jacobin that dared question Robespierre. In July, a group of surviving members of the Convention pre-empted their turn at the tribunals and overthrew Robespierre, promptly sending him to the guillotine instead.[1]

In 1795 the French changed their constitution again, creating two separate legislatures and an executive team of five members called the Directory. Some attempts at peace were made, but the war continued. Bonaparte, despite his achievement at Toulon, was initially distrusted by the Directory because of close ties with Robespierre's brother, but his successful quelling of a royalist uprising in Paris earned his promotion to command of the French army in Italy. Within two years he had defeated the Austrians there and forced them to make peace at Campo Formio in October 1797. The Treaty obliged Austria to recognise the French acquisition of Belgium, along with the left bank of the Rhine and relinquish Lombardy to a newly formed French satellite, dubbed the Cisalpine Republic. In return Austria was given the previously independent Republic of Venice.

The remaining enemy was Britain, but not for long. In 1798 Bonaparte invaded Egypt, then part of the Ottoman Empire, in the bold hope of threatening the British in India. On the way he captured the small island of Malta which was ruled by the Order of the Knights of St John. This offended the Tsar of Russia who had recently acquired the title of Grand Master of its Polish-Russian chapter. He subsequently joined the British and the Turks in a new coalition against France. Austria, encouraged by money from England and the opportunity of getting back what it lost at Campo-Formio, was coaxed back into the war and by 1799 the French Republic was once again on the defensive. Nelson's sinking of the French fleet off Alexandria isolated Bonaparte's army in Egypt. The unpopular Directory was perceived as incompetent and corrupt by the war-weary French people who were ready for change. In October Bonaparte suddenly appeared in Paris. A month later he emerged as the military leader of the coup d'état that made him the first and most powerful of three consuls of a new centralised government.

---

[1] Leeds pp.1-19

George treated the "Corsican tyrant's letter" with contempt. He did not think Bonaparte would last in power very long. To the Foreign Secretary, Lord Grenville, he complained that it was "impossible to treat with a new, impious, self-created aristocracy". There was no way he was going to reply in person. Grenville would make a formal reply, and not to Bonaparte directly, but to his Foreign Minister, Talleyrand.[1]

In the first week of the new year of 1800, the Cabinet met to consider the peace offer. The King's first minister was William Pitt, who held the post of Chancellor of the Exchequer. Pitt was a thin man with a sharp, slightly upturned and snooty-looking nose. Now in his early forties, he was increasingly susceptible to illnesses. Serious-minded, Pitt did not come across as sociable and was very shy. This often caused people to think him aloof and unfriendly; and with no wife or mistress, suggested the quip that he was stiff to all except the ladies.[2] In 1798 he had formed a fond attachment to the daughter of Lord Auckland, but considered there were "insurmountable obstacles" that barred the transition of their relationship to marriage. Henry Dundas, his War Minister, wagered £500 that Pitt had never touched a woman. However, when amongst friends, he drowned his inhibitions with alcohol that did not hamper a considerable wit.

Pitt was only twenty four years old when he had been appointed by the King in 1782. His great pre-war achievement was to reform the means of financing government. Increasing revenue by £4 million between 1783 and 1792, finding economies in expenditure and rationalising the accounting of it, Pitt managed to reduce the national debt that had accumulated significantly from the war against the American colonies by £10 million. Pitt's greatest challenge came in 1793 when England became embroiled in the war with France. As well as fighting the French, he cracked down on the growing radicalism in Britain. Thomas Paine, author of the *Rights of Man*, was prosecuted in 1792 for libel, obliging him to flee to France. In 1794 the legal principle of Habeas Corpus, restraining the state's ability to imprison without trial, was temporarily suspended. In 1795 public meetings of more than fifty people were forbidden unless sanctioned by a magistrate and the law defining

---

[1] *The Later Correspondence of George III, vol. III,* Cambridge 1967 (p 308). Cited in Cronin p.278

[2] Cited in Gattrell p.19

treason was extended to include merely speaking or writing it. Stamp duty on newspapers was increased; printing presses registered and magistrates given more power to act against blasphemous or seditious articles.[1]

Pitt's key colleagues in the Cabinet, as far as the war was concerned, were Lord Grenville the Foreign Secretary and Henry Dundas the Secretary of State for War. Henry Dundas, a Scottish MP in his late fifties and Pitt's regular drinking companion, had joined Pitt's Cabinet in 1791 as the Home Office minister where he vigorously frustrated attempts to abolish the slave trade. In 1794 Pitt appointed him to the War Office. William Grenville, a cousin of Pitt, had served in his government in the early days and joined the Cabinet as Home Secretary in 1789. In 1790 he became Lord Grenville and then Foreign Secretary in 1791.[2]

At the end of 1799 the war was not going badly for Britain and its allies. In Italy a Bourbon government had been restored to Naples, while Austrian forces controlled the north. England was supreme at sea and had managed to isolate the remnants of the French army Bonaparte had left in Egypt. There was unrest in western France, where pro-royalist insurgents were being supplied by England. There were problems, however. In Switzerland the Austrians had been defeated at Zurich, prompting the Russians to retreat and a British force under the Duke of York had just withdrawn from Holland. Bonaparte's peace offer must have caused the members of the British Cabinet to reflect what it was they were fighting for. For Grenville, who had always advocated the commitment of British forces to the continent, the goal was to restore the French monarchy. However, he did not necessarily insist that the restored monarchy be an absolute one. He would allow the French to have a constitutional model much like England's own. Dundas was more in favour of a colonial and economic struggle to effect the best terms in a compromise peace, but one that would restrict France to her frontiers of 1792. Pitt, although he sympathised with both Dundas and Grenville, was perhaps the most moderate of the three. He only wanted the French to get out of Belgium and take steps to contain its revolution.

Pitt inferred that the reference in Bonaparte's letter to the two countries being more powerful than their security required, suggested a

---

[1] Miller pp.1-14

[2] Derry pp.38-42, Hague p.308

willingness to give up something if England did the same. However, he shared the King's concern about the stability and reliability of the new regime and rather than speculate on probable terms decided they could "have nothing to do but decline all negotiation at the present moment." Despite advocating this firm rejection, Pitt wanted the French to know that England would be eager to treat as soon as it felt the French could be trusted. They should therefore tell the French that "the shortest road to peace is by effecting the restoration of Royalty" while not ruling out the possibility of "treating even with the present Government, if it should prevail and be able to establish itself firmly".[1] Lord Grenville and William Windham the junior Secretary for War agreed. Henry Dundas, Windham's superior, was in Scotland, but Pitt felt that he would be of the same mind. In the meantime they resumed their plans to destabilise the new French government by considering schemes to support royalist uprisings in the west of France.

Grenville replied to Talleyrand on 4 January: "The King has given frequent proofs of his sincere desire for the re-establishment of secure and permanent tranquillity in Europe. He neither is, nor has been, engaged in any contest for a vain and false glory." There was nothing to be gained from negotiating until the ultimate cause of the war ceased to operate – and that was the French revolutionary government and its aggressive policies. As long as this system prevailed, Britain could only offer open and steady hostility and as yet there were no signs that the threat to His Majesty's dominion's had disappeared. If the French really wanted peace they should restore the monarchy, but another form of government would be acceptable to His Majesty as long as long as it was one that did not threaten his interests. "Unhappily no such security hitherto exists: no sufficient evidence of the principles by which the new government will be directed; no reasonable ground to which to judge of its stability. In this situation, it remains only for His Majesty to pursue, in conjunction with other powers, those exertions of just and defensive war."[2]

Talleyrand's response insisted that France had never been the aggressor. It may have declared war on England and its allies but it had been provoked; and if former French governments had not always been

---

[1] Stanhope p.206

[2] OPRP p.3

moderate this was largely due to the animosity of England. But "why instead of attempting the apology of war, should not attention be rather paid to the means of terminating it? And what obstacles can prevent a mutual understanding [...] especially when the First Consul of the French Republic has personally given so many proofs of his eagerness to put an end to the calamities of war, and of his disposition to maintain the rigid observance of all treaties concluded."[1] Grenville retorted that he refused to continue a discourse that engaged him in endless refutations of claims by the French that everyone knew were false.[2]

---

[1] OPRP p.6

[2] OPRP p.8

2 William Pitt

Illustration from *Portraits of Illustrious Personages* by Edmund Lodge (Harding and Lepard, 1832). (Look and Learn Collections)

3 The House of Commons

Illustration from *A Short History of the English People* by J R Green (Macmillan, 1892). Based on a painting by Karl Anton Hickel. (Look and Learn Collections)

2. Peace, not its Shadow

Having rejected the French peace offer, it only remained for the government to explain its decision to Parliament and ask for its confidence. Pitt could usually depend on a healthy majority in both the House of Lords and the Commons. The only regular opposition to speak of was a small minority of Whig MPs led by Charles James Fox. He and many of his followers had absented themselves from attending Parliament for the last three years, a protest against the interference and influence of the Crown in politics.

After becoming an MP in 1768 at nineteen years of age, Fox earned the bitter enmity of King George by opposing the war against the American colonies after they had declared their independence from Britain in 1776. He acquired a reputation for pragmatism or hypocrisy, depending on one's point of view, when in 1781 he formed a government with Lord North who had been the prime minister responsible for prosecuting the war against the American rebels. This government fell when it failed to get sufficient backing for a bill that intended to change the way India was governed by transferring powers of appointment from the Crown to Parliament. Support for the bill collapsed when the King declared that he would regard anyone who voted for it as his personal enemy. Fox returned to opposition, now against Pitt's government. The nearest he came to toppling Pitt was in 1789 when King George went mad. He demanded the King's estranged son and Fox's friend, the Prince of Wales be made Regent, but the King recovered and Pitt held on to office. Fox continued in opposition, campaigning for parliamentary reform and abolition of the slave trade. Considering the French Revolution the "greatest event" in the "history of the world", he advocated peace when England became embroiled in the war with France. Although he deplored the excesses of the Revolution, he thought war would make things worse and would not be in the interests of the country. In 1794 a Whig faction led by Lord Portland deserted the opposition and joined the government, leaving Fox and his supporters increasingly isolated. In 1797 they considered the best strategy for resisting Pitt was to withdraw from Parliament, as conventional opposition seemed to achieve nothing but imply the acceptance of a corrupt system. His last attendance was in April 1798 to support another of Wilberforce's attempts to abolish slavery.[1]

Fox now spent most of his days in a modest country house surrounded by thirty acres of farmland at St Anne's Hill near the village of Chertsey in Surrey. He shared this "seat of true happiness", with its secluded gardens, trellised veranda, fine views of Surrey woodland and countryside, with his partner of over fifteen years, his "dearest Liz" - Mrs Armitstead. She was born Elizabeth Cane in 1750, blessed with little but good looks. Obliged by poverty to earn a living as a brothel prostitute, she attracted the attention of a string of Lords, a General, a Duke and the Prince of Wales, allowing her to rise to the rank of courtesan and own her own property, including St Anne's Hill.[2] Changing her name to Mrs Armitstead, she made friends among the Whigs, including Charles Fox who was whittling away his inheritance on gambling at card tables and horse races, and going through a string of mistresses, "fucking in cundums".[3] In 1784 they became lovers and Fox gradually settled down at St Anne's, restricting his indulgences to literature, conversation, and the charms of Mrs A, whose favours only Fox enjoyed from then on. Fox was now quite fat, but still had plenty of energy. Large sloping dark eyebrows imposed on him a permanent countenance of melancholic indifference or perhaps laid-back surprise, yet he was generally quite jovial, friendly and sociable. He dressed carelessly, often leaving buttons undone, and if cartoon caricatures of him could be trusted, frequently sported a shadow of stubble on his face.[4]

When Fox heard of the government's rejection of Bonaparte's peace offer, he thought that they "must be quite mad."[5] Friends and supporters urged him to return to Parliament to confront Pitt, suggesting that there was a general inclination towards peace and that the King and Cabinet had blundered. On 17 January, Fox wrote to his nephew, Lord

---

[1] Derry pp.14-38,42-51

[2] Davis pp.11-58

[3] Cited in Gattrell p.19

[4] Davis pp.58-114

[5] Cited in Mitchell p.166

Holland: "I have determined, against inclination, common sense, and philosophy to attend upon the question of Bonaparte's letter & etc, and shall be much obliged to you if you will enquire about the time and manner in which it will probably come on."[1] Pitt decided that the correspondence between them and the French would be laid before Parliament on 22 January and the debate would occur on the 27th. Fox left St Anne's Hill and stayed with his nephew at Holland House, planning only to stay two days (so reluctant was he to leave his blissful life with Mrs A). When he then learned that Pitt was ill and the debate was to be delayed he was devastated. His nephew watched him sit in silence, tears stealing down his cheeks, upset at "being detained from his garden, his books, and his cheerful life in the country".[2]

The Lords debated the issue on 28 January. Lord Grenville spoke for the government while Lord Holland and the Duke of Bedford made speeches against. Of the ninety-eight Lords who voted only six went with Lord Holland and the Duke. On 3 February, it was the turn of the Commons. Three hundred and twenty-nine MPs took their seats in the debating chamber of St Stephen's Chapel in the old Palace of Westminster. Pitt would normally enter the Commons "with a quick and firm step, his head erect and thrown back, looking neither to right nor left, nor favouring with a nod or a glance any of the individuals on either side."[3] In contrast, Fox would work his way gradually to the opposition front bench, nodding to a friend here, stopping and chatting to a friend there, exchanging news, gossips and jokes.[4] Henry Dundas began the proceedings by moving that the House approve of the government's decision to continue "the vigorous prosecution of the war".

When Pitt rose to speak, he usually stood stiffly and displayed little emotion. His speech on this occasion began by stating his view of "the French Revolution as the severest trial which the visitation of providence has ever yet inflicted upon the nations of the earth" and reminded the House why they were at war. In November 1793

---

[1] Russell p.195

[2] Cited in Ayling p.202

[3] Cited in Hague p.126(from Wraxall)

[4] Ayling p.139

Revolutionary France had forced the Austrians out of Belgium after defeating them at the battle of Jemappes. France declared their intention to open up the Scheldt estuary to shipping, violating the Treaty of Westphalia of 1648 in which France had agreed to allow the Dutch Republic to keep it closed. In addition the French government had ordered their generals to pursue enemy armies into any neutral country – an implicit threat to Holland. Britain could not tolerate the prospect of so much of the Channel coast closest to its own in the hands of its ancient enemy. To add insult to injury the French Revolutionary government decreed on 19 November in its Edict of Fraternity that it would support any nation in its struggle to free itself from another's control and support any people wishing to overthrow an undemocratic government. This seemed like an explicit threat to encourage discontent in England itself. Britain asked France for a satisfactory explanation of these actions in order to allay its concerns.

The French replied by dismissing Britain's worry about the Scheldt as trivial, suggesting France had a general and natural right to open it up for navigation that overrode any formal treaty. Belgium would be only retained by France as long as it was necessary to consolidate its liberty. As for the decree of 19 November, the French held that it did not encourage sedition in Britain as it only applied to countries where the majority of people were in favour of revolution. France demanded that England disarm and recognise its ambassador Monsieur Chauvelin, as well as accept its explanation of their actions. Any refusal to do so would be treated by France as a declaration of War. Pitt pointed out that it was only after these demands had been made and after the French King had been executed in January that Chauvelin was expelled from England under the Aliens Act as a foreigner suspected of revolutionary principles. In February France declared war on England and Holland. "And on a war thus originating, can it be doubted, by an English House of Commons, whether the aggression was not on the part of this country, or of France? Or whether the manifest aggression on the part of France was the result of anything but the principles which characterise the French Revolution?"

Pitt listed the aggressive actions of France:

- 1791: the seizure of Avignon in France from the Papacy.
- 1792: the seizure of Savoy from the Kingdom of Sardinia, justified by the claim that the Rhine and the Alps were the natural and therefore legitimate boundaries of France.

- The declaration of war on Austria the same year. The French claimed at the time they were provoked by Austria and Prussia's intention to dismember France, a reference to their joint declaration at Pilnitz the previous year. This, Pitt said, was untrue. The declaration's only aim was to rescue the King and only if a sufficiently strong coalition could be formed. The fate of France would have been decided by its restored King. The declaration "did not contain one word relative to the dismemberment of France".

- Then there was Italy in 1796 and 1797: the destruction of Italian states to make way for democratic republics such as Genoa and Tuscany.

When Pitt mentioned the transfer of the previously independent Republic of Venice to Austria as part of a peace deal between the latter and France, he noticed the reaction from the opposition benches: "I observe from the gestures of some honourable gentlemen, that they think we are precluded from the use of any argument founded on this last transaction. I already hear them saying that it was as criminal in Austria to receive, as it was for France to give." But just because Austria "was forced to accept an unjust and insufficient" compensation for what France had taken from it, "are we to be debarred from stating what, on the part of France, was not merely an unjust acquisition, but an act of the grossest and most aggravated perfidy and cruelty" and one of the most striking examples of the policy France applied to any nation within its grasp?

Pitt contrasted France's aggression with his own attempts to make peace. He would have been willing to make peace with France as long as it abandoned its conquests, withdrew to the limits of its territory and promised not to foment revolution against other governments. In return, England and the other powers of Europe would have promised not to interfere in French affairs. The only other terms they would have imposed would be those in the way of compensation for the expense of the war. In 1796 Pitt had tried to make peace from a position of strength on reasonable terms – no partition of France and only a return of some conquests. He dismissed opposition claims that the negotiation faltered only on England's refusal to allow France to keep Belgium – formerly the Austrian Netherlands. No, it failed because France had refused to consider the return of any annexations in any negotiations. Even when Pitt again attempted to make peace in 1797, this time from a much weaker position, it was France that again ruined this opportunity. England's only terms were that it be allowed to retain its Dutch conquests (Holland by then being an ally of France). Even this France rejected.

"Then tell me", Pitt continued, "whether the disasters of Europe are to be charged upon the provocation of this country and its allies, or on the inherent principles of the French Revolution, of which the natural result produced so much misery and carnage in France, and carried desolation and terror over so large a portion of the world [...] The all-searching eye of the French Revolution looks to every part of Europe, and every quarter of the world, in which can be found an object either of acquisition or plunder. Nothing is too great for the temerity of its ambition, nothing too small or insignificant for the grasp of its rapacity."

Pitt summed up the fundamental nature of the French Revolution (and its leaders up to and including Bonaparte) as being consumed by an insatiable love of aggrandizement. Its fundamental methods were bribery, incitement and treachery: bribery of the poor with the property of the rich; inciting the rest of the world with revolutionary ideas; and betraying the trust of others, unrestrained by normal human obligations. Should England have accepted a precarious security against so tremendous a danger? Had recent changes in the French government actually altered anything? Even if it had, how permanent a change would it be? Another feature of French Revolution was the instability of its short-lived governments, not one of which had lasted more than three years.

Nevertheless, it was worth considering whether the nature of the new government might be different. It was certainly more openly militaristic and despotic, wielding a sword instead of a sceptre. What confidence could be had from this system of government and from the conduct of Bonaparte? Not a lot was Pitt's judgement, quoting Bonaparte as saying "the Kingdom of Great Britain and the French Republic cannot exist together." And how could England trust Bonaparte's promises to governments of other countries if, by removing the Directory in his coup, he had failed to uphold the oath of allegiance to his own? All treaties made by the French had subsequently been broken by them and many of these treaties and their violations had involved Bonaparte to a significant degree. Bonaparte's promise to respect the property of Italian states was always followed by heavy taxes and plundering and in some cases, atrocities. At Bresanco he massacred civilians in retaliation for the capture of a French garrison. And of course it was Bonaparte who was responsible for giving Venice over to Austria at the Treaty of Campo-Formio. Could England really trust peace offers from a man who needed military success to sustain himself in power? Bonaparte was not a man to forego opportunities out of obligations to a treaty and military despotism was never a stable form of government.

"What, then," asked Pitt, "is the inference I draw from all that I have now stated? Is it, that we will in no case treat with Bonaparte? I say no such thing. But I say, as has been said in the answer returned to the French note, that we ought to wait for *experience*, and the evidence of facts, before we are convinced that such a treaty is admissible."

If France were to demonstrate it was now guided by different maxims and if the new French government were to show signs of stability, then Pitt would consider treating. He would even consider making peace if the risks of continuing the struggle were to increase, but now there was every reason to carry on fighting. There was active resistance within France against the new tyranny; continuing the struggle was more likely to improve their situation than worsen it; and, Pitt assured the House, the British could expect greater co-operation from their allies. Public finances were in a better state than they were in 1797, while the French army was under-supplied and under-resourced. How secure could England feel in a peace with an aggressive country allowed breathing space to strengthen itself, while England disbanded its armies and kept its fleet laid up in harbours?

Could Britain really feel safe by making peace with Bonaparte? While he was in power and while France maintained such large military resources, Pitt saw little hope of "permanent security [...] and as a sincere lover of peace, I cannot be content with its nominal attainment [...] As a sincere lover of peace, I will not sacrifice it by grasping at the shadow, when the reality is not substantially within my reach."[1]

---

[1] SPITT pp.1-57

4 Charles James Fox

Engraving by S.Freeman from a painting by H.Richter. (Author's private collection)

3. Is Peace a Rash System?

Unlike Pitt, Fox's facial expressions would match the sentiments of his words. Fox apologised for keeping the House up at such a late hour before focusing on Pitt's claim that France was exhausted, suggesting that victory was just around the corner:

> "What! At the end of seven years of the most burdensome and the most calamitous struggle that this country was ever engaged in, are we again to be amused with notions of finance and calculations of the exhausted resources of the enemy, as a ground of confidence and hope? Gracious God! Were we not told, five years ago, that France was not only on the brink, but that she was actually sunk in the gulph of bankruptcy? Were we not told, as an unanswerable argument against treating, that she could not hold out another campaign; that nothing but peace could save her; that she wanted only time to recruit her exhausted finances; that to grant her repose, was to grant her the means of again molesting this country, and that we had nothing to do but persevere for a short time, in order to save ourselves for ever from the consequences of her ambition and her Jacobinism? What! After having gone on from year to year upon assurances like these, and after having seen the repeated refutations of every prediction, are we again to be seriously told, that we have the same prospect of success on the same identical ground? [...] If the right honourable gentleman should succeed in prevailing on Parliament and the country to adopt the principles which he has advanced this night, I see no possible termination to the contest."

Fox lamented the language used in Grenville's response to the French offer and considered Pitt's bringing up the causes of the war as pointless, but felt he could not leave it unchallenged, repeating his belief that "this country was the aggressor in the war". He conceded this was debatable, "but with regard to Austria and Prussia; is there a man who, for one moment, can dispute that they were the aggressors?" There may not have been any formal treaty to dismember France but in the declaration at Pilnitz there was a very real intention to interfere in its internal affairs. Was it not the case that "in direct terms, it declared, that whenever the other powers should concur, they would attack France, then at peace with them, and then employed only in domestic and internal regulation?" If two powers said that they would attack Great Britain when circumstances were right would not Parliament and the people not consider it an act of "hostile aggression? [...] We must, then, respect in others the indignation which such an act would excite in ourselves..." Given the very public declaration at Pilnitz "it is idle to say, that as far as the Emperor and the King of Prussia were concerned, they were not the aggressors in the war."

As for the French decree of 19 November 1792, inciting revolution in other countries, the government should have paid it no heed. Instead they demanded a satisfactory explanation. But how could they expect a satisfactory answer when they failed to state what it was that would satisfy them? "I contend that when a nation refuses to state to another the thing which would satisfy her, she shows that she is not actuated by a desire to preserve peace between them: and I aver that this was the case here. The Scheldt for instance. You now say, that the navigation of the Scheldt was one of your causes of complaint. Did you explain yourself on that subject? Did you make it one of the grounds for the dismissal of M. Chauvelin? Sir, I repeat it, a nation, to justify itself in appealing to the last solemn resort, ought to prove that it had taken every possible means, consistent with dignity, to demand the reparation which would be satisfactory, and if she refused to explain what would be satisfactory, she did not do her duty, nor exonerate herself from the charge of being the aggressor."

Fox was not trying to praise the French. He admitted they had also been aggressive themselves and were guilty of terrible acts against other nations, but it was not the Revolution that made them so. As well as being provoked, they were only following in the footsteps of Louis XIV, who threatened Europe a hundred years earlier. The Bourbons had been just as rapacious and untrustworthy as the republicans and Britain had deigned to treat with the former so why not with the latter? And if the British government refused to make peace with France on account of its iniquity, should they not be just as scrupulous with her friends? Yet "what was the conduct of your own allies to Poland?" In 1794 what remained of the Kingdom of Poland was partitioned between Russia, Prussia and Austria after the Polish people rebelled against a government imposed by Russia. Fox reminded the House of the massacre of 20,000 inhabitants of Praga, a suburb of Warsaw, by Russian troops. "Men, women, and children, nay infants at the breast, were doomed to one indiscriminate massacre! Thousands of them were inhumanly, wantonly, butchered! And for what? Because they dared to join in a wish to meliorate their own condition as a people, and to improve their constitution, which had been confessed by their own sovereign to be in want of amendment."

Fox conceded that the handing over of Venice to Austria by France was "an abominable act" but insisted that the "receiver was as bad as the thief". To mitigate Austria's culpability by suggesting that it was owed compensation and not responsible for the means by which this was satisfied was no better than the "false and abominable reasoning" and "detestable sophistry" justifying the slave trade. Even the actions of Britain herself were not above reproach. The French may be blamed for its aggression towards Switzerland, but it was the English ambassador to the Swiss cantons that persuaded them to abandon their neutrality by suggesting "in such a contest neutrality was criminal". Then there was Britain's ultimatum to the Grand Duke of Tuscany threatening to bombard Leghorn if he did not dismiss the French ambassador there. As such conduct was not confined to the enemy "we have no right to refuse to treat with the French on this ground."

By claiming the French alone had provoked the other continental powers against her, Pitt was forfeiting the opportunity of taking his share of the credit. Had he not bribed those powers to remain in the war? "What Sir! Have all your negotiations, your declamation, all your money, been squandered in vain? Have you not succeeded in stirring the indignation, and engaging the assistance of a single power? But you do yourselves injustice." As for Russia's motives for entering the war, they could only be considered ridiculous. After his acquisition of Catholic Poland, the Tsar had made himself a Grand Master of the Knights of Malta and feigned indignity when the French took the island. Yet "his religion is as opposite to that of the Knights as ours is; and he is much considered a heretic by the Church of Rome as we are. The King of Britain might, with as much propriety, declare himself the head of the order of the Chartreuse monks."

Fox asked why England would not negotiate now when it was apparently willing to do so before, as Pitt claimed. Pitt had argued that the French had demonstrated their disinclination towards peace by refusing to negotiate a few years earlier. But, by refusing the French offer now, was he not demonstrating by his own standard his own unwillingness for peace? "But, they say, we have not refused all discussion. They have put a case. They have expressed a wish for the restoration of the House of Bourbon, and have declared that to be an event which would immediately remove every obstacle to negotiation [...] I cannot forget that the whole history of the century is little more than an account of the wars and calamities arising from the restless ambition, the intrigues, and the perfidy of the House of Bourbon".

Fox inferred from this that Pitt had not treated as sincerely for peace as he claimed. He had negotiated only in the hope that France would reject his terms, thereby winning back the public and Parliamentary support that would provide him with more revenue to continue the war. It was not honest of him to pursue in public a popular policy while undertaking one in secret that undermined it. "I know not whether this may be not honesty in the political ethics of the right honourable gentleman, but I know that it would be called by a very different name in the common transactions of society..."

The government said it wanted "experience, and the evidence of facts" that France had changed its spots. "Can there be any evidence of facts equal to that of a frank, open, and candid negotiation? Let us see whether Bonaparte will display the same temper as his predecessors. If he shall do so, then you will confirm the people of England in their opinion of the necessity of continuing the war, and you will revive all the vigour which you roused in 1797. Or will you not do this until you have a reverse of fortune?"

Fox returned to the government's suggestion it had not actually refused the offer of peace because it had suggested a condition which if satisfied by the French would bring them immediately to the table. Of course, this was the restoration of the monarchy, but the government was also trying to insist that this was not a necessary condition. "You deny that this is a sine qua non; and in your nonsensical language, which I do not understand, you talk of limited possibilities which may induce you to treat without the restoration of the House of Bourbon. But do you state what they are?" Surely, Fox argued, that if one does not state what the other conditions are then the only condition that is stated is effectively the only and necessary condition.

Perhaps these other conditions were the "evidence and facts" of good behaviour on the part of a stable French government. Pitt contended that he must have "experience that these foul crimes" of the past "are repented of, and that a purer and a better system of government is adopted by France" before he was willing to treat with them. "Sir, these are not conciliatory words; nor is this a practical ground to gain experience. Does he think it possible, that evidence of a peaceable demeanour can be obtained in war? What does he mean to say to the French Consul? Until you shall in war behave yourself in a peaceable manner, I will not treat with you. Is there not something ridiculous in this?" It reminded Fox of two men duelling, where mutual respect is only restored by the discharge of pistols. "There is something, bye the bye, ridiculous even in this; but between nations it is more than ridiculous – it is criminal." There was nothing wrong in expecting Bonaparte to abandon the aggressive behaviour of his predecessors and moderate his own, but "I ask you, Sir, if this is likely to be ascertained in war? It is the nature of war not to allay, but to inflame the passions."

How, asked Fox, was Bonaparte to demonstrate the stability of his government? According to Pitt, by the acceptance of his rule by the French people. As he had usurped power, that then seemed to rule out the possibility of stability as far as the English government were concerned. Yet, Fox pointed out, Cromwell had been a usurper, but this had not stopped France and Spain from treating with him. "No, Sir, these are not the maxims by which government are actuated". Furthermore, if Bonaparte was deceiving the English, and they refused his peace offer, he was more likely to gain the support of the French people much in the same way as Pitt had gained renewed support for the war in 1797. And if Bonaparte had the support of the French, would this not put him in a better bargaining position for a future peace treaty?

Fox mocked Pitt's other circumstances under which he would consider peace – if the allies and England were to be less successful in the war; or if the pressure of war would be too heavy to endure. "These are the other two possible emergencies in which the right honourable gentleman would treat even with Bonaparte. Sir, I have often blamed the right honourable gentleman for being disingenuous and insincere. On the present occasion I certainly cannot charge him with any such thing. He has made tonight a most honest confession. He is open and candid. He tells Bonaparte fairly what he has to expect. I mean, says he, to do everything in my power to raise up the people of France against you. I have engaged a number of allies, and our combined efforts shall be used to excite insurrection and civil war in France. I will strive to murder you, or get you sent away. If I succeed, well; but if I fail, then I will treat with you [...] Is this the language for one state to hold another? And what sort of peace does the right honourable gentleman expect to receive in that case? Does he think that Bonaparte would grant to baffled insolence, to humiliated pride, to disappointment and to imbecility, the same terms which he would be ready to give now?"

As for the military despotism of the new regime, how could Parliament disapprove of it in France and be so complacent of its presence in Britain's own realm – in Ireland. In 1798 the Irish had rebelled against English rule and this had been brutally suppressed by English troops, which still remained there. "Are not the persons and property of the people left, in many districts, at this moment, to the entire will of military commanders?" And the government and its supporters were insisting this was the best way to govern the Irish at the present time. "Now, really, Sir, I cannot think that gentlemen who talk in this way about Ireland, can with a good grace, rail at military despotism in France".

Bonaparte's breaking of oaths was of the least importance, but then there was his alleged claim that Britain and France could not exist together. "Well, and what is there in this absurd and puerile assertion, if it was ever made? Has not the right honourable gentleman, in this House, said the same thing? [...] May not these offences and charges be reciprocated without end? Are we ever to go on in this miserable squabble about words? [...] Sir, this temper must be corrected. It is a diabolical spirit, and would lead to interminable war. Our history is full of instances, that where we have overlooked a proffered occasion to treat, we have uniformly suffered by delay." Fox again argued that military despotism was not necessarily a short-lived mode of government, offering the example of ancient Rome. And peace was not necessarily against its interests. Bonaparte could conceivably not want to risk tarnishing his glory with a prolonged war that may end in his defeat. And even if he thirsted for more glory, why should he not overlook this in considering the interests of France? Could the government be sure what Bonaparte was really like? George Washington, the first American President, was originally thought as bad as Bonaparte was being viewed now.

The governments' suggestion to France that it restore the monarchy was considered by Fox to be wholly impractical. Unlike Pitt, he deemed the change of ownership of property in France was an insurmountable barrier to the return of the original owners along with their old rights and privileges. The exiled King-in-waiting, Louis XVIII, had let it be known that he intended to be restored to the throne with the full powers of an absolute monarch. This was unlikely to be a prospect welcomed by most French people, even those with some royalist sympathies.

Fox reminded the House of the atrocities of war with the example of one committed by Britain. In June 1799 a royalist Neapolitan force attacked a French army and local revolutionaries that had seized Naples. With the help of the Royal Navy under Nelson blockading the port, they pushed the French and the rebels into the city's fortress – the Castel de Uova. Eventually, a number of them surrendered on the understanding of an agreed amnesty that they would be given safe passage to France. Although Fox did not specifically mentioned him by name,

Nelson, backed by the King of Naples, refused to honour the amnesty he had not been a party to. A number of the prisoners were "thrown into dungeons, and some of them I understand, notwithstanding the British guarantee, actually executed. Where then Sir, is this war, which on every side is pregnant with such horrors, to be carried? Where is it to stop? Not till you establish the House of Bourbon! And this you cherish the hope of doing, because you have had a successful campaign. One campaign is successful to you – another to them; and in this way you may go on forever [...] And all this because you may gain a better peace a year or two hence [...] We must keep Bonaparte for some time longer at war, as a state of probation. Gracious God, Sir is war a state of probation? Is peace a rash system? Is it dangerous for nations to live in amity with each other?"

"But we must pause." Here Fox may have been referring to a comment by Lord Carnarvon in the Lords who seems to have suggested the wait-and-see strategy of the government could be considered as a pause in the war.

"What! Must the bowels of Great Britain be torn out – her best blood be spilt, - her treasure wasted – that you may make an experiment? Put yourselves – oh! That you would put yourselves – in the field of battle, and learn to judge the sort of horrors that you excite. In former wars a man might, at least, have some feeling, some interest, that served to balance in his mind the impressions which a scene of carnage and of death must inflict [...] But, if a man were present now at a field of slaughter, and were to inquire for what they were fighting. – 'Fighting!' would be the answer; 'they are not fighting, they are pausing.' 'Why is that man expiring? Why is that other writhing in agony? What means this implacable fury?' the answer must be, 'You are quite wrong, Sir, you deceive yourself – They are not fighting – Do not disturb them – they are merely pausing! – this man is not expiring with agony – that man not dead – he is only pausing! Lord help you Sir! They are not angry with one another; they have now no cause of quarrel – but their country thinks that there should be a pause. All that you see, Sir, is nothing like fighting – there is no harm, nor cruelty, nor bloodshed in it whatever – it is nothing more than a political pause. It is merely to try an experiment – to see whether Bonaparte will not behave himself better than heretofore; and in the mean time we have agreed to a pause, in pure friendship!' And is this the way, Sir, that you are to show yourselves the advocates of order? You take up a system calculated to uncivilize the world, to destroy order, to trample on religion, to stifle in the heart, not merely the generosity of noble sentiment, but the affections of social nature; and in the prosecution of this system, you spread terror and devastation all around you."

Fox claimed that despite the restraints on the expression of public opinion it was still clear that the people wanted peace. He pleaded with the independent members of the House of Commons who would have voted for the government had they accepted Bonaparte's offer to vote against them now. [1]

The House divided, the votes counted and the results read out: Yeas: 265. Noes: 64. The war would continue.

---

[1] SFOX pp. 678-715

5 The Union Club

Detail from the Union Club by James Gillray, published 1801. (Look and Learn Collection) Satire of British and Irish Whigs fraternizing at the Union Club, formed after the union of the two parliaments. Fox is dozing bottom left. The Irish Peer Lord Moira sits on the table. Below him, passed out on the floor, his legs crossed, is the Prince of Wales. Behind Moira to the left is Erskine and to the right is Sheridan. Lord Cholmondeley with two arms raised is in the background.

6 Henry Dundas

Illustration for *A Comprehensive History of India* by Henry Beveridge (Blackie, 1862). (Look and Learn Collection)

4. The Irish, the Madman and Monsieur Otto

Next to the war with France, the greatest concern for Pitt in 1800 was Ireland. Governed by a viceroy appointed by Westminster, Ireland had its own houses of parliament which provided an Irish cabinet. It was a predominantly Catholic country, and although property-owning Catholics were allowed to vote in sixty-four open boroughs, they were not allowed to stand for office or parliament. The other 300 seats in the Irish Commons were controlled by great Protestant County families.

The current viceroy, Lord Cornwallis had been appointed in 1798 to restore order following the rebellion that year. He suggested as an "ultimate settlement" to the Irish problem the union of the Irish Parliament with Britain and the emancipation of the Catholics. He advised Pitt that although Catholics would not be good subjects immediately, he hoped that once the most justifiable of their grievances had been addressed it would at least "check the rapid progress of discontent and disaffection."[1] He believed that until "the Catholics are admitted into a general participation of rights (which when incorporated with the British government they cannot abuse) there will be no peace or safety in Ireland."[2] In this he was supported by his deputy, the Chief Secretary, Lord Castlereagh, but many in the Irish cabinet, who represented the interests of the Protestant elite, were not so amenable to union and were downright hostile to allowing Catholics into government. For different reasons, the King shared this view. To Cornwallis he wrote on January 31 1800: "...though a strong friend to the Union of the two kingdoms, I should become an enemy to the movement if I thought a change of the situation of the Roman Catholics would attend this measure."[3] The King considered that allowing Catholics into Parliament and government would violate his coronation oath. After all, his claim to be King of England rested on Parliament's decision a hundred years earlier to exclude Catholics from the throne.

---

[1] Packenham p.338

[2] Hague p.436

[3] Hague p.454

Pitt embraced the idea of both the Union and Catholic Emancipation. It would offer the prospect of power to Irish Catholics while at the same time diluting it in a Protestant dominated British Parliament. However, as he became aware of the extent of Irish Protestant opposition to emancipation, he opted for the tactic of separating the two goals. Why risk defeat of both measures in the Irish Parliament when emancipation could be safely left to a United Parliament afterwards? As it was, getting the Irish MPs to accept union was not an easy task. The plan was to abolish the Irish Parliament and give Ireland one hundred seats in the British House of Commons and admit thirty-two Irish peers to the British House of Lords. To smooth the Act of Union in Ireland financial compensation would be given to the proprietors and patrons of the abolished Irish seats while new peerages or elevations in titles were offered to others. As well as these public inducements, state funds were also deployed to provide secret annuities for some Irish MPs.

On 5 February 1800, Lord Cornwallis informed the Irish Houses of Parliament that it was the King's desire that they should merge with that of Britain. Debates in both Houses followed and continued into March. On 10 February the Irish Lords voted in favour of Union. In the Irish House of Commons, an exchange between the Irish Chancellor of the Exchequer, Mr Corry, and Mr Grattan, a pro-Catholic anti-unionist, escalated into a duel, from which the Chancellor received a wound in his arm. By the end of March the Irish Commons had voted for the Union.

On 21 April it was the turn of the British Parliament. Grenville recommended the Union to the Lords, where Fox's nephew, Lord Holland opposed: "however desirable in their judgements the union of the two countries might appear, it ought not to be accepted, unless it were the pure and spontaneous offer of the Parliament of Ireland, uninfluenced by corruption and menace."[1] Fox himself remained in St Anne's Hill. Although he considered the Union as "one of the most unequivocal attempts at establishing the principles as well as the practice of despotism",[2] he declined to attend Parliament. In his absence, his ally Charles Grey suggested the House reject Union pending an appeal to the Irish people, but this failed to arouse sufficient support. By the end of the day both Houses had voted for Union. Royal assent was received two

---

[1] Gifford p.247

[2] Stanhope p.230

months later from the King, who declared: "This great measure [...] on which my wishes have been so long earnestly bent, I shall ever consider as the happiest event of my reign, being persuaded that nothing could so effectually contribute to extend to my Irish subjects the full participation of the blessings derived from the British Constitution".[1]

****

A few weeks after Parliament passed the Union Bill, on 15 May, the Drury Lane theatre was holding a royal command performance of two plays – *She would and she would not*, and *The Humorist*. As the doors opened to the pit of the theatre that evening, the crowds surged in. In the ensuing bustle, a young woman cried out "Oh sir! The handle of your umbrella is running into my breast!" The cause of her discomfort was concealed under the overcoat of the man she addressed, who sat down in the middle row of the pit, and with the rest of the crowd, waited patiently for the royal family to appear in their box. Some of them may have heard that earlier that day the King had attended a review of the Foot Guards, where a man from the Navy office had been wounded by a musket ball. As the soldiers should have been firing blanks and the wounded man had been standing near the King, the incident had aroused much anxiety. When the King appeared, he bowed in acknowledgement of the audience's warm reception of him. As the Queen and royal princesses were about to enter, the man in the overcoat stood up, drew a pistol, took careful aim and fired into the box. The King, remaining erect, motioned with his hand to the Queen not to come in. After a moment of frozen astonishment, some musicians in the orchestra leaned over and dragged the shooter out of the pit and bundled him into the music room.

Here, the man was restrained and visited by the proprietor of the theatre, the MP and playwright Sheridan, the King and his sons the Dukes of York and Cumberland. The would-be-assassin, who had a scar on his face and a soldier's jacket under his overcoat, gave his name as James Hadfield. On seeing the King, he said "God bless you your royal highness;

---

[1] Stanhope p.231

I like you very well, you are a good fellow." As a former soldier, he had served under the Duke of York, whom he also addressed with much respect, but told them he was now weary of life. He was taken into custody and the King was urged to leave the theatre. The King refused, believing that his absence would alarm an already angry and agitated audience. The orchestra played "God Save the King" three times, the King and his family took their seats in the box, and the performance began. For some of the princesses, all this excitement was too much. They fainted and had to be roused by smelling salts and cold water.[1] The loyalty demonstrated by the audience inside the theatre was not matched by the those outside who were disposed to jeer rather than cheer the news of the King's good fortune.[2]

Hadfield was indicted for regicide and tried at the Bar of the Court of the King's Bench on 26 June. The Attorney General, Sir John Mitford, who was prosecuting Hadfield, realised that the jury might consider him insane and fail to convict. He would not be able to deny that Hadfield had acted strangely since receiving a war wound to the head in 1794, at the Battle of Tourcoing, where he was captured by the French but presumed dead by his comrades. They were pleased to see him again when he re-joined them in Croydon in 1795, but the following year he was discharged for being insane. He found work as a silversmith, but became increasingly drawn to religion, believing the end of the world was nigh. A religious fanatic, Bannister Truelock, convinced Hadfield that the Messiah was about to come out of his mouth, but could not accomplish this second coming until George III had been eliminated. Hadfield, Truelock claimed, had been chosen to be the King's assassin. A few days before Hadfield's attempt on the King, he had tried to kill his own baby son under the conviction it would be for the benefit of mankind. Filled with remorse, he felt he deserved to die, but reluctant to commit suicide, he opted for an attempt on the King's life in the expectation that this would inevitably result in his execution for treason.

Mitford's aim therefore was not to deny there was insanity, but to deny that it was sufficient to absolve him of his responsibility. He clarified where the law stood on the insane. Those without a will – idiots, infants and madmen – were excused from punishment because they could not be

---

[1] Ashton pp.9-12

[2] Jay p.292

considered to have committed a crime any more than a weapon could. However, it was the job of a jury to determine the degree of discretion possessed by a defendant. Did they have sufficient faculties of reason to distinguish right from wrong? Hadfield knew he had done wrong because he recognized he would be punished for it, which was his ultimate goal. He was therefore demonstrating a competent use of his faculty of reason. He might have been insane, but not sufficiently so to have excused him from his crime. To bolster his case he brought up legal precedents where guilty verdicts were delivered despite the insanity of the accused.

Mitford also produced witnesses to testify that Hadfield had given no impression he had acted without reason. The steadiness of his aim, the quietness and patience with which he sat waiting in the pit in his well-chosen seat were all evidence of rationality. Among the witnesses was the Duke of York, who was asked: "In the whole course of the conversation which your royal highness had with this man [...] did he betray in his answers any irregularity, from which you could collect a then existing derangement of his understanding?" The Duke replied: "Not the least; on the contrary, he appeared to speak as connectedly as could possibly be." Mitford's last key point was that no matter how insane Hadfield might have appeared at other times, his culpability depended only on his reasoning skills during the commission of the crime itself.

The lawyer defending Hadfield was the Foxite Whig MP Thomas Erskine, who had previously defended Thomas Paine. The law, as it related to insanity, Erskine said, was problematic. It quite rightly acquitted a man who was deprived of his reason, but reason was too narrow a principle and neglected the more difficult cases of insanity. He admitted that conventional legal wisdom held that it was up to the jury to decide borderline cases of insanity. He also acknowledged that the same authority considered that for a man to avoid criminal responsibility by being insane he had to be totally deprived of memory and understanding. However, it was Erskine's contention that neither jury nor expert legal opinion should be expected to judge the mental health of a man, rather it should be done by medical professionals. Only they could assess whether the insanity was responsible for a crime rather than the will. To demonstrate his point he brought forward as witnesses a number of medical experts, all of whom testified that Hadfield was insane. He also showed the jury the nature of Hadfield's head wound, which had exposed the membrane of the brain.

The testimony of the experts made it clear that the mad did not generally lack memory and reason. The defects in their reasoning was not the reasoning itself, but in the assumptions they reasoned from – their delusions. Also, it was only on certain subjects, such as religion, that their delusions took hold. "Delusion", argued Erskine, "where there is no frenzy or raving madness, is the true character of insanity." Hadfield was insane under this expert definition and the crime of which he was accused was the direct consequence of his illness. Hadfield could distinguish between right and wrong, but his madness lay in what he thought was right – he thought he was doing something good for mankind. Madness showed itself, not just in irrational behaviour, but also in rational behaviour motivated by irrational beliefs. Other witnesses testified to the patriotism and loyalty of Hadfield. As this could not be contradicted by the prosecution, it was clear that his attempt to shoot the King could only have been the result of a strong delusion.

Erskine was about to call on Hadfield's family and neighbours to testify when Judge Kenyon interrupted. As the Attorney General could offer no evidence to contradict that presented by Erskine, Kenyon had come to the conclusion that Hadfield would be found insane and acquitted. However, as he was clearly dangerous, he could not possibly be discharged. Mitford, who acknowledged that he had no evidence to contradict Erskine's and accepting that acquittal was likely, suggested that common law allowed the judge to direct Hadfield's confinement. The judge confirmed this, but was concerned that he only had the power to remand him to the confinement from which he came – prison. He did not have the power to send him somewhere more suitable. One of the prosecuting team suggested that if the jury declared the grounds for acquittal – insanity – that would be a "legal and sufficient reason for his future confinement." The jury was directed as suggested, so when their foreman announced their verdict he said: "We find the prisoner is not guilty; he being under the influence of insanity at the time the act was committed." To prevent Hadfield's future release, Parliament was to pass a statute to provide for continuation of custody for those found not guilty by reason of their insanity. Hadfield was consequently sent to the Bethlam madhouse – notoriously known as Bedlam, where he was soon joined by Truelock, the religious fanatic who had incited him to regicide.[1]

****

---

[1] Kopans pp.61-76

Meanwhile, the government failed to take any firm action against France. The Royal Navy was successfully blockading French, Dutch and Spanish ports and isolating French land forces in Malta, Alexandria in Egypt and Belle-Île off the coast of northern France. However, plans to occupy Belle-Île and Walcheren off the coast of Holland were abandoned in favour of sending a force to the Mediterranean to attack France from the south. Then in late March, Dundas proposed that instead of sending an army to the Mediterranean, the government should switch to a naval strategy and seize the overseas territories of Spain, France's weak ally. Capturing New Orleans, Tenerife and some South American colonies would open up new markets for British trade. Grenville, who wanted to attack the Bordeaux region of France, was incensed: "Do this, or anything else you prefer, but for God's sake, for your own honour, and for the cause in which we are engaged, do not let us, after having by immense exertions collected a fine army, leave it unemployed, gaping after messengers from Genoa, Augsburg, and Vienna, till the moment for acting is irrecoverably past by. For this can lead to nothing but disgrace." Dundas was finding the business of government affecting his health, especially his sleep and implored Pitt, not for the first time, to allow him to retire. Pitt convinced him to stick to an earlier promise to not quit until the war was over. The original decision to send the army to the Mediterranean was upheld, but it achieved nothing, prompting Cornwallis to comment on "twenty thousand men floating round the greater part of Europe, the scorn and laughing stock of friends and foes".[1]

While the British dithered, Austria attacked the French in northern Italy and besieged Genoa. The Cabinet planned to land their army in Italy to support their allies, but they were too late. After the French General Moreau defeated the Austrians in Germany at Stockach, Bonaparte himself crossed the Alps into Italy and defeated them at Marengo in June. The best the British could do for now was to put further pressure on the French in Malta. Meanwhile, a new appeal for peace by Bonaparte was sent to Austria which agreed to an armistice in exchange for their evacuation of their recent Italian conquests. An Austrian envoy was sent to Paris where he agreed to French peace terms which were the same as Campo Formio. However, the Austrian monarch, Francis II of the Holy Roman Empire, encouraged by an English

---

[1] Hague pp.456-457, Stanhope p.243

£2million interest free loan to resume fighting, refused to ratify them. Instead, Austria requested another armistice in Germany where they agreed to withdraw to the river Inn while leaving besieged garrisons in Ulm, Ingolstadt and Philipsburg. Bonaparte consented and allowed the isolated garrisons to be re-provisioned every ten days. The Austrian foreign minister Baron Thugut then proposed a general peace conference involving Britain. In August, the British ambassador in Vienna, Lord Minto, conveyed his government's agreement to the idea of peace negotiations. It was willing to send plenipotentiaries as soon as the French declared a willingness to treat with Britain. On August 11 Thugut communicated this to the French Foreign Minister Talleyrand and suggested the peace talks take place in Lunéville.

About two weeks later, Grenville received a letter from the French commissioner for prisoners of war based in London, Monsieur Otto. Louis Guillaume Otto was a French Protestant from Strasbourg who had served as a diplomat for both the ancien régime and the Revolutionary governments. His previous postings included the United States, Prussia and Bavaria. He arrived in London in January 1800, installing himself at Hereford Street in Portman Square.

In the letter, Otto acknowledged the recent peace feelers made by Lord Minto and welcomed England's desire to end the war. However, it was impossible for France to negotiate a joint peace with Austria and Britain while in a truce with the former but not the latter. He therefore proposed on behalf of the First Consul a general armistice between their fleets and armies. Grenville declined to respond directly. Instead, he instructed the officer Otto normally dealt with regarding prisoners, Captain George, to communicate his response. Through him Grenville pointed out that this was the first time the idea of a naval truce as a preliminary step to negotiation had been suggested. It was more likely to obstruct a full peace because of the possibilities of disputes about its execution and a naval truce could not be compared to a land truce. Otto argued that the disadvantages to England of a maritime truce would be balanced by the drawbacks to France of the land truce in Germany. He needed an answer by 3 September. If England would not consent to a naval truce, France would break off its armistice with Austria. Grenville now wrote to Otto himself, but simply repeated what he had already said through Captain George. In Otto's reply to Grenville, he pointed out that the preliminary peace agreement with Austria had not been signed by Francis because England was still insisting on being included. Therefore the armistice would cease on 11 September. If England were to consider a naval truce, France would expect Malta and Egypt to be considered on same terms as those places under siege by the French.[1]

Grenville needed more details. Otto answered with seven suggestions: a suspension of hostilities; freedom of navigation; the return of recently captured vessels; Malta, Alexandria and Belle-Île to be equated with Ulm, Philipsburg and Ingolstadt and all neutral or French vessels to enter with provisions freely; the British blockade of Brest, Cadiz, Toulon and Flushing to be lifted and fleets to withdraw from the coast; the British should notify their squadrons of the armistice as soon as possible; and Spain and Holland, France's allies, were to be included.[2]

Grenville had kept the rest of the Cabinet informed. Pitt was worried that an absolute refusal would provoke immediate renewal of hostilities and perhaps oblige Austria into a separate peace on bad terms. This would make any separate treaty England might make with France less advantageous also. As long as England could retain its right to search French ships then an armistice now might be preferable to both losing Austria as an ally or a renewal of hostilities on the continent.[3] Grenville went back to Otto with a counter-proposal: provisioning of French forces in Malta and Alexandria should exclude anything that could aid their defence. The blockades of ports would be lifted, but the blockading fleets would remain where they were and these ports would not be allowed to receive any naval or military stores. Effectively they were to be treated the same as besieged land fortresses. Otto replied he would have to consult Paris.[4]

---

[1] PRCNP pp.4-17

[2] PRCNP pp.29-32

[3] Stanhope p.240

[4] PRCNP pp.39-50

7 Lord Grenville

Engraving after a painting by William Owen. (Look and Learn Collection)

8 Louis Guillaume Otto

Stipple engraving by P. Roberts after a painting by John Trumbull. (Yale University Art Gallery, Mabel Brady Garvan Collection).

5. Riots

While His Majesty's government continued to deal with the menace from France it also became increasingly concerned about the threat posed by more and more of his own subjects. At the end of the 18th century, Britain had become a net importer of cereals, the staple diet of most workers. 1799 had been a cold wet summer with prolonged rains in the harvesting season. About a quarter of the expected crop was lost causing wheat prices to rise. This combined with a downturn in the trade cycle, especially in the textile industries resulted in misery for countless working class families who were forced to spend everything they had on cereals. If they had nothing they could only beg or apply for relief. This was provided mainly by parish administrations financed by local ratepayers. Beggars might be liable to be treated as rogues or vagabonds and sent to houses of correction, while the sick and the aged went to alms-houses and youths were apprenticed. The able-bodied unemployed often laboured in workhouses, especially in the north, but in the south, many received outdoor relief, not only if they were jobless, but also if their wages were too low to match bread prices. In 1795 the parish administrators in Speenhamland in Berkshire supplemented wages of local workers and this practice was widely adopted in southern England. Pitt would have liked to have seen this rolled out on a national scale, but its perceived defects worried many others. Wage subsidies encouraged employers to keep their wages low, discouraged the free movement of labour and invited the poor to breed without worrying about the resources required to raise families. It was also clear that the steady increase in rates to pay for poor relief was not actually relieving all of the poor.[1]

On the streets of Manchester children competed with dogs for scraps of food, while in Wolverhampton youngsters scoured dunghills for potato skins. People sought alternatives to wheat, eating horse beans, turnips and even nettles, which now had a market price. Small businessmen were applying for food from soup kitchens in Leeds, Wakefield, York and Newcastle. The government's response was to rely on the free market, hoping that high prices in regions of scarcity would

---

[1] Miller 1979 pp.119-128

attract suppliers in regions of relative abundance. It did subsidise the import of cereals and also encouraged the consumption of unpopular alternative foods through the relief agencies, including rice, coarser wheat, maize, potatoes and fish soups. These had only minimal impact. It would ultimately use further state resources to deal with the anger the hunger produced.

The people, encouraged by radical societies, demanded the government impose a fixed maximum price for bread. An outburst of rioting in the spring, fuelled by rumours of profiteering, prompted the government to send troops to help the local magistrates and volunteers. By July the price of wheat was 135 shillings a quarter, almost double what it cost nine months previously. Early summer was hot and in the expectation of a normal harvest, prices calmed down. However, in mid-August widespread and heavy rains began and the prices rose again, sparking a chain of riots starting in Yorkshire and spreading to the Midlands in September. In Birmingham volunteers fired on the crowd, killing a boy and wounding many others.[1]

By Sunday 14 September, revolutionary graffiti and posters could be noticed in the streets of London and handbills were being widely distributed in the city. Two placards were posted on the Monument, the tall pillar commemorating the fire of London of 1666 standing on the north bank of the Thames near London Bridge. One of these placards read as follows:

Fellow Countrymen. How long will ye quietly and cowardly suffer yourselves to be imposed upon, and half starved by a set of mercenary slaves and government hirelings? Can you still suffer them to proceed in their extensive monopolies, while your children are crying for bread? No! Let them exist not a day longer. We are the sovereignty, rise then from your lethargy. Be at the Corn Market on Monday.

On 15 September at nine in the morning, a thousand people had assembled at the Corn Exchange on Mark Lane. An hour later the crowd, now doubled in size, hissed at the traders turning up to the market and pelted them with mud. At Eleven o'clock the Lord Mayor arrived and he tried to persuade people that their behaviour could not influence the market. He was met with hisses and cries of "Cheap bread! Birmingham and Nottingham forever! Three loaves for eighteen pence." Nearby

---

[1] Wells pp.179-194

windows were smashed. The Mayor read the riot act and the constables charged. The mob dispersed, but by the evening it was back, breaking bakers' windows and stealing faggots, no longer intimidated by the constables. The Mayor summoned volunteers and London militia, who blocked both ends of Mark Lane. The crowd jeered and hooted before being charged and dispersed west into Lombard Street and south into Fish Hill Street near the Monument. When most of them crossed London Bridge into the borough of Southwark, the volunteers retired. Unchallenged on the South Bank, the mob rampaged through Southwark, breaking the windows of cheesemongers and warehouses. Outside 6 Temple Place on Blackfriars Road they called for a Mr Rusby who had been tried and found guilty of profiteering from oats in July. The mob burst into his home, finding his wife in a room on her own. She told them they could do as they pleased with the house and furniture but begged them to spare her and her children. They assured her they would not harm them but searched for Mr Rusby with the intention of hanging him. He had fled to a neighbour's home through the back, so when the lynch mob failed to find him, they vented their frustration by destroying drawers and papers and stealing some money. By the time a detachment of Light Horse accompanied by London militia arrived, they had gone.

The next day, there was further unrest, despite a fall in the price of wheat. Encouraged by revolutionary ballads and cartoons demonising traders as profiteers, and urged by radical literature to pursue the cause of liberty with slogans such as "Bread or Blood", the mob kept the authorities busy. The Lord Mayor and aldermen declared that had it not been for the riots, the price would have fallen lower. They were therefore resolved to suppress by force "every attempt to impede, by acts of violence, the regular business of the markets of the Metropolis." The Mayor was determined to protect property and maintain the peace, advising residents to stay indoors and away from their windows if they saw the military. On 18 September Mansion House was warned of a mob that had assembled in Chiswell Street. The crowd had suspected some barrels of salted pork a shopkeeper had in a cellar contained commodities he was keeping from the market and were threatening to blow the place up. Constables were despatched and the mob was dispersed, but by the evening another crowd had re-emerged at Bishopsgate Street. From there it rampaged westwards though Sun Street and Finsbury Square. Undeterred by constables, the rioters continued their westward rampage from the Barbican into Smithfield, spreading up Saffron Hill, into Holborn and down Snow Hills, where they broke the windows of cheesemongers. With troops on their heels, they moved south. In Fleet market they destroyed anything breakable including another cheesemongers window and threw up anything they found not fixed to the ground. In Ludgate Hill they smashed all the street lamps. Moving east and then north they rampaged through Cheapside, Newgate Street, St Martins Le Grand and Barbican, smashing more lamps, before finally dispersing into the night at Old Street. The same day the King issued a proclamation urging all authorities to use the most effective means possible of suppressing the disturbance. More riots occurred the following evening, but the large number of troops in London ensured that the masses failed to achieve anything more than closing the Corn Exchange for two days and the damage of some property. On the 20 September crowds at Clare Market and Monmouth Street were respectively dispersed by the Horse Guards and the Westminster volunteers.[1]

After a week of rioting, the mob had gone, allowing the police to wash off the graffiti chalked on the walls. The Home Secretary, the Duke of Portland, wrote to local authorities, telling them they were indulging the rioters by fixing prices. This, he said, was counter-productive and an intolerable breach of the sanctity of private property. The sole answer to the economic problem was to ensure the unrestricted operation of the free market. The reason for the scarcity was not, as the public believed, the result of profiteering, but another bad harvest. These letters were widely published and criticised as rioting spread to Kent and the south-east and then to South Wales.[2]

While the London Corn Exchange was being besieged, Otto had received further instructions from France. On 16 September he sent Grenville Bonaparte's response: because the terms offered by England gave no advantage to the French it did not compensate for the inconvenience of the continental truce. Such terms could only be considered in a separate treaty with France and England. So England could either join the negotiations with Austria by agreeing to the naval truce offered by France, or have separate negotiations on the naval truce terms of England. On the 20th Grenville refused both options. Otto replied the next day with another suggestion: six French frigates should be free to sail from Toulon to Alexandria and return without being searched

---

[1] Ashton pp.16-26

[2] Wells p.182

while only ships of the line need be withdrawn from the blockaded coasts.[1]

On 22 September, Dundas, perhaps concerned that the negotiations were being dominated by the hawks in the government, decided to submit his feelings to Pitt in writing. He wanted Pitt to be clear about the different positions in Cabinet. "Some [...] think that the only solid hope of peace lies in the restoration of the Bourbons. Some [...] think that there should be no peace with a Revolutionary Government and that the present Government of France is such. Some are for negotiating with the present Government of France" in conjunction with Austria. He himself saw nothing wrong in negotiating a separate peace with France "with a just sense of our dignity and honour, and of the conquests we have made out of Europe. It is earnestly hoped that Mr Pitt will take these observations into his most serious consideration before it is too late."[2]

The next day Grenville received another letter from Otto. It was regrettable, Otto lamented, that he was not allowed to communicate more directly with English minister. The First Consul had given the armistice another eight days, which had now run out. Grenville's reply the day after accused Bonaparte of duplicity and fraud. France could only prove the sincerity of its requests for peace by engaging in a joint negotiation with England and Austria. Nobody could believe that "if the present war is to be terminated by a succession of treaties between the different powers now engaged in it, any permanent or solid basis of general tranquillity could be established." Grenville still declined to see Otto in person, but had appointed Mr Hammond, Under-Secretary of State, to continue any further discussions. They met the next day. Otto told Hammond that the key parts of a naval armistice for France were the equating of Malta, Alexandria and Belle-Île with German sieges and the withdrawal of English fleets from blockaded coasts. On these terms it could not budge.[3]

While these negotiations were going on another matter was pre-occupying Pitt again. Castlereagh was over from Ireland with some issues

[1] PRCNP pp.51-.71

[2] Stanhope p.242

[3] PRCNP pp.81-111

for the government to consider and Pitt therefore arranged a Cabinet meeting for Tuesday 30 September to discuss Catholic Emancipation. Amongst those Pitt wanted to attend was the Lord Chancellor, Lord Loughborough, who was currently in Weymouth with the King. Pitt wrote to him on the 25th, apologising for the need to shorten his stay and explaining in brief what was to be discussed.[1] At the Cabinet meeting, Pitt revealed that he wanted to replace the anti-Catholic religious Test Act with an anti-Jacobin political one, to be imposed on all persons sitting in Parliament, government officials, ministers of religion and teachers. Instead of an oath of loyalty to the Church of England, it would require and oath of loyalty to the King, his government and the established constitution. It would also specifically require the rejection of the notion of the sovereignty of the people. In addition, tithe payments to the Anglican Church in Ireland would be commuted to rents. Lord Loughborough immediately objected. He was willing to commute the tithes, but he insisted that Catholics remain for ever excluded from Parliament and office. Pitt was disappointed. As well as the King, the highest law authority in the land was against the scheme. He decided to postpone any decision for two or three months and planned to speak to the King on it as soon as possible. He never did.

Catholic Emancipation could perhaps be put off, but what to do with the floating army in the Mediterranean could not. The Cabinet was as divided as ever. Windham and Grenville had been advocating intervention in Europe. Windham believed that simply landing an army of 20,000 men in France would be sufficient to encourage the French to rise up and overthrow Bonaparte. Dundas now favoured sending the troops to evict the French from Egypt, which provoked Windham to accuse him of wanting to throw away an army to the plague in addition to that lost to yellow fever in the West Indies.[2] By 3 October, Dundas got his way. British forces would attack the French in Egypt.

Meanwhile, the peace talks between France and Austria were getting nowhere. Otto told Hammond in a meeting on 7 October that France was still prepared to negotiate a separate peace with England and would let England decide where these negotiations would take place. If in London, the First Consul would grant Otto necessary powers to negotiate

---

[1] Stanhope p.268

[2] Grainger p.14

on behalf of France.[1] Otto was informed two days later by Hammond that His Majesty declined to enter into any measure tending to separate his interest from those of his allies.[2]

On the home front, public opinion was growing against the government's response to the scarcity crisis. *The Times* newspaper attacked Portland's letters to local authorities, calling them "injudicious". Convictions of wholesalers for commercial malpractice in the courts seemed to contradict Portland's rejection of profiteering as a cause of the crisis. Even the right-wing *Anti-Jacobin Review* criticised Portland as well as the Royal Proclamation. It claimed they had made matters worse by encouraging farmers and dealers to withhold stocks while prices were rising. Magistrates were angry and insisted that civil order depended on a parliamentary solution. The Tory press called for a parliamentary enquiry. A nation-wide petition movement re-emerged, led by London, demanding an emergency recall of Parliament, which was not expected to meet again until January next year. The government initially refused to consider an emergency session, and the King refused to receive the London petition. This inflamed public opinion further and encouraged other towns to submit their own petitions.[3] In Manchester seditious graffiti appeared on it streets demanding bread or peace and always "No King". These sights and the overnight circulation of handbills calling for insurrection in the Midlands provoked fears of an imminent uprising. By 9 October Pitt was now convinced that a "speedy meeting of Parliament" was perhaps the best thing to "prevent the progress of discontent and internal mischief" and that "even if no important legislative measure could be taken, the result of Parliamentary enquiry and discussion would go further than anything towards quietening men's minds, and checking erroneous opinions".[4] The government decided to recall Parliament to meet in a month's time on 11 November.

Pitt was ill. His bowels were acting up again and he had no appetite. Physically weak, he needed both hands to hold a glass of beer to

---

[1] PRCNP p.134

[2] PRCNP p.135

[3] Wells p.182

[4] Stanhope p.245

his lips.[1] His doctor advised him to go to a spa in Cheltenham or Bath. Once the decisions about where to send the army, whether to make peace and to recall Parliament had been made, Pitt felt he could afford some time to recuperate. However, instead of a spa, he opted to stay with his old friend the Speaker of the House of Commons, Henry Addington, at his home in Woodley, near Reading in Berkshire. Pitt had known Addington since childhood, as the son of his father's personal physician. In recent years Pitt often consulted the Speaker on the issues of the day, treating him effectively as an informal member of the Cabinet. Addington and his family welcomed him to their home in mid-October, where Pitt's health improved but not sufficiently to ease his friend's concern.[2] While there, Pitt anxiously followed the price of corn in Reading, noting with relief it had fallen by seven shillings.[3] By 26 October Pitt seemed to have recovered and returned to London in the first week of November to prepare for the opening of Parliament on the 11th.

Before Parliament met, the government had to deal with a public meeting on Kennington Common on 9 November. It had been advertised in advance by handbills calling for a meeting of mechanics to petition the King to redress their grievances. An anonymous letter to Pitt in late October warned him "that a plan is in agitation to remove his Majesty's ministers from this world by a cowardly and diabolical scheme".[4] Although not necessarily related, the Privy Council did not want to take any chances and mobilised a large force of constables and volunteers. On the morning of that day, Bow street officers arrived early and took up position at The Horns public house. By nine o'clock small groups of six or seven people congregated to form a modest crowd of about a hundred. The constables summoned help, but succeeded in dispersing the gathering themselves. However, when more people arrived and others had returned, the constables decided to wait for the Surrey Yeomanry. When they arrived, they moved on a crowd that had grown to 500. By ten in the morning, the Southwark Volunteers and more constables appeared. The

---

[1] Hague p.459

[2] Pellew vol. 1 p.266

[3] Stanhope p.247

[4] Wells p.206

large force, the arrest of a few men and the onset of rain ended the resolve of others to re-assemble.[1]

The scarcity issue was referred to select committees of both Houses of Parliament. Their conclusion was that the scarcity was caused by a deficiency in cereal yields. It recommended the prohibition of using corn in distilleries, forbidding its use in the manufacture of starch and preventing the use of fine wheat flour in bread as the sole ingredient. It also proposed the continuation of paying bounties to importers of foodstuffs such as rice from India. Pitt supported this approach: "I recognize the freedom of trade in its full extent; but I do not mean to deny that some regulation may be necessary in the present situation of the country."[2] All these measures were duly approved by Parliament. What their effect would be remained to be seen.

On the continent the truce between France and Austria ended. On 3 December the Austrians were decisively beaten at Hohenlinden by General Moreau, exposing Vienna. By Christmas Austria was suing for peace. Just as England was about to lose an ally it gained a new enemy. Tsar Paul I of Russia was upset that England had not restored Malta to the Knights of St John of which he was a Grand Master. He was also annoyed with England's policy of enforcing their blockade of France by stopping and searching the ships of neutral countries like Russia. Together with Sweden and Denmark, he formed the League of Armed Neutrality to "oblige England to allow neutral ships to pass without search". As the year 1800 drew to a close, things were looking bleak for Pitt's government and they were about to get much bleaker in the New Year.

---

[1] Ashton p.26-28

[2] Stanhope p.251

LORD SIDMOUTH.   FROM AN AUTHENTIC PORTRAIT.

9 Henry Addington

Illustration from John Cassell's *Illustrated History of England* (W Kent, 1857/1858). (Look and Learn Collection)

6. Pitt's Fall, the Speaker's Rise and the King's Madness

King George was livid. He had heard that Castlereagh was over from Ireland and that the Cabinet had begun to discuss Catholic Emancipation again. At his levee at St James's Palace on 28 January 1801 he told Windham that he would be "personally indisposed towards" anyone who voted for emancipation.[1] At the same reception he shouted at Dundas:

"What! [...] What is the question which you are all about to force upon me? What is this Catholic Emancipation which this young lord, this Irish Secretary has brought over, that you are going to throw at my head? [...] I will tell you, that I shall look on every man as my personal enemy who proposes that Question to me – the most Jacobinal thing I ever heard of! […] I hope all my friends will not desert me."

Dundas tried to placate the King: "Your Majesty will find [...] among those who are friendly to that measure some whom you never supposed to be your enemies".[2] "None of your Scotch metaphysics!" was believed to have been the King's response.[3]

George was determined that his government should not pursue this issue any further. The next day he wrote to the Speaker, Henry Addington, asking him to convince Pitt to drop it. Addington obliged, and after meeting Pitt, reported to the King at Buckingham Palace that he felt he had succeeded. But on the last day of January the King received a letter from Pitt. In it he argued why he thought Catholic Emancipation was necessary and pleaded with the King to reconsider his objection. If not, Pitt wrote, then "it must be personally Mr Pitt's first wish to be released from a situation which he is conscious that, under such circumstances, he could not continue to fill, but with the greatest disadvantage."

---

[1] Jesse vol. IV p.466

[2] Stanhope p.274

[3] Jesse vol. IV p.466

The next day, Sunday 1 February, the King wrote back: "I shall hope [...] Mr Pitt's sense of duty will prevent his retiring from the present situation to the end of my life". George suggested a compromise: he would not mention the subject again if Pitt promised never to bring it forward. "But [...] further, I cannot go." Now it was Pitt's turn to be stubborn. In a letter to the King on 3 February, he said he was unable to continue on these terms. Two days later the King wrote to Pitt telling him he was obliged to accept his resignation despite the grief it caused him. George turned to Addington and asked him to form a government. Addington still hoped Pitt would reconsider and doubted he was the best candidate, but the King pleaded: "Lay your hand upon your heart," he said, "and ask yourself where I am to turn for support if you do not stand by me".[1] Addington tried to persuade Pitt from resigning once again, mentioning that the King had asked him to form a ministry. "I see nothing but ruin, Addington, if you hesitate" was Pitt's advice.[2] On 5 February Addington accepted the King's request and a few days later when he called on the King in person, he was warmly embraced by George who said: "My dear Addington, you have saved your country".[3]

Pitt promised his support for the new government and encouraged others to do likewise, expecting no-one to resign along with him. However, Grenville, Dundas, Spencer, Castlereagh, Cornwallis and Windham all resigned, as they had been committed to Catholic Emancipation as much as the prime minister. Canning, Rose and others did the same out of fanatic devotion. Rose claimed he would sooner consent to the prostitution of his daughter than stay in office.[4] The Duke of Portland, Westmorland and Lord Chatam, Pitt's elder brother, decided to remain. On 16 February in the Commons, Sheridan compared the resignation of key ministers in the middle of a war to that of a battleship preparing for battle but clearing its decks of guns rather than lumber. Pitt refused to explain the details of his resignation except to say that he and his ministers met with circumstances which rendered it impossible for them to propose Catholic Emancipation, adding that they "felt it

---

[1] Pellew vol. I p.287, Zeigler p.93

[2] Zeigler p.93

[3] Zeigler p.94

[4] Glenbervie 17 Feb 1801. Cited in Zeigler, p.98

inconsistent with our duty and honour any longer to remain a part of that Government".[1]

Pitt was to present his last budget on 18 February and after that it was presumed he and other resigning ministers would surrender their seals of office to the King. Unfortunately, reports of the King's behaviour suggested he would not be in a fit state to receive them. On Friday 13 February, after attending a church service, the King had caught a chill, developing cramps, constipation, sickness and a hoarse voice – symptoms that preceded his earlier bout of madness in 1788. Addington, after meeting the King, thought him worryingly heated and hurried, while Portland noted he was speaking in a loud voice. On Sunday the King was observed in his chapel loudly repeating a well-known verse in the Morning Service.[2] It was not until Saturday the 21st he fell into a fever and doctors were summoned. Dr Francis Willis, who had treated him in 1788, was too old to come so Dr John Willis answered the call, followed by his brother Rev Thomas Willis a few days later. To Thomas Willis the King said: "I do feel myself very ill" because of worrying about the Catholic question. "I am much weaker than I was, and I have prayed to God all night that I might die, or that He would spare my reason [...] For God's sake keep me from your father and a regency". George became delirious that night and it took three doctors over an hour to get him to bed. The next day, he was able to see Addington, who found him "much deranged on some subjects" while perfectly sensible on others.

The King's illness prompted the question: who was in charge of government – Pitt's outgoing Cabinet or Addington's new administration? Pitt was quite clear on what should happen. His government should wind-down and hand over responsibility to Addington's. In the mean-time both Pitt and Addington would hold their own Cabinet meetings until either the King recovered or his son, the Prince of Wales, became Regent. However, Pitt was concerned that the Prince might exploit his father's illness and invite Fox to form a ministry. The Prince had certainly not seemed too concerned over his father's illness. The day after the King developed a fever, music and dancing could be enjoyed at the Prince's residence at Carlton House. Pitt warned the Prince that he was prepared to resurrect the Regency Bill he had advocated during the last crisis in

---

[1] Cited in Stanhope, p.285

[2] Cited in Stanhope, p.294

1788 which would curtail the powers of the regent. On 27 February the Commons were told this Bill would be introduced if the King had not recovered by the middle of March.

Meanwhile the King was showing signs of improvement. He had had two hours of uninterrupted sleep. His familiar, former habit of saying "what, what, what?" returned and he was beginning to eat and drink normally. But then his health declined again. His pulse rose. On 2 March it was feared the King was going to die. The Prince of Wales and the Queen were called to his bedside. Hot vinegar was applied to the feet and blisters to the head. Musk, quinine and tartar emetics were administered. At Addington's suggestion, a pillow of warm hops was placed under His Majesty's head to cure his insomnia. Although the King then slept for several hours and awoke feeling better, he deteriorated again over the next few days, becoming nervous, irritable and finding it difficult to swallow. He convulsively clenched his teeth and obsessively rolled up his handkerchiefs at a rate of fifty per day while an inability to concentrate reduced him to tears. A backlog of 800 unsigned official documents piled up, so Dr John Willis was allowed to supervise the King while he carried out his duties. Then suddenly on 5 March the King was sitting up in bed eating his meals unaided. Two days later, after noting his son, the Duke of York, was reluctant to answer his question about public affairs, George said: "Frederick, you are more nervous than I am. I really feel quite well and know full well how ill I have been."[1]

In the meantime, Addington formed his government. As he had no personal following, he had to fill his Cabinet with influential colleagues, the most important of whom were suggested by either Pitt or the King. Perhaps the key post was that of Foreign Secretary. Pitt recommended Robert Banks Jenkinson, Lord Hawkesbury. Hawkesbury, with the help of his father Lord Liverpool, became an MP in the 1790s and held a number of minor offices in government where he had impressed Pitt and the King. Hawkesbury was a tall gangly man with an awkward gait and a melancholic expression that suggested to one contemporary wit that he looked like someone who had been on the rack for several turns and expected suffering several more. He was to become Addington's closest confidante in the Cabinet. Pitt also suggested Lord Hobart, an ex-army officer and former political ally from the 1780s, serving as Chief Secretary for Ireland for five years. He was persuaded by

---

[1] Cited in Hibbert, p.316

Pitt to accept the post of Minister of War. At the Admiralty Addington appointed Lord St Vincent. Addington disliked him, but St Vincent was a war-hero to the mob and much respected amongst naval officials. He was also determined to reform the Navy, a goal they both shared.

Lord Loughborough, who was suspected of leaking Pitt's plans for Catholic Emancipation to the King, was dismissed as Lord Chancellor and replaced by Lord Eldon, but when Addington held his first cabinet meeting, Loughborough was the first to turn up. It was thought to be some kind of farewell gesture, but when he attended the next meeting as well, Addington had to make it clear there was no place for him there. If Loughborough seemed reluctant to leave, Eldon was just as reluctant to join. Eldon was the King's choice, but he hesitated to join Addington's administration for fear of losing his job if Pitt returned to office. He was only persuaded to accept after Pitt promised him a pension in the event of his dismissal on his return. Eldon nevertheless made it quite clear that he owed his position to the King and not to Addington. Another choice of the King – and his son the Duke of York – was Lord Pelham, a Portland Whig who had been Chief Secretary of Ireland on two occasions. The King and the Duke suggested the War Office, but Pelham refused. When a reluctant Addington offered him the Board of Trade, Pelham insisted on a Cabinet post. Addington, in desperation exclaimed to the King's friends: "Would you have me go on my knees to him?" The issue was resolved when Portland agreed to vacate the Home Office, a role Pelham finally felt obliged to accept. Lord Ellenborough was offered the position of Attorney General, which he did not hesitate to take.

Other members of the government included a few friends in minor posts and Addington's brother Hiley as one of the secretaries of the Treasury. Pitt's older brother, Lord Chatham, known as "the late Lord Chatam" for his tardiness at attending meetings, was retained. Addington told his colleagues that he did not expect them to be against Catholic Emancipation, but simply recognise that this was not the time to consider it. He expected only character, talent and friendship.

Reaction to the new government was mixed. The appointment of a doctor's son as prime minister jarred with the prejudices of many who expected their leaders to be aristocrats. If they were not aristocrats then they should at least have talent and Addington appeared to have none. Certainly, his speaking skills were inadequate for parliamentary debates. He could not deal with interruptions, was unable to talk confidently on unfamiliar topics and would become renowned for being incoherent. His background and perceived weaknesses earned himself the nickname of "the Doctor" and his Cabinet the labels of the "dumpling" and "goose" administration.

The MP George Canning seemed to take a personal dislike to Addington, expressing his contempt with barely disguised personal insults in witty doggerels. When Canning first learned from Pitt that Addington had told him the King was to appoint him as the head of a new administration, Canning's response was: "Did you not kick him downstairs?"[1] Canning seemed more upset by Pitt's downfall than Pitt himself and did everything he could to return his leader to power. When Pitt was informed by Dr Willis that the King had considered his illness had been caused by Pitt's raising the question of Catholic Emancipation, he asked the doctor to convey his promise to the King to never to bring it up again. Canning, Dundas and others considered this promise effectively negated his reason for leaving office and urged him to rescind his resignation. On 8 March Canning wrote to him insisting that the public interest required he stay in power, suggesting that "nothing but miserable, petty, personal considerations" could motivate his refusal. Pitt, however, would only act if Addington made the first move. Enquiries were made through the Duke of Portland to see if Addington would step aside. He would not: he had only given up his beloved role as Speaker on the understanding he would be prime minister. Pitt then made it clear to Dundas that he would only resume office if that was the spontaneous desire – not just the acquiescence – of Addington.[2]

Not everyone had a negative view of Addington's government. One independent MP thanked God for a ministry "without one of those confounded men of genius in it"[3]. Others closer to Addington were more positive. Lord Eldon considered him a man of strong Protestant principles, while Pitt's brother Lord Chatham held that the King could not have acted more wisely. Many others were just relieved that Fox – the only other alternative to Pitt – was not prime minister.

[1] Foreman p.344

[2] Hague pp.481-484

[3] Fedorak p.44

10 Lord Hawkesbury

Engraving by H. Robinson after a painting by Sir Thomas Lawrence. (Author's private Collection).

7. Peace Talks and Trouble up North

On 19 March, less than a week after officially becoming the new government, Addington's Cabinet asked the King's permission to resume peace talks with France. Addington himself conveyed this request to George, who consented the same day. The new Foreign Secretary, Lord Hawkesbury, invited Otto for talks at his London home in Sackville Street. Otto had only recently returned to London, as he had been recalled to France in protest after Dundas had ordered the Royal Navy to arrest French fishermen in the Channel in January.

A week later Addington made his first speech to Parliament as prime minister. He declared "that it was the determination of His Majesty's servants to take such steps as appeared to them best calculated for the restoration of peace; that no consideration, arising from the form of government in France would, on their part, obstruct negotiation: and that if there were a corresponding disposition on the part of the enemy, the grand object to which the efforts of government would be directed would, he trusted, be accomplished."[1] The speech was well received by the county members, the Whigs and *The Times* newspaper. Only Windham and others had reservations. Pitt declared he would support any peace that did not threaten vital interests of the country. Behind the scenes he continued to offer support and advice to Addington's government, dining every fortnight with Hawkesbury.

At the beginning of 1801 Britain had three allies: Portugal, the Kingdom of Naples and the Turks of the Ottoman Empire. Against them were France, Spain and Holland. Britain was also fighting the League of Armed Neutrality led by Russia. The French side had the upper hand in mainland Europe. By the end of March, Naples was out of the war and allowed French troops to occupy some of its ports, closing them to British and Ottoman ships. The main battleground was the Mediterranean: Britain had captured Minorca from Spain and had ejected the French from Malta and was attempting to drive them out of Egypt. In other areas of the world Britain had, over the course of the last seven

---

[1] Ziegler p.118

years of war, accumulated a number of other conquests: in India it had taken Mysore from the French ally Tipu Sultan, Pondicherry and Chandernagore from the French and Mahé and Ceylon from the Dutch; in the East Indies Britain seized from the Dutch Malacca and the Spice islands of Amboyna and Banda (also from the Dutch it had appropriated Cape Town in South Africa); in the West Indies Britain had acquired French sugar-producing islands (including Martinique, Guadeloupe, Tobago and St. Lucia), and relieved Spain of Trinidad; from the Dutch it swiped Curacao, Surinam and its Guyanese possessions of Demerary, Essequibo and Berbice. In North America Britain had captured the French territories of St Pierre and Miquelon in the Gulf of St. Lawrence. It could use all these conquests to bargain for a more favourable situation in Europe and the Mediterranean.

When Pitt's Cabinet had been negotiating with Otto the previous year it had sketched out a peace plan in case the talks moved on from the stumbling block of the preliminary naval truce, on which they had been unable to agree terms. The main concerns at the time were the French occupation of Egypt and their influence over the Dutch Republic. Britain's treaty with the Turks obliged the British to seek nothing less than the evacuation of the French from Egypt, but towards the Netherlands they were inclined to be more flexible. The preferred option of Pitt and his colleagues was for the Prince of Orange to be restored to the position of Stadtholder but they realised this was unrealistic. Other options included giving Holland to either the Elector of Bavaria, the Duke of Tuscany or some lesser prince as part of an arrangement that France might be induced to make with Austria which had not yet made peace at that time. Now that Austria was out of the war the only realistic option Britain could adopt was merely to hope that Holland would be allowed to form an independent republic modelled as much as possible on its native ancient institutions and provide the Prince of Orange with compensation.

The peace plan also revealed the relative importance of its conquests to Pitt's government. The most important conquests were the Cape, Ceylon and Chochin, which were to be kept at all costs. Then came the West Indian French sugar islands of St Lucia and Martinique. After that were the islands of Trinidad and Tobago. The return of the Spice Islands, Surinam and Demerara to Holland were not considered a big loss for Britain, while the French and Dutch trading posts in India could be returned and continue trading as long as they were not fortified in any way and did not threaten British interests.[1]

In early April the Foreign Secretary Lord Hawkesbury dismissed Otto's suggestion of a preliminary naval truce, but this did not stall the talks this time. Otto offered the option of Britain retaining all its conquests if France were allowed to keep Egypt. Otherwise these countries should all be restored to their previous owners. Hawkesbury refused, but indicated later that Britain would be prepared to give up some of its acquisitions if France left Egypt. Otto said that France would quit Egypt and allow Britain to keep Mysore as long as it returned all other territories, including Malta which would be restored to the Knights of St John.

Hawkesbury wanted to keep more of Britain's conquests. In a second meeting on 14 April he handed Otto a note written in his own hand, offering to restore the following if the French abandoned Egypt:

- in India – Pondicherry, Chandernagore, Mahé and Cochin;
- in the East Indies – Negepatam, Malacca and the spice island of Amboyna and Banda;
- the islands of St Marcou, off the Normandy coast;
- in South America – Surinam;
- in the West Indies: Curacao, St Lucia, and the Sainte islands;
- off the West African coast: the island of Gorée;
- in the Mediterranean – Minorca;
- and in North America – St. Pierre and Miquelon.

In Southern Africa the Cape would be returned to the Dutch but would become a free port. What was not mentioned were Ceylon, Malta, Martinique, Trinidad, Tobago, Demerary, Essequibo and Berbice which were to be retained by Britain. He also insisted that the Prince of Orange should receive territorial compensation for loss of his Dutch lands. The

---

[1] Yonge p.50

offer would be withdrawn if news arrived of the French being defeated in Egypt.[1]

The proposal was transmitted to Bonaparte, who though that it was just an attempt by the British to gain time. The official French reply was that they could "not leave in the hands of England countries and establishments of such considerable weight".[2] In a letter sent to Hawkesbury by Otto on 16 April the French accused Britain of being involved in the bomb plot against Bonaparte the previous year and supporting militant royalists in western France. The communication also complained of personal attacks on Bonaparte in the English press. Otto suggested they resume their negotiations as verbal discussions rather than exchanges of letters. Hawkesbury denied British involvement in the bomb plot but agreed to revert to face-to-face meetings.[3]

Meanwhile, Britain's threat from Russia, Denmark and other countries of the League of Armed Neutrality was abating. On 13 April Hawkesbury received a letter from the Russian chancellor announcing the death of Tsar Paul. He had been assassinated and was succeeded by his son Alexander who was to divert Russian foreign policy away from the recent pro-French stance of his father. Then on April 15 it was announced that Nelson had destroyed the Danish fleet at Copenhagen.

****

The social unrest that Pitt faced in 1800 did not go away in 1801. In November 1800 there was a general fear of a mass uprising in the north of England. Some of the volunteer militia were considered unreliable and troops were sent to the West Midlands, much to the annoyance of local magistrates who had not asked for them and thought they were inflaming

[1] OPRP p.38

[2] Liverpool p.149

[3] Grainger p.35

the situation. Nevertheless, the Home Secretary, Lord Portland was reluctant to remove the troops in the New Year.

The incessant rise in prices during the winter and the resulting discontent with the government among the unrepresented populace produced various forms of political expression. One was a revived petition movement for peace and parliamentary reform, led by men like Major John Cartwright and supported by the middle classes. This movement also attracted workers and the poor, but its lack of success persuaded many of those that if petitioning failed, they should simply revolt. Many joined underground political societies like the United Britons and United Englishmen, realising that for an insurrection to succeed, it had to be organised. Leading the United Britons was a national executive committee, co-ordinating it members by various tiers of messengers, superintendents and conductors.

In March, on the day circuit judges convened the seasonal courts of the Warwickshire assizes, food riots broke out in Birmingham, where bakers were singled out for attack by the mob. Similar unrest occurred in Worcester and Coventry. In mid-March, in Lancashire and West Yorkshire, meetings were arranged to induct people into the cause by administering oaths. As many as 50,000 people may have been willing to take such oaths in Oldham, Ashton, Saddleworth and Rochdale. The arrest of oath administrators in Bolton provoked a riot. Fires in Manchester factories and an outbreak of thieving revived fears of an uprising. The army was reinforced and the Lord Lieutenant of the West Riding urged magistrates to be vigilant and advised that the volunteer cavalry should be recruited from the conservative farming community. Meetings continued to be held in late March and April. At Tandle Hills in Lancashire, thousands turned up from Oldham and Rochdale to listen to speakers articulate their complaints and propose solutions. A tree poster summed these up as "an equal representation of all the people of England by universal suffrage", a reduction of the national debt and a lowering of prices. Orators considered that the war was the "sole cause of unparalleled high price" of food. It enriched contractors "at the expense of the great body of the labouring poor." They complained of high taxes and high prices, the decline of manufacturing and commerce and low wages. Because of this, most of the "community are literally starving." A similar meeting in the West Riding in April also complained of the inflated cost of food, oppressive taxes and the national debt, suggesting the war was the cause of all the present calamities because it shut off three-quarters of world trade. As well as peace, attendees called for the care of the sick and elderly. They proposed an end to hereditary government and fairer representation in the House of Commons, but wondered whether petitioning Parliament was like asking a corrupt agent to remove itself. A more radical gathering in Nottingham saw the main question as whether to wait for the French to invade or rise up without them. Petitioning was only useful in that it allowed them to test their strength prior to a revolution.

On 1 April Addington formed a secret committee to review the state of unrest in Ireland and England. The Act suspending Habeas Corpus had expired in March, obliging the government to release its political prisoners. A radical dinner celebrating their release was held in the Green Dragon pub, but this joy was short-lived. On 13 April, Addington's committee noted that the revolutionaries had been encouraged by the resumption of Habeas Corpus and urgently recommended its suspension be renewed along with a new Seditious Meetings Act. When Habeas Corpus was once again suspended arrest warrants were issued on 19 April against twenty radicals who had attended the Green Dragon dinner. Ten days later a new Seditious Meetings Act also came into force. Addington's committee concluded, based on evidence of oath taking, that there was a "very dangerous conspiracy" with links to the United Britons who were directing insurrectionary activity within the petitioning movement and that activity was being undertaken on the pretext of high prices.

In May meetings continued, but some were interrupted by the authorities. On 3 May dragoons were sent to Buckton Castle near Manchester to prevent a widely publicised mass meeting that was drafting a petition. People arrived as early as four in the morning, but it was not until ten o'clock, when a sizable crowd had assembled, that they were told to move on. When they kept defiantly returning, three of four shots were fired. Most eventually left by the afternoon and those that remained were arrested, but were released after they had given their names and were not prosecuted. On 24 May a Rivington meeting was infiltrated by volunteer corps with concealed bayonets. Two hundred miners and weavers turned up, but fled when the cavalry arrived. Magistrates were again lenient with prisoners, releasing those who had been vouched for by respected persons.

By the summer trade was reviving, prices were falling and the enthusiasm for political protest had waned or gone further underground. The petitioning movement had been discredited by reports of revolutionary plans in London and plotting with the Irish. At the summer assizes in Lancashire thirty men were prosecuted for oath taking, some of whom were sentenced to transportation. Some employers tracked the political opinions of their employees and sacked suspected Jacobins. In May the United Britons executive in London had considered some of their northern colleagues as too reckless and hasty, urging them to stop their open meetings. In Lancashire the high visibility of cavalry and artillery forced radicals into more secret activities. Smaller groups of ten with agreed signals were formed. Some groups started to arm and drill. In Sheffield, pike heads were produced and buried in gardens. The United Britons issued a new constitution, specifying its aims as the independence of Great Britain and Ireland and the equality of civil, political and religious rights. These objectives were printed on a card and new members would signify their assent by kissing it, an act equivalent to the taking of an oath.[1]

---

[1] Wells pp.192-220

8. Pride and Progress

The face-to-face talks dragged. At the end of May, Otto complained to Hawkesbury that "two months had passed away without being able to fix the basis of a pacification so important to the two nations and all Europe". By then France had persuaded Spain to invade Portugal, supported by French troops. After a brief campaign Portugal was ready to cede some territory to Spain and close her ports to Britain. News had also arrived from Egypt of a British victory, but not a decisive one. The French were still clinging on. Otto suggested that the negotiations "assume a more official character" and asked that Britain communicate in writing what it proposed for peace terms.[1]

On 6 June Hawkesbury denied delaying tactics and said that Britain would only ever give up all its conquests if the powers of Europe were restored to their boundaries of 1792. If France could not accept this then Britain would have the right to retain some of its conquests "as a counterpoise to the important acquisitions of territory obtained by France on the Continent". Britain's proposal remained the same as those made on 14 April. This, Hawkesbury claimed, was actually a concession, as Britain's fortunes had improved since then. Otherwise, "if the French government has any propositions to make different from those that have been mentioned, and which in its judgement may conduce to peace, His Majesty is ready to give them the highest consideration".[2]

In mid-June a disappointed Otto complained to Hawkesbury that "the sincere disposition to peace is not visible" in the propositions presented on 14 April. Bonaparte was not prepared to trade French European acquisitions for the return of just a few colonies and would only withdraw French troops from the territories of Britain's allies – Portugal, Naples and the Ottomans. If Britain refused to relinquish its colonial conquests, France would continue to occupy Italy and Portugal,

---

[1] OPRP p.39

[2] OPRP p.40

threatening British commercial and strategic interests in the Mediterranean.

"Nevertheless, it is acknowledged, that the great events that have happened in Europe and the changes that have taken place in the boundaries of the Great States of the Continent, might authorise a part of the demands of the British Government, but how can it demand, as an ultimatum, the keeping of Malta, of Ceylon, of all the countries conquered from Tipoo Sahib, of Trinidad, Martinique, &c.?"

Otto asked: if France allowed Britain to keep its conquests in the East Indies and restored Portugal to its state before the war, would Britain consent to the restoration of the Americas and the Mediterranean to their pre-war state as well?[1] Before Hawkesbury had a chance to reply he received a second letter from Otto informing him of the terms Portugal was being obliged to accept. As well as closing its ports to British ships and ceding a Portuguese province to Spain it also agreed to relinquish some Guyanese territory in South America to France in addition to paying an indemnity. Despite this, Bonaparte was refusing to ratify the agreement and was prepared to resume his attack on Portugal unless Britain would consider a restoration of the pre-war state of the Americas for the pre-war state of Portugal.[2]

A week later Hawkesbury replied, his confidence perhaps boosted by the Anglo-Russian Convention of 17 June that re-opened Baltic ports to British trade. What did Otto mean by the status before the war? Was he referring to 1793? If so, then France should restore Egypt to the Turks, Nice to Piedmont, Piedmont to the King of Sardinia and Tuscany to the Habsburgs. If France would not accept 1792 why would they agree to 1793? If French "influence" in Italy continued, Britain would have to hold on to Malta.   Also, the *status ante bellum* in the Americas could in no way be considered equivalent to the *status ante bellum* for Portugal. The immense number of conquests by Britain of French, Dutch and Spanish possessions far outweighed the gains France had made at the expense of Portugal. Nevertheless, if the French endorsed Britain's proposal regarding the Mediterranean and agreed that Britain could keep its conquests in the East Indies plus Martinique, Tobago, Demerary,

---

[1] OPRP p.43

[2] OPRP p.43

Essequibo and Berbice, His Majesty would grant the restoration of Spain's status before the war in exchange for that of Portugal's.[1]

This was not well received by the French. Anthony Merry, who had been sent to Paris by Hawkesbury, reported soon after he arrived that the French had not found the Foreign Secretary's last communication very helpful. Merry tried to emphasise to the French foreign ministry that the reference to 1792 was not meant to imply that British policy was to overthrow Bonaparte, but simply to seek peace with him.[2] On 15 July, Hawkesbury received an indignant letter from Otto, referring to the former's proposal of the 14 April and complaining that Britain had added further demands to this, obliging France to threaten a resumption of the campaign against Portugal unless these additional claims were withdrawn: "Can it be believed that the French people are reduced to such a sad extremity as to sign a disgraceful peace?"[3]

On 20 July Hawkesbury denied that Britain was making more demands, even though it had every right to, considering its progress against the French in Egypt. British terms still remained the same as those of 14 April. He reminded Otto that "the French government has distinctly admitted, in the note presented by M. Otto, 18th June, that which could not, indeed, be contested, that His Majesty was justified in retaining from his own conquests a compensation for the important acquisitions of territory that France has made on the continent". Hawkesbury asked that the French declare exactly what part of the British proposals they objected to and what conditions they deemed would bring the "negotiations to a prompt and happy conclusion".[4]

This prompted Otto to respond five days later with a detailed statement of French terms. In the Mediterranean the French would restore Egypt to the Ottoman Empire and evacuate Papal and Neapolitan ports in Italy. Britain would return Minorca to Spain and Malta to the Knights of St John. Malta's fortifications would be razed. The Dutch

---

[1] OPRP p.45

[2] Grainger p.42

[3] OPRP p.47

[4] OPRP p.49

would cede Ceylon to Britain, but all other British conquests should be restored. As for Martinique, "France would never renounce her right to it." It was now up to the British Cabinet to decide whether to accept these terms. If they did not "it will be proved in the face of the world that the First Consul has neglected nothing, and that he has evinced his disposition to make every kind of sacrifice, to re-establish peace, and to spare to humanity the tears and blood which will be inevitable consequences of a new campaign."[1]

The latest French terms were discussed by the Cabinet two days later. They decided that Otto must be persuaded to improve the French offer. On 5 August Hawkesbury wrote to Otto arguing that Martinique had been placed under British protection by its own inhabitants and therefore was not technically a conquest. Britain's proposals were reasonable and, unlike the French, guided by honourable principles. The British had every right to expect the French to agree to them and the French had no right to object. However, His Majesty was prepared to give "a new proof of his moderation and sentiments". If the French would be reasonable over the East Indies, the British would consider discussing an arrangement regarding Malta "which would render it independent both of Great Britain and France".[2]

Despite Hawkesbury's arrogant jibe at French principles, Otto welcomed this latest gesture. In the East, France was ready to abandon its ally Mysore and cede Ceylon while Britain's willingness to give up Malta removed the "sole obstacle" to peace as far as the Mediterranean was concerned.[3] Otto had an agreeable meeting with Hawkesbury on 13 August, after which Otto dined with an English friend, Sir John Macpherson, before sending off a dispatch to France. Otto had heard reports that Cairo had fallen to the British, leaving only Alexandria in French hands. He recommended to Talleyrand that the French accept Hawkesbury's offer of 5 August without delay. Macpherson reported his dinner conversation with Otto to Addington the next day: Otto "is literally fighting your battle with his own government" and getting to abate its terms. Otto had persuaded them to drop a proposition

---

[1] OPRP p.51

[2] OPRP p.53

[3] OPRP p.55

concerning Mysore, hoped for a positive reception to his recommendations and was considering resigning if his advice was "not attended to". Macpherson went on to say: "On the arrival of the answer he trusts that you will likewise meet concession with some concession, and then close at once a work which will render the greatest service to your country and mankind. If peace is not very shortly concluded, he has no hopes for it."[1]

Hawkesbury made some further helpful suggestions a few days later: "if the possession of Martinique by His Majesty be considered by the French government as an insurmountable obstacle to the return of peace, His Majesty might be induced to renounce his just pretension in this respect" on condition that the French accepted one of the following alternatives: either Britain be allowed to keep Trinidad and Tobago or be allowed to retain St Lucia and Tobago along with Demerary, Essequibo, and Berbice.[2] Otto again urged Talleyrand to accept this latest offer, but it was declined because it was felt both options would leave Britain with too much power in the Americas. Although the French had been determined that the peace ought not to cost their Republic any personal sacrifice, they were prepared to offer Tobago and Curacao instead.[3]

The British rejected this, but by 7 September both Otto and Hawkesbury were optimistic enough to consider the provisional articles of a preliminary peace treaty. Otto made the suggestion that they only enumerate conquests to be restored, as France had no authority to cede territories of its allies to Britain. He claimed that the most they could do in the preliminaries was agree not to oppose British demands for these lands at the definitive treaty conference. Hawkesbury retorted that as France's allies were relying on France to get their colonies returned then France had the right to decide what they should give up to achieve this. Otto indignantly replied that only the French government could determine what obligations and rights it had in respect of its own allies. An exasperated Hawkesbury declared that either Otto had the authority to cede Spanish and Dutch colonies or he would have to cede French ones instead. If neither of these were acceptable then Britain would be obliged

---

[1] Pellew vol 1 p.450

[2] OPRP p.56

[3] Fedorak p.64, Gifford p.358

to make a separate peace with each country, making it pointless to continue the current negotiation.

Otto complained that the cessions demanded by Britain did not derive from any right, but was simply an accessory advantage Bonaparte was allowing Britain out of his desire for peace. Hawkesbury contradicted him: Britain had only agreed to negotiate on the principle that the retention of conquests was compensation for territories acquired by France on the continent and this principle had been admitted by France. Omitting any reference to the colonies to be retained "would give the treaty an equivocal meaning", exposing it to be interpreted by France and its allies as implying they were never given up, but only put off for further discussion. Otto made one last attempt to get his way, suggesting a secret article enumerating what was to be retained by Britain and keeping the preliminary articles secret until the signing of the definitive treaty. Hawkesbury did not think preliminaries could be kept a secret in practice and besides, it was not usual to do so for such an important peace treaty.

They moved on, quickly agreeing to the return of the Cape to the Dutch before turning to Malta. Hawkesbury complained that the article proposed by the French was not sufficiently explicit – it did not mention a guarantor or protector. He read out his own proposal, involving the reinstatement of the Knights of St John under the protection of Russia, which would provide a garrison for the island. Otto said that Bonaparte would not refuse Russia as a guarantor but questioned the need to ask the Tsar, as he had already effectively pledged his support of the Knights through their Russian chapter. Otto was also concerned that the numerous conditions relating to Malta would delay the signing of the definitive treaty and its execution. Hawkesbury defended the conditions as necessary to ensure they were confident that the Knights, currently disordered by internal schism, were capable of defending the island against possible future French aggression. Otto asserted that if there was a delay in the evacuation of Malta the French would be justified in postponing their withdrawal from the Neapolitan and Papal states. Hawkesbury conceded, but insisted that any French troops left in southern Italy should be proportionate to those of Britain's in Malta. Otto thought this precaution was misplaced as France had nothing to gain by these delays.

After Malta they agreed on the evacuation of Egypt by France and then discussed the article stipulating the integrity of the Kingdom of Portugal. Hawkesbury wanted the definition to cover "territories and possessions". Otto objected as it might contradict the arrangement made at Badajoz between Spain and Portugal in respect of Guyana.

Another contentious article was prisoner expenses. Hawkesbury wanted to insert a clause borrowed from the last peace treaty with France in 1783, which provided that France and Britain would repay the expenses the other had incurred for maintaining enemy captives. Otto objected: this would be too much for France to bear as it would have the most to repay. He argued that the French had maintained the prisoners of Britain's allies such as Russia throughout the war at their own expense, while the article he was proposing was consistent with the Lunéville treaty with Austria. In 1783 the number of prisoners each side had maintained was equal and therefore incomparable to the current war. Hawkesbury countered that Russian and other prisoners of France had no bearing on a treaty with Britain.

Nothing was agreed so the discussion moved on to the article asserting French fishing rights in Newfoundland. Hawkesbury claimed that Britain's superiority at sea gave her the sole right to determine this issue. The British were willing to agree the same rights that prevailed before the war, but wanted to defer this to a commercial treaty on the grounds it would take a long time to consult with the necessary experts on the matter. Otto made the point that it had been part of the preliminaries to the 1783 treaty so should be included in their preliminary treaty as well. Hawkesbury would not give way. It had taken three months, he said, to settle the issue in 1783 and would take even longer now. Otto did not think the delay would be as long as that. He admitted that the fisheries were not particularly valuable, but thought the issue needed to be resolved to cement the peace more firmly. Britain's refusal to discuss this threatened the future tranquillity of the region. Hawkesbury was tied by the Cabinet's decision to abide by same terms of the 1783 treaty, so he and Otto agreed to defer it to a later discussion.

A French proposal that Britain should promise not to seize French fishermen in any possible future war was rejected by Hawkesbury. He said the current freedom of French fishermen was an indulgence allowed by Britain on the grounds of humanity and could not be considered a right. Otto tried to persuade Hawkesbury that it could only be honourable for a nation that controlled the sea to fix the limit of its activities to prevent future injustices. Hawkesbury was unmoved, declaring that war gives nations the right and duty to exercise their full powers to defeat an enemy.

The meeting ended with both sides agreeing to admit the allies of France to the conference. Hawkesbury wanted Britain's allies to attend as well, but Otto pointed out they were not sacrificing anything in this treaty, while separate peace agreements were being made with Portugal and the Ottoman Empire. Hawkesbury conceded, but suggested they should be at least invited to approve the final settlement.[1]

---

[1] OPRP p.58-65

11 William Windham

Engraving from The National Gallery (Jones, c 1850) (Look and Learn Collection).

9. A Welcome and Shameful Peace

Despite an announcement confirming the capitulation of French forces at Cairo, Otto's recommendation to his masters was still not heeded. Bonaparte instructed Otto to reject as many of the British demands as possible. On 11 September a letter from Talleyrand told him that the First Consul "will never subscribe to conditions in which the honour of the nation is compromised. It is prescribed to you, citizen, to give a formal assurance of it." Otto was instructed to add verbally "that the First Consul having gone so far as honour would permit him, there was no room to hope that he would make one step more"[1]

On 17 September Otto conveyed the latest French position to Hawkesbury: Egypt, the Neapolitan coast, Port Mahon and Malta should be restored to their original owners. The French consented to the idea that Malta should be protected by a guarantor if this was insisted on, but would not allow that power to garrison the island as it would infringe the sovereignty of the Knights. The evacuation of the island by Britain should not be delayed any longer than that agreed for other withdrawals. In the East Indies the French felt both sides now understood what was being restored and retained. The indemnity for the Prince of Orange should be settled separately in Berlin. The main problem for the French was Britain's demands in the Americas, where it thought Britain was already too powerful. Britain wanted both Trinidad and Tobago, rich islands close to the South American mainland and therefore of high financial and strategic value. The British also wanted Demerara, Berbice and Essequibo to be free ports – an arrangement that would be more advantageous to Britain than any other nation.[2] Two days later, to break the deadlock, Otto decided to play a card Talleyrand had authorised him to use earlier. He suggested to Hawkesbury that Britain could keep Trinidad but only if they renounced Tobago, Demerara, Essequibo and Berbice.[3] Hawkesbury insisted on retaining both Trinidad and Tobago,

[1] OPRP p.65

[2] OPRP p.66

[3] Fedorak p.65

but on 22 September said he would renounce Britain's claims to Demerara, Essequibo and Berbice if France allowed Russia – or any other power willing to be the protector and guarantor of the Knights – to take effective charge of the defences of Malta after the British had left. France would also be allowed to extend its Guyanese territory into Portuguese Brazil as long as the integrity of Portuguese European territory was maintained.

"From the disposition that his Majesty has shown to get rid of every other difficulty, he cannot suppose that the French government will raise a new obstacle on the possession of the island of Tobago. It is an ancient property of his crown; the people are almost entirely English colonists; and is not of any value or interest to France."[1]

Bonaparte, however, had been getting impatient. Two days earlier he had instructed Talleyrand that peace must be signed by the 2 October or not at all, but refused to offer more concessions to Britain. "They risk losing all [...] if they seek for more".[2] After Otto delivered this ultimatum, Hawkesbury and Addington disagreed over their response. Hawkesbury was opposed to making further concessions to France, while Addington's view was that peace was too important not to consider doing so. To bridge their own deadlock they asked Pitt for advice. On 26 September the three of them stayed up most of that night discussing the latest French terms. France was demanding Britain return all its conquests except Ceylon and Trinidad. It was also to return Malta to the Knights of St John under the guarantee of an unnamed third power to be agreed at a formal peace congress at Amiens, which would finalise any outstanding issues. In return, France would restore Egypt to the Ottoman Empire, evacuate Naples and the Papal States, while the Cape would be opened to all as a free port.

Pitt had reviewed the country's finances with Addington and was convinced that Britain could not afford to continue fighting. The French terms should be accepted.[3] Eventually, with Pitt's help, Addington persuaded Hawkesbury that peace was worth the price of further

---

[1] OPRP p.68

[2] Fedorak p.65

[3] Zeigler p.123

concessions if the effective neutrality of Malta could be assured and Portugal and Naples were allowed to accede to the treaty.[1]

On 28 September both Addington and Hawkesbury met with Otto. Addington declared that the mutual goal of Britain and France was not merely to cease hostilities, but to reconcile their two nations. The neutrality of Malta was essential to avoid future contention. He suggested that Portugal and Naples be invited to accede to the treaty as a matter of diplomatic courtesy. The next day Otto delivered another draft treaty to which minor modifications were made by both sides before they shook hands. On 1 October the deal was presented to the Cabinet. Many doubts were expressed but a consensus in favour emerged when the meeting ended in the afternoon. Later the same day, Addington asked the King to approve their decision, saying he would have to resign if His Majesty declined, as it was not possible to get better terms from the French. George reluctantly acquiesced. Hawkesbury summoned Otto to the Foreign Office and in the early evening they signed the Preliminaries of London.[2] The same day, Hawkesbury wrote to the Lord Mayor, asking him to inform the City. When he received the letter at his private residence in Clapham, the Mayor went to the Stock Exchange and Lloyds Coffee House to read it out to the assembled businessmen. They reacted with joyful smiles and mutual handshaking, raising the price of government stocks by ten per cent. News was carried to the provinces by the mail coaches displaying "Peace with France" on placards.

The next day dispatches from the British forces in Egypt were delivered to Hawkesbury. A month earlier the French general Menou had offered to surrender Alexandria. However, it was the news of the peace that was foremost in people's minds. By the evening illuminations began appearing in the windows and exteriors of buildings in London. The details of the Treaty could be read in the newspapers which wasted no time in offering their own opinions. The *Morning Chronicle*, the *Morning Post*, the *Star*, the *St James's Chronicle*, the *Porcupine*, and the *Heart of Oak* all condemned the peace while *The Times*, *True Briton*, the *Sun*, and the *Herald* welcomed the news. In this they were joined by the masses. Nearly 4,000 of them assembled in St James's Park, waiting for the French envoy to bring the ratification from France. This was General Lauriston, who

---

[1] Fedorak p.66

[2] Fedorak p.67

arrived in London at noon on 10 October in a coach and horses bedecked with blue ribbons bearing the word "peace". Inside a golden box was the French ratification. Crowds surrounded his carriage shouting "Long Live Bonaparte!" accompanying it to Otto's residence at Portman square. Otto joined Lauriston in the carriage which set off for Downing Street. The cheering crowd unhitched the horses and drew them down Bond and St James's Streets to Whitehall, proceeding to the gates of the Admiralty. There, Lord St Vincent addressed the crowd: "Gentlemen! Gentlemen!" he shouted, as they interrupted him with three cheers. "Let me request," he continued, "you to be as orderly as possible; and if you are determined to draw the gentleman accompanied by Mr Otto, I request you to be careful, and not to overturn the carriage."

By three in the afternoon the guns in the Tower of London announced the exchange of the ratifications had completed. Three hours later, the streets of the city were lit up by a seemingly limitless number of candles. On all the public buildings were hung transparencies or multi-coloured lamps arranged into words proclaiming "Peace", "G.R.", "Long Live the King, Peace & Commerce", "Peace and Prosperity", "Peace and Universal Happiness" accompanied by symbols of doves, crowns, cornucopias and olive branches. Otto's house in Portman square was among the most brilliantly lit. He had been obliged to take down lights declaring the word "Concorde" when two sailors complained, after reading it as the word "Conquered".[1] He replaced it with the word "Amity". On a building opposite hung an image of Bonaparte bearing the legend "Saviour of the universe". As well as public buildings, private residences were also illuminated. Many in the West End were obliged to do so by crowds crying "Lights! Lights!" and smashing the windows of those who failed to comply. In Bond Street, Lord Camelford refused and when he went out to remonstrate with the mob he was beaten with a brickbat and had to be rescued by his servants from a violent kicking.[2] The crowds were finally dispersed by a thunderstorm at eleven at night that lasted until three in the morning.

On the same day that Lauriston arrived in London, a dinner was held at the Shakespeare Tavern to celebrate the anniversary of Fox's election to Westminster. Fox could not restrain his delight at the turn of

---

[1] Cited in Pocock p.28

[2] Cited in Gattrell p.73

events in the last ten months and made a controversial speech that made even a few of his own supporters wince. He suggested that if the peace was more favourable and glorious to France that was only fair, given her struggle for independence against a confederacy of all the great kingdoms of Europe. "Some complain that we have not gained the object of the war. The object of the war we have not gained most certainly, and I like the peace by so much the better."[1]

A definitive treaty remained to be agreed, but the fighting was at an end. On 13 October the London Gazette printed George III's proclamation of "the cessation of arms" at land and sea. A week later the artillery and fortifications along the frontiers of the French Republic were placed on a peace footing.

In November Parliament debated the peace conditions. Pitt was supportive: "It was undoubtedly the duty of every government in negotiating a treaty of peace to obtain the best possible terms; but it was sometimes difficult to know how far particular points might be pressed without running the risk of breaking off negotiations." He defended the surrender of the colonies by arguing that they "would only give us a little more wealth; but a little more wealth would be badly purchased by a little more war". He insisted that "the government had undoubtedly endeavoured to obtain the best terms they could." In the Lords Grenville criticised the government for not basing the peace on the either the situation before the war or on the situation at its end. He claimed that the surrender of the colonies and other spoils of war would weaken Britain's strategic position. Grenville was contradicted by Lord Nelson who claimed that Malta "was of no sort of consequence to this country" and "in any hands but the French it became immaterial to us".[2] Dundas, despite approving of peace in principle, lamented the surrender of the colonies, especially the Cape and Malta. As he did not want to differ from Pitt in public, he abstained from the debate. Thomas Grenville was disgusted that – despite being victorious – Britain had treated as if it were a vanquished nation. Fox pointed out that war had increased poverty while charity had failed to deal with it. One of the immediate benefits of the peace was the fall in the price of wheat: "Can any man doubt under such circumstances whether it be not better for the people to eat, than

---

[1] Mitchell p.170

[2] Pocock p.35

that we should possess the Cape, or even Malta?" He noted that they were so weary of the war "that they preferred peace almost upon any terms". He only regretted it had not come sooner.[1] Perhaps Sheridan best summed up the mood of politicians when he said this was "a peace which every man ought to be glad of, but no man can be proud of".

When Windham received the news of the preliminary treaty from Addington he replied that "I must not omit to thank you for your note, however dreadful the intelligence it contains" adding that "the country has received its death blow".[2] An illness delayed his own speech in Parliament until the evening of 4 November. He considered that Addington and Hawkesbury "in a moment of rashness and weakness [...] have signed the death warrant of their country. They have given it a blow [...] from which I do not conceive how it is possible for it ever to recover".[3] Commenting on the previous speeches he said: "All that I heard, and all that I saw [...] tends only to confirm more and more the deep despair in which I am plunged, in contemplating the probable consequences of the present Treaty." He summarised their arguments as a recognition that as France had the power to destroy Britain, they could only hope she did not have the inclination. France had told them: "we can hold out, and you cannot; make peace, or we will ruin you." Bonaparte was as much Britain's master as he was of Spain or any other of those supposedly independent countries.

The issue for Windham was whether peace was better than the continuation of hostilities. Peace could not be measured purely in terms of assets lost, but also by its effects on Britain's character and reputation. After all, past wars were not fought merely over resources. Windham reminded the House of a conflict over the Falkland Islands, "a barren rock, an object of competition for nothing but seals and seagulls". A nation that gave way in a single instance was like a woman who admitted one familiarity. They both become inclined to further submission. Statesmen had to consider the reputation of their nation every time they considered conceding something to another. This principle had been ignored: "France gives nothing, and, excepting Trinidad and Ceylon,

---

[1] Cited in Fedorak p.75

[2] Windham Papers Vol. II, p.172

[3] Windham Papers Vol. II, p.178

England gives everything". Windham listed instances of French influence in Europe and of its now effective control in Asia, Africa, the West Indies, North and South America. "Such is the power which we are required to contemplate without dismay!" Their ancestors, he suggested, would turn in their graves. He dismissed the argument that Britain's wealth would protect it from future French aggression as ridiculous. Had they not just treated for peace because they were too poor to afford further war? If peace failed to suit Bonaparte he would soon pick a fight with Britain, which was about to hand back all his colonies, thirty thousand of his seamen and leave Egypt and Malta defenceless. What was to stop France from persuading Spain to give up all its remaining colonies just as it had already done so with Louisiana and its share of San Domingo? Or if they invaded Malta or Egypt? If British foreign policy was to be conducted according to the same principles as the peace just made, then France would be allowed to do anything it liked.

Britain could only hope that "the progress of the Revolution will stop where it is; and that Buonaparte [...] instead of proceeding to the conquest of new worlds, will be willing to sit down contented in the enjoyment of those which he has already." This was unlikely. If Windham's fellow MPs examined the French Revolution carefully they would see that the "scheme of universal empire" was its ultimate goal. It needed political power to destroy morality and religion. As there was no reason to believe these designs had been renounced, they could only hope that Bonaparte, being effectively a monarch himself, would join Britain in its support of monarchical principles. He may have already shown anti-Jacobin tendencies by suppressing their ideas in France, but he still permitted the export of Jacobinism abroad. Yet Bonaparte could not be trusted. He had already demonstrated his duplicity as recently as the peace negotiations. He had agreed to respect the territorial integrity of Portugal while hiding from Britain the details of his treaty with Portugal, which encroached on that integrity. He consented to evacuate Egypt because he knew before Britain did that his forces there had already surrendered it. Nor could they hope that internal dissensions in France would save them. France had already proved its ability to fight a war in Europe despite a civil war in the Vendée at home.

"What can France want with any of the possessions which she has compelled us to surrender, but with a view of rivalling our power, or of subverting it, or of removing out of our hands the means of controlling her further projects of ambition?" The only possible reason why Bonaparte insisted on the surrender of Malta was to deprive the British of a base from which they might thwart his designs in the Mediterranean. As long as France had the aim of overthrowing Britain, the two countries would remain at war, whether anyone thought so or not. This peace was not an end to that war, but simply a major French victory. If this peace was then nothing but an armed truce, would it not have been better for Britain to have actually made a transparent truce, which would not have relinquished the means of prosecuting an inevitable future war more effectively?

Windham considered the supposed advantages of peace. Resumption of economic activity interrupted by the war would be offset by competition from France for Britain's export trade. The expense of a large navy and army could not be reduced until Bonaparte could be fully trusted. If peace brought economic decline rather than prosperity, Britain's sacrifices for it would have all been for nothing. He contrasted these qualified advantages with the dangers of peace. It was clear that France's economy would grow and rival that of Britain's and if war was resumed they would be faced with a far more powerful enemy. What Windham feared perhaps most of all though was the uncontainable flood of revolutionary ideas into Britain. Bonaparte may be restraining them in France, but would not stop their export abroad. Even if political ideas were being restrained, immoral practices were still being tolerated. France had not only abandoned religion, but also the institution of marriage. What was one to think of a system that, by allowing men and women to divorce each other as if they were giving notice on a furnished flat, had "turned the whole country into one universal brothel?" Lastly, he lamented the danger inherent in Britain's loss of reputation for loyalty to allies, especially the Bourbons whose cause had been shamefully abandoned. If anybody agreed with Windham that these fears were not imaginary, yet approved the peace purely from the temporary and personal gains it afforded them, then they were "a disgrace to their country and to their species."[1]

Both Houses approved the peace, which improved the popularity of Addington's government. Nevertheless, a future government majority could never be certain, especially if the negotiations for the definitive treaty dragged. Although the administration currently enjoyed the support of Pitt and those influenced by him, there were signs that Lord Grenville and his followers might slide into more permanent opposition and take others with him. Pitt had urged Grenville not to vote against the peace,

---

[1] Walsh pp.44-77

arguing that this position would alienate himself from the government. Grenville promised to back Addington, but he could not be persuaded to change his mind on the peace. If Addington did lose the support of Grenville, this might be offset by gaining it from Foxite Whigs. From November to December attempts were made to lure them. Fox could not be approached himself, because the King hated him too much, but his exclusion did not deter his colleagues from considering their options. Fox's indifference to and absence from Parliament had made them more independent. While Addington had talks with Tierney, St Vincent talked with Grey and Lord Moira. They got nowhere, because Lord Moira refused to work with Lord Portland and Grey was disappointed that Addington refused to contemplate parliamentary reform or Catholic Emancipation. Another obstacle was that Addington would only consider offering them minor posts in government.

The Consequences of Honour

12 Peace Illuminations

Engraving of Otto's House in Portman Square, illuminated to celebrate the Peace. (Look and Learn Collections) This actually shows the illuminations of April 29 1802 to celebrate the definitive Treaty of Amiens.

13 Lord Cornwallis

Illustration from *Portraits of Illustrious Personages* by Edmund Lodge (Harding and Lepard, 1832) (Look and Learn Collection).

14 Talleyrand

Engraving by S. Freeman after painting by Gerard. (Author's private collection).

10. Paris

The British government appointed Lord Cornwallis to be its negotiator at Amiens. The Marquess Cornwallis was over sixty years old with considerable military experience that included surrendering to the Franco-American forces at Yorktown in 1781 during the American War of Independence. He had governed India for seven years before being appointed viceroy for Ireland. After his appointment as the British plenipotentiary, he was invited to Paris by Bonaparte to attend the peace celebrations there on 9 November, so he set off for Dover at the beginning of that month. Accompanying him to France were his son Lord Brome, his illegitimate son Colonel Nightingale, his son-in law Captain Singleton, a Colonel Littlehales and Francis Moore, the brother of Major General John Moore, one of his ablest and more moderate subordinates from his time as viceroy of Ireland. They travelled in a convoy of three four-horse coaches. Cornwallis journeyed in an emblazoned yellow carriage decorated with his coat of arms, its interior furnished with silk, lace and cushions. At mid-day on 3 November, they crossed the Channel, enduring a stormy ten-hour passage before arriving in Calais in the late evening, where they were welcomed at the pier by local dignitaries. The next day, with a French cavalry escort, they were on the recently repaired road to Paris. Passing through Boulogne, Cornwallis was presented with a bouquet of flowers from a young woman, his age and serious countenance giving the young lady the impression of a grumpy old man.[1]

The British legation arrived in Paris on 7 November, settling into the Hotel Grange Batelière, an old mansion with spacious grounds and pleasant gardens. The next morning Cornwallis met the French Foreign Minister. Charles Maurice de Talleyrand-Périgord was the eldest son of an aristocratic family, but was passed over from inheriting the family title and estate because of a clubbed foot. Instead, he was expected to pursue a career in the Catholic Church in which, despite his atheism but because of his connections, he became Bishop of Autun in 1789. Talleyrand welcomed the Revolution that year and as a clerical member of the Estates General served its early leaders in subordinating the Church to the

---

[1] Warren pp.216-217

State. It was at his suggestion that the State seized all Church property, provoking the Pope to excommunicate him. Despite sharing the concerns of enlightenment philosophes for the welfare of humanity, his primary concern was his own, considering it best served by women and money. He was still at seminary when he had his first mistress, later attracting many others with sallies of wit in the salons of Paris. Money had to be earned as effortlessly as possible. On the same day he presided over the celebration of the anniversary of the Revolution in July 1790, he won a small fortune at the gaming tables. When The Terror came, he was on a diplomatic assignment in England, where he decided to remain after the Convention issued a warrant for his arrest. In 1794 He was obliged to make a commercial living in the United States after he was expelled from Britain by Pitt's Aliens Act. Once the Directory came to power in France, he was able to return and managed to secure himself the position of Foreign Minister, which he retained after supporting Bonaparte's coup.

The French Foreign Ministry was situated in an imposing building fronted by ninety-nine pillars on the Rue de Bac. The coach entrance was guarded by a tall, strong Swiss man who had no problem telling visiting diplomats that Talleyrand was out when he was in or carrying out a Countess after she had managed to slip past him. Talleyrand started the working day very late and spent it mainly in his office at the Ministry or in meetings with the First Consul in the Tuileries Palace. He had persuaded Bonaparte that as foreign affairs were of a highly sensitive nature, their discussion should be usually limited to between themselves while the business of other ministries was often discussed in the Council of State. These conversations with Bonaparte would often digress into areas beyond foreign policy as Bonaparte valued Talleyrand as a talking companion. While he enjoyed the First Consul's confidence, partly achieved by flattery, Talleyrand had some influence in shaping French foreign policy. When he thought Bonaparte had acted too rashly in a rage, he would delay sending an angrily dictated dispatch until the next morning when his master had usually calmed down and had second thoughts.[1] He was noted for his composure, which prompted the remark that were anyone to kick him up the backside his countenance would remain unchanged. Hawkesbury warned Cornwallis that Talleyrand "is a person who is likely to take every unfair advantage in conducting business with others, and should therefore be treated with more than usual caution and circumspection." When Talleyrand suggested that the

---

[1] Lawday pp.128-130

talks could be held in Paris, Cornwallis could not be persuaded, objecting that it would have given the French delegation an unfair advantage in the speed with which they could communicate with their respective political masters. Talleyrand would certainly not have missed any opportunity to exploit any advantage in France's favour, but he was genuinely interested in securing peace with England, hoping that the two countries would not only never fight again, but become permanent friends.[1]

Talleyrand told Cornwallis that Bonaparte was very keen to see him, but was unlikely to do so the next day as no carriages were to be allowed on the streets on account of the peace celebrations. Cornwallis had planned to attend the fireworks display at the Tuileries gardens that evening, but if he could not be driven there he would probably stay in as he did not relish the prospect of wading through the muddy streets on foot. An exception was then made for his coach and the following day he duly joined the celebrations. From their position at Pont Neuf the British diplomats watched a balloon ascend into a clear sky from the Seine. An animal was thrown out with a parachute and descended safely to the ground. Bonaparte, with the other two consuls, Cambacérès and Lebrun, appeared on the balcony of the Tuileries palace, presenting themselves to a crowd cheering "Vive Bonaparte! Vive le Premier Consul!" As darkness descended, the main buildings lit up with magnificent illuminations while the sky exploded with spectacular fireworks.[2] The festivities were marred when a spectator stand collapsed, injuring eighty people, including an Englishman. Charles John Clarke, who was visiting with his wife, fractured his spine. When Bonaparte heard about it he offered his own surgeon, but nothing could be done and he was to die a month later.[3]

The morning after the fireworks Cornwallis met Talleyrand and Bonaparte together. British expectations of Bonaparte's appearance were often negative – a hollow-eyed, yellow-skinned, long-haired pygmy was one image that came to mind. Certainly he used to wear his hair long in the revolutionary manner and in his twenties he may have had a hungry haunted look about him. He was small, but his features were reasonably

---

[1] Churton p.235, Ross p.392, Colmache p.181

[2] Ross p.390, Lemaistre, Pellew vol. 2 p.5

[3] Clarke had recently inherited Addiscombe Place, the residence leased by Lord Hawkesbury's father Lord Liverpool. Alger p.23-24

handsome and his body well proportioned. Now in his early thirties, his dark hair was cut short, revealing more clearly an olive complexion, intelligent, spirited eyes and a firm, severe mouth.[1] Bonaparte received Cornwallis graciously, asking after the King's health and telling him he had a great respect for Great Britain. As long as it was friends with France, there would be peace in Europe. Cornwallis responded just as warmly, praising his host for restoring order and tranquillity to France, thereby allaying the fears of Europe, which had only known him previously as a conqueror.[2]

For the next two weeks Cornwallis remained in Paris attending dinners and other social events, waiting for an opportunity to talk to Bonaparte in private. At a dinner given in his honour by Joseph Bonaparte, the First Consul's elder brother and the French delegate to Amiens, Cornwallis looked around at the other guests and enquired about Lafayette, the French general who had fought against him in the American War of independence. He knew Lafayette was a friend of Joseph's, but guessed he had not invited him in case it reminded Cornwallis of his defeat at Yorktown. Cornwallis was touched by this gesture, but disappointed: "It would have given me much pleasure to have met him here," he told Joseph. He suggested they each try not to be overly diplomatic in future, but simply strive for a prompt and solid peace.[3] Lord Brome, Cornwallis's son, was not impressed by his French dining companions, whom he described as having the "dress of mountebanks and manners of assassins". He took a particular dislike to Talleyrand and his mistress – the divorcee and former ancien régime courtesan Catherine Grand – observing that "she is very like him, and he is like everything that is detestable".

On 20 November, Cornwallis attended the opening session of the Corps Législatif. This was one of the law-making bodies that constituted the Consular regime. Its 300 members approved laws drawn up by the Council of State. The assembly could only vote for or against a bill, it could not debate it. This was the prerogative of the Tribunate who could debate and vote, but whose vote had no legislative effect. The

---

[1] Jackson p.19

[2] Ross p.390

[3] Abbot p.85

members of both bodies were chosen by the Senate from a national list of notable Frenchmen. The names on the national list were selected from ten per cent of a departmental list who in turn were selected from ten per cent of a communal list who were voted there by all adult males. Senators were also drawn from the national list, but they were appointed by the three consuls. The First Consul alone made appointments to the Council of State and government ministries.

At the Palace of the Corps Législatif, formerly the Palais Bourbon, situated in front of Pont Louis XVI next to the Champs-Élysées, Cornwallis was received with military honours, introduced to some of the key members and then ushered into the hall where they took their seats in a box. The octagonal chamber had a high arched ceiling sheltering an amphitheatre, behind which was a ring of seats in a public gallery for spectators admitted by a silver ticket. The seats faced a tribune – a kind of pulpit – where orators would address the assembly. Just in front of the tribune was a small pillar upon which rested the constitution and which was known as the altar of the country. The doors flew open and the costumed members entered, marching in pairs to military music, preceded by a guard of honour. They wore a kind of blue uniform embroidered with gold, gold laced hussar boots and cocked hats, a tricolour sash around their waists.

While they took their places in the chamber, guards with fixed bayonets positioned themselves by the doors. Outside, detachments of troops were posted in the avenues leading to the building. "No puppet show could be more ridiculous" thought Lord Brome. Littlehales agreed it was more like a theatre than a solemn proceeding of a legislative body.[1] Then the Minister of the Interior made a speech asking the assembly to choose their president. Brome could not help thinking that he was dressed in the manner of someone about to walk the tightrope.[2] A visitor in the public gallery overheard some Frenchmen there commenting on the boots of the members, which they considered as pointless as their wearers: "We pay them 10,000 francs for doing nothing. I am astonished Bonaparte does not get rid of these fellows."[3]

---

[1] Ross p.397

[2] Ross p.410, Warren p.121-123

[3] Lemaistre pp.63-69

The well-heeled members wrote down their nominations on a piece of paper, which they placed in one of four vases. These were then tipped out and counted by an official, who conveyed the result to a temporary president, who announced the new President as M. Depuis. Depuis would probably not have been Bonaparte's choice. He was the author of the anti-religious *Origine de tous les cultes* and close to liberal intellectuals who had become increasingly critical of Bonaparte, despite his achievements. The assembly was reminded of these by the Councillor of State Thibadeau the next day. In a state of the Republic speech, Thibadeau highlighted the re-establishment of internal security. The civil war against the royalist and Catholic Chouans and Vendeans in the west of France had ended. To achieve this, rebels had been pardoned, religion tolerated and émigrés encouraged to return. The elimination of highway brigands and the repair of twenty roads, the opening of new routes over the Alps, the reclamation of land, the building of canals and bridges all contributed to an improved economic infrastructure in which the industries of Lyon, Lille, St. Quentin and Rouen were all now flourishing. Peace had been made with Russia, the Ottoman Empire and Portugal while peace with Great Britain was expected to be concluded soon. Yet there was still much to be done – including hospital improvements and provisions for foundlings.[1]

On 24 November Cornwallis was visited by Joseph Bonaparte, who declared his intention to deal fairly and open. As he was a stranger to diplomacy, he would not try to gain anything by cunning and chicanery and did not doubt that Cornwallis would observe the same principles. Joseph was being disingenuously modest, as he had been the principal negotiator with the Austrians at Lunéville. He was not a career diplomat, but was advised by the wily Talleyrand, who had briefed him thoroughly since his appointment as France's plenipotentiary ten days earlier. Joseph was given Otto's despatches and told to familiarise himself thoroughly with all the key issues of interest to France. He was to take note of what Cornwallis considered important. There were certain subjects he should refuse to discuss – the King of Sardinia, the Dutch Stadtholder and the internal affairs of Batavia, Germany, Switzerland and Italian Republics. All these were to be considered as irrelevant to their discussions with England. The formal conferences should alternate between their residences and Joseph was to make sure the points discussed and agreed were recorded in accurate protocol documents.

---

[1] Villefosse p.144-145

After declaring his honesty, Joseph told Cornwallis what he thought about Malta. He suggested that the King of Naples as well as being the suzerain power for Malta should also be its guarantor. Cornwallis immediately disagreed. Naples was simply not sufficiently powerful. A guarantor had to be a major power, like Russia, which any future enemy of Malta would have to risk reckoning with if it was tempted to invade. Joseph acknowledged the point but insisted that Russia could not be allowed to garrison Malta. If it did so, it would claim the right to pass through the Dardanelles from the Black Sea into the Mediterranean from where it could threaten the Ottoman Empire. Cornwallis had been informed by Hawkesbury that Russia did not think it would be practical for them to garrison Malta so it was not difficult to agree with this. Joseph then appeared to propose what seemed to be a plan identical to the one Hawkesbury had recently suggested. Malta was to be a semi-autonomous island run by the Knights of St John, but ultimately under the sovereignty of the King of Naples who would protect the island from foreign invasion by providing a garrison to be funded by England and France. The order would admit Maltese natives and the whole arrangement would be guaranteed by the Tsar of Russia. Despite Joseph's qualification that he could not formally agree to this idea until he conferred with his government, Cornwallis was pleased to find that his counterpart's sentiments were consistent with the spirit and meaning of the preliminary articles.

Half-heartedly, Cornwallis suggested that Spain should give up its conquest of the Portuguese territory of Olivenza, but would not press this as he appreciated that France would already find it difficult to convince Spain to relinquish the Caribbean island of Trinidad. Of more importance to Cornwallis was the question of reimbursing Britain for the expense of maintaining French prisoners of war. The bill he presented to Joseph was £1 million. Joseph was surprised, both at the demand and the amount itself. Cornwallis told him that Britain had been obliged to contribute to the upkeep of its soldiers held as prisoners by France so it seemed only fair that they should be compensated for this double expenditure. He appreciated the amount was considerable so promised to provide a detailed account. Cornwallis had anticipated this might be an area of contention with the French, so he suggested that Britain might be prepared to accept another West Indian island –Tobago – in part payment if necessary. Joseph's instructions from his brother through Talleyrand on this were clear. Although France had agreed this subject could be deferred to the definitive discussions, they had not made any commitment to comply with British demands, either for money or Tobago. He was to reject all their claims on this point and use the same arguments made by

Otto. Questions of money could not be mixed with that of territory. If it was recognized by France that it owed money, it would pay it, but only after taking into account prisoners maintained at French expense that were in the pay of Britain.

Joseph wanted to discuss the arrangement for the fishing rights around the Gulf of St Lawrence. Bonaparte expected Britain to suggest a return to the treaty of 1783, but this had been bad for France, so Joseph was instructed to get a better deal. Not only should the French be permitted to fish on the north-east coast, they should also be allowed to make permanent settlements there. At the very least, rights should be obtained for St Pierre and Miquelon to cut wood from Newfoundland. Cornwallis pleaded he was insufficiently informed on this issue to talk about it at that time.[1]

A few days later Cornwallis was able to have a private meeting with the First Consul. Bonaparte assured him of his earnest desire for peace, which was desperately wanted by France, it having lost much of its commerce and resources: "You see that I conceal nothing and that I speak frankly." He desired only to adhere in the definitive treaty to the full intent and meaning of the preliminary articles. As he expected Cornwallis to find his brother a just and fair man, he did not doubt a speedy conclusion. Cornwallis assured him of the King's desire for a lasting peace, adding that Britain had no concern what mode of Government France adopted providing it did not threaten the happiness and safety of its neighbour and congratulated Bonaparte from rescuing France from confusion and anarchy.

As proof that Britain had no ill-will towards France and was willing to make sacrifices to cultivate mutual understanding Cornwallis reminded Bonaparte of Britain's recent consent to the sailing of a French fleet to the West Indies. This fleet was to send troops to the island of San Domingo to restore French authority there following the take-over of the island by its former slaves, led by Toussaint L'Ouverture. Once the preliminaries had been signed the French had notified the British of their intention to send this force. Britain had been alarmed at the size of the fleet and number of troops and felt obliged to ready its own ships to keep an eye on the expedition. Bonaparte complained he had been much chagrined by Britain's earlier objections. If they had persisted he would

---

[1] Ross pp.397-399, Du Casse pp.22-30

have had to abandon the plan and come to some less satisfying arrangement with Toussaint. This would have been to the disadvantage of both Britain and France as Toussaint would set up some piratical state threatening all nations with colonial possessions in that region.

When Cornwallis pressed for compensation for the Prince of Orange, Bonaparte claimed he had always intended for the Prince to be recompensed and, as the King of England himself had a personal interest in this, he would now treat it with greater consideration. Reassured, Cornwallis then broached the subject of the King of Sardinia. Britain wanted Piedmont, in North West Italy and currently occupied by France, to be returned to its original King. Bonaparte said this was beyond his power. All he could do was establish him in Sardinia with a pension from France. The King of Sardinia had rejected an earlier offer which would have restored his Piedmontese territories, but had then sought protection from Russia. Bonaparte claimed that if he were to make another offer now, he would expose himself to too much discontent at home.

Bonaparte raised the issue of Malta, declaring that a Russian garrison was out of the question. Even if Malta was held in trust by a weaker state such as Naples it would be a constant source of conflict between England and France, coveted as it was by both. One of them would sooner or later exert an unfair influence over Naples. The best thing to do, he suggested, was to blow up the fortifications, making it an object of no material advantage to either party. Cornwallis objected that the Knights might not want to return without the necessary fortifications to defend the island from the Barbary pirates, but Bonaparte replied that the battlements were much stronger than was necessary to protect against such a threat. Cornwallis had no answer to this except to say that his government had not briefed him on this option.

On the subject of reimbursing Britain for the upkeep of French prisoners, Bonaparte doubted that there was any justification for charging France for this and deemed it dishonourable to give up Tobago in exchange. If Britain wanted Tobago because it had English planters, they could get it in return for a former French island they held or even a slice of India. Cornwallis reposted that there was no possibility that Britain would exchange another island for Tobago, but would pass this idea on to his government nevertheless. Britain was also unlikely to give up territory in India as this would increase tensions between them and France in that region. Bonaparte smiled and said "Vous êtes bien dur". He expressed the hope that – if it turned out France did owe a significant amount for the prisoners – he would be given time to pay it off. Bonaparte ended the conversation with a suggestion that France would ban the United Irishmen from France if Britain would expel French Royalists from Britain. Cornwallis decided not to comment. The next day, impatient to start the talks, Cornwallis exhorted Talleyrand to hasten the arrival of the Dutch and Spanish plenipotentiaries. The day after he left Paris for Amiens.[1]

Once Bonaparte had received the consent of Britain to his Caribbean expedition he set its wheels in motion. Two young men were brought to him. They were Isaac and Placide, the son and adopted son of Toussaint L'Ouverture, the rebel slave leader of San Domingo. Toussaint had sent them to Paris for their education and as a pledge of his fidelity to France, where they studied at the Collège La Marche. Josephine had befriended them, often inviting them to lunch and dinner. To Isaac, the natural son of Toussaint and the younger of the two, Bonaparte said: "Your father is a great man; he has rendered eminent services to France. You will tell him that I, the first magistrate of the French people, promise him protection, glory, and honour. Do not think that France intends to carry war to Saint Domingo. The army which it sends thither is destined, not to attack the troops of the country, but to augment their numbers."

He introduced General Leclerc, his blond-haired brother-in-law who had been appointed to lead the expedition in October. Leclerc was married to Bonaparte's favourite and prettiest sister Pauline, who was to accompany her husband on his mission. Isaac and his step-brother Placide were to go with them and were expected to convey to their father the peaceful intentions of France. The next day the Minister of Marine entertained the two brothers to a lavish meal and presented them with gifts of a suit of armour and a brilliant military costume.[2] A few weeks later they were on their way across the Atlantic.

---

[1] Ross p.399-404

[2] James p.262, pp.301-302, Beard p.155

15 Napoleon Bonaparte

From the painting by Jean Auguste Dominique Ingres, engraved by T. Johnson. Illustration for the
Life of Napoleon Bonaparte by William Milligan Sloane (The Century Co, 1896) (Look and Learn
Collections)

16 Cambaceres

From the painting by Henri-Frederic Schopin, engraved by Henry Wolf. Illustration for the *Life of Napoleon Bonaparte* by William Milligan Sloane (The Century Co, 1896) (Look and Learn Collection)

11. Civil Codes

At the end of November 1801 the Tribunate was presented with the first draft of the Civil Code, an attempt to consolidate and rationalise French civil law into a single set of rules. Driving this legislation, with the engaged support of Bonaparte, was the Second Consul Jean Jacques Régis de Cambacérès. He was a hypochondriac lawyer with a taste for fine food so refined that he would request fellow diners to be silent while he could hear himself eat. The Second Consul was also known for his flamboyant costumes and the company of bachelors. Although the French Revolution had de-criminalised homosexuality, the police of the Consular regime would use surviving laws against indecent behaviour to prosecute the less discrete manifestations of what was called a man's "little flaw". Cambacérès did not hide his disposition, but never openly declared it either, so the most he had to endure was the ridicule of his society, Bonaparte included. When Cambacérès once arrived late for a council meeting, explaining he had been detained by a lady, the First Consul could not resist offering some advice: "Next time you are detained by a lady, you must say, 'Get your hat and stick and leave, monsieur. The Council is waiting for me.'" If Cambacérès was upset by this treatment and the laughter it invited at his expense, he never complained and served his master faithfully.[1]

Before the Revolution there were effectively two distinct legal frameworks in France – Roman written law, which predominated in the south and customary laws in the north. The latter varied so much between regions that it prompted Voltaire to claim that a traveller changed laws as frequently as he changed horses. In addition to these differences, there were canon laws regulating marriages and families laid down by the Church and Royal Ordinances issued by the monarchy. French philosophes like Rousseau and Montesquieu had suggested that law should be the product of human reason and therefore established by statute. They should be simple and uniform. Feudal privilege, regional antagonisms and vested interest of the parlements, (pre-revolutionary provincial courts), resisted attempts to rationalise the law, but the

---

[1] Merrick pp.80-84, McLynn pp.263-291, D'Abrantes, Vol. 1, p.357

Revolution would sweep these obstacles aside. A common grievance collected by the deputies of the Estates General in 1789 was that the law was so confusing to people that they had little confidence in the courts ability to dispense justice. In 1790 the Constituent Assembly voted for a codification and the constitution of 1791 promised one. Cambacérès, influenced by the philosophes, presented some draft legislation, arguing that a legislator "should not aspire to declare everything; but, after having laid down the generative principles anticipatory of many doubtful points, he should undertake an elaboration leaving but a few questions for determination". Although the obstacles to codification had gone and most accepted its desirability, there was no consensus on what the content of the code should be. Robespierre believed that legislation could be sufficiently clear that there would be no need of experts in jurisprudence to interpret the law. The Convention rejected Cambacérès' proposals as being too complicated and insufficiently radical or philosophical. He tried again in 1793, attempting to keep it simple but his proposal was again rebuffed on the grounds that it was more like a list of morals than a code of laws. Under the Directory Cambacérès submitted a new draft in 1796, but this was never considered.

In August 1800 Bonaparte appointed a commission under the direction of Cambacérès to look into it. Four months later they produced a draft and by July 1801 it was ready to be discussed by the Council of State. The sessions of the council discussing the code continued to the end of the year and Bonaparte would often attend. He took an active part in the debates, surprising the legal experts in the Council with his grasp of the issues, the novelty of his ideas and soundness of his arguments. Bonaparte intervened especially where the rights of fathers and women were being discussed, stamping his patriarchal inclinations on the emerging articles. Fathers would have the right to imprison their children, control their property until they were eighteen and veto their marriages until they were in their twenties. Divorce by mutual consent, allowed by the Revolution, would now have to be approved by both the parents of the divorcing couple. While a woman could now be imprisoned for adultery, she could only divorce a husband on the same grounds if it had been committed in the conjugal dwelling. The wife would not be allowed to engage in any legal contract without her husband's permission.[1]

---

[1] Homberg(Thibadeau, Marmont), Lyons, pp.94-102

In November 1801 the preliminary articles of the draft code was presented to the Tribunate by Jean-Étienne-Marie Portalis – an expert in Roman Law and the Minister of Religion. He considered that it was the duty of the legislator to: "establish, by broad views, the general maxims of the law, to set down fruitful principles, and not to descend into the details of questions that may arise on every subject [...] There are a multitude of details that escape him, or are too contentious or too mutable to be dealt with by an enactment".

A "code, however, is not so soon finished, that thousands of unexpected questions present themselves to the magistrate [...] A multitude of things are therefore necessarily abandoned to the empire of common practice, the discussion of educated men, the arbitration of judges [...] one can no more do without jurisprudence than without legislation [...] It is to jurisprudence that we leave those rare and extraordinary cases which do not fall within the framework of a reasonable legislation [...] To foresee everything is a goal impossible to achieve". The preliminary articles related when, where and how the code was to take effect and to whom. It was not to be retrospective. Judges could not defer decisions – if they refused to decide on grounds that the law was silent they could be prosecuted. Their decision was only local and could not be considered as a precedent.

The reaction of the Tribunate was hostile. Andrieux, a brilliant dramatist, journalist and lawyer suggested that the preliminary articles were "ill arranged and incoherent". As they should be general maxims – theoretical principles of scientific law – they belonged in the constitution rather than the head of the civil code. One speaker suggested the non-retrospective principle was counter-revolutionary. Another criticism was that it was nothing new, that it was a "servile imitation" of Roman and customary law and a "vapid compilation devoid of originality." Portalis pointed out it was not meant to be novel, just lucid and just. No new society was being constituted, but an old one being reformed. The point was to review the old laws and expel from them everything that was repugnant to the spirit of the present time – like feudalism – and to draw up the remaining prescriptions in a language that removed ambiguities and scope for dispute. To the objection that it contained no grand conceptions Portalis retorted that there was a danger in grand conceptions. The Tribunate however, was not impressed with his arguments and voted against the preliminary articles.

Watching the debate with interest was a Genevan writer Etienne Dumont. He had arrived in France a few weeks earlier and was working on a book to be published in Paris that was to expound the views of a little-know contemporary English philosopher, Jeremy Bentham. The book – *Traités de législation civile et pénale* – a treatise on civil and penal codes, was to be a presentation of Bentham's views on law based on compilations of published and unpublished manuscripts he had written before the Revolution. Bentham had been promoting the idea of a civil code in England since 1780. English Common Law contained no pre-established rules, but emerged from precedents established by court decisions over time, so was set forth as judges saw fit. For Bentham the Common Law was "dog-law". If your dog did something you did not want him to do, you beat him when he did it. "This is the way you make laws for your dog: and this is the way judges make the law for you and me [...] Multitudes are thus doomed to inevitable ruin, for the crime of not knowing a judge's opinion, some 10 or 20 years before the question had ever entered into his head." Law by precedent was just as arbitrary as that made by an unenlightened absolute despot, but what was worse, it was applied retrospectively.

Dumont had been obliged by his liberal views and political circumstances to live the life of an exile. In England he enjoyed the patronage of the liberal Whig aristocrat Lord Shelbourne, later Lord Lansdowne, while in France he wrote speeches for the French revolutionary Mirabeau. Like many, he shared the optimism encouraged by the French Revolution, but was deeply disillusioned by its descent into Terror. His search for what had gone wrong and what path it should have taken, led him to the discovery of the writings of Jeremy Bentham, whose ideas seemed to offer a pragmatic alternative to the heady idealism of radicals and the prejudiced inertia of conservatives.

In the late 1790's Dumont had succeeded in attracting the attention of the French chattering world to Bentham's ideas through the periodical, *Biblioteque brittanique*, founded by fellow Genevans. One of those intrigued by Bentham was Talleyrand. When the preliminaries of peace between England and France had been signed in London in October 1801, Dumont came to Paris to arrange the publication of his book. He arrived on 8 November and went straight to the Foreign Ministry to meet Talleyrand, who invited him to dinner. Talleyrand advised Dumont to publish as soon as possible before any opposition had time to block it. The two men shared a low opinion of the current disciples of Voltaire, who incited the violent overthrow of society only to replace it with a system governed by useless abstractions. Talleyrand was particularly wary of Sieyès, whose principles made no allowance for the weakness of human nature and who would not tolerate being contradicted by the pragmatic, down-to-earth ideas of Bentham. When Cambacérès once told Talleyrand that he thought Sieyès profound, the Foreign Minister replied: "Profound is not the word, no, no; hollow, very hollow, you mean." Other enemies might be those promoting the Civil Code in France who might see Bentham's book as undermining their project. Talleyrand deputed one of his own officials, Hauterive – another fan of Bentham – to assist Dumont with the publication, while he discussed with the publisher Bossange what paper and font was to be used. When Bossange wanted to acquire the ownership of the book by offering the sales of the first 300 copies as Dumont's cut, Talleyrand suspected a bestseller. He encouraged Dumont to retain ownership by promising to underwrite the costs of a complete edition.

Dumont was unimpressed with the French legislators. After listening to the speech by Portalis he commented: "I am always fascinated by this love of fine phrases, this avidity for clichés, this obligation to go all sentimental at the mention of the family, father, fatherland, human &c, &c. – endless tirades – endless rhetorical non-senses – not a single clear idea – those who were around us in the gallery were going into rhapsodies over his facility – it was as though they were watching a high-wire artist jumping and admiring the way he kept on alighting back on the cord – what a bullshitting people! – not even ten years of suffering have cured them!" [1]

On 15 December, after hearing speakers from the Tribunate and the government, the President of the Corps Législatif announced the debate to be closed and asked his colleagues to proceed to the ballot. Two green urns were placed either side of the tribune, and as a secretary called out the list of members, each one walked to one of the containers where they were given a black and a white ball. White was a yes vote. The ball representing the vote was placed in the left hand urn, while the other was discarded into the right-hand vessel. When the list of names had been read, the left-hand urn's contents were tipped into a basket. First, they were counted: 281 balls in total. Then they were separated into black and white. The black balls were then counted quietly into another basket. By the time the last one was counted a deathly silence hung over the chamber. As the total count was called out – 142 – there was a burst of applause that had to be silenced by the President with the help of some of

---

[1] Blamires p.247, Churton pp.231-252

the sentries. After the white balls were tallied and found to be 139, the President rose and said "The Law is rejected." [1]

Bonaparte was disappointed and worried that other sections of the Code being debated in the Tribunate would be rejected as well. He was particularly inflamed by a complaint by Siméon that the new law neglected to say that a person born of French parents in the colonies was French. "When I hear an able man like Siméon questioning whether people born in our own colonies are Frenchmen, I begin to wonder whether I am standing on my head or my heels. Of course they are Frenchmen; it is as clear as daylight." At a meeting of the Council of State Bonaparte expressed his wider concerns about the legislature:

"What would you do with persons who before discussion say that the councillors of state and the consuls are nothing but asses and that their labours ought to be flung at their head? What will you do when such a one as Siméon accuses the law of being incomplete because it does not declare that infants born of Frenchmen in French colonies are French? In truth, one stands astounded in the midst of these strange mental aberrations. Even with all the good faith brought to this discussion in the bosom of the council of state, we have had the greatest difficulty to come to an agreement; how is it possible then to succeed in an assembly 5 or 6 times more numerous, discussing with no sincerity at all? [...] How is an entire code to be drawn up under such circumstances? I have read the speech of Portalis to the legislative body, in reply to the orators of the Tribunate; he has left them nothing to say; he has drawn their teeth. But let a man be ever so eloquent; let him speak 24 hours in succession, he can do nothing against an assembly which is prejudiced and determined to listen to nothing."

Bonaparte asked his council for suggestions. A number of proposals were made – including presenting the Code as a whole rather than in pieces, but nothing attracted much enthusiasm. Tronchet finally suggested waiting to see what happened to the next two sets of articles. Bonaparte agreed. "Yes, we can risk two more battles. If we gain them, we can continue the march that has commenced. If we lose them we must go into winter quarters, and consider what course we shall adopt".

---

[1] Warren p.121-123

The next set of clauses – "Keeping of the Acts of the Civil State" – giving the responsibility of registering births, deaths and marriages to civil servants rather than priests – passed. On 1 January however, the articles "On the enjoyment and privation of civil rights" was rejected by the Tribunate. Bonaparte was also angry to learn that the Senate were considering as a Senator an opposition candidate nominated by the Tribunate and Legislative assembly – M. Daunaou – rather than his own choice. On 2 January he addressed them personally: "You are determined then to nominate no more generals? You are indebted to them for peace. This would be a good time for showing them your gratitude." Bonaparte looked at Sieyès: "There are people who want to give us a grand elector, and who are thinking of a prince of the house of Orleans. This system has its supporters, I know, even in the Senate." Addressing the senators as a whole he said "I declare to you, that if you nominate M. Daunaou, I will take it as a personal affront, and as you know, I have never put up with one."

After this meeting Bonaparte conferred with Cambacérès who would have shared the First Consul's frustration. Together they considered their options in dealing with a difficult legislature. The consular government was still popular with the people, but the constitution did not allow them to dissolve the assemblies and call for an election in the hope of returning a pro-government majority. Bonaparte wanted to withdraw the Code and submit nothing but finance bills in the hope that the French would tire of their representatives and allow him to dilute their power without any protest. Cambacérès agreed that they should temporarily abandon the Code, but cautioned that the reduction of legislative power should not be too radical. The Directory had done the same and been rewarded with the contempt of people. Instead he suggested they exploit Article Thirty Eight of the constitution. This gave the government the right to determine when in the year the legislative bodies renewed a fifth of their members. They then only had to persuade the Senate to remove and appoint members by ballot rather than lottery and to dismiss the most troublesome fifth and appoint their own candidates.

On 3 January the Legislative Assembly was informed that "the government has resolved to withdraw the bills of the law of the civil code".[1]

---

[1] Thiers p.319-325, Holmberg (www)

17 Joseph Bonaparte

Engraving by François Louis Couché. (Author's private collection)

12. Delays, Details and Distrust

Accompanying Joseph Bonaparte to Amiens was a small staff of advisors and assistants. Secretary to the legation and highly regarded by Joseph was André-Julien Dupuy who was supported by two young men, Antoine-Marie Roederer and Joseph-Marie Portalis, both sons of prominent government ministers. The others included Hattement, an apprentice diplomat and fluent in English, Fluery, who was with Joseph at Lunéville, and Méneval his personal secretary. On their way, they worried about how they should treat their counterparts. They needed to be friendly and respect British sensitivities, but being patriotic republicans, they did not want to be seen fawning over foreign aristocrats. One question that vexed Joseph in particular was: who was obliged to make the first visit? He need not have worried. When he arrived at his residence in Amiens on 3 December, Cornwallis was there to greet him and opened the door of his carriage himself. Shaking his hand Cornwallis said: "I hope it is thus you will deal with me and that all our etiquette will not retard for a single hour the conclusion of peace. Such forms are not necessary where frankness and honest intentions rule."[1]

That evening Cornwallis immediately stressed the importance to Britain of the Dutch and Spanish representatives formally agreeing to their ceding of Ceylon and Trinidad respectively. Joseph replied that the Dutch delegate would arrive soon, but the Spanish plenipotentiary was delayed by an illness. In the meantime one of them should draw up a plan for the treaty based on the preliminary articles. Joseph would allow Cornwallis to choose which of them should do this and Cornwallis proposed himself.

By 11 December, after further input from Hawkesbury, the British plan was ready. The greatest issue was Malta: it had to be independent of both Britain and France. Hawkesbury did not anticipate Naples garrisoning Malta for longer than five years and was concerned how the long term defence of the island was to be provided for. If a French chapter of the Knights of St John remained on the island then an

---

[1] Abbot p.88

English one would have to be established as well.[1] Joseph told Cornwallis that the French could not restore the French lodge as a qualification for membership to the Knights was proof of nobility, which was currently prohibited in egalitarian France while England would not be allowed to form a lodge as it was not a Catholic country. Cornwallis recognised these current restrictions, but considered that neither were necessarily permanent. Britain, he said, would not object to the French restoring their chapter in the future if they could establish their own.

Joseph repeated his brother's suggestion of blowing up Malta's forts. Cornwallis privately had much sympathy with this, recommending it to Addington. He did not think the British should rule it out simply because they were suspicious of Bonaparte's motives. He doubted the ability of Naples to control the island and thought they would be easily influenced by the French in a new war. However, as long as his government disliked the idea, he could not agree to it. Instead, he suggested that Malta be garrisoned by both the French and the British until the Knights were considered ready to defend themselves.

Although Hawkesbury hoped that Portugal either be relieved of the indemnity they owed the French or their territory of Olivenza be returned by Spain, Joseph would not accept this. Cornwallis pulled out of his pocket some documents to show Joseph, proving that Otto had agreed to abide by the Treaty of Badajoz. Hawkesbury had assumed that the indemnity was only liable under the Madrid treaty, which had been superseded by the Badajoz settlement. Joseph pointed out that the latter also required the payment of the indemnity and that Otto had already pointed this out in one of the documents the Englishman was holding.

Hawkesbury had told Cornwallis to insist on a single treaty signed by all parties and there should be no separate pacts between the participating powers. Joseph consented without any qualifications. Cornwallis felt the meeting had gone well. Malta was still an issue and the French were still resisting Hawkesbury's insistence that Britain be reimbursed for prisoner expenses, but Joseph had seemed to agree with Cornwallis on many other points.[2] He was also getting to like Joseph personally, seeing him as "a very sensible, modest, gentlemanlike man,

---

[1] Ross p.406

[2] Ross p.411, Du Casse p.39

totally free from diplomatic chicanery, and fair and open in all his dealings".[1]

In the next few weeks, Cornwallis's optimism subsided. On 19 December Joseph refused to admit the emissary from Portugal, who was waiting in London for France to issue the necessary passports to join the talks. Joseph was acting on specific instructions from Talleyrand, who told him to explain to the English delegate that as France was at peace with Portugal it could not be considered as being in the same situation as Spain or Holland. Joseph explained to Cornwallis that the preliminaries only allowed the British to negotiate on behalf of its former ally, not to permit it to the conference. Cornwallis disagreed, claiming they allowed for the final treaty to be decided by all the powers involved in the war.

The British claim for Tobago was rejected in an official note by Joseph, who reminded Cornwallis that his brother had already told him he would not yield an inch of French territory. As for compensation for the Prince of Orange, Joseph had no instructions to include this in the treaty and was disappointed to find Cornwallis talking about issues that were foreign to the preliminaries. Cornwallis sent Joseph his own note, claiming that British issues with the Dutch were relevant to a definitive treaty, even if the preliminary articles did not explicitly mention them. As an inducement, he suggested Britain would convince the Prince to recognise the Batavian Republic in return, adding that they had only agreed to withdraw this issue from the preliminaries on the understanding that a settlement would have been reached separately before the final treaty, but this had not happened.[2]

Further developments threatened any speedy conclusion. Cornwallis received a letter from Hawkesbury telling him that Britain had not submitted the full amount of prisoner expenses to the French. Instead of £1 million the amount was double that. A few days later he learned that the First Consul was going to Lyon, attending an assembly of delegates of the north Italian Cisalpine Republic. This would delay the negotiations. Cornwallis could also not help feeling that Britain's repeated demands for Tobago were annoying Bonaparte and that its

---

[1] Ross p.413

[2] Du Casse pp.48-57

representations on behalf of the Prince of Orange may have provoked the French to make further claims themselves.[1]

Talleyrand, receiving regular dispatches from Joseph and Otto, had been disappointed with the progress at Amiens. He complained that minor issues were being blown up beyond their importance and lamented that Cornwallis did not follow Talleyrand's idea of professional diplomatic practice of writing up regular protocol documents to record what had been agreed and what remained unresolved and signed by both parties. Instead, he was simply exchanging official notes. The French Foreign Minister remembered that the aborted negotiations the Directory had with England a few years earlier were disrupted by the same types of delays. He found it difficult to avoid suspecting there was some ulterior motive for them in London, some intrigues of which Cornwallis was perhaps the unwitting instrument. Talleyrand was aware there were reports in London of France being in turmoil, reports which he knew to be untrue and which he suspected emanated from the British representative in Paris, Francis Jackson. Talleyrand speculated that such rumours were being used by those in Britain who were against the peace and trying to obstruct the negotiations. After meeting with Bonaparte, the French Foreign Minister instructed Joseph to ignore demands for Tobago and convince Cornwallis to defer the issue of prisoner expenses to a commission. Joseph could allow a Maltese order of the Knights as long as it was not required to limit members to the nobility. Malta should be evacuated in one month, not three. As there were too many obstacles to satisfy France's ideal fishing rights in the New World, Joseph could settle for their pre-war situation but attempt to gain more if he could. Joseph was authorised to admit a secret article regarding the Prince of Orange, but not to promise compensation with German land. French relations with Portugal were to be considered as settled by the Treaty of Madrid. Badajoz only applied to relations between Portugal and Spain.[2]

Around Christmas time Joseph presented Cornwallis with a new French plan, complaining that the British draft was written in a dated style. To Cornwallis, the new scheme contained many more potential areas for disagreement. The French were again proposing that Naples be the guarantor as well as protector for Malta. In addition, they wanted

---

[1] Ross p.415, p.416, p.418, p.418

[2] Du Casse pp.58-62, pp.65-68

more territory and fishing rights in Newfoundland, the abolition of the salute at sea, an agreement to treat fishermen as neutral in any future war between France and Britain and the French outposts in India to be restored in a satisfactory condition. Missing from the French proposal were the reimbursement of prisoner expenses, compensation for the Prince of Orange, the extradition of British traitors, the relinquishing of Tobago and any commitment to guarantee the territorial integrity of Portugal. Neither was there any mention of Spain and the Batavian Republic agreeing to the cessions of Trinidad and Ceylon.

Cornwallis fell ill. When he recovered, two disagreeable days of meetings with Joseph followed. On the first day Cornwallis demanded to know why such important articles had been excluded by the French and why the King of Naples rather than the Tsar of Russia was to be the guarantor of Malta. Joseph replied that as the ultimate ruler of Malta, it was only natural to make him the guarantor. As for the missing articles, Joseph pointed out that his draft clearly stated it admitted those clauses in the English plan. There was just no point in including these as items for discussion until the Spanish and Dutch delegates had formally joined the conference. The following day Cornwallis declared that Britain would never accept Naples as guarantor for Malta and re-iterated his government's objection to destroying its forts. When asked to explain the French position of Malta, Joseph seemed to admit he had been evasive. He claimed he did not want to reveal the real reason why the French objected to the Tsar, which was because they feared Russia would eventually take possession of the island, given recent intensive Russian involvement with the Knights of St John. Cornwallis found this explanation difficult to swallow. Even when Joseph declared he could personally see no objection to the Tsar of Russia as guarantor, promising to write to Paris immediately recommending this, Cornwallis thought the French were being dishonest and deliberately delaying the treaty.

Joseph also tried to justify the omission of the Dutch Republic's consent to the cession of Ceylon. He argued they had to be consulted before the article on Ceylon could be inserted, but complained he did not have full powers to call the Dutch representative to the meeting. However, he assured Cornwallis he would send a messenger immediately to ask for full powers to do so. The attendance of Portugal was no longer insisted on by Britain, but no agreement was reached on what position the definitive treaty would take on Portuguese territory. Cornwallis wanted to conclude soon and was willing to let Spain accede after it had been signed rather than delay it any longer. He stressed to Joseph that Addington's government depended on prevailing public opinion which could change rapidly especially if the negotiations were perceived as advancing unfavourably against Britain. The horrible possibility of another war obliged them both to conclude quickly. He was finding Joseph more difficult. He would agree on a point one day and then disagree on the same one the next.[1]

Before Bonaparte left Paris for Lyon, to attend the assembly of delegates from the Italian Cisalpine Republic, Talleyrand had gone on ahead of him, leaving his deputy Hauterive to mediate between the two brothers. Hauterive would visit the First Consul every day, carrying foreign office despatches, including those from Joseph and Otto. Bonaparte would then dictate his thoughts, instructions and expectations to Hauterive, who would transmit these to Joseph. Bonaparte was particularly insistent that his brother keep pressing for the destruction of the Maltese forts. The fact that the British were so against this measure suggested that they had ulterior motives and was a good reason for Joseph to redouble his efforts to persuade the British to agree to it. Bonaparte was impatient for the peace to be concluded so that he could get on with other affairs on the continent. Writing directly to Joseph on 29 December, he said: "I hope that before I go you will let me hear three or four times from Amiens and tell me for certain the day on which the definitive treaty is to be signed. It appears to me that there is no longer any serious obstacle."[2] After Joseph received this letter from his brother and further instructions from Hauterive, Cornwallis found the talks had begun to change for the better, guessing that some circumstance had obliged Bonaparte to seek a speedy conclusion.[3]

At a conference in the first week of January, Cornwallis reminded Joseph of an understanding between Lord Hawkesbury and Otto that Tobago could be kept by Britain in return for waiving the prisoner expenses France owed. When Joseph had first been told this by Cornwallis he had been unaware of any verbal agreement and could only insist on the preliminaries. Joseph again referred to the preliminary articles, reminding the English Lord that these were dated later than any alleged bargain and they specified that these expenses would be dealt with

---

[1] Ross pp.420-423, Du Casse pp.84-93

[2] CCNBJ p.56, Du Casse pp.73-76, pp.101-108

[3] Ross p.424

in the customary manner. This, as he was instructed to say by his brother through Hauterive, was the principle that each nation paid for the upkeep of its own prisoners. France could not be expected to deviate from this custom just because the Directory had voluntarily opted to pay for French prisoners in England. There had been only two treaties in the whole of the 18th century that had required the reciprocal reimbursement of prisoner expenses. If Britain insisted, then France would have to claim the expenses it had incurred for maintaining the captives of its allies in the pay of Britain.

The Consequences of Honour

18 Josephine Bonaparte

Lithograph from the painting by Pierre-Paul Prud'hon. Illustration for the *Life of Napoleon Bonaparte* by William Milligan Sloane (The Century Co, 1896) (Look and Learn Collections)

19 Hortense

Engraving by Ch. Paquien (Author's private collection)

13. Tears of the Bride and Death at Dinner

Time in France was measured by the French Revolutionary Calendar. The 1st of January 1802 was not the start of a new year, but the 11th day of Nivôse – the month of snow – of Year X. The calendar also dispensed with the traditional seven-day week. Instead there was the ten-day décade. For every ten days there was a day and a half of rest and Bonaparte would spend this with Josephine at the Chateau of Malmaison eight miles from Paris. This was a yellowish, three-story building with a slate roof surrounded by three-hundred acres of wheat fields, vineyards and extensive gardens, landscaped in the unregimented English style, close to the river Seine. The chateau was Josephine's choice and she had borrowed a lot of money to purchase it in 1799 while Bonaparte was campaigning in Egypt.

It was in Egypt that Bonaparte learned of her affair with an army officer – Hippolyte Charles. The news devastated him, but he consoled himself with the wife of another officer. When Bonaparte returned to France prior to the coup of 1799 he was determined to divorce Josephine. He almost went through with it, but was dissuaded by the agonising cries of remorse from Josephine and the pleas of her teenage daughter Hortense and her son Eugène who had campaigned with Bonaparte in Egypt. They effected a reconciliation, much to the disappointment of most of Bonaparte's brothers and sisters, who never liked their sister-in-law. However, the relationship between the couple had changed. Until he had discovered Josephine's affair, Napoleon had been faithful and had worshipped his wife with the most extravagant displays of affection. Josephine had never reciprocated these sentiments with the same ardour and had demonstrated her infidelity with Hippolyte Charles. Now that Napoleon was First Consul, he continued to love Josephine and express his love for her, but never with the same passion as before. He no longer idolised her and was easily irritated by the most trivial of her flaws, venting his anger by snapping the blooms off her precious plants or taking pot-shots at her exotic swans.[1] He no longer felt the obligation to remain faithful and although he did not stop sleeping with Josephine, he

---

[1] Asprey p.437

began to seek sexual satisfaction elsewhere from younger women. Josephine, however, seemed to develop a stronger and more sincere affection for and dependence on her husband, despite his unreasonable rages. Even Napoleon's affairs failed to shake her fondness for him in any lasting way. They upset her terribly and she would despise Napoleon for having them, but not enough to stop loving him. In October 1801 Josephine wrote to her mother that "Bonaparte [...] makes your daughter very happy. He is kind, amiable, in a word a charming man."[1]

At Malmaison both Napoleon and Josephine relaxed. They were often accompanied by Eugène and Hortense and other guests of young officers, generals and ministers with their wives, secretaries, actors and friends. In the grounds they would play games like prisoners base, where two opposing groups would run at each other trying to capture players from the other team. A seized player would have to remain inside a designated area until rescued by someone of their own side. If Josephine got taken, Napoleon would shout "A rescue! A rescue!" He was not a good runner and would often fall, pick himself up and laugh heartily before inevitably getting caught, despite his best efforts to cheat. Hortense and Eugène were the best runners.[2] When Talleyrand visited Malmaison one day, he found everyone outside sitting on the grass. Preferring the salons of Paris where he could wear his silk breeches and stockings without fear of soiling them, he did not share his master's taste for the outdoor life which was "nothing to him with his camp habits, his riding boots and his leather breeches". The Foreign Minister could not tolerate the idea of sitting with the First Consul on the lawn himself: "I'm crippled with rheumatism as it is. What a man. He always thinks he is camping out!"

More suitable for the month of snow were the many indoor entertainments. To indulge her taste for amateur theatricals, Josephine had erected a stage and seating for 200. On quieter evenings Josephine might knit, play the harp or backgammon, while Napoleon would cheat at chess, read books out loud with Hortense or tell Corsican ghost stories after dimming the candles with gauzes.

---

[1] Cited in Cronin p.228

[2] Memes p.190

The conversation was often playful. On one evening at Malmaison, just after the peace preliminaries with Britain had been signed in October 1801, Napoleon had been perusing the English newspapers. He normally had them translated, but sensed his interpreters were not telling him everything, so attempted to read them himself. The guests that day included Cambacérès, General Junot and his wife Laure – a young woman Napoleon had known since she was a child. Aides-de-camp Christophe Duroc and Jean Rapp and General Berthier the Minister of War were also present. They were all assembling in a salon for dinner when Napoleon approached Cambacérès with an English journal in his hands and asked: "Citizen Cambacérès, do you know why I went to Egypt?" Cambacérès was taken aback by the question and said nothing. Napoleon now addressed the rest of them. "Yes, I should like to know whether any of you divine the true motive which induced me to go to Egypt? [...] I have no doubt that you believe it was to flatter the fancies of certain learned enthusiasts in antiquities, who would sacrifice an army to obtain a marble column from Palmyra, or a mummy from Thebes." He struck the back of his hand on the newspaper, citing the journal's claim he went to Egypt to make himself King of Jerusalem. "The King of Jerusalem! Forsooth," he said, laughing loudly. Cambacérès bantered with Napoleon in the same vein when another guest remarked he did not see anything wrong in the comparison considering what the crusaders achieved. Napoleon frowned, but then resumed his jovial countenance. "Truly you do us Republican soldiers great honour in comparing us with the crusaders." But then, Napoleon wondered aloud, which of his generals had assumed the role of the womanising crusader Rinaldo?

"Junot, you are fond of running after the pretty women – but hush, Madame Junot is here, we must say nothing on that subject, though I suppose she knows she was not your first love. Do you know that your husband kept a complete seraglio in those distant quarters, Madame Junot?"

If Napoleon hoped to shock Laure, he was disappointed. She replied: "He has told me something of the kind, General; and I have even a pretty portrait hanging over the chimney piece in my room." Napoleon stared at her for a moment before wandering outside into the garden.[1]

---

[1] D'Abrantes vol. 1 pp.504-505

When Josephine returned from her annual health pilgrimage to Plombières in 1801 she decided that Hortense – at seventeen years of age – was more than old enough to marry. She was being courted by Napoleon's aide-de-camp, Christophe Duroc who, when accompanying the First Consul to Malmaison, had often played prisoners base. Napoleon's brother Lucien had proposed to Hortense, but was disappointed when his older brother disapproved of the idea. Duroc, however, was, he felt, a better match. Josephine disagreed and tried to persuade Hortense that Duroc was only interested in her for the power he would attain from marriage. She was more successful in persuading Napoleon to test the sincerity of Duroc's passion. One day he summoned his secretary, Bourrienne and asked: "Where is Duroc?" Bourrienne told him he had gone the opera. "As soon as he returns, tell him he can have Hortense. The wedding must take place within two days. I will give him half a million francs and the command of a division at Toulon. They must go there the day after the wedding. I will have no sons-in-law around me. I must know immediately if this suits him." When Duroc heard of the offer from Bourrienne he was indignant: "Tell him he can keep his daughter," he shouted. "I am off to the brothel." Josephine told Hortense herself that Duroc had declined the offer.[1]

Now that Duroc was out of the way, Josephine considered her own candidate for Hortense. She did not feel her own marriage was secure while she was unable to provide her husband with children. Napoleon's brothers Joseph and Lucien seemed to be constantly scheming to arrange a divorce and the regular visits to Plombières were not making her any more fertile. The possibility that the problem was on Napoleon's side was not discounted. Just before one of these trips, Lucien brazenly advised her to secretly sleep with another man to secure an heir for Napoleon. A marriage of her daughter to a younger Bonaparte would tighten the bonds of their own and relieve the expectation on her to deliver an heir. When Josephine suggested this to Napoleon he agreed that Hortense should marry his brother Louis, but insisted that they both approve the betrothal themselves. He arranged for Bourrienne to ask Hortense the delicate question.

Bourrienne duly met with Hortense and got to the point quickly: "I have been commissioned to suggest something to you that your mother and the Consul desire ardently. They wish to unite you with Colonel Louis

---

[1] Cited in Hibbert 2002 p.115-116

Bonaparte." He persuaded her that Louis was kind, that their marriage would strengthen that of the consular couple, who would consider any child as their heir. Hortense asked for a week to decide. She would have asked her brother Eugène for advice, but he was away so had to think things through herself. She had liked Duroc, but had convinced herself that he failed to live up to her ideal and suspected that no man would ever do so. Marriage might help her mother and all she had to lose were hopeless romantic aspirations. She accepted, but Josephine, who sensed from her lack of enthusiasm that Hortense was sacrificing herself for her, burst into tears.[1]

On 4 January 1802 Hortense and Louis were married in the State Rooms of the Tuileries palace. Cambacérès and Lebrun were among the witnesses. Hortense wore a simple white crepe dress, pearls and a bouquet of orange blossoms, having rejected the more elaborate dress trimmed with flowers that her mother had arranged. Neither did she wear the diamonds given to her by Napoleon. She arrived with Josephine from Napoleon's private stairs, while Louis was obliged to enter from the main staircase which annoyed him. When asked to consent to take Louis as her husband she forced herself to say "Yes" as loudly as she could, as she was worried that she might have said it too weakly. Hortense and Louis avoided eye contact throughout the ceremony and it was noticed by one onlooker that Hortense seemed to be weeping at one point.[2]

After the civil ceremony, they went to the Rue de la Victoire, their new home, to be blessed by Cardinal Caprara. Napoleon's sister Caroline and her husband Murat were also blessed immediately afterwards. The other couple's obvious happiness made Hortense even gloomier. After the ceremony, they went to the drawing room to see the wedding gifts. Louis noticed Hortense seemed uninterested, which prompted her to try harder to appear happy. Josephine, far from cheerful herself, was still crying the next day. The marriage was celebrated by a ball held by Madame de Montesson, a former ancient regime hostess and morganatic widow of the late Duke of Orleans. Still attractive at sixty-five, the grand lady resurrected the refinement of former times. Her rooms were perfumed with fresh flowers from the south of France. A large circular room was lit by a "superb" chandelier and reflected by twelve

---

[1] Hortense pp.72-75

[2] Constant vol. 1 p.107-108

"magnificent" mirrors. Her banquet tables were covered with the finest Saxony linen tablecloth on which were laid plates of Sèvres porcelain bearing the arms of the House of Orleans. The hostess wore an old-style lace and satin gown, a pale-cream cashmere shawl and an ornate, high piled white wig, which would not have been out of place at the court of Marie Antoinette. Her guests, obliged to dress up for the occasion, adorned themselves with jewellery, coloured plumes and heron feathers. First among them was Hortense, wearing a dress copied from a statuette from Herculaneum and flowers in her hair, betraying no hint of her misery as she enjoyed waltzes and gavottes with the best dancers in Paris.[1]

Soon after the wedding Napoleon and Josephine left to attend the conference of Italian delegates from the Cisalpine Republic in Lyon. While they were away, the newly wedded couple stayed at Malmaison accompanied by a school friend of Hortense and a gawky officer companion of Louis'. The officer was unable to solve a puzzle, provoking the girls into fits of laughter. Louis was angry with his new wife. When they were alone he told her: "Who do you take me for? Do you believe I am prepared to be your plaything? I warn you, only a woman of light morals dares laugh at her husband and make sport of him. I would rather leave you than allow myself to be humiliated!"

****

In Lyon the Italian deputies were invited to draw up lists of candidates for three electoral colleges, which were to elect the members of a commission, who would in turn appoint the members of the key state institutions: a senate to deal with state security and foreign affairs, a council of state to propose laws and a legislative body to approve them. Talleyrand had gone on ahead of the First Consul and to smooth the whole process invited the deputies to a grand dinner, trusting that the cuisine of his chef Marie-Antoine Carême would put the delegates in a favourable mood. An oversight caused the Archbishop of Milan to be omitted from the invitation list, an error Talleyrand quickly corrected by

---

[1] Erickson p.219-220, Warren p.170

placing the Archbishop to the right of his own seat. The Archbishop was a large, heavy man with a melancholy expression and laboured breathing, but a lively interest in food. Throughout the dinner, he asked Talleyrand the name of each dish served, and the servants of their ingredients. As every new plate arrived he chuckled and clapped his hands with delight. Standing behind the Archbishop was his private servant Nino, a short fat man in bright multi-coloured livery, who he despatched to the kitchens to enquire about his favourite dishes. As the two talked, Talleyrand noticed that a purple colour in the Archbishop's ears was spreading to the rest of his face: "Your grandeur is ill," Talleyrand whispered. "Allow me to order yon window to be opened above your head, or would you prefer to retire for a moment to breathe the air upon the staircase?"

"No, no, I have not finished dinner yet" replied the Archbishop as he helped himself to copious servings of artichokes à la Barigoule, eating them with the gusto of someone who had not eaten all day. As they talked, the Archbishop seemed to be agreeing with everything Talleyrand suggested regarding the conference, but as the Frenchman asked one last question, the priest suddenly raised his head, gazed vacantly at him and bent forward as if to whisper something. To Talleyrand's horror, the Archbishop's head continued to lean and fell onto his chest, a dull gurgling sound coming from his throat as his goggling, protruding eyeballs attempted to burst from his face. Talleyrand, straining to retain his posture and composure from the pressure of the poor man's body against his own, called for Nino without alerting any of the other diners of his predicament. When Nino arrived he seized his master by the collar, pulling him back into his chair where he sat motionless. By now, the scene had everyone's attention. As some screamed and others gathered round offering advice, Nino told them to leave this to him, explaining this had happened before and that he could not breathe because his teeth were closed. He set about trying to prise them open with an enormous iron door key, but after this proved futile, eventually accepted his master was dead with a yell of despair. When the body was removed, the dinner was resumed with the same background of chat and laughter as before, the only reminder of the Archbishop's former presence his empty chair.[1]

Bonaparte arrived in a freezing Lyon on 11 January. The next few days he met with a small committee of deputies to review the electoral college candidates. There was some discussion about who was to become

---

[1] Colmache p.195

the President of the Cisalpine Republic and the outcome was to consider Bonaparte himself. This was approved by the assembly on 25 January. At the Hotel de Ville, a deputation made the offer to Bonaparte, who had just reviewed the remains of his recently returned army of Egypt amongst the ruins of the Place Bellecour. He accepted, and the next day addressed the assembly in the church where they had been holding their sessions and announced the names of selected candidates for government positions. The new constitution was read out and the country's new name declared – the Italian Republic. Cheers filled the chamber: "Long Live Bonaparte! Long Live the First Consul! Long live the President of the Italian Republic!"[1]

While in Lyon, Bonaparte had not forgotten the French legislature. Writing to Cambacérès he said: "I beg you particularly to see that the 20 and the 60 unruly members whom we have in the constituted authorities, are everyone got rid of." By mid-January Cambacérès had persuaded the Senate to agree to renew the chambers by ballot and not by lot. Legislators who protested were warned that their remonstrance to the Senate could only draw attention to their suitability for removal. The ballot was to nominate the members to be retained and was carried out at the end of January. The results matched a secret list of candidates preferred by the government. When Bonaparte returned to Paris on 31 January he was pleased to find that "unruly members" likes Benjamin Constant and Daunaou were gone, to be replaced by more friendly faces such as his own brother Lucien.[2]

---

[1] Thiers pp.330-333

[2] Thiers pp.333-335

20 Assembly of Lyon

Bonaparte presiding over the assembly of deputies from the Cisalpine Republic at Lyon. Drawing by Girardet, engraving by Torlet after a pinting by Nicolas-André Monsiau. (Author's private collection).

14. The Trying Dutchman

Cornwallis asked about the Dutch delegate, Schimmelpenninck, who had arrived in Amiens three weeks earlier. He said they could not go on discussing issues in his absence and reminded Joseph of his request to get from both Holland and Spain their formal consent to their cessions of Ceylon and Trinidad to end the anxiety of the British government. If, as Joseph had suggested, the presence of Schimmelpenninck testified to his government's acceptance, why was there yet no formal confirmation? Joseph's refusal to include these cessions into a draft treaty until they were admitted to the conference only increased Britain's anxiety. Joseph remarked that what he had said earlier could not be considered as expressing his formal position, but realised that inviting the Dutchman to join the talks was not something that could be put off much longer.

Rutger Jan Schimmelpenninck was a Dutch lawyer, politician and diplomat who had been acting head of State of the Batavian Republic twice since the Dutch had expelled the Prince of Orange as hereditary Stadtholder. Before the Prince fled, the Dutch had been enemies of France, a relationship that was reversed when the French armies marched into Holland to the general approval of its inhabitants in 1795. However, the terms of their friendship with France were to disappoint the Dutch. At the Treaty of The Hague, in the same year, they were obliged to cede territory including Flushing, Maastricht and Flanders, pay an indemnity for their previous enmity with France, maintain a French army at their own expense and then lend the French a large sum at low interest. On their part, the French promised, but only when hostilities ended, to pay compensation for the cessions and withdraw their troops.

Schimmelpenninck, like a number of powerful Dutch politicians, had become disillusioned with the stalemate that democratic legislatures seemed to impose on their state. Although he was in favour of devolving more power to the Dutch provinces, he thought there should be a stronger executive like a presidency, while the electorate ought to be limited to independent and well-to-do citizens that freed them from partisanship. He therefore welcomed the move in March 1801 by reformist Directors to consider constitutional changes. Although this was opposed by the Dutch assemblies, they were kept in check by French troops. Bonaparte was also disappointed with the state of affairs in

Holland, especially when the Dutch refused to offer a cheap loan for his Marengo campaign. A referendum was held in October for a new constitution. This was not open to all Dutch people, but only to their primary assemblies – a total of 400,000 citizens. Fewer than 80,000 took the trouble to vote, and while 50,000 of them said "No", the abstentions were counted as "tacit affirmations". The new constitution, thereby sanctioned by indifference, created a twelve-member executive council including three former reformist directors, whose proposals had to be accepted by a thirty-five-member legislature. Much administrative power was given to local government.

When Schimmelpenninck had arrived at Amiens in early December he alarmed Joseph by telling him he was not prepared to formally accede to his country's cession of Ceylon before he joined the negotiations. He assured Joseph that his country was prepared to make a sacrifice for peace, but wanted something in return. Joseph had not been briefed on this eventuality, and as he had no formal powers to negotiate with the Dutch, he could only express his personal opinion. He told the Dutchman that nobody could think his presence at Amiens did not signal his adherence to the preliminaries and that if he persisted in bringing in Dutch demands, which were not the affairs of England, this could only alarm their former foe. Joseph urged him to at least write a note or make a verbal statement, but Schimmelpenninck would only promise to avoid Cornwallis and persuade his own government to sacrifice Ceylon as long as the British reimburse the Dutch living there for any subsequent loss of property. After this conversation Joseph asked Talleyrand to either give him the powers to negotiate with the Batavian government or oblige them to send Schimmelpenninck the necessary instructions.[1] Schimmelpenninck, alluding to the preliminaries, had complained to Talleyrand that the French had ignored their pledges to Holland to guarantee all Dutch colonies and not make a peace deal without it. Talleyrand told him that "the whole world has need of peace and your country above all."[2]

Joseph had to wait nearly a month before getting clear directions from Paris. A dispatch from Hauterive told him that he could include Schimmelpenninck as long as the Dutchman formally agreed to the

---

[1] Du Casse pp.37-39

[2] Schama 2005 p.439

cession of Ceylon in a note to both Joseph and Cornwallis. If Schimmelpenninck hesitated, or his statement was not full and frank, Joseph was not to admit him. Bonaparte was worried that allowing the Dutch to join the talks without this pre-condition would encourage them to use the conference to get concessions from the French and make common cause with the English against them. His opinion was that the discussions at Amiens should only finalise what was in the preliminaries and the relations between the Batavian Republic and France were not part of these discussions. Joseph had no need of powers to negotiate with Schimmelpenninck because his mission was only to deal with England. If the preliminaries had been particularly detrimental to the Dutch, Bonaparte would have had reason to listen to their complaints, but the war had actually ended better for them than they could have hoped. If either Spain or the Dutch refused to acknowledge their cessions before the treaty was signed, the French would sign without them and give them fifteen days to agree to it.

After receiving these instructions Joseph told Schimmelpenninck that he would be admitted to the conference, but only if he formally and clearly agreed to the preliminary articles and relinquish Ceylon beforehand. Two days later a note from Schimmelpenninck informed Joseph that he had full powers to negotiate according to the preliminaries. Joseph was still worried that he would refuse to sign the final treaty until France had fulfilled all its obligations to the Dutch it had promised in the Treaty of The Hague. Schimmelpenninck told him that it would be too shameful of him to give up Ceylon without first settling his country's issues with France and was prepared to resign rather than sign.

Bonaparte dismissed Dutch complaints on the grounds that their Republic only existed because the French supported it: "We owe them nothing and they owe us everything [...] if France and England make peace, what can a secondary power like Holland do but to adhere to it?" Besides, Amiens was no more the place to discuss Dutch affairs than Italian ones. Nevertheless, Bonaparte considered the Batavian delegate's statement sufficient for him to be admitted to the conference, as long as he consented that his adherence to the preliminaries was inserted into the protocol and that he did not bring up the affairs of Holland in the presence of Cornwallis.

When Schimmelpenninck finally joined the talks he told Cornwallis that he had already given the French formal notice of acceding to the preliminary articles, so was as much surprised as the British at not being admitted earlier.[1] Schimmelpenninck also asserted that he had been told by the French that it had been Britain's wish to negotiate only with France and then present a fait accompli to the minor powers, but was not unduly surprised to be told by Cornwallis that this idea had originated with the French. Anthony Merry, who had joined the British delegation, asked the Dutchman why the French were so Machiavellian. Because, he answered, "they want to make an abrupt peace and steal from you all that you have gained". Afterwards, they would still interfere in Spain and Holland. "They know very well that by including us in the same treaty, you will give us an importance which can only be harmful to their ambitions and unreasonable views."[2]

As well as the formal talks that usually took place in the Hotel de Ville at Amiens, the delegates and local dignitaries entertained each other once or twice a week with evening dinners. Joseph played host at the large house of Madame de Folleville, a former beauty with a tomboy upbringing of riding, fencing and swimming. Now she was the widow of a French politician and grieving mother of a son whose embalmed body rested beneath her bed. Cornwallis' dinners, which employed twelve servants in rich liveries as well as six valets de chambre, were generally appreciated, but Schimmelpenninck provided the best food. At his dinners they ate turbot and eels from Holland, pike and perch from the Rhine, game from Provence and drank exceptional wines. His tea parties, intimate gatherings hosted by his attractive wife and eldest daughter, became a regular highlight, especially for the younger men, and sometimes lasted late into the night. Despite this, Nightingall complained of there being nothing fit to eat or drink. He also complained about his hosts and their wives. While Schimmelpenninck and his wife were acceptable, the French men were all rogues, while the nature of French women was too despicable to commit to writing. He considered Joseph Bonaparte to be the best of the men, but he still lacked the manners of a gentleman. "His wife is a very short, very thin, very ugly and very vulgar little woman without anything to say for herself." The Prefect of the Department, Nicholas Quinette, was an ill-looking scoundrel who, as a member of the Convention in 1792, had voted for the French King's death. His wife was a tall, plain vulgar woman, while the Mayor of Amiens' spouse was good

---

[1] Ross p.432

[2] Schama 2005 p.437

looking but rumoured to be of "easy virtue".[1] Even Cornwallis thought that the new French "have all the disagreeable qualities of the old French without the accomplishments".[2] The British delegation therefore often preferred to dine amongst themselves and their regular habit of drinking in the evening was noted by the French. A lull in the talks, when both sides were obliged to wait for dispatches from their respective governments, would allow a trip to the seaside at Saint-Valéry-sur-Somme or a visit to the cloth and carpet factories at Abbeville. Apart from these outings and dinners, the only other regular recreation the British enjoyed was a daily ride with Cornwallis. However, the weather was getting cold and Cornwallis was beginning to suffer from an old complaint of a swelling in his heel.

In early January, shortly after the British Cabinet received a copy of the latest French plan submitted by Joseph, Otto had a two-hour evening meeting with Addington. Apparently the French plan had caused some alarm and Otto detected anxiety in the Prime Minister's eyes as he relayed his government's concerns. Addington declared he had already sacrificed too much in the preliminaries and could not make any more without prejudicing the dignity of the King. The greatest concern was the cession of Trinidad, which Spain had not yet formally acknowledged. It seemed to Britain that the Spanish had taken advantage of the armistice but had not yet decided for peace. Addington asked: were they supposed to sign without Spain's consent? This seemed to be the only alternative to getting Spain's accession by force, but to delay the restoration of all territories until after Spain had acceded to the treaty would make peace illusory, a point on which Otto agreed. Britain therefore had no other option but to refrain from signing until Spain accepted the loss of Trinidad.

On Malta, Addington argued that the destruction of the forts would not neutralise the island as the key to their strength relied on the rocks on which they were built. Furthermore, the Maltese would revolt against any force that demolished them. On Portugal he would no longer insist their delegate attend, despite his opinion that the preliminaries did allow for it.

---

[1] Ross p.435, Méneval pp.96-98

[2] Ross p.406

On the reimbursement of prisoner expenses, he did not consider foreign troops merely financed by Britain should be treated the same as foreign troops paid and commanded by His Majesty's government. The former were commanded by foreign sovereigns. He did not deny there were Bavarian, Swiss and Italian troops paid by Britain acting on their behalf, but they would never agree to pay the debts of those not under their orders. They were not asking for payment immediately but only as and when the French Treasury could afford it. Otto, who would have refused to sign the preliminaries if the British had insisted on repayment, found it more difficult to argue with Addington than Hawkesbury on this issue. Addington still wanted Britain to retain Tobago especially because it had only been the promise of Tobago by Otto that had persuaded the King to consent to the preliminaries. This and compensation for the Prince of Orange were the two issues of most concern to the King. The retaining of Tobago would also satisfy the merchants and go a long way to improving relations between France and England.

Otto thought that the British government was ruled as much by the country's creditors at the Stock exchange as by the court of St James. Ministers did not take one step without first consulting committees of merchants and ship owners. This was even more the case with Addington, whom Otto realised could not rely on powerful aristocratic family allegiances like previous prime ministers. To them, he was a new man, a nobody for whom they professed an absolute neutrality. He was therefore forced to appeal to the trade interests represented in the House of Commons. Otto might have sympathised with Addington's predicament, but his duty and honour obliged him to tell the First Minister that his promise of Tobago had never been absolute and would have been considered by his government only for a fair equivalent. Addington complained that he did not have the power to dispose of a single English possession and that this remedy was worse than the disease, while Tobago itself was of no use to the French.

Furthermore, Addington claimed, French demands in the North American fisheries and India would be too unpopular to accept, adding that if their refusal on this point resulted in the resumption of war, it would be heartily supported by Parliament and the people. In calmer times, when less mistrust prevailed, this could be more negotiable, he suggested in consolation. Addington ended the meeting by expressing his hope that he would be able to announce the final peace at the opening session of Parliament on 26 January.

Otto understood that British interests in India were determined by its commerce, which would be threatened by French trade. He advised Talleyrand to drop French demands in the fisheries, but not before persuading the English it would be making a big sacrifice by doing so.[1]

Just before the admission of Schimmelpenninck, Cornwallis had received fresh instructions from Hawkesbury on Malta and presented these to Joseph. The British would evacuate within three months after the ratification of the treaty, after which there should be a Neapolitan garrison to remain for a fixed number of years, but after six months half the garrison could be native Maltese. The Neapolitan garrison would be funded by Britain and France equally. The ports of Malta should always remain neutral except to Barbary Coast ships if they were still at war with the Kingdom of Sicily. The Knights ought to admit a Maltese chapter and give up the principle of perpetual war against unbelievers.[2] Britain refused to blow up the forts but would consent to guarantees from the major European powers. Joseph had a few objections: it would not be possible to open the port for all nations and the renunciation of war against the infidels would be pointless while the Barbary States continued to threaten Italy. Also, France would not be prepared to pay for the upkeep of a garrison. Joseph sensed that Cornwallis felt uncomfortable with the role he was expected to play and decided to hold off admitting an article on compensation for the Prince of Orange in case he could gain concessions without it. In particular he hoped Cornwallis would recognise the Ligurian and Cisalpine republics. Anthony Merry, who had joined the English delegation in Amiens and spoke far better French than Cornwallis, felt no restraint in asking for compensation for the King of Sardinia in exchange for these. Joseph, surprised at Merry's independence, wondered whether he had a different agenda to Cornwallis.[3]

A few days later, Joseph conceded that the ports of Malta should remain neutral and open to all shipping except for Barbary Coast nations hostile to Malta and that Britain be allowed three months before evacuating the island. However, he was still not having a Neapolitan garrison, but proposed instead one that was garrisoned by the Knights

---

[1] Du Casse pp.119-138

[2] Ross p.424, OPRP Part II, p.3

[3] Du Casse pp.143-148

themselves who would recruit half the force from countries that still had chapters and the other half from native Maltese.[1] Cornwallis began to feel optimistic about Malta again and was reasonably confident that the Prince of Orange would be compensated given what Bonaparte had told him in November. At a meeting on 22 January, Joseph informed him that the Prince would get some German territory and this would be made public in the treaty, despite criticising the Englishman for assuming too much from what the First Consul had previously said.

Joseph was still resisting the reimbursement of prisoner costs. He thought a reciprocal repayment would not favour France and insisted that the customary practice of nations maintaining prisoners at their own expense was their best position. Dispatches from Talleyrand were firm on this. The First Consul still refused to pay the charges for French prisoners by relinquishing Tobago and considered these expenses were only higher than those to maintain British prisoners because civilians abducted by Britain from commercial vessels were treated as prisoners of war. However, he agreed with Joseph that the best strategy was to recognise only the principle that prisoners were maintained at the expense of the detaining power.[2] Cornwallis suggested a compromise remarkably similar to the one the French were considering. Why not defer the matter to a committee of French and English commissioners appointed after the treaty was signed? By now, Cornwallis did not expect the French to pay a penny. He did not want to jeopardise the chances of peace with a squabble over money, but he needed to preserve England's honour as this was an article in the preliminaries which they could not be seen to give way on. After welcoming this suggestion, Joseph then asked Cornwallis whether His Majesty's government would recognise the Ligurian and Cisalpine republics in northern Italy. Cornwallis repeated the suggestion first proposed by Merry, that this might be possible if some compensation for the King of Sardinia could be arranged.[3]

---

[1] OPRP Part II p.5

[2] Du Casse pp.150-158

[3] Ross p.442

15. Is the King of Naples the Order of St John of Jerusalem?

When Bonaparte returned to Paris from Lyon he seemed pleased with the progress at Amiens, but became increasingly enraged by articles published in England in the French émigré newspaper *L'Ambigu* by the royalist journalist Jean-Gabrielle Peltier. The November articles were very close to encouraging the First Consul's assassination. On 1 February Bonaparte wrote to Joseph: "I beg you to speak to Cornwallis about the infamous pamphlet which I enclose. Impress upon him how little it suits the dignity of either country to allow such nonsense to be published in London by an emigrant, at a time when I am particularly anxious to put an end to all that can excite complaint from England." He was also annoyed with the English diplomat in Paris, Jackson, perhaps because he was fuelling rumours of instability in France and claiming that Bonaparte had insisted on the presidency of the Italian Republic. He instructed Joseph to tell Cornwallis not to trust Jackson. He kept bad company and got his information from swindlers who only wanted money.[1]

In Amiens Cornwallis was temporarily cheered by a meeting with Schimmelpenninck who agreed to a clause consenting to compensation for the Prince of Orange for the loss of personal property in Holland. Also, the Dutchman would no longer demand the return of Dutch ships held by Britain on the Prince's behalf as long as their value would be deducted from the total compensation.[2] The Dutchman reported his meeting to Joseph, asking him if the French expected the Dutch to pay or whether it was still hoped that Prince would be recompensed with German lands. If the latter was the case, the Dutch would still claim from Britain their seized assets. Joseph forwarded the question to Talleyrand, who informed Joseph a few days later that the Dutch should pay nothing.

---

[1] CCNBJ p.57

[2] Ross p.444

It was in the hands of France and compensation would be in the form of German territory and be arranged with Berlin and Vienna.[1]

At the end of January, Spain's representative, the elderly Chevalier Jose Nicolas De Azara y Perera arrived. Azara was the Spanish ambassador to Paris, a post held effectively since 1798. Talleyrand treated him with the same contempt Bonaparte had for his masters, the Spanish Bourbons, albeit with a little more discretion. Ever since Azara had expected payment for some Spanish chocolate he had acquired for the French Foreign Minister, the latter decided the Spaniard was an avaricious old fool and to be played accordingly. When visiting Azara, Talleyrand bribed his host's footmen to "accidentally" break his precious plate just to enjoy the effect it produced on the ambassador's face. Another time Talleyrand was able to convince Azara some intelligence he had uncovered was untrue just by assuring him confidentially of the opposite.[2]

When Cornwallis met Azara, the latter candidly told him that Bonaparte would renew the war if it suddenly became convenient to France, before handing Cornwallis a note on behalf of the King of Spain requesting the return of Trinidad, to which Cornwallis replied with his own saying this was impossible. Azara proceeded to lay down Spain's other demands: Portuguese territory should be determined by the Treaty of Badajoz (allowing Spain to keep Olivenza), Britain should recognize the Bourbon King of Tuscany and Spain should be allowed to navigate to the Cape and trade in the East Indies. Hawkesbury instructed Cornwallis to only recognise the King of Tuscany if Olivenza was restored to Portugal. When Azara was formally admitted to the conference he confirmed his adherence to the preliminaries, thereby accepting the loss of Trinidad.

On the last day of January, Cornwallis visited Joseph in the evening, informing him of a letter from Addington, who was complaining Cornwallis was being too conciliatory on Malta. The British prime minister was insisting the French pay for Neapolitan troops as the Knights were unpopular with the Maltese. Joseph told him the French would refuse and doubted the necessity of a garrison to bolster the Knights. Cornwallis assured him the Neapolitan garrison was absolutely

---

[1] Du Casse p.189, p.199

[2] Churton p.155, p.269

necessary to allow the Knights to re-assert their authority over Malta. Joseph promised to consult his government, but a few days later he was taking an even harder line. He rejected a temporary Neapolitan garrison altogether, complaining that by suggesting this peculiar idea the British were deviating from the preliminaries. Cornwallis showed him the letter from Addington that referred to a Maltese delegation petitioning the British government. As the Maltese despised the Knights, Cornwallis argued it was essential that time be given to inspire confidence in them. If the French refused the article admitting a Neapolitan garrison, they would be suspected of not wanting peace. Joseph asked about prisoner expenses and recognition of the King of Etruria and the Ligurian Republic, but found Cornwallis evasive: he was still awaiting his government's instructions. The Frenchman also read out the letter from his brother complaining about Peltier's article. Cornwallis could only reply that, as Britain had a tradition of free speech, it was difficult for a government to suppress libellous articles.[1]

Cornwallis was still sympathetic to the French suggestion of blowing up the forts, suggesting this to Hawkesbury, if the Knights were unable to establish themselves. If he thought the French were getting annoyed by the British insistence on a Neapolitan garrison, he was to be shortly proved right. Soon after his last meeting with Joseph, Cornwallis received from him the protocol document that recorded and commented on what they had discussed. These documents would often note the differences that had arisen during a meeting, but in language that was impartial and diplomatic. Cornwallis was surprised to read Joseph's position being advocated in the following terms: "What do the preliminaries say? That Malta shall be restored to the Order of St. John of Jerusalem. Is the King of Naples the order of St. John of Jerusalem? Is the order too weak?" If so, the guarantors would protect them. The preliminaries suggested one guarantor but France had agreed to a joint guarantee by all the great powers of Europe. Joseph insisted on the insertion in the treaty of either the latest French proposal or the preliminary article itself.[2] Joseph had transcribed the wording in the protocol almost directly from his last dispatch from Talleyrand, conveying his brother's feelings. Bonaparte was unimpressed by the supposed protest of the Maltese, considering this childish and ridiculous. He

---

[1] Ross pp.445, Du Casse p.201

[2] OPRP p.16

claimed he had also received letters from Malta which indicated the opposite of what the British were claiming. The Maltese wanted the Knights to return. Any culture, commerce or political unity that rock had was thanks to them. Talleyrand instructed Joseph to stand firm and see if the British would become more reasonable.[1]

On 8 February Cornwallis asked if the change in style and tenor of the protocol reflected a change in the French position. Joseph denied this, claiming that the document was just written in firmer language, to make clear that Naples could not take too much for granted regarding Malta. Cornwallis declared that if the French were still sincere about peace there must be some way they could demonstrate it. Joseph suggested Britain could remain in Malta for six months after the ratification rather than three. The Grand Master should be allowed to recruit 200 men from each country that had a chapter or engage 1,000 men from a German prince. The principal powers of Europe would be ultimate guarantors. Cornwallis did not think this was practical. If the only problem France had with the Neapolitan garrison was funding it then he was sure some arrangement could be made. Joseph said nothing so Cornwallis did not pursue this any further at the time. A few days later he was more direct. He explicitly asked Joseph: was the reason why France objected to a Neapolitan garrison because they did not want to pay for it? If that was all, he hoped that Britain would simply agree to pay it all. Joseph explained the objection was with Naples itself: it had been an ally of Britain. Cornwallis then asked: whose troops would France prefer? Malta still needed a garrison for one to three years while the Knights re-established themselves. Joseph replied that three months would be enough and the Grand Master of the Knights should hire troops from European powers that had chapters, excluding Britain and France. Cornwallis insisted that three months was insufficient time and as the new Grand Master had not yet been elected, this would require Britain to remain in Malta for at least six months after the ratification of the treaty. He also suggested – emphasising it was a personal and therefore only a provisional suggestion – that France would not be obliged to finance anything. Joseph agreed to write to his government immediately recommending this.

Cornwallis also challenged the French understanding of the preliminary article allowing for a guarantor and a protector. A protector,

---

[1] Du Casse p.204

Cornwallis argued, could not just be an ideal protector, but an actual and effective one that could support the defence of Malta until the Knights could do so on their own. He reminded Joseph that he himself had proposed a Neapolitan garrison in Paris in November and more recently suggested the King of Naples be both guarantor and protector. Cornwallis insisted a garrison of some sort was necessary until the Knights were ready and re-iterated the British proposals.[1]

Bonaparte was getting impatient and suspicious of the British. He instructed Talleyrand to tell Joseph to draw up a new draft treaty that deviated from the preliminaries as little as possible, while accommodating British proposals as far as possible, except for those that were completely unacceptable. He was to submit this to Cornwallis with a note highlighting the concessions France had made since the preliminaries and declare that there should be no reason to discuss anything further as the French had done all they possibly could and no further changes could be expected from them. If three months was insufficient for the re-establishment of the Knights, then Britain could be allowed to remain in Malta for six months or more as long as the French were allowed to remain in the Neapolitan port of Otranto. In the matter of prisoner expenses, prisoners had to be clearly defined and exclude women and the elderly and if an article on reimbursement had to be admitted, Joseph was to ensure it was sufficiently vague to avoid any pre-determined outcome. More preferable would be an understanding that nations maintained their own prisoners, a principle dictated by humanity and morality and one that could not be repeated too often. On the mutual extradition of traitors, forgerers and bankrupt fraudsters, Bonaparte had no objection and hoped that it could be extended to pamphleteers like Peltier. He claimed to be surprised that a civilized country like Britain tolerated disgusting libels and their miserable authors and had asked Otto to complain about a disrespectful article on the marriage of his brother Louis to Hortense. However, he accepted that as his exhortations for the extradition of conspirators and the deportation of Bourbons were not being well received in London, he allowed Joseph to accept the extradition criteria of the preliminaries.[2]

On 19 February Joseph requested it was noted that he could not find any evidence in any official records of preceding meetings of the

---

[1] Ross pp.450-456, Du Casse p.223

[2] Du Casse p.199, p.242

French ever proposing Neapolitan troops for Malta and rejected Cornwallis' suggestion that this could be inferred from the preliminaries. Any remarks made by himself in an informal meeting in Paris could not be construed as being part of the formal treaty-making process. The proposal he had made more recently as part of this process was only that Naples be the guarantor and protector and mentioned nothing about a Neapolitan garrison: "France has never consented to Neapolitan troops being installed at Malta". Nevertheless France was now prepared to offer two options for a garrison: Malta could either have a garrison of 1,000 Swiss troops to be funded equally by Britain and France for one year, after which it would be paid for by Malta. Or it could have a Neapolitan garrison of 1,000 troops.[1]

A few days earlier Cornwallis had received a letter from Hawkesbury. The election of Bonaparte to the presidency of the Italian Republic had alarmed many in Britain who had previously supported the peace and now wanted to resume the war. It was necessary therefore for Cornwallis to be firm with the French. Joseph should be told that Peltier had no connection with the English government and received no pension from them.[2]

By 22 February Azara was softening Spain's position, telling Cornwallis that Spain was ready to sign even if Britain refused to recognise the King of Tuscany. Joseph also seemed to be reluctantly accepting Britain's refusal to acknowledge this King and the Italian and Ligurian Republics. However, by doing so, Joseph claimed that Britain was abrogating any right to object if those countries sought further protection and support from France.[3] Cornwallis may have begun to sense the endgame was drawing close. Worried that the slightest mistake might renew the bloody and hopeless war – or worse – that he might dishonour or degrade his country, he confessed to a friend that he would rather be still fighting in the backwoods of North America than peace-making in Amiens.[4]

---

[1] OPRP Part II p.23

[2] Ross p.457

[3] Ross p.448, p.458, Du Casse p.189

[4] Ross p.460

Compensation for the Prince of Orange was still eluding Cornwallis. Schimmelpenninck had agreed on behalf of the Dutch, but this was now being blocked by the French. Joseph claimed the Dutch government had requested the French to do so, but assured Cornwallis that the French would still try and get compensation, and even declare this in the treaty, they just did not want to commit to anything specific. However, by 26 February, Joseph had relented and would insert the obligation in the treaty if the British insisted. A few days later, at an evening meeting at Azara's residence, Joseph claimed he had the authority to do so and would arrange it once the issue of Malta was settled. Joseph told Merry that he had said his last word on Malta. If Britain wanted peace, Malta's future had to be settled by either the Swiss or Neapolitan plan.[1]

---

[1] Ross pp.460-461

16. Great Pleasure

Joseph, having had his draft treaty approved by his brother, was ready to present it to Cornwallis, pending the latter's official response to the two alternative projects for Malta. Cornwallis had told Joseph that he thought the Swiss plan was the best, but believed his government would reject it because it would take too long to establish itself, leaving French troops in Neapolitan territory for much longer, exposing Britain to accusations of abandoning its allies. Days went by, and each day a dispatch arrived for Cornwallis from London, but no response from Cornwallis was forthcoming. Joseph was getting impatient and thought the Englishman's manner towards him had changed. Rumours in Paris and London about the outcome of the negotiations prompted him to send Dupuy to see Mr Merry. The British had received a letter from the Turkish ambassador in Paris who was ready to join the conference at Amiens if invited. This seemed to contradict what they had been told by the French, who had refused to invite the ambassador because his powers were to negotiate a separate peace with France.[1]

By 6 March Cornwallis had finally received the latest British plan for Malta and exchanged it for Joseph's draft treaty. An agreement on the garrison was almost in place. Joseph consented to 1,000 Neapolitan troops for a year. He would allow the force to increase to 2,000 if the British insisted, but would not extend the period. Instructions from Talleyrand had told him to resist both prolonging the stay and increasing the size of the garrison. Joseph agreed that the stay should be no more than a year, but thought that if they conceded on the size, they were more likely to get the British to agree to limit the stay. The French draft also had a secret article stipulating that French troops would remain in Otranto until the British left Malta. Cornwallis protested that the number of troops was too small and the time allowed too short. The latest instructions from Hawkesbury were more precise and left him less room to manoeuvre. The article inviting the Ottoman Porte to accede to the treaty would be insisted on. He could not possibly ignore his orders on

---

[1] Du Casse p.242, p.287

this. He had already brushed off too many reproaches for having abandoned other former allies to abandon this one as well.[1]

By early March, Bonaparte had received a copy of the British plan and wrote to Joseph on 7 March: "I do not think there is now much difference between the different proposals. The last wording on the English proposals respecting Malta is not far from ours." Bonaparte also seemed to welcome Cornwallis' compromise on "the matter of the prisoners". He was still as impatient as ever to get the treaty signed: "I do not see what there is to prevent the immediate conclusion of the treaty. If Lord Cornwallis means what he says, peace ought to be signed by noon on the 12th. If this is not done, it will be evident that some change has taken place in the plans of the British Cabinet, and this, in the present state of Europe, would be madness [...] I have yielded to all the demands of England. If peace is not made immediately, I do not fear war. Express yourself strongly on this subject, and let me know by noon on the 19th what I am to expect; for as it seems the English are arming at Plymouth, I must look to the safety of our fleet." Regarding Britain's insistence that the Ottoman Porte be invited to accede to the treaty, he said: "it is impossible to discuss again a matter on which our decision has been often repeated. Our peace with Turkey will not be made at Amiens, but this is no objection to the article which guarantees the integrity of the Ottoman Empire." The next day he decided to back down: "I adopt, though against my will, this formula: 'the sublime Porte is invited to accede to this treaty'. I do not, however, give up my intention of making a separate treaty with the Porte, for the present one does not settle all our differences." Bonaparte again urged haste. "I am of your opinion that it is extremely important not to lose another minute. Do all in your power therefore, to finish and to sign." Two days later Bonaparte was still stressing the urgency of concluding the peace to his brother: "Otto's dispatches and all the letters from England confirm the report that she is making considerable armaments, and that squadron after squadron are being sent off". Bonaparte related that Lord Hawkesbury had told Otto that Cornwallis had received his final instructions. The differences at Amiens were not worth making such a noise about. One of the British delegates may be telling London that he did not want peace. In these circumstances delay would cause real mischief and be of great consequence to the French expeditions. Bonaparte ordered his brother: "send special couriers to inform me of what you are doing, and of what you hear, for it is clear

---

[1] Ross p.463, Du Casse 1855 p.224

170

to me that, if the peace is not already signed or agreed on, there is a change of plans in London."[1]

Meanwhile, in Amiens, Cornwallis and Joseph had compared their plans. There were still differences they had to reconcile. The French were now agreeing to a Neapolitan garrison for Malta, but objected to the clause that endorsed Russia's claim to supervise the election of the new Grand Master of the Knights. Cornwallis suggested the clause just state that the order would be restored by the great powers of Europe, which included Russia. As the clause still adopted the words of the Tsar – insisting on the aristocratic integrity of the Knights and the procedure for electing the Grand Master – he did not think Russia could be offended. The French draft also expected the British recognise the Ligurian Republic and allow French troops to remain in Otranto in southern Italy until the British had evacuated Malta. However, Joseph said he would withdraw these clauses if the British continued to object to them. Cornwallis also resisted the French clause specifying that territories of Spain and Portugal be defined by the Treaty of Badajoz, but Joseph did not think that it could be withdrawn. The points of accord and contention were submitted to their respective masters for confirmation and further instructions.[2]

Bonaparte was the first to reply. On 11 March he wrote to his brother, expressing surprise they had not yet signed, despite having come to an agreement: "I see then no obstacles to peace" he said, but then told Joseph to take care with the wording of the article regarding prisoners lest it inadvertently exclude the Ottoman Porte's indemnity to France. He was also disappointed that Britain was still not recognising the Italian Republic and told his brother to tell Cornwallis that Prussia, Austria and all the sovereigns of Italy had done so.[3]

While the delegates waited for London's response to the latest plan, Joseph was able to tell Cornwallis on the 12th that the French had agreed to invite the Ottoman Porte to accede to the treaty and that they had withdrawn their threat to retain troops in Neapolitan states if Britain

---

[1] CCNBJ p.58-59

[2] Ross p.463

[3] CCNBJ p.60

had not evacuated Malta. Cornwallis thought the only issue remaining was the agreement to extradite traitors. Joseph pointed out that high treason was not a recognised crime in France so Cornwallis suggested the article cover any conspiracy against the state instead, to which Joseph gave his consent. In the evening Schimmelpenninck objected to Spain being given the same access to the Cape as Britain and France, but was eventually persuaded to agree that they should all be charged no more than Dutch ships.[1]

In mid-March Cornwallis received a letter from Hawkesbury with his response to the French plan. He also enclosed a draft treaty that he was authorised to sign. If the French did not sign within eight days of its presentation, he was instructed to leave Amiens.[2] On the 17th he met with Joseph to present it. Regarding the prisoners, Hawkesbury was insisting on reimbursement but proposed that the French could offset their liabilities with any expenses they incurred in maintaining any foreign soldiers under the command of British officers. Cornwallis was personally embarrassed by this position, as it contradicted everything he had been saying, so would do his utmost to rectify it and tried to reassure Joseph that they did not expect the French to pay, but they did not want to publicly acknowledge this. He implored Joseph not to communicate or respond officially to this until his next courier arrived.

Hawkesbury had allowed the changing of the wording regarding the election of the Grand Master, but only as long as the French accepted that the office was currently vacant. Ferdinand von Hompesch, the last holder of the post, had resigned in 1799, but Azara had pointed out to Cornwallis that he was technically still the Grand Master until the Pope had consented, which had not yet happened. Hawkesbury had also refused to accept the French condition that the Maltese garrison should only be of native Neapolitans. This would exclude the effective Swiss and Albanian regiments. The wording should be changed to only exclude troops of a major European power which might then control Malta.

Joseph was bitterly disappointed with the latest British proposals. He refused to declare the office of Grand Master vacant as he considered it superfluous do so, adding that it would also be dishonourable. He also

---

[1] Ross p.469

[2] Ross p.472

insisted that France could not allow French émigrés or Swiss to be part of the garrison. As for the prisoner expenses, he could not promise to delay any official response and would be obliged to inform his brother immediately. He thought these latest proposals negated several important articles and had put back the negotiation, endangering its fate just at the moment when a deal was so close. Some of the changes appeared to be written in a spirit of malice against France and its allies, without being of any benefit to Britain. He declared his astonishment at what he was hearing and reminded Cornwallis of all the sacrifices France had made already. He told the Englishman he had no hope of getting the French government to be more conciliatory than it had already been. Cornwallis claimed he was also personally disappointed by this setback and expressed his hope that his government would desist in some of its demands and hoped for better news in his next dispatch from London. When Joseph spoke angrily about members of the Cabinet who wanted war, Cornwallis argued that it was only because Addington wanted to confound those colleagues with an advantageous peace that he risked the break-up of the negotiations. Joseph did not want the Englishman to think he would walk out of the negotiations, so did not refuse to discuss the proposals to which the French were not implacably opposed. However, the meeting, lasting seven hours, ended with no satisfactory result. Joseph had asked Cornwallis to provide a copy of the latest proposals to which he consented. As an afterthought following their conference, he sent Dupuy to ask Cornwallis to sign it as it would be a useful official document clearly showing that if peace was not concluded it was because the British had changed their minds about the prisoners and other items. Cornwallis refused. Joseph informed both his brother and Talleyrand of the latest developments. He also wrote to Otto. As Cornwallis did not appear to enjoy the confidence of his masters, perhaps a direct appeal to Hawkesbury would settle the issues. In particular he wanted Otto to point out that Cornwallis had assured him two months ago that the article on the prisoners would satisfy the honour of both nations and that France would not pay a penny. Joseph had been so satisfied with Cornwallis's assurances on this subject that he had postponed discussion of it and was consequently more conciliatory on other issues. It seemed impossible to Joseph that, if London wanted peace, they would undermine an article the justice of which was acknowledged by Cornwallis and confirmed in a note in the handwriting of Mr Merry.[1]

---

[1] Ross p.477, OPRP p.48-52, Du Casse p.323, p.326, Du Casse 1855, p.230

Schimmelpenninck, after a lively conversation with Merry, went to Cornwallis. Speaking in English, the Dutchman convinced him that the French would not yield, pointing out that if the negotiations broke down, Cornwallis's reputation would be tarnished. The English Lord offered to see Joseph, promising to sign a project that was midway between what had been discussed on 13 March and the proposals he had presented on the 17th, if Joseph would compromise on the wording. Cornwallis, who had decided it was bad timing to present his government's ultimatum, showed Schimmelpenninck his letter from Hawkesbury. The Dutchman informed Joseph of the offer and the contents of the letter, which demonstrated that Britain wanted peace, but only if it was deemed honourable. The refusal of France to the latest British proposals would be considered as a signal for renewed hostilities. A grateful Joseph thanked the Dutchman for his mediation, and promised to be as reasonable as he could with Cornwallis in their next meeting. If Schimmelpenninck was hoping to be rewarded with a promise by the French to withdraw troops from Holland he was disappointed, being told by Talleyrand that negotiations between allies were outside the terms of reference of the settlement.[1]

When the First Consul was apprised he wrote to Joseph on the 21st, approving of his conduct and reserve. Regarding the prisoners, he had heard from Otto in London that the English government were going to take into account the expenses incurred by France in holding Britain's allies: "This seems right". Regarding the occupancy of the role of Grand Master, Bonaparte did not see much of an issue. As no Frenchman or Englishman could be a Knight of St John and vote for a new Grand Master "there can be no harm in declaring, since it is a fact, that the post of Grand Master is vacant". Bonaparte then addressed the issue of the garrison for Malta: "The words 'forming part of the Neapolitan army' which they want to substitute for the term 'native', are rather important if their secret wish is to introduce French emigrants or Englishmen; if this be not the motive for the change of words, it is of less importance."[2]

Hawkesbury praised Cornwallis' judgement in not issuing the ultimatum and acquiesced to the alterations to the draft treaty, but said that if this did not result in the signing, Cornwallis was to carry out his

---

[1] Du Casse p.329, Schama 2005, p.438

[2] CCNBJ p.62

earlier instructions without fail. Hawkesbury had met with Otto who promised to convince the French government to accept the latest proposals on the Prince of Orange and prisoner expenses, and hoped the treaty would be concluded soon. The Treasury was almost exhausted. Addington needed to complete his budget and could not arrange a new loan on favourable terms in the present state of uncertainty. A letter from Addington reinforced the point that the speedy conclusion of the treaty was vital for government finances.[1]

On the evening of 24 March Cornwallis met with Joseph and Schimmelpenninck and they began what was to be their final discussion at ten o'clock. It ended at three in the morning. Britain was to restore all its conquests except Trinidad and Ceylon. The Cape, returned to Holland, was to be a free port that would not expect from French, British or Spanish ships any more in duties than it would charge the Dutch. France was to keep the Portuguese territories it had added to French Guyana while Spain was to retain the Portuguese province of Olivenza. In article X, Malta was to be restored to the Knights of the St John who were to elect a new Grand Master. No English or French chapters of the order were to be re-established. A Maltese chapter would be set up which would allow non-noble members. The Knights and the island were to always remain neutral in any future wars and its ports open to all shipping, except to those of the Barbary States until they ceased to be hostile. The independence and security of Malta would be guaranteed and protected by Britain, France, Austria, Russia, Spain and Prussia. Britain was to evacuate Malta within three months of the exchange of ratifications of the treaty, after which they would be replaced by a garrison of 2,000 troops provided by the King of Naples which would be composed only of natives of his dominions. This would be just for one year, after which the Knights were to defend the island themselves. If the guaranteeing powers did not consider the Knights to be strong enough by then, the Neapolitan garrison would remain until they could be relieved by another force that was adequate. The French had to evacuate their troops from the Kingdom of Naples and the Papal States. The Newfoundland fisheries were to remain in the same state as they were at the beginning of the war. Commissioners would be appointed by France and Britain to assess the reimbursement of prisoner expenses incurred by both sides. The Treaty promised compensation for the Prince of Orange and the Ottoman government was to be invited to accept its terms.

---

[1]Ross pp.481-483

Cornwallis wrote to Hawkesbury declaring that "peace is made", while Joseph sent Dupuy with a copy of the treaty to Paris, recommending its bearer to both Talleyrand and Bonaparte for ministerial appointment. The final four copies of the treaty, one for each of the signatories were drawn up and completed on 26 March. On that day, at eleven in the morning, detachments of infantry and cavalry marched to the residences of Joseph and Cornwallis, escorting them to the town hall to the accompaniment of military music and a large crowd. The delegates were received by the Mayor of Amiens and congratulated by the Prefect. They went into the room where the signing was to take place and closed the doors. Joseph presently announced they were ready to sign, the doors were opened and an orderly crowd entered the room. After they applied their signatures, Joseph and Cornwallis embraced to loud cheers from those in the room, many of whom were overcome with emotion. Half an hour later Joseph entrusted the signed treaty to the young Portalis who sped to Paris. Joseph then wrote to Otto, praising the character of Cornwallis, who left for London the next day.[1]

Talleyrand was the first in Paris to receive the French copy. He placed it in his briefcase along with other diplomatic documents and met with Bonaparte, but did not produce it immediately. First he discussed routine matters and after about an hour, took the peace pact out of his case and said: "Now, I am going to give you great pleasure. The Treaty is signed. Here it is." Standing up, Bonaparte said: "Why didn't you tell me at once?"

"Ah, because you would not have listened to all the rest. When you are happy I am unable to reach you." [2]

---

[1] Méneval pp.90-97

[2] Lawday p.128

PART II: PURSUITS OF PEACE

17. Peace Approved and Pitt Praised

At nine o'clock on the morning of 29 March, Francis Moore arrived at Downing Street with the definitive Treaty of Amiens. Addington immediately invited financiers to bid for a loan to the government. On the 31st, after being presented with seven proposals, he agreed to borrow £97.9 million pounds, allowing him to complete the budget he had purposely delayed to realise the better terms afforded by the peace. He estimated an expenditure of £63 million, nearly of half of which would be interest charges on the national debt which was well over £400 million. The other half was on the military, especially the Navy. Addington was not prepared to reduce this dramatically because France could not wholly be trusted. The loan would create £30 million of government stock and cover £11 million of exchequer bills. The rest would offset the liability of £56 million that Pitt's government had incurred using income tax revenue as security. Not only was income tax unpopular, it had also failed to raise the revenue expected of it, so after receiving a petition from the City, Addington decided to repeal it. The new loan would incur an additional £3 million of interest charges for which new taxes were raised on malt and beer along with further import and export duties. Addington also reformed the system of paying salaries to government employees. This was now done through the budget instead of the civil list, now purely for royal expenses. To ease this through, he settled the outstanding civil list bill. He introduced the budget in the Commons on 5 April. It was well received by most members. Even Canning felt obliged to concede that it was no longer essential for the country to have Pitt at the Treasury. Fox questioned the need to maintain such large military resources in peacetime, while Grenville objected it was too small.[1]

Although the definitive Treaty was welcomed with illuminations at the end of April, the activities of France during the negotiations had alarmed many, both inside and outside of Parliament. In January, William Cobbett, a friend of William Windham, published his *Letters to the Right Honourable Henry Addington, On the Fatal Effects of the Peace with Bonaparte*. Cobbett, who had his windows smashed by the mob for refusing to

---

[1] Zeigler pp.147-150, Fedorak pp.89-94

illuminate them with candles, told Addington that the peace was so bad it had swallowed all the other evils the government was responsible for. The Treaty would ruin the colonies, commerce, manufactures and the constitution of Britain. The French and their satellite acquisitions on the South American coastline provided the perfect bases from which they could threaten Britain's remaining West Indian colonies, which brought much needed revenue. This income, deriving mainly from trade, was vital to pay off the massive national debt. Much of the economic growth during the war had come from indirect trade with San Domingo and acquisitions of enemy territory now lost by the peace. Meanwhile, the proceeds from existing colonies had declined and by the restorations Britain had given up half its West Indian market. The peace would open the European market to competition from France which had a larger population, a cheaper workforce and abundant resources now including the Belgian coal pits of Namur and Liege. The French would impose trade agreements on its neighbours more favourable to France than Britain, thereby controlling the supply of fine woollen cloth from Spain and admitting French woollens into Portugal. French looms would process the finest cotton from Demerara, while Britain would now have to get its cotton from Brazil and Georgia. Britain could no longer be complacent about its exports to the United States, which was becoming increasingly self-sufficient and now had the option of buying its manufactured goods from a revived Europe.[1]

In Parliament, Grenville had expressed his concern about the French Brest fleet sailing to the West Indies in December 1801 and although the government had shadowed this with its own ships – provoking a mutiny amongst war-weary sailors at Bantry Bay – his anxiety was not diminished. In March, when another French fleet was expected to follow, Lord Carlisle resurrected this concern amongst others: in January it was confirmed that Spain was to return Louisiana to France. In the same month Bonaparte became president of the new Italian Republic, which was augmented with Parma, Placenta and part of Piedmont in February. These encroachments by France since the preliminaries encouraged worries that peace was insecure. Elliot declared in the House of Commons that France would build a navy and claim it was to promote

---

[1] Cobbett's Letters to Addington, 1802 pp.5-115

the liberty of the seas, while in fact its true purpose was the "annihilation of the commerce and consequence of Great Britain".[1]

Windham was the most vigorous opponent of the definitive Treaty in the Commons. In May he justified his call for a debate on it for four reasons:

- First, the secret gains of France unknown at the time of the preliminary treaty. Of these he highlighted the surrender of Elba to France, the redrawing of the boundary of Guyana in France's favour and the cession of Louisiana to France by Spain.
- Secondly, there were the French actions after the preliminaries, which included the creation and extension of the Italian Republic with Bonaparte as President and the French expedition to St Domingo. The former was tantamount to the virtual annexation of northern Italy and proof that Bonaparte did not intend to respect the balance of power the treaty was supposed to maintain. The latter was a direct threat to British interests in the West Indies.
- The third reason was what the Treaty left out: the most significant omission being that there was no binding guarantee to indemnify the Prince of Orange, who had thereby been most shabbily treated.
- Fourthly and finally, there were two noticeable differences between the preliminary and definitive treaties. The first was that the French were being allowed to offset their debt to Britain for prisoner expenses against the expenses they incurred for keeping Russian prisoners. The second difference was that the increase in French power in Italy since the preliminary Treaty effectively exposed the island of Malta to future French possession, given the weakness of the Knights and the Kingdom of Naples.

Addington was obliged to counter these points: Elba was ceded by Tuscany, not Britain. Guyanese boundaries were agreed by Portugal. Louisiana had never been a threat to Britain when formerly owned by France and it was not a threat now. The Italian Republic was recognised by Russia, Austria and Prussia and did not justify breaking off talks. Regarding St Domingo, Britain had no right to stop another power from suppressing a revolt in one of its colonies and to have allowed a revolt to be successful would have encouraged similar revolts in British colonies.

---

[1] Cobbett's Annual Register for 1802. p.115

Russian troops were not only British allies, they were under British pay and control. As for the Prince of Orange, the unbinding promise of compensation was the best they could do for him in the circumstances without jeopardising the peace. Addington dismissed Windham's concerns over Malta: the Knights would grow in strength and Naples would not give in so easily to French pressure. To the popular criticism of restoring so many French colonies, Castlereagh supported Addington by noting that France would have more to lose if she resumed war again.[1]

In another speech on 13 May, Windham blamed the British government for its part in destroying the independence of Malta and degrading its Knights. The Neapolitan garrison was a farce, as Naples was under the control of France. Because the order included a Maltese chapter allowing non-noble members, it had been diluted, not with just common water, but with water from the puddle and was no longer an institution in which German Knights were prepared to serve. France was now a colossal power, something not seen in Europe since the Roman Empire. In ten years it had acquired more than the Romans had in fifty-three. Britain might be safe with the Channel protecting it, but its colonies were seriously threatened by a French empire that in the Americas now controlled the Mississippi and Amazon rivers and would soon probably take from the Dutch the Cape of Good Hope – a vital stopover on the way to India. It was obvious that the object of France was universal empire. When he criticised Britain's strategy of focusing too much on colonies during the war and not combating the Jacobin menace directly, Pitt objected: Windham's revelation of opinions in the previous Cabinet of which he had been a member, opinions given in confidence, was out of order. Windham nevertheless insisted that the only military decisions which deserved praise were those that attacked France directly such as the support of the uprising in Toulon. War strategy could not be divorced from ultimate goals and the nation had never been told the real reason why they had been at war. They had fought because the nature of the French government precluded any possibility of peace. Because the people had not been aware of this, they were not alerted to the perils of this peace. The dangers of Jacobinism were now even greater especially because most people were now wholly insensible to them.[2] Despite

---

[1] Pellew vol. II pp.36-45

[2] Hazlitt 1810 p.575, Cobbett's Annual register for 1802, p.150

Windham's efforts, both Houses of Parliament approved the definitive Treaty with only sixteen Lords and twenty Commoners opposing.

As well as the budget and the peace, another subject that attracted the attention of Parliament was the previous Prime Minister. On 12 April Sir Francis Burdett proposed a committee was formed to investigate the previous administration and expressed his opinion of Pitt in the bitterest terms. Pitt's supporters were indignant and one of them, Lord Belgrave, suggested an amendment. Instead of investigating the former Cabinet, Parliament should thank them for their wise conduct of the war. Although the Speaker allowed this, Pitt himself objected to it on the grounds that such an amendment was contrary to parliamentary procedure. Belgrave withdrew his amendment and Burdett's motion was voted on and defeated by a vast majority. When Belgrave announced his intention of proposing a motion of thanks to the previous government Mr Nicholls pre-empted it by accusing Pitt of "criminality of the deepest dye" and suggesting that Parliament should offer its thanks to the King for having dismissed him. In response, Belgrave pointed out that Pitt had not been dismissed, he had resigned. Parliament was being asked to thank the King for doing something he had never done. Belgrave then proposed his own motion of thanking the former government. Although this was resisted by Fox, Grey, Erskine and others, the motion was carried by 222 against fifty-two. Another Pittite stood up suggesting a motion to thank Pitt personally and this motion was also carried. The fanatical support for Pitt spilled outside Parliament when on 28 May a dinner for 823 was organised to celebrate his birthday at Merchant Taylor's Hall. Although Pitt did not attend himself, this did not stop Canning from rendering a sonnet he had composed for the occasion. Gushing with praise for "a statesman unbiased by int'rest or fear, by power uncorrupted, untainted by gold", the song ended dramatically: [1]

> "And O! If again the rude whirlwind should rise
> The dawning of peace should fresh darkness deform
> The regrets of the good and the fears of the wise
> Shall turn to the pilot that weathered the storm"

---

[1] Stanhope vol. III pp.375-381

The Consequences of Honour

With the peace approved, the budget passed and Pitt praised, the King dissolved Parliament on 29 June, obliging members of the Commons to fight for their seats in a summer election.

18. Mass and Gratitude

On Easter Sunday 18 April, the First Consul rose early. Bonaparte was normally an early riser, but today was a special occasion. As he was helped by his attendants into knee breeches and a scarlet coat embroidered with golden palms on the seams and a black collar, his brother Joseph and Cambacérès entered. "Well, we are going to mass" said Bonaparte to the latter. "What do they think of that in Paris?" Cambacérès replied that he thought some people might be going to hiss at the ceremony. "If anyone takes a notion to hiss, I will have him turned out of the doors by the grenadiers of the consular guard," retorted Bonaparte. "But what if the grenadiers begin to hiss like the others?" asked Cambacérès. "As to that, I have no fears. My moustaches will go to Notre Dame here, just as they went to the mosque in Cairo. They will look to see what I am doing, and seeing me behaving seriously and decently, will do the same..." "I am afraid that the Generals may not be so accommodating," Joseph told him. "I have just left Augereau who is spitting fire and flame at what he calls your pious affectations. He and several others will not be so easy to bring into the bosom of our holy mother the church." "Bah!" exclaimed Bonaparte. "Is Augereau like that? He's a brawler who makes a good deal of racket". Bonaparte suggested that Augereau would have no problem with the Church if he had an imbecile relation who would only be suitable for the post of a chaplain. The final accessories to Bonaparte's costume were added: a sabre from Egypt suspended by a narrow, finely wrought, richly embroidered shoulder belt and a hat with three coloured plumes.[1]

The mass they were about to attend at Notre Dame cathedral was the first public state endorsed ceremony of its kind to be held in France since The Terror had outlawed the Catholic Church years earlier. It was to celebrate the recently ratified Treaty of Amiens and the Concordat with the Pope which re-established Catholicism in France. The seizure of Church assets in 1789 had been followed by the abolition of its right to collect tithes, cutting off its main source of revenue. The Civil Constitution of the Clergy in 1790 subjected priests and bishops to

---

[1] Constant p.115

elections and made them dependent on a state salary. In 1791 they had to pledge obedience to the government. Many refused, and when the Pope condemned the oath in 1792, many more recanted. When war broke out, refractory clergy – those who refused or retracted their oaths – were associated with counter-revolutionaries and mercilessly persecuted, forcing 30,000 to flee France. In 1793 the Revolution turned against the remaining constitutional clergy and Christianity in general. State funding of the Constitutional Church stopped in 1794. Under the courageous leadership of Bishop Henri Grégoire, it barely survived The Terror and although the Church was left alone during the Directory, it had to do without state support or protection. Bonaparte realised that the attack on the Church had divided France and had motivated much of the support in Europe for war against the Republic. On becoming First Consul he declared his intention to make the Pope a gift of thirty million Frenchmen. Negotiations between Paris and Rome were initiated, concluding in the signing of the Concordat in July 1801.

Although Catholicism would be professed by the consuls and recognised as the religion of the "vast majority of French citizens" and the state would pay the salaries of its clergy, it would be subject to police regulation and there would be liberty to worship other faiths. The Pope would be allowed to appoint bishops, but only those nominated by the state. The ten-day décade was to be replaced by the traditional seven-day week with Sunday reclaiming its position as the day of rest and worship. A completely new and streamlined episcopate was formed. Former bishops were asked to resign or dismissed by the Pope and replaced by only ten archbishops and fifty bishops from a pool of both constitutional and refractory clergy.[1]

The Concordat had been published in February 1802 and presented to the legislative bodies earlier in April with the "Organic articles" of the new civil regulations for the Church. Large majorities in its favour were delivered in both the Tribunate and the Legislative Assembly. The articles disappointed the Pope as they interfered in the internal administration of the Church, something he understood the Concordat had avoided. The Pope complained, but was no match for the determination of the French to tolerate religion on their own terms. The evening before Easter Sunday, Cardinal Caprara, the Papal legate to France, was still insisting that newly appointed French bishops should

[1] Duffy pp.254-266

recant their previous adherence to the civil constitution of the clergy imposed by French Revolution. He only backed down when Portalis went to him and told him the ceremony would be cancelled and the Concordat suspended if he persisted with this.

Bonaparte was not the only early riser on Sunday morning. Assailed by a few passing showers, the whole city, swelled with visitors from the provinces, was in motion. The first public ceremony Bonaparte attended was the monthly reception of foreign ambassadors at the Tuileries. Francis Jackson, the British representative, was returning to England and took his formal leave of the First Consul who wished him well in his next posting. He was being replaced by Anthony Merry, recently returned from Amiens. After the reception, about 11 a.m., a long procession of carriages wound its way through troop-lined streets to Notre Dame Cathedral. Bonaparte and the other two consuls were in the same green liveried coach driven by eight horses. All three wore gilded velvet red coats and triple plumed hats. Lebrun had hair curls and pleated pigtails, while Cambacérès opted for a wig with three rows of curls. Beside them rode seven of Bonaparte's generals, including Junot. Behind the consular carriage trailed the coaches of his ministers and officials, the diplomats and the wives, mothers and daughters of all these important men. Among the procession, watched by thousands waving white handkerchiefs from the streets, windows, balconies and rooftops, was a troop of Mameluke cavalrymen in baggy trousers, green caftans and turbans. The councillors of state were obliged to travel in ordinary ramshackle hackney carriages with their number plates removed because there were not enough state coaches available for the occasion. They themselves were more suitably dressed in long dark overcoats with square lapels embroidered with gold or blue silk. The ubiquitous tricolour sash and a cockaded three-corner hat completed their uniform. As for the ladies, Laure Junot thought Bonaparte's sister, Caroline Murat, stood out most of all. She was wearing a pink satin hat and feathers, a fine muslin dress lined with pink satin and trimmed with Brussels lace. A muslin scarf was draped over her shoulder. By now the rain had stopped and the sun had come out.

Notre Dame Cathedral, whose crowned figures decorating its facade had been decapitated during the Revolution, was transformed. Flowers hung in its arches and incense burned on its altars, while the damage to its pillars was masked by wall hangings. By the time Bonaparte had arrived, most of the congregation had been waiting two hours. Access to the cathedral was restricted to ticket holders, and was packed to excess. The First Consul was met at the door by the Bishop of Paris who presented him with holy water. The Senators, Tribunes and members of the Legislative body took their places either side of the altar which had been decorated with a crucifix and candles from Arras. Behind the place reserved for Bonaparte were his generals in full uniform. About sixty of them, under orders to attend from General Berthier the Minister of War, had reluctantly turned up to the Cathedral to find no seats arranged for them. When they noticed a group of clerics obviously amused at their predicament, General Masséna walked over and struck one of them, encouraging the other generals to follow his example. As they evicted their frocked mockers and occupied their seats, some of the congregation applauded. Although General Moreau absented himself, his wife and her mother did attend, but had taken the seats reserved for Josephine and Bonaparte's mother in the Ladies gallery. A furious row erupted, ending only when Moreau's wife fainted, obliging the Bonaparte women to back off.

The ceremony began soon after Bonaparte entered the Cathedral, preceded by priests behind a cross and taper. Mass was read by Cardinal Caprara, twenty-four bishops took their oaths and a chorus of clergy chanted the words "Domine, salvam fac republicam; domine, salvos fac consulus". As the Archbishop of Tours read a sermon from the pulpit, he was serenaded by the generals sitting beneath him who laughed at his Latin and scoffed at his cassock.[1] General Augereau affected to mutter loudly while the priests were at the altar. His rudeness was matched by many of the congregation eating chocolate cakes and bread throughout the ceremony.[2]

Other than these incidents, the concerns of Cambacérès and Joseph proved unwarranted. When evening fell, Paris was lit up by illuminations of multi-coloured tinted lamps adorning its houses and public buildings. The Palace of the Legislative Assembly (formerly the Palais Bourbon) looked like a palace of jewels. The Tuileries was covered in lamps, flowers and flags of all nations and part of its gardens similarly illuminated. Military bands and fireworks competed for everybody's attention.

---

[1] Augustin-Thierry pp.1-39, Thiers, pp.347-349

[2] Goodrich p.100, Bourrienne

Bonaparte was not deeply religious. He saw the Church as a useful resource for the state. To set an example, Bonaparte endeavoured to observe mass every Sunday, but all this involved was that the doors between his room where he was working and the room in which mass was conducted were kept open. However, he was sentimental about it. One day he was walking through the grounds of Malmaison along a shaded path with Josephine and some noisy company when he motioned to them with his hand to be quiet. The church bells of neighbouring villages chiming their vespers could be heard in the distance. "Those bells remind me of the days of my boyhood. It seems to me, when I hear them, that I am still at Brienne."[1]

****

After the ratification of the Concordat two more important legislative successes for the government were quickly achieved. After a discussion in the Council of State on 16 April, a general amnesty for all émigrés – with only 1,000 exceptions – was granted on the 26th. A few days later an education law authorised the creation of state supported Lycées – secondary schools modelled on the Prytanée – the former Louis le Grand – whose most infamous recent pupil was the late Robespierre. A lycée was to be set up in every appeal court district to train the military and civil elites of the future, some of whose education would be funded by 6,400 scholarships, 2,400 to be awarded to sons of officers and government officials. The rest would go to the brightest pupils. Private schools were to be tolerated, while elementary schools would remain the responsibility of local authorities.

On 6 May the president of the Tribunate, M. Chabot de l'Allier, addressed his colleagues in the Luxembourg Palace. As well as presenting them with Treaty of Amiens, he proposed that they should manifest their gratitude to the First Consul in some way and invite the other chambers to do the same. This was not a spontaneous suggestion. Cambacérès and Bonaparte had been discussing ways of making the government more stable, but agreed they should not do anything too radical. Bonaparte claimed he had no personal desire for more power, but he still thought the position of the head of state was too precarious. He had several ideas about what to change, but was too personally interested so felt he should not take any initiative. He asked Cambacérès to find out what other

---

[1] Muhlbach p.234

people thought on the matter and Cambacérès approached de l'Allier who now asked his colleagues in the Tribunate to consider thanking the First Consul. They and the Senate agreed, but nobody was sure what form this gratitude should take.

The next day a deputation of Tribunes visited Bonaparte at the Tuileries, hoping to find out what he wanted. Bonaparte pretended not to understand what they wanted. He claimed he desired no reward beyond the gratitude of his fellow citizens. Death itself would lose its sting if with his dying eyes he could see the assured happiness and glory of the Republic. The Tuileries and Cambacérès residence teemed with senators trying to find out how they should act. Bonaparte, when asked, would reply that anything they awarded him would be sufficient. Cambacérès and Lebrun hinted to the senators that they should offer him consulship for life. Some of them believed this was more than he wanted and felt that he would be satisfied with a further ten years as consul. When Cambacérès and Lebrun warned Bonaparte that his reserve would be exploited by his enemies, Bonaparte remained convinced that the Senate would always do more than what was expected of them.

On the 8 May the Senate deliberated all day. Some were disgusted at Bonaparte's pretensions, but most were in favour of awarding him some extension of power. Garat protested against life consulship and proposed an extra ten years in office instead. This met with near universal approval with sixty senators in favour. Only one voted against it: "How", he said, "can any Frenchman be so craven as to accept as a master a foreigner from a nation which the Romans did not even want for slaves."

Bonaparte was with his brothers Lucien and Joseph when he heard the news. He was furious and considered refusing the offer. He sent for Cambacérès who suggested a plan. The following day, Bonaparte sent the Senate a reply, thanking them for their "honourable proof of esteem", but reminded them that it was the people who had given him power and to assure himself of their confidence he felt obliged to ask them directly whether his magistry should be extended. On 10 May a Council of State was held in Bonaparte's absence. It agreed that the stability of the government was of the utmost concern. Foreign powers, credit, prosperity – all had need of confidence – and the perpetuity of the First Consul's powers seemed the most certain means to inspire it. Ten years would not be sufficient. The question to be put to the people would therefore be: "Shall the First Consul be consul for life?" A second question was added: should he have the power to designate a successor? When Bonaparte was presented with the Council's proposal by

Cambacérès he objected to the second question, but approved the first. The next day it was announced in the *Moniteur* that a plebiscite would be held on the question of consulship for life. Polls would be opened in all town halls, registrars and lawyers officers.[1]

---

[1] Villefosse pp.159-160, Lefebvre pp.144-145, Thiers pp.357-365

19. Honour, Hunger and Human Bondage

Although Bonaparte wanted France to prosper, he hoped to encourage in the French people aspirations other than wealth: "Affluence carries no merit," he said. "The rich are often a pack of undeserving idlers, and a rich merchant usually gets his wealth either by selling dear or by outright thievery."[1] To foster higher goals and to inspire personal loyalty he proposed forming an order of notable patriots admitted on merit: a Legion of Honour. Many in the Council of State objected on the grounds that it was a return to aristocracy. Bonaparte insisted it was not: "What is there aristocratic in a distinction, merely personal, given only for life, given to a man who has displayed civil or military benefit, and to him alone, nor descending to his children?" But, countered one councillor, baubles were distinctions of monarchy.

"I defy you", Bonaparte replied, "to show me a republic, ancient or modern, in which there were no distinctions. You spoke of baubles. Well it is by baubles that we delude mankind. I should not say this to a tribune, but in a council of sages and statesmen we ought to say everything. I do not believe that the French people love liberty or equality. The French are not changed by ten years of revolution. They have only one sentiment – honour. We must therefore give aliment to this sentiment. We must create distinctions."[2]

The Council of State approved his scheme by a narrow majority of four. It passed through the Tribunate and Legislative Assembly, but only just. On 19 May the Legion was established. Fifteen cohorts of 350 legionaries were to be appointed by Bonaparte, each cohort granted 200,000 francs to come from the sale of state assets appropriated from the Church and former aristocrats during the Revolution. This was to pay for salaries, lodgings and rest homes for legionaries who were expected to "dedicate themselves to the service of the Republic" by combating all

---

[1] Cited in Lefebvre p.155

[2] Cited in Thiers p.355

attempts to restore the feudal order and unite to preserve "liberty and equality".[1]

The legislative chambers also approved Bonaparte's budget for Year X (September 1801 to October 1802). When Bonaparte came to power in 1799 he found only 16,000 Francs in the government coffers. Under the Directory constant deficits had swelled the national debt, while depreciated paper money and a shortage of coins inflated prices, especially of basic commodities and thereby contributing to discontent. The Directory had attempted to deal with the debt by swapping two thirds of it for bonds that allowed the holder to buy state assets, and tried to increase its revenue by creating a new agency to collect land taxes and forcing the wealthy to lend them money. The bonds lost their value, the new collection agency valued land using old inaccurate surveys and the forced loans proved difficult to collect, obliging the Directory to rely on occupied territories for a quarter of its revenue.

Bonaparte wanted to eliminate the public debt and curb inflation, issues he considered responsible for the demise of the *ancien régime*. He set up a Sinking Fund to start paying it off, but as his own first budgets could not be balanced, in 1800 he established the Bank of France to lend to the government. The Bank's initial capital of 30 million Francs came partly from the Sinking Fund and partly from private investors, the wealthiest of whom became its directors. To reduce the national debt accrued by the Directory, Bonaparte effectively defaulted by converting two-thirds of it to five per cent stock at only five per cent of its value.

To increase his revenue, Bonaparte appointed Martin Gaudin, an experienced financial administrator, as his Finance Minister, while from 1801, expenditure would be under the control of the Treasury Minister, François Barbé-Marbois. In the budget of year X, this amounted to about 500 million Francs. The Ministry of War spent 210 million of this. Continental peace had brought savings of forty million from the previous year, but a large standing army, no longer able to live off the resources of conquered countries, limited its impact. Also, because of Bonaparte's colonial projects the Ministry of Marine increased its expenditure, pushing it to about 100 million francs. The next largest expense was the settling of liabilities the government owed to its creditors and pensioners, some 70 million Francs.

---

[1] Lefebvre p.144, Thiers pp.353-357, Villefosse pp.157-158

To meet these outgoings was a revenue of roughly 500 million, allowing the government to balance its books and estimate a modest surplus. Most of the incomings – about 275 million – came from direct taxes on property. The agency for collecting direct taxes set up by the Directory was abolished and in its place were appointed tax collecting officials in each department and *arrondissement*, appointed mostly by Gaudin. Bonaparte would appoint those for large wealthy towns. These collectors were obliged to make advance deposits of expected returns into the Sinking Fund and remit the taxes collected on a monthly basis. The greatest portion of direct taxes came from the land tax, where the amount a landowner was expected to pay was based on an estimate of his agricultural income. Other direct levies were imposed on the employment of domestic servants and personal property of urban dwellers such as their horses, carriages and chimneys. Although the propertied classes thus bore the brunt of the state's fiscal demands, the poor would bear an increasing portion of the burden through indirect taxes on consumables. The Revolution had abolished many duties, but the Directory had re-introduced levies on tobacco, playing cards, carriages, gold and silverware and alcoholic drinks. Bonaparte not only retained these taxes, but saw them as an important source of further revenue by increasing their rate and by taxing a wider range of goods.[1]

The last day of the legislative session, 20 May, was reserved to legitimate once again a practice that the Revolution had abolished. The Peace of Amiens was to return to France its colonies in the West Indies, prompting the question: what was to be done about the slave plantations that had been maintained in these colonies while under British rule? Human bondage had been abolished by the National Convention in 1794, but the prospect of freeing all the slaves in the restored territories was not one that was welcomed by those with economic power and unprincipled profits to make.

Bonaparte's key peacetime goal was to cultivate the commercial prosperity of France and much of his support lay with the business community. Deputies for Nantes, Bordeaux and Marseilles urged him to revive the slave trade. The council of Commerce for Bordeaux was to argue that "the supreme object of African commerce has always been to sustain our western colonies [...] Cultivation cannot be usefully carried on

---

[1] Thiers pp.365-366, Lefebvre, NBCG Vol. III pp.1237-1247, Alexander Grab, *State, Society and Tax Policy in Napoleonic Europe*, in Dwyer pp.169-176

except with the strong arms of Africans."[1] Meanwhile, news of the expedition to San Domingo was hardening French attitudes to rebel black slaves. Bonaparte's brother-in-law Leclerc had failed to persuade Toussaint to accept French hegemony and was obliged to use force instead. By the end of March he had taken a key rebel stronghold at Crête-à-Pierrot and wrote to the Minister of Marine and Colonies: "You can have no idea of the atrocities committed here [...] More than 10,000 whites and black or mulatto inhabitants have had their throats cut on the orders of Toussaint or Dessalines and Christophe. In our expeditions we found more than 6,000 men, women, and children whom they had led into the woods and whom they intended to kill."[2]   A returned émigré, François-René de Chateaubriand, published a book called the *Genius of Christianity*, in which he declared that the crimes by the blacks in San Domingo had erased any pity they once aroused. Other émigrés who favoured the return of slavery included former plantation owners and ancien regime officials in the French ministry of Marine and Commerce such as Pierre-Victor Malouet. They argued that slavery was required to force blacks to work and ensure the security of colonial whites.[3]

Bonaparte discussed government policy towards its colonial black populations with his Council of State. A wide spectrum of suggestions emerged, from upholding the illegality of slavery to decimating those who had terrorised the Caribbean. Admiral Bruix, who came from a plantation-owning family, was in favour of restoring slavery, suggesting that the sentiment of freedom should not be carried too far. Bonaparte, noticing that the Senator Henri Grégoire had remained silent, asked him his opinion. The former Bishop of Blois had long opposed slavery and had been an influential member of the abolitionist group *Société des amis des Noirs*. Grégoire replied: "I think that listening to such speeches is sufficient to show that they are spoken by whites. If these gentlemen were this moment to change colour they would talk differently." Bonaparte laughed sarcastically and accused him of being incorrigible.[4]   As early as August 1800 the First Consul had decided slavery should be maintained in

---

[1] Thomas p.546

[2] Fraser p.65

[3] Jennings pp.1-5

[4] Carnot, pp.120-122

those colonies where it had never been abolished.[1] He declared his intentions publicly in an address to the legislature in November 1801. Referring to Guadeloupe and San Domingo, he said: "In these two islands there are no more slaves; all are free; and so they shall remain. In Martinique, a different policy has been pursued: the practice of slavery has been there continued, and it must be preserved. It would cost too much to humanity, to attempt there a new revolution."[2]

He would endorse slavery, but only in the restored colonies where it had been maintained and would resurrect the slave trade until such a time that it could be multilaterally abolished by an agreement with the other European powers, especially Great Britain. It would have been difficult for a calculating mercantilist like Bonaparte to forgo the perceived commercial advantages of slavery while his country's main rival continued to reap them without any competition. While the peace negotiations were being conducted at Amiens, in London Otto had suggested to William Wilberforce the idea of including the abolition of slavery in the treaty. When Wilberforce enthusiastically urged this on Addington, he was disappointed by the prime minister's refusal to countenance this. Addington was no supporter of slavery, but would have realised that an abolition article would have made the treaty less palatable to a Parliament that had a track record of opposing Wilberforce's abolition bills. Peace was his priority, so abolition would have to wait.

With the peace finally signed in March, Bonaparte instructed Cambacérès in April to make the necessary arrangements to legalise human bondage once again. On 17 May it was argued in the Tribunate by Adet that the new policy was a pledge of good relations renewed with England. While its amoral character was acknowledged, this could not override the vital economic necessity of slavery. Legislators could no more renounce slavery than they could renounce war. By repudiating the latter, they would abandon the right to defend themselves and by upsetting the balance of power in Europe, they would expose it to the very evils they would attempt to avoid. Similarly, the French could not renounce slavery without endangering other nations. They had to reject gradual as well as immediate emancipation – both would be the signal for bloody insurrection. They could not afford to pity the plight of blacks,

[1] NBCG III p.1227

[2] Cobbett in Crisis of the Sugar Colonies p.35

wrenched from their homeland, any more than a general could risk retreating from battle at the first sight of blood: "You would sacrifice to the blacks the interests of your country, by destroying an institution necessary to the colonies, themselves become necessary to our existence." Adet suggested he and his colleagues content themselves with the hope that Europeans would treat their slaves humanely: "However limited may be the intelligence of the African relative to our own, whatever may be the difference between their species and ours, let us never forget they are men." Their consciences thus relieved, they agreed to suppress their patronising pity with a majority of fifty-four to twenty-seven.

On 18 May the Legislative Assembly was told that ideas of freedom and equality were inappropriate for the colonies and that their introduction there resulted in the evils of death and despair. Jaubert declared that liberty was a poisonous fruit to some people and urged the legislature to "obey the great law of empires, necessity. Let us not trouble the world with theories." Two hundred and eleven of them swallowed this against sixty-three queasier stomachs.[1]

On 19 May the proposal was discussed in the Senate. Admiral Bruix argued that there was no inconsistency in cherishing liberty and owning slaves. The ancient Greeks and Romans, often seen as enlightenment role models, kept slaves, so why should not modern Europeans be allowed to have them? "The commercial prosperity of France renders it necessary that a certain quantity of the produce of the country, in wine and cereals, should be sent to the Antilles for consumption by the blacks. Now these Negroes, were they free, would prefer manioc to wheat, and the juice of the sugar cane to our wines; it is therefore indispensable that they should be slaves." It was the difference in skin colour and social customs that justified the separation of humanity into masters and slaves. It was necessary for property and power to be in the hands of less numerous whites. It was necessary for the more numerous blacks to be slaves.[2] Regnaud Saint-Jean d'Angély urged the Senate that they could not afford to pity the few and procure for them the doubtful good of freedom at the risk of exposing the wider human race to certain and terrible evils. This law would ensure the duration of the peace of the world. The Senate, considering that the disparity in the status of

---

[1] Cochin pp.42-47

[2] Fauriel pp.31-34

blacks in different colonies would be unconstitutional, invited Bonaparte to adopt a single system of restoring slavery everywhere, but he refused. On 20 May the slave trade was resumed in the ports of France and slavery was maintained in the restored colonies according to the laws and regulations of 1789. This was followed in July by a consular decree signed by Bonaparte which forbade blacks, mulattoes and people of colour to set foot in France without the permission of colonial authorities and the Ministry of Marine and Colonies. Any person fitting this description without such approval would be arrested and detained until they could be deported.

****

At eleven o'clock in the evening, two financiers hurried to Malmaison, summoned by the First Consul. It was late spring, and France was on the verge of a famine, threatening to bring with it all the unrest suffered during the Revolution. The situation had been precarious ever since Bonaparte assumed power. A bad harvest in 1799 combined with increased circulation of more untrustworthy bank notes increased the price of a four-pound loaf of bread to thirteen sous. The victory over the Austrians at Marengo coincided with a fall in prices, but by Spring 1801, bread prices had risen again and by the summer of 1801 a four-pound loaf was costing eighteen sous in Paris. Prices in the outskirts of the city were actually higher, encouraging inhabitants there to come into the capital, lengthening the queues outside bakeries that were forming at 4 a.m. In Rue Saint-Honoré, a convoy was attacked and similar pillaging occurred throughout France.

Unlike Britain, where ratepayers were obliged to fund poor relief at a local level, France had no established state institutions to deal with widespread scarcity and poverty. A charitable Committee of Beneficence was set up by some members of the Department of Agriculture for the Seine region. This organisation invited rich individuals and public institutions to donate funds by purchasing, for eighteen Francs each, subscriptions of 240 rations of soup. Seven soup kitchens were set up throughout Paris, charging two sous per ration or providing it free to those who had been given a coloured ration card. The card, issued to those in distress, would indicate the time and the place where it could be redeemed for about twenty-eight ounces of broth and just over an ounce of bread. Subscribers included Josephine Bonaparte, who paid for the establishment of a soup kitchen near Malmaison, and the Senate, who set up a similar one near the Luxembourg Palace.

The First Consul was also a subscriber, but he realised that charity alone was insufficient. In November 1801 Bonaparte summoned a Council of State, including the Ministers of Police and the Interior, Fouché and Chaptal. The press was forbidden to report on the crisis, Chaptal was ordered to purchase foreign grain and five bankers were commissioned to import into Paris 50,000 quintals of grain per month. Despite these measures, scarcity still threatened France in the spring of 1802. At the Malmaison meeting, Bonaparte asked the two financiers to offer their advice and propose a solution, telling them he would provide them with as much money as they needed. The financiers, Ouvrard and Vanderberge, agreed to help on the condition of receiving a small commission of two per cent. They immediately despatched agents to the ports of England and Holland with instructions to buy all the grain they found there, plus any that was expected. One million quintals of grain was bought for twenty-two million francs and then resold at a loss to the state of 15 million francs. Within three weeks the threat of famine was averted and by the end of 1802 the scarcity crisis was over.[1]

---

[1] Lefebvre p.131, Tulard p.111, Ouvrard p.68, Yorke p.166

21 Fouché

From the painting by Claude-Marie Dubufe, engraved by H. Davidson. Illustration for the *Life of Napoleon Bonaparte* by William Milligan Sloane (The Century Co, 1896) (Look and Learn Collections)

20. The Notched Letter "R"

On 28 May a woman named Felice called at the offices of the Prefect of Police for Paris near the Pont Neuf. The Prefect Dubois was out, so Felice spoke to the divisional chief, Bertrand. She showed him some Placards. On one Bertrand read the following:

> *"Appeal to the armies of France by their comrades. Soldiers of the fatherland! [...] How long will you suffer a tyrant to make slaves of you? [...] Soldiers, you have no longer a fatherland. The republic is no more! [...] A tyrant has usurped authority, and who is this tyrant? Bonaparte [...] Ask your brothers of Egypt and they will tell you to what horrible sufferings he exposed them by his abandonment [...] What was the object in fighting for the Republic? To annihilate every caste of nobility or priesthood, to establish the most perfect equality [...] The émigrés are back again everywhere: the hypocritical priests are in the pay of the tyrant. You have conquered in vain [...] Soldiers, you have not a moment to lose, if you wish to preserve your liberty, your existence and your honour [...] If you delay longer, shame and infamy will be your portion, your names will no longer recall the glorious days of our triumphs; they will only be synonymous with cowards and slaves!"*

A second placard was an "Address to the army [...] and officers on half-pay":

> *"Brave Brothers in Arms! [...] Soon a Bourbon will be on the throne, unless Bonaparte gets himself proclaimed emperor or king [...] By what right does this bastard manikin of Corsica, this republican pygmy try to make himself a Lycurgus and a Solon? [...] Let our generals stand forth and compel respect for their glory and that of the army! Our bayonets are ready for the work of vengeance [...] Let them say the word, and the Republic is saved!"*

Bertrand asked Felice how she had come into possession of these libels. In a butter-crock, she replied. A butter-crock was a cylindrical piece of pottery used to preserve butter. It had been sent from Rennes in a hamper to her friend Captain August Rapatel. He had brought the basket round to her place without opening it: "I alone have discovered the libels" she insisted. She said that the sender's name had been torn off and the placards had been addressed not to Rapatel but to others, including his brother François, who was an aide-de-camp to General Moreau.

When the Prefect Dubois returned, Bertrand presented him with the story. They both believed it was evidence of a plot against the First Consul concocted by General Moreau in Paris. Dubois set off for Malmaison to report this development to Bonaparte in person. Dubois had regular meetings with the First Consul to keep him abreast of police matters in Paris. Discontent with Bonaparte amongst some Jacobin army officers was surfacing. There was an on-going trial against two officers, Fournier and Donnadieu, for conspiring to assassinate him at a Carousel review. Joseph Fouché, the Minister of Police was suspected of delaying the trial and hampering the search for other conspirators. Fouché was an ex-Jacobin who would always be remembered for his role in the Terror, especially for the enthusiasm with which he dealt with rebels in Lyon in 1793. Groups of prisoners were chained together and blasted with grapeshot, any mutilated survivors being finished off by sabres and muskets. A clash with Robespierre over religion obliged Fouché to play a leading part in his downfall, ensuring not only his survival but also his acceptance by the Directory, who appointed him Minister of Police in 1799, a position Bonaparte allowed him to keep, despite suspicions of his Jacobin sympathies.

These suspicions were reinforced by reports from General Davout who had contacts with a spy who claimed Fouché was intriguing with General Bernadotte who was in league with General Moreau. Moreau did not hide his contempt for Bonaparte's regime. He had mocked the Legion of Honour by awarding a scullion with a saucepan of honour and had a collar of honour made for a dog.

Bonaparte ordered Dubois and Chamans-Lavallette, the Director of the Post Office, who was at Malmaison that evening, to search the mail for suspicious packets before the post went out that night. Fouché was not to be told. Two hours later, they met at the Post Office on Rue Coq Heron and began their work. They discovered a number of red and blue envelopes, inside of which were the same placards.

The next day Lavallete received someone from Fouché requesting the letters they had found. Lavallete told him that they had been handed to the Prefect of Police. Fouché approached Bonaparte, who refused to allow him to see the placards and reproached him for negligence and prevarication. On 31 May, however, Fouché's ministry received similar placards from a Prefect in Tours. One of the Prefect's staff had been given what seemed to be a hamper of Breton dainties posted from Rennes, but inside were letters in red and blue envelopes addressed to seventy-five army officers with more of the placards. Desmaret, one of

Fouché's officials, immediately wrote to the Prefect of Ille-et-Vilaine based in Rennes, telling him there was a royalist plot concocted in London to make common cause with Jacobins in the army. For different reasons, both were against the Concordat. Everything had been printed there, smuggled to France and put in the post by Chouan agents. This was a royalist plot and not a Jacobin one because there was no mention of the expense of bread as a complaint; military rebels would never have advocated unlimited liberty; and Rennes was not Jacobin, but rather known for its royalist leanings.

Meanwhile, in Rennes, the Prefect of Ille-et-Vilaine, Jean Joseph Mounier, a returned émigré, had been visited by General Delaborde, the commander of the local army barracks. Delaborde showed him a bundle of seditious pamphlets a colonel had received from Rennes. One was addressed to the Minister of War Berthier and to Delaborde himself. Delaborde had gone to the coach company and discovered that similar parcels, despatched by the same sender "Thomas", had been sent to six other locations in France. Mounier summoned the Mayor, two local magistrates and the police commissioner, asking them who they thought was behind the pamphlets. At the Mayor's suggestion that monarchists were involved they decide to investigate a royalist printer in Rennes.

When the police went to this man's workshop and interrogated him, they found nothing suspicious. The printer asked if he could look at one of the placards to see if he could be of any help. He observed that the letter R in ARMIES had a notch – a white streak, suggesting the type should have been replaced. One of the police officers, Simoneau, remembered this. He later noticed a bill advertising a theatrical event: a performance of the play *Irato*. Irato had been misspelt in capitals at the top of the bill as "IRRATO". The second of the two R's had a white streak in its tail. Simoneau noted the name of the printer, went to the Prefecture and told Mounier it was Chausseblanche – a man with Jacobin sympathies who had previously been warned not to print anything anarchic.

The next morning Mounier insisted that the Mayor and magistrate arrest Chausseblanche immediately and search his workshop. Despite some objections, they agreed, but decided to a have a long lunch before meeting up with Simoneau and some gendarmes at the Place Egalité. By the time they got to the printer's premises their suspect had gone. Simoneau searched the property and found the printing equipment with the typeface that matched the notched R. While the Mayor and the

magistrates reported the bad news to the Prefect, Simoneau hid and
waited and when Chausseblanche returned, arrested him.

In Paris on 7 June Captain Rapatel was sent to the Temple
prison. Dubois had established that the sender of the hamper to the
Captain was a person named Jourdeuil. After monitoring the mail, a
package was uncovered from a Jourdeuil of Rennes to a lady's maid called
Duret. Inside was a box containing, among Jourdeuil's things, more
placards and anti-Bonapartist verses written on red paper. It was also
learned that the sender was to follow his package in a few days. The lady's
maid, now in custody, was persuaded to tell him to collect his parcel from
the lost property office at Cour Neuve. He was arrested the moment he
arrived. Dubois interrogated him personally. Jourdeuil said he found the
red paper in a gutter and admitted writing the couplet, but pleaded he had
done nothing wrong.

After two days in a galbanon – an insanitary black hole in the
notoriously damp Bicêtre prison – Jourdeuil wrote a confession. He was
the valet to François Bertrand, an officer of the 82nd demi-brigade
garrisoned at Rennes, and who had once been Bernadotte's quartermaster.
On Bertrand's instructions, he had spent ten days delivering hampers to
the coach house at Rennes, each day using a different name as the sender.
The man who was directing the plot lived somewhere in the countryside.
Dubois interrogated him again: why had he come to Paris? To work for
an old master, Captain Fourcart at Versailles, he said. Dubois discovered
that Fourcart had been one of General Bernadotte's officers and was
recently appointed to a position in Rouen, but was delaying his departure.
He had received his orders a month ago, but remained in the Golden
Chariot Inn with his wife in a deserted part of town, often going in to
Paris to work with Bernadotte, sometimes not returning in the evening.

Dubois told Bonaparte that he thought the instigator of the plot
was Bernadotte. Bonaparte ordered Dubois to arrest Fourcart and any
officers connected to him. Dubois, informing Fouché of their arrest,
pressed him for the immediate apprehension of Bertrand in Rennes.
Fouché sent a warrant for his arrest and on 13 June at mid-day, Mounier
sent two squads of gendarmes to Bertrand's lodgings in Rue d'Horloge.
When they arrived, a neighbour spoke to the officer in charge, Caron:
"Nobody upstairs sergeant! The officer is out. He is at dinner." They
waited for him to return, but when he did, they managed to let him get
inside and shut his door before they could follow. An order to open the
door was ignored. Caron, unsure of what powers he had, sent a request
for further instructions to his superior who was equally indecisive.

Meanwhile the gendarmes could hear a lot of noise coming from inside Bertrand's lodgings. The sound of a chimney roaring and the smell of burning pervaded the house. When Caron's superior arrived with his commandant, the police commissioner and a magistrate, Bertrand finally opened the door. He was ordered to hand over his sword and told he was arrested. "Where are your papers?" they demanded. Pointing to the smoking cinders on a grate, he replied "They are there."

"What! Have you destroyed your papers?"

"Bah, they were only love letters! A French soldier must never compromise ladies." He was led off in hand-cuffs to the prison of Tour-Lebat. An angry Mounier visited the lodgings himself, where a single surviving letter was found. It read: "At the beginning of Prairial (late May) one of our friends will pass through Rennes. He will deliver to Bertrand the expected packets. Ursule C, 20th Floreal (10 May)". The letter bore a stamp of St Malo.

Mounier interrogated Bertrand himself: "You know Jourdeuil, your servant?"

"Of course, I have dismissed him; he's a rascal, an emissary of the Chouans"

"Emissary of the Chouans?"

"Certainly! He was a groom in the stables of an ex-nobleman."

"You know Chausseblanche too, Chausseblanche the printer?"

"Let me see...Yes, I remember. I have sometimes bought sealing wax off him."

"Some outrageous libels on the First Consul have been handed in at the coach office in Rennes."

"You make me shudder. Why, it's abominable."

The Prefect showed him six blue and red envelopes and asked "Do you know this writing?"

"Not at all."

"It is said nevertheless to resemble yours."

"This scrawl? [...] I pride myself on my penmanship."

"The experts will contradict you."

"Ignorant fellows."

"Well then. Here is a pen. Write."

"Are you joking? Am I before a court-martial? As a soldier, I don't know you."

"I wish to have a specimen of your handwriting."

"Do you? Then go to Mainz, I used to live there. You will find lots of my autographs there."

"Take care. Do not defy the severity of the law."

"Ouf. How warm it is Citizen Prefect. This summer is really tropical and the Tour-Lebat is like an oven. All this emotion has exhausted me. Could I not be left in peace?"

When the Rennes garrison heard that Bertrand had been arrested, they sent a delegation to the Prefect, demanding news of their comrade. Had he been tortured? Was he still alive? The Prefect assured them that he was very much alive and in excellent health, but they demanded to see for themselves. The Prefect obliged, after which the soldiers left, but when another band of comrades demanded to see him they were turned away.

Although Fouché criticised Mounier's actions, advising him not to be constrained by formalities and sensitivities and to focus his attention on royalists, the Prefect was not convinced they were responsible and expressed his views to Chaptal, the Minister of the Interior: "I persist in my belief that the anarchists alone are concerned in the plot [...] I repeat, the Chouans have nothing to do with it. Someone has tried to throw you off the scent with stories of émigrés and English boats." Fouché ordered Mounier to send Bertrand and Chausseblanche to Paris without delay, but the Prefect had not finished with them yet.

As Bertrand was not talking, Mounier had Chausseblanche brought to him. The printer had been moaning about his gout, three ulcers on his leg and the dampness of the prison and was worried about his wife, his large brood of children and his elderly mother. Mounier told him that Fouché had orders to send him to the Temple in Paris, where his illnesses would be even more difficult to endure. "Come, citizen. Think of your family. After all, you are not so guilty." The real culprit was the one who took advantage of his distress and need of money. "He is a soldier, a general, is he not? [...] A general, we know all about him. Now write and tell this man that he would do well to fly as quickly as possible. We do not care to arrest him, for we wish to avoid a scandal. Render us this service, Chausseblanche, and you will soon be rewarded."

The printer agreed to write a letter: "To General Simon, La Moinerie, Thorigné-les-Rennes. Citizen, the Prefect has given me permission to warn the authors of the proclamations that they may place themselves in safety before their names are made known. You are strongly suspected. I recommend you, therefore, to fly..."

Mounier sent the letter and waited. On 24 June an army officer with a sabre-scar across his face presented himself to the Prefect as General Simon and had come to offer his confession:

"Nothing was talked of at Rennes but the Concordat and the victories of obscurantism, the life consulship and its dictatorial power. I listened, and my heart was devoured by rage; my sleepless nights were tortured by fever. No, France could not submit to such dishonour! [....] One day, in the Place d' Égalité, I met Citizen Bertrand [....] We exchanged ideas [...] Then we resolved to utter a cry of alarm to our legions." Returning to his cottage, he had composed his addresses. "My friend knew a printer [...] who struck off 3,000 copies." His wife was "good enough to write some addresses [...] But Citizen prefect [...] Citizeness Simon has always been ignorant of the text of the placards."

Mounier promised him she would not be interfered with, but was curious about the General's motives: "I do not understand you. What did you hope for?"

"Liberty, citizen prefect, Liberty!" was the General's reply.

Mounier was unconvinced. "So a simple brigadier-general presumed to cause an insurrection in the army? That won't do! [...] You must have an accomplice, an advisor, an instigator; be frank, name him!"

Simon lost his temper. "I swear it on my honour as a soldier: I alone planned the attempt, and I intended to execute it alone." After putting down his confession in writing, he was dispatched to Paris that night.

On Saturday June 26 General Delaborde received instructions from Paris. Four demi-brigades were to leave Brittany immediately. The 82nd was to proceed to Brest. Delaborde summoned Colonel Pinoteau to relay his orders to angry officers at the St Cyr barracks, some of whom suspected they were going to be deported. Some of the troops were becoming unruly and considering mutiny. They went into Rennes, drinking with canteen girls in the cafés, damning Bonaparte, praising Moreau and inciting the pro-Jacobin civilians. Seditious bills were posted in the suburbs and Gendarmes had to tear down placards proclaiming "War to the death against Bonaparte! Long live Moreau!" General Delaborde received Pinoteau's resignation and then a delegation of loyal soldiers petitioning him to arrest Pinoteau and their mutinous comrades who had gone to Rennes. Delaborde refused, but on Monday he confined the whole demi-brigade to their barracks where he waved his sword at them, shouting "Long Live the First Consul!" He was met with silence and murmuring.

"Why don't you shout Long Live Bonaparte?" he asked a private, only to be met with silence. "Come, be frank. Has Colonel Pinoteau been trying to make you revolt? Yes or No?" The men protested, claiming he was incapable of treason. The next day the 82nd were on the march to Brest where they were split up. The troublemakers were sent to San Domingo, the rest to Martinique.

General Simon's coach arrived at the Ministry of Police in Paris on 27 June, where he was handed over to Desmaret, who informed Fouché of his arrival. Desmaret told Simon that he knew about his financial plight caused by a banker running off with his funds and sympathised. When the General acknowledged his poverty, Desmaret asked: who then supplied him with the necessary funds for the plot? A messenger arrived, informing them that Simon was to see Fouché. After a private meeting between the General and the Minister of Police, Simon was taken to the Temple and put in a narrow cell near the roof which in the summer became an oven.

After five days he wrote to the First Consul, accepting his actions were wrong and misguided by anger:

"Since then, I have returned to my senses, I have reflected on the terrible consequences to which this act of folly might have led and I have not hesitated to expose myself to the just punishment which it deserves, by making myself known." He hoped that the frankness of his confession would end the suspicion of others who were innocent: "My actions are unconnected with any plot and have no ramifications. I assure you by all that honour holds most sacred, that no-one, either above or below me, has prompted me in this [...] The First Consul is too just, General Bonaparte is too great not to alleviate the sufferings of a culprit who repents, and who is already sufficiently punished by remorse." In a note addressed to the Minister of Police, he pleaded that "I am not a victim sacrificing himself for others."

Further days in solitary confinement made him more desperate. In another letter to Bonaparte he implored: "In the name of humanity, in the name of your renown, General, have pity! Eight poor creatures have none but me to depend on. What is to become of them if I fail them?" He appealed again to Fouché: "Humanity cannot be incompatible with the duties of your office! I therefore appeal to your feelings of loyalty [...] I am writing today for the fourth time to the Minister, and I claim the fulfilment of his promise to treat me as a brother..."

Another letter to Fouché enclosed a letter for Bonaparte: "I will enter into no explanation of its contents; but you will be able perfectly to judge of it and appreciate its motive and its importance. The time has come, I think, to serve me as a brother." Fouché was not moved. After fifty days in prison rumours reached Simon that his wife was ill and that bailiffs had seized his furniture and sold his uniform. More certain news was that he was to be dismissed from the army, sent to the isle of Oléron from where he would be transported to the penal colony of Cayenne in Guiana.[1]

---

[1] Augustin-Thierry pp.41-285

22 Sir Francis Burdett

Illustration from *The Gallery of Engravings* edited by C H Timperley (Fisher, 1846) (Look and Learn Collections)

21. Summer of Discontent

Peace did not end the disaffection in Britain. Throughout the spring and summer of 1802, the underground radical organisation the United Britons continued to hold meetings and recruit new members. In a printed address to its members and potential converts to the cause, the United Britons declared that the people laboured under a tyrannical political system threatening ruin to all. There was danger in indifference, it told its audience, so why not unite and "by one bold and decisive effort rescue ourselves from the horror that awaits us [...] If you are determined to be free you must first be united [...] Have you any friends in whom you can place confidence – have you a friend that can confide in you – if you have, is it not evident that you can unite in spite of all the artifices of your enemies?" Since a union founded on such friendship would evade the authorities and was "the only means of averting the ruin of yourselves and country, make no delay in carrying it into effect."

The Northern United Britons had their own executive, below which were departmental committees of twelve which co-ordinated with each other by electing five chiefs or superintendents. Orders to the members, organised into groups of ten, were conveyed by conductors, who also collected money to finance their activities. Members were expected to recruit and arm themselves and others. In March the Sheffield committee ordered its conductors to arm their men with a pike, gun or sword. By May it was claimed 1,000 spears had been made in the town. An informer from Nottingham reported to the authorities he had received two pike heads and something to throw on the ground to lame horses of the cavalry. In July an ex-soldier was approached by a conductor to train his men. Under orders to arm himself, a member in Chesterfield asked a local whitesmith to make some spear blades, which he buried in a box with shafts made from wood collected from a forest.

A common way to recruit new members was to hold nocturnal meetings, where initiates could pledge their service to the cause by kissing numbered oath cards. In May, a mysterious Fred Flower told Addington of secret night-time gatherings near Wakefield, Dewsbury and Leeds. In Huddersfield a magistrate reported rumours that seditious assemblies were very common. The lower ranks would often talk about the coming time when "a sudden and midnight insurrection shall lead them to assert and regain their natural rights". In the same town pamphlets were circulating, including one entitled *Rights of Swine,* first printed in 1794, as well as the new address to United Briton members. On 17 July a meeting of 5,000 was held at Bruntcliffe Thorn near Leeds. The Mayor of Leeds observed a smaller gathering of 300–400 labourers. He noted that most were spectators, watching a central ring of conspirators, carrying oath cards, on which were printed their aims of preserving their rights and privileges.

In February the United Britons estimated their strength in Lancashire, Yorkshire, Derbyshire and Cheshire at 17,120. In March 1802 the Leeds department reported themselves as having 1,822 members – recruited from a population of 30,000. In the same month Sheffield had 1,615 and Wakefield 645. June counts from Lancashire noted 574 members in Stockport, 330 in Buxton and 133 in Wilmslow. In London it was claimed there were 57,000 English and 15,000 Irish United men.

In the summer of 1802, many in the West Riding thought that a rising was imminent. In some cases, talk was getting bolder and more open. In Sheffield a man damned the King in front of soldiers and declared himself a Jacobin. Magistrates received threatening letters and in July, in Huddersfield market, bets could be placed on the possibility of a general insurrection in less than one month. The Mayor of Leeds noticed that meetings of croppers to form combinations to demand better wages and conditions from employers was being copied by other trades. He expected these unions to expand and make more extensive and more political demands, believing that thousands secretly hoped that matters were growing ripe for a better order of things. When he reported his concerns to the Lord Lieutenant of the West Riding, William FitzWilliam, the latter was dismissive. FitzWilliam was convinced that the unrest was mainly caused by conflicts between employers and workers and resisted attempts to impose further legal restrictions on union activity. A strike by croppers convinced him that they and other unions had been mistaken for seditious societies. They could be dealt with simply by bringing in new machinery such as sheering mills. Referring to the croppers, he said that "if merchants had the firmness to do without them [...] their combinations would fall to the ground". FitzWilliam was also disinclined to be too worried because intelligence from Sheffield suggested everything was quiet and many alarming reports were from unreliable spies. One of these, whom he considered a "consummate rascal", declared a national rising was imminent and that well known Whig politicians were implicated. His orders to magistrates was to prevent meetings and arrest the leaders who convened them. However, when Halifax magistrates reported a recent assembly of a thousand near Morley and that an ex-militiaman had been approached to drill a group of ten he agreed to support their request for soldiers. The Home Office obliged by strengthening the garrisons at Sheffield and York, while Bradford, Pontefract, Barnsley and Doncaster each received a troop of dragoons.

The United Britons of Leeds, whose town was allocated two troops of dragoons by the government, had asked the central committee for financial support and received a sum greater than any former payment. In late May a delegate from Leeds was sent to meet the national committee in London, who were pleased by his report on the situation in the north. At another meeting to which the Leeds delegate was invited, the committee was joined by a leader of the United Irishmen, two guardsmen and a light dragoon. Claiming to represent over 4,000 comrades, the soldiers presented a paper with six articles recommending capturing the Tower of London, the Bank of England, the Woolwich Arsenal and both Houses of Parliament while they were sitting. They demanded that during the coming struggle, soldiers should receive one guinea per week and ten acres of land plus investment capital afterwards. Meanwhile they would try to enlist sailors to the cause. It was agreed that the Tower and the Bank should be seized, but not until Parliament had dissolved. No private property was to be meddled with on any pretence whatsoever. Towns involved in the plot would be informed as soon as London had risen. In Sheffield it was understood that on hearing from London they would capture barracks, disarm and imprison the soldiers and then take possession of the town.[1]

Radicalism also manifested itself during the parliamentary elections that summer. On 29 June the King dissolved Parliament, obliging MPs to fight for their seats in July and August. Many did not have to fight very hard if they were the candidate for a local powerful landowner who influenced a small electorate. In more open constituencies, where the electorate was a larger proportion of the population, the contest could be less predictable. On 5 July a radicalised electorate forced Windham out of Norwich. The Marquis of Buckingham consoled him with the seat of St Mawes, promising that the only thing the voters expected of him was to agree that "Pilchard is the best of all possible fish".[2] In Liverpool where riots erupted, two people were shot

[1] Wells pp.226-246

[2] Windham Papers volume 2 p.195

by a man who was subsequently trampled to death by the crowd. In Nottingham troops had to be called out to restore the peace. At Westminster, Fox was challenged by a candidate more radical than himself. Deeply disillusioned with politics, Fox had considered retiring, but was persuaded to stand once again by his agent. On 15 July Fox was declared elected by the High bailiff from the constituency hustings, the wooden framework of which was then demolished within twenty minutes by the mob, bringing it down on top of themselves, breaking one man's back and thighs.[1]

In the other London constituency of Middlesex, Sir Francis Burdett was invited to stand as radical candidate. As an MP since 1796, Burdett had opposed the war with France and supported parliamentary reform. In 1800 he had protested against the suspension of Habeas Corpus and the renewal of the Sedition Bill. His greatest success had been to persuade Parliament to set up a commission to investigate the management of Coldbath Fields prison in Clerckwell. This had been built by Middlesex magistrates under the authority of an Act of Parliament and became known as the Bastille. After visiting the prison, Burdett had first alerted Parliament of the poor condition of the jail and its inmates in 1798 and continued to do so, despite the best efforts of prison authorities, the Middlesex magistrates and the Home Office to frustrate him.

As well as mutineers, Burdett highlighted the case of prisoners indefinitely retained on suspicion, cases like that of Colonel Despard, who spent seven months with an ulcerated leg in a small damp cell, with no fire, candle, book, chair, table, knife or fork. Shuttered windows forced the choice between blocking out the sunlight or the cold. Armed with two-hundred and ten pages of letters and affidavits from prisoners, Burdett castigated the governor who extorted tips from prisoners to pay for their upkeep and expected presents from visitors as the price of their admission. Those who would or could not pay were threatened with dark cold cells, close confinement without exercise and insufficient food. Prohibited to write or read, heavily ironed, prisoners who complained were met with punishments, some resulting in death. As well as the governor, Burdett singled out the jailer Aris, who had refused to let the mutineers keep his gifts of tobacco and admitted striking prisoners. Perhaps the most scandalous case was that of Mary Rich, who had been detained to prevent her from testifying against her rapist. Described as a

---

[1] Annual Register 1802, p.426

worthless girl, the justices investigating this incident had concluded she had been properly treated. Burdett was outraged: "A scene of iniquity hardly to be paralleled was declared by twelve magistrates to be innocent and not to attach the smallest blame to the author." Burdett's motion in July 1800 to set up an enquiry in to the prison was carried.

The Commission found that no provision had been made to warm the cells in cold and damp weather. Regulations were not displayed, records were irregularly and incorrectly kept. There was overcrowding, with inmates having to share their bedding and no proper classification of prisoners. Persons not yet convicted but detained on suspicion were being improperly treated. The commission also recommended that charges against Aris for embezzlement and bribery should be investigated by the courts.

When Burdett received the invitation to stand for Middlesex, he had become disgusted with the government and was thinking of migrating to France. He accepted, on the understanding he would be advocating parliamentary reform: "I think our country may still be saved, but by one means only – by a fair representation of the people in Parliament." He ran his campaign from the ground floor of the Stratton street house of his father-in-law, the banker Thomas Coutts, whose embarrassment at playing host for a radical politician was overcome by his delight at having his daughter and grandchildren so close. Burdett met the other candidates at a dinner on July 8: Mr Byng – a Whig; and Mr Mainwaring – a banker and magistrate. When Mr Mainwaring's health was proposed at the dinner, another diner mischievously suggested that the health of the jailer Aris should be coupled with it. Mr Mainwaring, noting the implied insult by the association, remarked that this proposal was unkind and un-gentlemanly. Burdett asked: "Sir, you confess that you are ashamed of your friend". "No sir," replied Mainwaring. "I always considered him an honest, humane, and upright character."

On the first day of the poll, 13 July, Burdett set out from Piccadilly for the hustings at Brentford with an enormous cavalcade. A long line of carriages, his own attended with gentlemen outriders, was accompanied by musical bands, twenty butchers in white jackets with marrow bones and cleavers and supporters wearing his blue cockade and carrying banners and flags with the words "Burdett and no Bastille". When the procession reached Kew Bridge at 9.30 a.m., Burdett's horses were unharnessed and his carriage drawn to Brentford with considerable cheering, especially from the lower classes and women. In front of the large hustings erected for the election was a man whipping a handbill portraying a prisoner and another pretending to be in agony with his hands tied by a rusty chain. Above them on the hustings the three candidates were proposed and seconded. While Burdett was recommended for both his financial and political independence, Mainwaring was attacked for supporting Pitt's gagging Acts and as a defender of Aris – a man worse than Robespierre. Burdett reminded the crowd of their sovereignty and rights, promising to procure for them a "fair and equal representation in Parliament". He would however, fight the election chiefly on the question of Coldbath Fields prison. Mainwaring, as an abettor and defender of all the cruelties and atrocities committed within the walls of that Bastille, was not a fit person to represent Middlesex. This tactic certainly aroused the emotions of the crowd who subjected Mainwaring to tirades of personal abuse throughout his campaign. The sheriff overseeing the election proceedings was less accommodating. He did not let the father of Mary Rich speak on prison practices when invited by Burdett to do so. The day ended with Burdett returning to Piccadilly with the same cavalcade of coaches as before, but whose drivers and passengers were a little less sober.

The next day, 14 July, the anniversary of the storming of the Bastille, was an occasion for much semi-rioting. Despite the obvious support for Burdett from the crowds, it was the vote of property qualified constituents that counted. For the first thirteen days, Burdett was trailing behind Mainwaring by 400 to 500 votes. Burdett accused the government of exercising undue influence over the election, while Mainwaring and his friends accused Burdett and his partisans of treasonable practices, pointing to his association with Colonel Despard and the Irish rebel Arthur O'Connor. An anagram of Burdett's name proclaimed him as a "frantic disturber". The spirits of his supporters were kept high by dinners at the Crown and Anchor tavern on Arundel Street near the Strand, a regular haunt of radicals. The healths of Fox, the Duchess of Devonshire and other female canvassers were drunk there on the sixth day of the election. When on the thirteenth day Fox and Lord Russell organised a dinner at the Crown in Burdett's support, enthusiastic crowds filled the streets, blocking the Strand, Pall Mall, St James Street and Piccadilly. The windows of the house where Mainwaring was dining were broken.

On the last day of the polling, 29 July, the results were announced: Byng, 3,848; Burdett, 3,207; Mainwaring, 2,936. Byng and Burdett were declared the new MPs for Middlesex. In an address to his constituents, Burdett suggested that the votes for Mainwaring did not show they approved of his conduct, but merely that there were voters unacquainted with it: "When I assert that secret imprisonment, trial and execution are engines of oppression and tyranny and that innocence can only be protected by public custody, trial and execution, I am conscious that I stand upon a rock from which no hired magistrate, parliament or King can remove me." Byng and Burdett were carried in chairs by the crowd before returning to their carriages from which their horses were unharnessed. They were then manually dragged the whole way to London in a line of carriages, four abreast and three miles long, with the people following on foot, looked on by spectators in the windows and rooftops. Passing the King's palace at Kew, the mob sang the French revolutionary song "Ça Ira". When the procession stopped at Piccadilly and the Strand the crowd cheered. A dinner for six hundred was held at the Crown and Anchor to celebrate. The celebrations were premature. Mainwaring challenged the result, alleging the sheriffs had not been impartial and had allowed many to vote who had no right to do so. The House of Commons would order a new election in 1804. Burdett's father-in-law, Thomas Coutts, upset at accusations of Jacobinism, tried to explain his position to Pitt and other friends. Most understood, but his bank was not spared the loss of the Foreign Office accounts, withdrawn by Hawkesbury.[1]

Despite the radicalism on display, the election had not changed the House of Commons in any way to threaten the government more than before. Hawkesbury noted that there were many new members, but still much scope for intrigue among the old ones. Of those was Fox, who reckoned there were fifty-eight Pittites, thirty-six Grenvillites, sixty-nine Foxites and "all the rest Ministerial". The latter were MPs in the pocket of influential aristocrats with government connections or independent country gentlemen, whose assurances of support for Addington were, according to his Foreign Secretary, "as satisfactory as he could possibly expect."[2] The main threat seemed to be outside Parliament. By September the authorities were convinced from the reports of their spies and informants that there was a plot to overthrow the government and this was centred in London. Suspected conspirators were closely watched, especially a man named by a spy from the north as "Major General Despot".

---

[1] Annual Register 1802 p.185, Patterson pp.66-78, pp.132-142

[2] Mitchell p.195

23 Malmaison

Artist unknown. (Author's private collection)

24 Madame Junot

Lithograph by J. Champagne. Illustration from *The Court of Napoleon* by F. B. Goodrich, (Derby and Jackson 1857) (Author's private collection)

22. Malmaison in the Summer

In June Josephine went to Plombières for her annual attempt to improve her health and fertility. Her daughter Hortense, now pregnant, was temporarily mistress of Malmaison. Keeping her company there was the seventeen-year-old Laure Junot. Bonaparte was also staying at the chateau. On the 19th he wrote to his wife, complaining that "it is rather dull for us here, although your charming daughter does the honours of the house to perfection. For the last two days I have suffered slightly from my complaint [...] I love you as I did the first hour, because you are kind and sweet beyond compare [...] Best wishes, and a love-kiss, Yours ever, Bonaparte."[1]

Josephine's son Eugène was also visiting. Eugène had been a little unwell, but was recovering and seemed a tad fat to his father-in-law. Bonaparte was in a good mood, enjoying hunting boars in good weather, watching the ladies put on plays and spending the evenings chatting and laughing, playing and cheating at chess and cards.

One night Laure Junot woke up to find Bonaparte sitting at her bedside. Rubbing her eyes, her uninvited guest laughed: "Is it really I? Why so astonished?" he said. In answer, she gestured to the darkness beyond the window she had left open because of the summer heat and showed the time on the clock to Bonaparte. It was five in the morning. "Really?" he acknowledged. "No later than that? So much the better. We are going to chat." He placed an armchair at the foot of her bed, sat in it and crossed his legs. In his hands was a large bundle of documents. In large letters she could read: *For the First Consul, for himself, for him alone, personally*. That was a lot of reading, she remarked, adding that he should get someone else to do it. "Perhaps," he replied, "At present it is impossible. I must answer all. At the commencement of the return of order, I must not be ignorant of any want, any complaint."

Laure pointed out a large letter which was so badly written that it could not be from anybody important – probably a request that could be

---

[1] Hall p.51

handled by a secretary. Bonaparte scanned it and told her this letter illustrated his point: "Here, read it." It was from a widow whose son had died in the Egyptian campaign and who had no means of support. She had written already ten times to the Ministry of War, the First Consul and his secretary, but had received no answer. Bonaparte got up to get a pen, asking Laure if she now understood why he had to read the mail himself. After marking the letter he opened another one scented with roses. "Here is a trap," he exclaimed, laughing, "It is a declaration, not of war, but of love. It is a beautiful lady, who has loved me, she says, from the day she beheld me present the treaty of Campo Formio to the Directory. And if I wish to see her, I have only to give the order to the sentinel at the iron gate, on the side of Bougivale, to let a woman pass dressed in white, and giving the word Napoleon!" He looked at the date on the letter. "Faith! This very evening."

"Mon Dieu!" cried Laura. "You will not be so imprudent?"

"What is it to you if I do? What harm can it do me?"

"What is it to me! What harm can it do! Really General, those are strange questions. May not this woman be bribed by your enemies?"

Bonaparte looked at Laure and laughed again: "I said it in joke. Do you think me so simple, so stupid, as to nibble at such bait? I am receiving such letters every day, with meetings appointed sometimes at the Tuileries, sometimes at the Luxembourg, but the only answer I make to such worthy missives is that which they deserve." He stepped towards the table and wrote on the letter that it be referred to the Minister of Police. A clock chimed. "The deuce, there is six o'clock." He collected his papers, pinched Laure's feet through the bedclothes and left her room smiling and singing his favourite tune, "Non, non, z'il est impossible d'avoir un plus amiable enfant..." (No, No it is impossible to have a more amiable child...)

That evening, as everyone was relaxing in one of the salons at Malmaison, Bonaparte whispered to Laure: "I am going to the Bougivale gate."

"I do not believe a word of it," she replied. "You know too well the irreparable loss to France should any evil befall you. If you say another such word I will tell Madame Hortense or Junot."

Bonaparte pinched her ear. "You are a little simpleton." Threatening her with his finger he said: "If you think of telling one word of what I have said to you, I shall not only be displeased, but pained."

Laure was indignant, suggesting the latter reaction would have been sufficient to discourage her from telling. Bonaparte gazed at her, saying, "The mother's head, the mother's head absolutely." When she did not reply, he walked into the billiards room.

The next morning Laure was awoken early again, this time by a knock at her maid's chamber door. Bonaparte walked in with papers and letters in his hands and apologised for waking her three hours too early. "Why do you sleep with your window open? It is fatal for women who, like you, have teeth of pearl. You must not risk the loss of your teeth; they resemble your mother's, and resemble real little pearls." Bonaparte read his journals, making lines with his nails, shrugging his shoulders and muttering. There was a scandal about Prince Württemberg and a young woman he had seduced. He criticised the Duke: "He is one of those young fools, who think themselves privileged in all things because they are princes." The father of the girl should have demanded much more in compensation from him. Then he slapped the back of the paper and praised the character of the Austrian Archduke Charles. After reading a few more journals and letters, Bonaparte left, pinching Laure's foot through the bedclothes again.

Later that day Laure joined an outing to Butard forest. Bonaparte complimented her on her courage she showed a year ago, when she had stood up to him in one of his foul moods with Josephine. After retiring to bed in the evening she had a restless night's sleep. She woke early and checked to make sure her maid's door to the corridor was locked as she had asked. She was annoyed to find that the key was on the outside and the bolt was unfastened. Locking the door and taking the key, she returned to bed. At six o'clock she heard footsteps in the corridor and then a knock at her maid's door. As she listened, she heard her maid explain to Bonaparte that Madame Junot had taken the key. As she listened to his footsteps walk way, she was overcome with guilt for depriving him of a moment's distraction with a child he had known since birth. She fell back to sleep, but was awoken by the sound of her door being violently opened.

"Are you afraid of being assassinated then?" It was Bonaparte.

Laure was too scared to tell him the truth. She explained she had risen early and decided her chamber should be entered only by her own door. Bonaparte scrutinised her like an eagle. "Tomorrow is the hunting party at Butard [...] We set out early [...] I shall come myself to wake you; and as you are not among a horde of Tartars, do not barricade yourself again as you have done. You see that your precaution against an old friend has not prevented his reaching you. Adieu!" He left without singing. She found out from her maid that Bonaparte had got into her room using a master key.

Laure was worried about staying another night at Malmaison, but she would not know what to say to Hortense if she asked for a carriage. If she wrote to her husband Junot telling him she was ill, transport would not arrive until the next day and she felt she had to leave that day. Later, her husband unexpectedly arrived and Bonaparte invited him to stay for dinner. Laure was overjoyed with relief. Bonaparte was in a good mood and played chess with her in the evening. When it was time for Junot to return to Paris, Laure asked him to come to her room while she wrote a letter for him to give to her mother. There, she tried to persuade him to take her back to Paris with him that night. He suspected someone had insulted her and became enraged, obliging her to convince him this was not the case. He calmed down, but he refused to take her back to Paris. Her only option was to persuade him to remain there. As Junot was on duty, he was supposed to return to the city. Laure had to tempt him with all her feminine charms to stay the night and risk a reprimand.

At five o'clock the next morning she awoke to admire the face of her husband lying beside her. Half an hour later, she heard footsteps at the door. It opened noisily and Bonaparte could be heard exclaiming "What! Still asleep, Madame Junot, on a hunting day! I told you that..." As he stood at the foot of the bed and drew the curtains he noticed Junot, who, just waking up, was astonished to see Bonaparte. "Why General, what are you doing in a lady's chamber at this hour?" Junot asked in good humour. "I came to awake Madame Junot for the chase," Bonaparte explained, staring at Laure. "But I find her provided with an alarm still earlier than myself. I might scold you, for you are contraband here, Monsieur Junot."

"My General, if ever a fault deserved a pardon, it is mine. Had you seen that little siren last night exercising all her magic for more than an hour to seduce me, I think you would pardon me."

"I absolve you then entirely" he said, forcing a smile. "It is Madame Junot that shall be punished." He laughed, but it seemed hollow. "To prove that I am not angry I permit you to accompany us to the chase." He promised to arrange a horse for him. "Adieu Madame Junot; Come get up, and be diligent."

As Bonaparte left them, Junot said "Faith! That is an admirable man. What goodness! Instead of scolding. Instead of sending me sneaking back to my duty in Paris. Confess, my Laura, that he is not only an astonishing being, but above the sphere of human nature."

Later that day, as the carriages and horses were assembling for the outing, Bonaparte seated himself in the first carriage and beckoned to Laure, smiling: "Madame Junot, will you honour me with your company?" She got in without saying anything. After a while, Bonaparte turned to her and crossing his arms, said: "You think yourself very clever; do you not?"

"I do not give myself credit for extraordinary sense, but I think I am not a simpleton." She replied.

"A simpleton no, but a fool."

Laure remained silent.

"Can you explain the reason why you made your husband stay?"

"The explanation is clear and brief, General. I love Junot; we are married and I thought there was no scandal in a husband remaining with his wife."

Bonaparte was not satisfied. She knew, he insisted, that he was not allowed to stay at Malmaison last night "and you knew too, that my orders ought to be obeyed." Laure responded: when the consuls were to dictate the law specifying the hours and degree of intimacy allowed between a married couple "then I shall think of submitting; till then, I confess, General, my good pleasure shall be my only law."

"You had no other reason, then, but love for your husband in making him stay?"

"No, General."

"You have told a lie there."

"General..."

"Yes, you have told a lie." He claimed he understood why. "You have a distrust of me, which you ought not to have. Ah! You have no answer," he declared in triumph.

"And if I have been impelled by a different motive from the distrust you speak of, General – if I have perceived that your visit at such an hour in the chamber of a young woman of my age might compromise me [...] in the eyes of other inhabitants of this house?"

Bonaparte gave this explanation some thought. "If that be true, why did you not tell me of your uneasiness? Have I not shown you friendship enough, naughty child, within the last week to obtain your confidence!"

"There I was perhaps in fault." She should, she admitted, have reminded herself of his friendship with her family, especially his attachment to her mother. Bonaparte looked out of the window as Laure continued to concede her mistake. She should have confided in him rather than risk his anger being directed at her husband "the man who loves you best in the world [...] This morning when I heard your steps when you were about to enter my chamber, I confess I had some fear of your resentment..." However, when she looked at her husband's scars, "received partly for your glory, I assured myself that you would never be the cause of suffering to the noble and excellent heart which beats, perhaps more strongly for you than for me, in the mutilated breast of Junot."

"Who talks of afflicting Junot? Why not have spoken to me?"

"And how was I to do so?" She argued that her attempt to lock him out of her apartment should have given him the hint that she thought his conduct unbecoming. His subsequent behaviour did not inspire any confidence that he would have listened to her. "I was left then to my own resources, and my judgement has perhaps erred."

"Is there none of your mother's advice in all this?"

"My mother, General! How could my mother direct me? My poor mother. I have not seen her this month."

"You can write."

"General, I have not written to my mother that I was not in safety under your roof; it would have given her too much pain."

Bonaparte was getting annoyed. He warned her that if she continued to speak to him in this manner she risked losing his friendship and would not be surprised if she had told Junot what she thought.

"If you grant me neither sense nor judgement, allow me at least a heart that would not wantonly wound one whom I know, and whom you know also."

"Again!" He striked the carriage with a clenched fist. "Again, hold your tongue!"

"No General, I shall not [...] I entreat you to believe that neither my mother, husband, not any one of my friends, has been informed of what has passed within the last week". She simply thought it absurd to complain to Bonaparte about his friendly conduct because of her fear it might compromise her, "but I thought it proper to put a stop to it at whatever price; and in so doing, my youth has no doubt led me into error, since I have displeased you. I am sorry for it; but that is all I can say."

A clamour of barking dogs and horns indicated they were about to arrive. Bonaparte seemed calmer now. "And you give me your word of honour that Junot knows nothing of this foolish affair?"

"Good Heaven! General, how can you conceive such an idea, knowing Junot as you do?" He would be too quick tempered to judge rationally all this. She was about to add something and paused.

"Well, what then?"

"Well General, if I had told Junot what had passed this week, neither he nor I would have been here this morning; you know Junot well enough for that, do you not?"

Bonaparte's fingers played with the inside of the carriage as he thought. He turned towards Laure. "You will not believe then, that I meant you no harm?"

"On the contrary General, I am so convinced that you had no ill intention towards me, that I can assure you that neither my attachment for you, an attachment dating from infancy, nor the admiration which I feel even more strongly than others, is at all lessened by it: and there is my hand as the pledge of my words."

Bonaparte shook his head gently, half smiling, but refused to take her hand.

"We are at variance then," she inferred, suggesting he seemed to insist on bearing some kind of Corsican grudge. Bonaparte looked onto the road, then un-gloved his hand, extending it towards Laure. "Be assured of my friendship Madame Junot; you might, had you chosen, have strengthened it." He wondered whether she had learned to despise him from an early age. "You do not like me, and I am sure..."

"I take the liberty of interrupting you General, to request that you will not talk thus. You afflict me; and so much the more as your arguments and inference are both false. Tell me that you do not believe them; it would be too painful to me to leave you in such a persuasion."

Bonaparte, who had been looking at the dogs being led in couples by their handler, suddenly turned round, so quickly that it shook the carriage. "You are going?" he asked her.

"On our return from the hunt, I have induced Junot to take me home." She showed him a letter from her sick mother she had received this morning urging her to come and visit.

"And when do you return here?"

"Whenever I am wanted, for my part General; but you may dispose of my apartment, I shall never again occupy it."

"As you will. For the rest, you are right to go this morning; after this foolish affair, you and I should not meet with much satisfaction at present. You are quite right. Jardin! My horse!" Bonaparte opened the door, mounted his horse and galloped off.[1]

On 1 July, Bonaparte wrote to Josephine: "I see you expect to be home in a week; that is good news for your lover, who is tired of being alone! [...] Rest assured of my love, and that I await your return impatiently. Without you everything here is dreary."[2]

---

[1] D'Abrantes pp.407-421

[2] Hall p.52

Maria Edgeworth

From a Drawing by Joseph Slater

25 Maria Edgeworth

Illustration from *English Literature An Illustrated Record* by Richard Garnett (William Heinemann, 1903). (Look and Learn Collection)

23. Visitors and Artists

Two weeks after the preliminaries had been signed in London, Bonaparte instructed Fouché to admit visitors from Britain, as long as they were not French émigrés, who were allowed to return in 1802. Almost immediately, curious English men and women took advantage of the opportunity that had not been possible or practical for nearly ten years. Regular Dover–Calais mail packet ships began crossing the channel again on 18 November 1801. Through tickets to Paris from London could be bought for £4 and 13 shillings. A coach to Dover would leave London at 4.30 a.m. or alternatively one could get a night coach leaving from Charing Cross. The Channel crossing to Calais was about eight hours, so passengers were advised to take their own light refreshments. A curious crowd of spectators might assemble on the pier at Calais to watch the English disembark. Some ships went to Boulogne, but here, if the tide was out on arrival, passengers had to be rowed inland and then carried ashore on the backs of fishermen's wives. Similar inconveniences occurred at Calais too. The artist William Turner, arriving there in mid-July 1802, had to be taken ashore in a boat that was nearly swamped by the waves and then obliged to wade through the surf onto the beach. The number of visitors arriving in Calais varied. One of the earliest packets disembarked sixty-three ladies. The busiest period saw 798 passengers alighting there in ten days, overwhelming the local hotels. By June 1802 the influx was just under 100 arrivals every ten days, but this grew as the summer progressed.

The first night in France would often be spent in Calais before continuing the journey the next day. Two visitors who never went beyond the port were the poet William Wordsworth and his sister Dorothy. Soon after the preliminaries had been announced in October 1801 Wordsworth and his sister had received a letter from across the Channel. It was from Annette Vallon, a woman with whom Wordsworth had a passionate affair in France nearly ten years previously and the mother of his only child, a daughter called Caroline whom he had never seen. Their correspondence had been interrupted by the war. Passionate, desperate letters from Annette were never received by Wordsworth, whose own desire for her had subsided. He was now in love with a childhood friend, Mary Hutchinson, with whom he was engaged to be married. More mail from Annette followed. When a fourth letter arrived on 22 March both brother and sister resolved to visit her in France.

Wordsworth had first gone to France in 1790, to Paris and then to Orleans to learn French with the plan of becoming a tutor to rich gentry and write poetry in his spare time. He met Annette and he remained with her until October 1792, when he returned to Paris. In December their daughter Caroline was born. He acknowledged her as his, but had to leave for England because he was running out of funds. There he tried to persuade his guardians – his uncles – to release more money due to him so that he could return to France, marry Annette and bring her and Caroline back to England, where they would share a cottage with him and his sister. His uncles refused and when war broke out Annette and Caroline were abandoned. Wordsworth hated the war and declined to celebrate English victories. Although the Terror disillusioned him, he remained a republican while Annette became a royalist Chouan sympathiser.

After the publication of *Lyrical Ballads* with Coleridge in 1800, Wordsworth and his sister Dorothy moved into Dove Cottage in Grasmere, in the Lake District, where in the winter of 1801–1802 Mary Hutchinson visited them. William and Mary fell in love and they resolved to marry as soon as it was financially possible. In May 1802 a cousin informed them that Lord Lonsdale, who owed their late father a lot of money, had died. In June his heir announced in the press that he would settle all the Earl's just debts. With his financial future seemingly secure, he arranged to marry Mary that year. But first, he had to settle things with Annette.

In July he and his sister left Grasmere, made a brief visit to Mary at Gallow Hill near Scarborough and then set off for France. On Sunday 1 August they arrived at Calais at 4 a.m. and a few hours later met Annette and Caroline at their lodgings with Madame Avril's in Rue de la Tête d'Or. They spent four weeks in Calais, walking and talking in French with Annette and ten-year old Caroline along the sea shore, with William sometimes bathing in the sea. William the republican was disappointed by developments in France, remarking of the greeting "Good Morrow Citizen" that it was "a hollow word, as if a dead man spoke it."

Some visitors did not go to Paris immediately from Calais, preferring to visit Belgium and the Netherlands first. This was Fox's preference, as he set out for the continent with Liz and two other companions from St Anne's Hill at the end of July, a few weeks after his re-election for Westminster. Just before he left he announced to his friends that he had been secretly married to Mrs A, his "dearest Liz", for seven years. In 1795 Fox had unwittingly attracted the attention of the youngest daughter of the banker Thomas Coutts. When her parents suggested a lock of his hair as a suitable gift for their daughter, Liz recognized this as an opportunity for Fox to lead a respectable family life and told him she was prepared to step aside. Fox responded in writing: "I love you more than life itself [...] I can not figure myself any possible idea of happiness without you [...] I could not endure the thought of belonging to any other woman [...] God bless my dearest mistress friend & wife, and make her love old Kins, and believe (what is true) that he is & always will be entirely hers, yes every bit of him." To prove his devotion, he convinced her to marry him in secret on 28 September 1795 at Wyton Rectory in Huntingdonshire.[1]

In July 1802 a large throng of people followed the Fox party to the shore at Dover and after a brief crossing in fine weather with favourable gales, they arrived at an equally crowded Calais quayside. Almost as soon as he had checked into his inn, an officer and his colleagues of the town authorities came round personally to welcome him to France, declaring "the highest gratification which he and his fellow citizens felt in seeing in their city the great statesman, whose counsels, had they been seasonably adopted, would have prevented the calamities that have distracted the world". In the evening Fox dined with the exiled Irish radical Arthur O'Connor. They then travelled to the Low Countries, taking in Lisle, Ghent, Antwerp, The Hague and Brussels. At Lisle a circus performance was held in his honour and a regiment of the town garrison serenaded him outside his lodgings. On 17 August they left Brussels for Paris, with Trotter – his personal secretary – reading the novel *Tom Jones* to them on the way. After a gruelling journey in which their carriage kept breaking down they finally arrived in a stiflingly hot Paris on the 19th, where they met up with Fox's nephew and his wife Lord and Lady Holland.[2]

Another group that opted for a less direct route to Paris were the Edgeworths. Richard Lovell Edgeworth was a fifty-year-old Anglo-Irish land owner, inventor, politician and writer. Amongst his inventions was a semaphore telegraph system and a device to measure the area of a plot of land. As a politician he had served as an MP in the pre Union Irish Parliament and unlike most of his other Protestant colleagues, supported

---

[1] Davis pp.116-121

[2] Annual Register 1806 p.908

Catholic Emancipation. Edgeworth's reputation as a writer was to be surpassed by that of his daughter Maria. Her first novel, *Castle Rackrent*, published in 1800, was an instant success. In 1802 father and daughter co-wrote an *Essay on Irish Bulls*, an attempt to show off the wit and talents of the Irish lower classes to English readers only recently terrified by reports of their atrocities in the 1798 rebellion.

Mr Edgeworth had decided on the trip to France after hearing an account of Paris from a visiting professor from Geneva. In mid-September, he took his wife and daughters across the Irish Sea by the Dublin to Bangor ferry. Leaving Wales, impressed by Carnarvon Castle but less so by Welsh peasants unwilling to speak English, they travelled to London, visiting Josiah Wedgewood and his steam powered flint mill on the way. They arrived at their London hotel on 27 September, where they washed off the red sand and chalk that had caked their faces and hands on the journey. Buying a roomy coach, they proceeded to Dover. After landing at Calais they drove through a bustling, ugly Dunkirk to Bruges, then onto Ghent, reaching Brussels in mid-October where Maria was amazed to find carts and carriages drawn by dogs, four abreast.

The route to Paris took them through the ruined houses and churches of Valenciennes, the entertaining talk of a busty inn-keeper's daughter in Roye and the ruins of the palace at Chantilly with its dark forest. When the road went uphill, the French postilions would walk awkwardly in their large jackboots alongside their horses. To Maria, it looked like they were dragging their feet and considered them so amusing they would make a pig laugh. When the Edgeworths arrived in Paris, they took up residence in a hotel in the Place de la Concorde, where Maria soberly reminded herself that this was where the French King and Queen had both been guillotined.

The coach ride from Calais to Paris took about fifty-eight hours, but this could be cut to about forty hours by hiring a faster three-horse handsome carriage carrying four to five travellers. This journey might involve overnight stays at Montreuil, Amiens and Chantilly. After an uncomfortable ride on bad roads interrupted by numerous turnpikes, the English traveller would alight at the stage posts of these towns and be greeted by lame, blind and elderly beggars who had been anticipating their arrival and climb onto their carriages, pressing their faces against its windows. The last leg of the journey – from Chantilly to Paris – was on a finely paved road. At the gates of the capital, they would be asked for their passports.

Paris was a city of large white-stone buildings separated by narrow, muddy streets guttered in their centre. Vehicles were driven recklessly, splashing pedestrians who were obliged to walk on unpaved footways, themselves often covered in thick, inky-black mud. Visitors could choose from a large selection of hotels in Paris, where they were to find the servants and waiters very polite and civil, but much too familiar for their tastes. Breakfast and dinner could be included, but that might mean eating in your bedroom. A dinner might offer many dishes, but portions were small and rarely consisted of a roast joint of meat. One would be obliged to use the same knife for all courses. If invited to dine out with French friends, an English guest might be disappointed by the briefness of time spent at the table, allowing no time to drink more of the very weak wine. At night the streets were badly lit from lanterns which visitors learned had been used as improvised gallows by the Paris mob during the Revolution. In the morning, women travellers may well have been disturbed to find their beds being made by men rather than chambermaids.

When visitors took to the crowded streets on foot, they found pedestrians just as careless as the coachmen. Nobody apologised for stepping on someone else's heels or soiling a person's coat with a cane or umbrella tucked under an arm. Equally shocking to the English, was the habit the French had of spitting on the floor. On the streets were shops catering to all tastes. Every street had a *cabinet literaire* selling newspapers. Stores were open every day of the republican week, even on the *decadi* – the day of rest when public business was suspended. A good bookshop was run by Pougens the blind bookseller on Quai Voltaire. The Paris print shops sold pictures more indecent that those in London. Inside, they were obliged to haggle with rude shopkeepers. By April 1802, the English mission in Paris was inundated with visitors complaining they were being extorted by French retailers. As more and more English arrived in Paris, their number grew to a peak of about 5,000.

Perhaps the greatest cultural attraction for English visitors in Paris was the Louvre, the palace where French Kings since Louis XIV kept their art collections and was used by the art academies until the Revolution. From 1793 it was opened to the public as a museum and although closed for structural repairs for a while, by the time of the Consulate it had re-opened. Situated by the Seine and close to the Tuileries Palace, for six days out of the ten-day week, the Louvre was reserved for students and closed on the seventh. The other three days it was open to the French people for free. Foreigners and artists were allowed access on any day. A similar arrangement was made when the seven-day week returned.

On the ground floor, in rooms with well painted, gilded ceilings and marble inlaid floors were the galleries of antiquities – statues, busts and reliefs from Ancient Rome and Greece. This was a mixture of the royal collection and objects acquired from the Vatican during the recent wars in Italy. The most notable items from the latter were the two statues known as the Apollo Belvedere and the Laocoon. The catalogue entry for the Apollo boldly announced its presence in the Seine as permanent. The other statue, in white marble, depicted the mythical figure of Laocoon and his sons being strangled by serpents sent by the Gods as a punishment. Some of the original arms were missing, but temporarily replaced with Plaster of Paris copies until marble versions had been made. Another popular statue was that of the dying gladiator.

Upstairs, accessed by a grand staircase adorned with modern sculptures were the galleries of paintings. As well as old and contemporary French works, the Louvre also exhibited Dutch and Italian masters. Of the latter, many of these were Renaissance paintings also acquired after Bonaparte's conquests. Visitors often complained of the lighting in the Louvre. Paintings were hung between windows on opposite walls. One wall was too dark and the other too well lit so either the varnish reflecting off the paintings or the glare from windows detracted from the viewing experience. Maria Edgeworth strained her neck and eyes looking at the paintings. She was disappointed by some of the restored works, especially a Raphael which had "eyes of a very odd sort of modern blue".

Among the regular English visitors to the Louvre was the young artist and future essayist William Hazlitt. He had been commissioned to copy ten paintings for a Mr Railton and had promised James Northcote a reproduction of Titian's portrait of Cardinal Ippolito de Medici, which Northcote considered "one of the finest pictures in the world". Finding the countryside outside Paris barren, miserable and full of beggars, the city itself disagreeable, Hazlitt preferred its riverside, especially the Louvre. "If thou hast not seen the Louvre, thou art damned" he was to write many years later. He had read a catalogue of the museum a friend had sent him, firing up his imagination with high expectations that were not disappointed by the real thing. On his first day, however, he could not get into the old masters gallery, but only peep at it through a door. "It was like looking out of purgatory into paradise." He soon realised that to gain access to some galleries the museum staff had to be bribed. He was admitted to an inner room where some works were being repaired. The

Transfiguration, the *St Peter the Martyr* and *St Jerome* of Domenichino, rested on the floor. He browsed the galleries in a dreamlike state, recognising original paintings he had only been acquainted with through engravings. Walking past an easel with its back to him, he turned round and saw Titian's *Ippolito de Medici* that seemed to him a "thing of life with supernatural force and grandeur". Each day at the Louvre ended with the words "Quatre heures passées. Il faut fermer, Citoyens," muttered in a coarse provincial French. He obtained a permit to copy the paintings through a French official Mérimée. One day Mérimée asked him what he thought of one French landscape. "It is too clear," Hazlitt replied. "Mais, c'est impossible!" Mérimée objected.

"What I meant is that the various parts of the several objects are painted with too much distinctness across the picture; the leaves of the trees in shadow are as distinct as those in the light; the branches of the trees at a distance are as plain as those nearby. Perspective arises in this picture only from the diminution of objects, and there is no interposition of air."

Mérimée stared at him with an expression of incredulity. Hazlitt tried to explain further: "Look, there: one can see the leaves of a tree a mile off!" The Frenchman just shook his head.

Hazlitt was not the only visitor copying paintings. Maria Cosway – rumoured to be a mistress of Thomas Jefferson when they were both in Paris before the Revolution – could be seen making copies of the key paintings from which prints were to be made and published. When her sixty-year old husband Richard from whom she had separated arrived in Paris to visit her, Hazlitt was invited for tea. Despite their split-up, they were still very fond of each other. William Turner spent only a week at the Louvre, making a study of *St Jerome in the Desert*, before setting off for a tour of Switzerland. St Jerome was the subject of one of Fox's favourite paintings by Domenichino. Hazlitt first noticed Fox at the Louvre, while he was finishing his copy of Titian's *Man in Black*. He overheard Fox commenting on painting to his friends and turned to see a man with grey hair, pale face and furrowed brow, suggesting age and fragility. When complemented by strangers, Hazlitt approved of Fox's warm response in a frank, simple and unaffected manner. The Foxes visited the Louvre two days after their arrival. It was there, while admiring Raphael's *Transfiguration* and through the windows overlooking the Carousel that they caught a glimpse of the First Consul with his troops and Mamelukes.

Liz noted that for a republican Bonaparte seemed very fond of state and show.[1]

---

[1] Wu pp.79-85, Mitchell p.174

26 Thomas Paine

Engraving from painting by Romney (Courtesy of Library of Congress).

24. Attractions of Paris

A key attraction for visitors was the Palace of Versailles, a few miles outside Paris. They found the town gloomy and poverty stricken with many half-starved, semi-naked beggars. The Palace itself, built by Louis XIV, was neglected; its exterior had been vandalised and ornamentations of royalist symbols had been destroyed. Inside was no better preserved. There was damage to the painted ceilings and the elaborately gilded cornices of the salons. Some rooms were mouldy and damp, moistened by rain seeping in through apertures in the roof. Almost all the windows were missing panes, while only a few doors and shutters remained intact. No paintings or mirrors hung on the walls, exposing magnificently carved but empty frames. There were a few items of furniture, but most were damaged. The apartments were now being inhabited by soldiers and guides. The formal gardens were dirty and desolate, the fountains choked with mud. A statue of Louis XIV as Apollo had been desecrated. Le Petit Trianon, the small chateau where Marie Antoinette escaped from the formality of court life had become an inn and restaurant. The former was considered so expensive by one English guest that he felt obliged to take the landlady to a local magistrate to remonstrate, successfully, about his bill.

Another popular place to go was the Palais Royale – or as it was supposed to be known – Le Palais et Jardins de la Revolution. This had been a private palace owned by the Dukes of Orleans. Just before the Revolution the gardens and surrounding structures were opened to the public as a shopping and entertainment complex. During the Revolution, orators would harangue the crowds that gathered there. Now, under the Consulate, the only orations allowed here were those that were sanctioned in the part occupied by the Tribunate. The rest of the complex resumed its hedonistic character both night and day, prompting one English observer to describe it as "a receptacle of all that is vile of either sex".[1]

Amongst the arcades of the Palace that enveloped its garden were over a hundred shops of all descriptions: booksellers, milliners,

[1] Warren p.194

confectioners, tailors, haberdashers, opticians selling opera glasses and telescopes, jewellers, silversmiths and watchmakers all jostled for custom. As well as boutiques, there were some of the most renowned restaurants, taverns and coffee houses in Paris, where people could be seen playing chess, cautiously talking politics or reading newspapers. The more inferior eateries were in the cellars, where diners would be constantly entertained by bands of musicians. The upper rooms hosted crowded cafés serving liquors as well as coffee, each decorated with distinguishing themes – one with walls of glass, another with walls illustrated with Alpine scenes. Upstairs also were the gambling salons. Beneath them the pawn brokers and in the cellars below unlicensed gambling to attract the most desperate chancers. A few theatres and puppet shows could also be found in the Palace. The central garden, hosting orange trees, had a gravel walk, chairs for the weary and ices for the thirsty.

Prostitutes strolled around looking for clients. Bonaparte himself had picked up a prostitute here as a junior officer. The Revolution freed them from state persecution, but soon after Bonaparte became Consul, Fouché raided the Palais Royale and arrested many women. They were released six months later and resumed their trade in the arcades, but their numbers declined and they were only allowed to parade themselves after 8 p.m. In 1803 the Prefect of Police compelled prostitutes to pay for health checks, a system exploited by the appointed physician.[1] English visitors would often be hailed by strangers offering to introduce their beautiful cousin or friend. Lightly dressed women without a male escort would be accosted by passers-by, so Englishmen advised their compatriots about the unsuitability of the Palais Royale for their own womenfolk. If the English visitors found the openness of prostitution in this area quite shocking, their hosts were no less appalled by the sight of drunken Englishmen reeling in the arcades, behaving like animals.

In the spring of 1802, a thirty-year old Englishman asked at a bookshop in the Palais Royale if they knew where Thomas Paine could be found. The bookseller, his wife and a bystander all responded in the same unfriendly tone. "Scelerat", "bandit", "coquina", were the words they used to refer to the man asked for. The Englishman beat a retreat, and decided to look elsewhere. At a house called hôtel de Philadelpie, he was told that Mr Paine was sometimes found at the adjoining coffee house. It

---

[1] Laborie vol. 1 p.30, Sanger p.137

transpired that he had not been there for several days, but they knew roughly where he lived – a bookseller in Rue du Théâtre Français.

Wary of French bookshops, the Englishman thankfully discovered an American bookseller at number four. He climbed the stairs to the second floor and rang the bell to the apartment. A woman opened the door. Did Mr Paine live there? asked the inquisitor. She looked him up and down, said he did, thought he was not in, but asked him to enter. She held a candle close to his face? "Do you wish to see Mr Paine?"

"I am just come from England, and am extremely anxious to see him, as I am an old acquaintance whom he has not seen these ten years." She smiled. "He is taking a nap; but I'll go and wake him." Two minutes later, she ushered him into a small dirty room with a wooden table and two chairs. "This is Mr Paine's room!" she said. The chimney hearth was a heap of dirt. Pasteboard boxes sat on three shelves, with labels revealing their contents as correspondence ordered geographically and political leaflets. In one corner of the room were several huge curiously shaped bars of iron. Opposite the fireplace was a sideboard covered with pamphlets and journals.

A man entered the room in a long flannel gown, whom his visitor instantly recognised as his old friend Tom Paine. He had aged badly and had a melancholy countenance. Paine, who did not recognise him, asked his visitor to be seated. The guest tried to nudge Paine's memory by mentioning experiences they had shared. His host often struck his head declaring, "Ah I know that voice, but my recollection fails." Finally, an incident was recalled that instantly made Paine's face change. His guest was Henry RedHead Yorke. In the early 1790s they had both written articles for the *Sheffield Register*, a radical newspaper printed by Joseph Gales. Paine avoided his trial for his seditious *Rights of Man* by establishing himself in France. Yorke had not been so lucky and was imprisoned at Dorchester Castle for two years.

He pressed Yorke by the hand with a tear rolling down his cheek. "Thus are we met once more Mr Paine, after a long separation of ten years, and after having both of us severely weather-beaten."

"Aye, and who would have thought that we should meet again at Paris." After explaining how he came to be there, Yorke listened to his old friend moan about the French. "They have shed blood enough for liberty, and now they have it in perfection. This is not a country for an honest man to live in. They do not understand anything at all of the principles of free government, and the best way (for foreigners) is to leave them to themselves. You see they have conquered all Europe only to make it more miserable than it was before". Yorke was surprised to hear him so despondent, suggesting there was much that might yet be done for the Republic.

"Republic! Do you call this a republic? Why they are worse off than the slaves at Constantinople, for they are ever expecting to be bashaws in heaven by submitting to be slaves below; but here they believe in neither heaven nor hell and yet are slaves by choice. I know of no republic in the world except America, which is the only country for such men as you and I. It is my intention to get away from this place as soon as possible, and I hope to be off in autumn. You are a young man and may see better times, but I have done with Europe and its slavish politics."

Yorke was not sure about America and was worried about yellow fever. Paine assured him that the United States was in some respects better than England, that yellow fever no longer posed the same threat as previously and was confident it could be managed. He showed his visitor a letter from President Jefferson, who was pleased that Paine was exchanging the old for the new world. The President wrote that Paine would be happy in America, where his principles were daily practiced and assured him of a hearty welcome. "It would be a curious circumstance," Paine said laughing, "if I should hereafter be sent as Secretary of Legation to the English court, which outlawed me. What a hubbub it would create at the King's levee, to see Tom Paine presented by the American ambassador! All the bishops and women would faint away; the women would suppose I came to ravish them, and the bishop, to ravish their tythes. I think it would be good joke."

Yorke wondered whether this daydream suggested he had not abandoned the possibility of returning to Europe. Possibly, but probably not, given the stage of his life, Paine replied. He would probably sell his estate there and live off the interest to complete his memoirs.[1]

---

[1] Yorke pp.337-347

****

Although Englishwomen were advised to avoid the Palais Royale, there were plenty of other more respectable places to promenade. Most of the streets, squares and courtyards were dirty and muddy, so these were generally avoided. The Tuileries gardens were open to the public and this was considered a clean and dry place to walk. It was a formal garden of raised terraces, octagonal basins with fountains, with copies of ancient statues, marble urns and vases placed along its straight paths. A statue of Voltaire also stood here. Many of the French men walking there sported beards and almost all military men had moustaches. Evening walks could be had in the illuminated Frascati and Tivoli gardens. Frascati's was a privately run, but allowed free entry in the expectation that visitors would buy the ices, cakes, tea, punch and lemonade it offered. The Tivoli was larger with bigger attractions – bands of music, tumblers and roundabouts on which French adults would ride, surprising some English visitors by the childish fun they derived from them.

The Champs-Élysées was considered impassable in the early months of 1802. In December 1801 a great storm struck Paris, causing the Seine to spill over its banks and the drains to regurgitate their waste into the streets. The Champs Elysees was flooded to a level of fourteen inches above its curb stones.[1] When the waters receded, a thick sediment of mud remained, putting off even the most intrepid pedestrians. Finally, in spring, its gravel walks, shaded by lofty trees, came alive with pedestrians and rows of chairs on which people sat eating ices or reading newspapers. In the late afternoon it was congested with carriages and horsemen, many of them on their way to the Bois de Boulogne, the wood on the north eastern edge of Paris. Many of its trees had been cut down during the Revolution for fuel, but it was still a pleasant place to spend a spring or summers day. The gate leading to it from the centre of Paris would get very crowded with carriages, horsemen and pedestrians obliged to mingle closely to get through. Inside the vast park, one could acquire chairs and buy ices, oranges, fruit, lemonade and flowers. A walk in the Bois de Boulogne was also an opportunity for public display. The most ostentatious exhibition of fashion occurred on the annual public promenade to Longchamp in spring. This had started many years before

---

[1] Hugo p.108

the Revolution as an annual pilgrimage to the Abbey of Longchamp where Parisians flocked to hear a monk with a heavenly voice singing mass. After his death, the annual excursions continued, becoming more of a fashion parade. It ceased during the Revolution, but under a Consulate which actively promoted the French clothing industry, the custom revived.

Weeks before the promenade of 1802, a small boom erupted for the tailors and milliners of Paris who were being asked to come up with new designs for hats and dresses. On the day itself, military guards were posted at the start of the Champs-Élysées at 2 p.m. By 3 p.m. a line of carriages stretching from the Bois de Boulogne to the Place de la Concorde had formed. Any pedestrians would have been smothered in dust. Many of the carriages were copies of those which some English visitors had brought over with them. However, only the authentic English vehicles would have had coats of arms on display as foreigners alone were permitted these. There were restrictions even the British had to observe. Nobody was allowed to fit their servants with badges on their caps in case they were mistaken for government officials. During certain hours, driving along the Champs-Élysées was forbidden, a prohibition rigidly enforced, as Lady Cholmondeley found out when she was arrested for breaking it.

Horsemen would often be accompanied by finely dressed grooms. Frenchmen aped the English style of dressing, wearing boots, leather breeches, blue frock coats and high crowned hats, but could be distinguished from their English role models by their earrings, coloured capes and pointed toes. The Ladies of Paris wore showy silks, embroidered muslins, pearl necklaces and lace capes. Transparent petticoats would barely disguise their "pommes d'albâtre".

The English noted that despite these public promenades, the French did not walk very much. What they did do a lot was dance. After the austerities of the Terror, Parisians seemed to make up for the fun that had been denied them. Clubs sprang up throughout the city putting on public balls and this love of dancing continued into the Consulate. The Salon des Étrangers was an exclusive gentlemen's club admitting citizens by ballot, but allowing foreigners to join by paying an annual subscription. It was based in a large house on la rue de la Grange-Batelière with windows overlooking the boulevard. Inside were several large rooms opened every morning and evening for use of members. There was a reading room supplied with the latest journals and salons where one could play billiards or cards. Every ten days a ball was held. They usually started at midnight and arrivals might have to queue in their carriages outside for nearly an hour. Inside it was crowded with men and women of all ages. The women, with naked necks and backs, showed off the rest of their body through their transparent petticoats, an attire that at least had the virtue of being practical in the stiflingly hot dance rooms. Their head-dress were often classically inspired and adorned with diamonds and pearls. The two most popular types of dances were the cotillon and the waltz. The cotillion was a formal affair originally made up of four couples in a square formation who swapped partners as the music changed, allowing participants to introduce themselves and flirt with other partners. More shocking to the English was the waltz, because it allowed partners to get much closer to each other. This indecency was only partially mitigated by the Frenchmen who restrained themselves from any improper actions.[1]

---

[1] Lemaistre pp.92-98,175-180,205-212; Alger pp.126-173 , Warren pp.36-37,39-44,85,211-215

27 Madame Récamier

Photogravure of painting by Gerard by Gebbie & Husson Co Ltd for Paris Exposition 1889 (Author's private collection)

25. Plays, Parties and Proposals.

There was perhaps only one thing the French liked more than dancing and that was the theatre. There were twenty-six theatres in Paris, most of them situated around La rue de la Loi, all open and crowded every night, offering a wide selection of entertainment. Magnificent operas with up to two-hundred dancers on stage could be seen at La Théâtre de la République et des Arts. Hortense had her own crimson-and-gold box here, directly above that of her father-in-law. Comic operas could be watched at the Le Théâtre Comique on rue Feydeau. Multiple short acts were performed at the Vaudeville theatre. The most important theatre was the Comédie-Française, the French national theatre founded by Louis XIV and still funded by the state, which performed the tragedies of Racine, Corneille and Voltaire and the comedies of Molière. The cheaper seats were at the front in the pit. Women, who were excluded from these seats, evaded this restriction by dressing up and behaving like the men. One English visitor found himself sitting behind a girl in male attire, ostentatiously kissing her female friend to attract his attention. An Englishman commenting about the costumes of the actresses thought the "Bishop of Durham would expire" on seeing them. It was also observed that the audience rarely dressed well at the theatre, except for opening nights. Another complaint about French theatre goers was that they rarely returned copies of the play they had borrowed unless specifically asked.

One of the most respected actresses of the day was the forty-five year-old Mademoiselle Raucourt. The daughter of an actor, Raucourt started her stage career at the age of twelve. She became successful in Rouen and by the age of eighteen she was acting at the Comédie-Française. A preference for women led to an affair with the famous opera singer Sophie Arnoud, who indulged her own insatiable taste for the female body by enjoying as many of them as she could at the same time. Raucourt expressed her sexuality in a fictional pornographic text *Confessions of a young girl*, in which she suggested that lesbianism existed throughout time and was tolerated because it aroused men. This tolerance may have been over-estimated. She was suspected to be the author of an anonymous pamphlet, which purported to reveal the secrets of a man-hating Anadryne sect of "cunt-sisters" which had "renounced fucking in the usual forms [...] to make use of pricks and balls no longer" and "agreed to fuck and tongue each other so as to pick the roses of pleasure without being exposed to the prick of the thorns."

The lesbian affairs made her notorious, she was often imprisoned for debt and pursued by scandal wherever she went in Europe. Marie Antoinette rescued her career, but her patronage fuelled rumours the two were lovers and her association with royalists ensured her imprisonment during the Revolution. It was in prison however, that she found the beautiful Madame de Ponty, who was to become the love of her life: "You are so necessary to my existence that far from you I am nothing but a shadow," she told her. "I will love you till my last days."[1] Her career and her private life revived again during the Directory and the Consulate.

The audience coming to watch Raucourt also began to notice her young fifteen-year-old pupil, Mademoiselle Georges, who was expected to make her debut in 1802. Georges, known as Mimi to her family, was discovered in Amiens in 1801 by Raucourt, who had been commissioned by the government to find a talented pupil who would benefit from her instruction. Mimi had taken to the stage at the age of five in a theatre managed by her father. Singing in a little milkmaid outfit, she proved a local sensation. By 1801, the little girl had blossomed into a beautiful teenager looking more like eighteen than her actual age. After giving a crowded farewell performance rewarded with flowers and boxes of bonbons, Mimi left Amiens for Paris, where the pressure from audiences and competition between actors were intense. At one of the first performances at the Comédie-Française that Mimi attended, an actor called Larrive was being hissed by the audience who cried: "Be off with you!" and ridiculed him when he forgot his lines. Mimi was impressed by actresses who seemed to be weeping real tears and by the two greatest actors of the day, Talma and Lafont, but especially by the comedy. When Mimi began to be recognised as the pupil of Raucourt and was noticed in the balcony box she was often applauded. After performances she went to her teacher's dressing room where she would be shown off to admirers paying their compliments.

Three times a week, Mimi went to Mademoiselle Raucourt's house shared with Madame de Ponty in the Champs-Élysées to receive her lessons which her teacher conducted wearing trousers and a dressing gown. The older actress would often take a break at her country residence at La Chapelle near Orleans. On one occasion, Madame de Ponty persuaded her to take Mimi with her to be free from distractions. However, the lessons there were often interrupted by visits from the

---

[1] Rupp p.119

leading ladies of Paris, such as Madame Talleyrand and Madame Tallien, and Mimi would be obliged to recite to them. The actor Lafont visited and contrived to seduce Mimi in the woods after parting her from the rest of the company. He declared he wanted to marry her, but was prepared to wait until after her debut performance, to give her time for reflection. Mademoiselle Raucourt would play children's games with Mimi, but preferred the more manly pursuit of hunting. She persuaded her pupil to go with her one day. Reluctantly, Mimi accompanied her gun-toting teacher, who wore a knee-length white skirt and game bag for the expedition, but refused to fetch the dead rabbits her mentor had shot.

Raucourt showed off her new pupil to Parisian society, taking her to visit her own mentor, Mademoiselle Clairon, whom Mimi remembered as a bitter old woman. More enjoyable were outings to members of the Bonaparte family. Both Lucien and his mother were friendly, as were Eugène and Hortense, who gave Mimi a shawl. She was presented to their mother Josephine at the Palace of St Cloud, where Mimi successfully induced her host to cry when asked to recite some lines. "My child, your talent will be maternity. You have moved my heart," Josephine said. "Bring back this little rogue who has made me weep," she added to Raucourt as they were leaving. When Mademoiselle Raucourt indignantly learned that Mademoiselle Duschenois, a rival pupil, was to make her debut before Mimi, she did just that, hoping that the First Consul's wife could exert some influence.

Josephine listened patiently as Raucourt complained, then offered her advice: "Well, my dear Fanny, don't disturb yourself so; you will be ill my dear. Come, let us talk a little and be calm. What harm can the debuts of Mlle Duschenois do to this charming child? The lady is twenty-eight, they say. She is made; she must already be all she ever will be. What comparison can be established between a woman of twenty-eight and a child of fourteen? None; be reasonable then. And you, dear child, what do you think about it? You are not so upset as your professor are you?"

Mimi burst into tears.

"Ah, see, she is crying!" exclaimed Josephine, "There, since it is such a great mortification, since you absolutely consider that she should make her debut first, I will beg the First Consul to come to me. He will decide."

"Oh no, Madame, please don't send for him. I much prefer to remain with you quite alone, you are so kind, and I am not afraid of you. Besides, Madame, I should bungle my business; I should be like an idiot before him. Then, as a matter of fact it is all the same to me to make my debut after that lady. That will make me work with more ardour." Mimi implored: "Do you consent Madame? It is not necessary to bother him, nor Madame either, who is so kind."

Josephine laughed and took Mimi in her arms: "You see Fanny, she is more reasonable than we are. We must do as she says; that will bring her good luck. Then we shall all be there to applaud our little protégé."

On the way back in the carriage Raucourt was not pleased: "Little idiot, you've made a mess of it; the Consul would have given the order. The good Josephine did not insist when she saw you so stupid, and I yielded. Come now, no more reproaches, and take your courage in both hands."[1]

The day after Fox and his party arrived in Paris they went to watch Mimi's rival – Mademoiselle Duschenois – perform in a play at the Comédie-Française. Fox thought the new actress ugly and ungraceful, but a competent performer and he disliked Talma. The actors and actresses were not the only ones being watched. When Fox was recognised by the audience in the pit the whole theatre resounded with shouts of Fox! Fox! Fox! as they stood up and applauded. The First Consul, who arrived later, received similar attention, but not as loudly, thought Fox's personal secretary, Trotter. Wherever Fox went in Paris, he was hailed as "the English patriot" and "benefactor of the human race". Some of the gratitude Fox received was deeply felt. When he attended a sitting of the Tribunate, the captain of that body's troop of guards approached him. He explained that when he and his comrades had been prisoners in England during the war, Fox had advocated an improvement in their conditions, an act for which the captain now had the opportunity to thank Fox personally.[2]

---

[1] Cheramy pp.35-70

[2] Annual Register 1806 p.909, Fox's 1802 journal

One of Fox's main reasons for visiting Paris was to undertake research for his book *The History of the Revolution of 1688*. He did this from eleven to three each day at the archives of the French Foreign Office, where he was given his own room and attended to by a polite and helpful archivist. While working there, Fox was pleasantly surprised by a visit from an old acquaintance, Lafayette, who invited him to his country house. Despite Liz falling ill with a cold and a fever, they spent a pleasant week there, celebrating the anniversary of their secret marriage, that "day of happiness, day of joy" that neither Liz nor he would ever repent.

The Foxes were also frequent guests at Talleyrand's chateau in Neuilly, which he now shared with his new wife and former mistress Catherine Grand whom he married on 10 September. Catherine had the reputation of being extremely stupid. They met for the first time a few years earlier, when she had waited at his home for him to return from a late night's gambling spree. In a state of despair, she had come to see him on the recommendation of Talleyrand's friend Montrond. Apparently she had just heard that Bonaparte was planning to reward his troops with the deposits of the Bank of England when they invaded Britain, deposits that included her own savings. Talleyrand was too gallant to explain she was the dupe of Montrond's joke and wrote out a letter assuring her of the security of her savings in the event of a French army entering the City of London. Despite her naivety, Talleyrand was charmed by her beauty. Her reputation for stupidity rested mainly on a story of her encounter with the traveller and director of the Louvre Vivant Denon, whom she supposedly mistook for Robinson Crusoe and whom she allegedly told: "How happy you must have been the day you found Friday!" Talleyrand was to later claim the story was a fanciful fabrication.

Bonaparte, who wanted his regime to have at least the semblance of propriety, had expressed his displeasure with the situation of having an excommunicated priest for a foreign minister cavorting with a divorcee and former courtesan who was hosting dinners for foreign dignitaries. After Bonaparte persuaded the Pope to absolve Talleyrand from his former priestly vows in July, Talleyrand obliged both his master and mistress by agreeing to marry the latter in September. Despite this, Bonaparte refused to receive Madame Talleyrand at court and Talleyrand threatened to resign. A compromise was reached: she could attend only once as a public recognition of her right to appear, but that she would never do so ever again. On receiving her, Bonaparte said: "I hope that the good conduct of Citoyenne Talleyrand will soon cause the indiscretions of Madame Grand to be forgotten." Catherine replied: "In that respect, I surely cannot do better than follow the example of Citoyenne Bonaparte."[1]

Talleyrand's dinners were often memorable occasions. Enjoying furnishings of velvet and gold, lit by branches of flickering candles in baskets supported by marble statues standing in niches, up to eighty guests of intellectuals, literati or foreign dignitaries would entertain each other with conversations on the highest and lowest of topics. At one dinner Talleyrand gave for diplomats and their wives, the Austrian ambassador Count Phillip Cobenzl, a man who imposed on himself the highest standard of appearance, shared the following story.

"This adventure is perfectly true, and I can assure you it actually happened to me. I was at one of my country-houses some leagues distant from Vienna, when a courier arrived with a letter from the Emperor Joseph II, who wished to see me immediately. Without losing a moment, I got into my carriage, after due attention to my toilet. When I reached the suburb of Vienna, I was suddenly seized with so violent a pain in my bowels, that I was absolutely obliged to stop. It had been dark for more than an hour, and after having looked about for a place of refuge, with the assistance of my servant I at last discovered a low public house, which I was obliged to enter, although in a court-dress, with my sword on, and covered with orders, so that I was pointed at by all the people I found in the abominable place. Obliged to make the best of a bad case, I addressed the landlord, and explained the urgency of my want. He conducted me...you know where. But I found the place so dirty and so disgusting, that I determined to stand upon the seat. No sooner had I mounted, than the boards gave way, and I was actually precipitated into the soil, so suddenly that I thought my last hour was at hand."

Talleyrand asked him how deep he had fallen in. "Faith, up to here", answered the count, placing his right hand just below his mouth.

"That is to say, up to the lower lip?"

"Yes my Lord."

---

[1] Stuart p.270, from J.F. Bernard – *Talleyrand* p.240

A tense silence followed, broken by Talleyrand who appeared to be puzzled as to why the Count thought he was about to die if his immersion had not been total. "But, Monsieur le Comte, are you not mistaken? …Was it not as far as the upper lip you meant?" The image of the impeccably dressed ambassador submerged and gurgling in bodily waste must have been too much for the other guests to bear as they burst into laughter. [1]

When they met, Talleyrand asked Fox if he approved of the peace. Fox replied that he liked peace better than war, but admitted that Britain could not have made a worse one. Talleyrand said that it was lucky for France that Britain had given way, as the First Consul would have conceded the chief points in dispute as he urgently wanted his Brest fleet to sail.[2]

Among Fox's many French admirers was the celebrated beauty, Madame Récamier. Juliette Récamier was the twenty-five year old wife of the fifty year old banker Jacques-Rose Récamier. They had been married since 1793 and were widely presumed to have never consummated their marriage, the age gap fuelling the rumour that Juliette was his illegitimate daughter whom he had married to secure her inheritance. Madame Récamier asked Fox to accompany her on a carriage ride through Paris. Fox hesitated, but Récamier persuaded him: "I must keep my promise and show you on the promenade. The good people of Paris must always have a spectacle. Before you came, I was the fashion so it is a point of honour, therefore, that I shall not appear jealous of you."

Madame Récamier invited Fox and his party to a gathering at her chateau at Clichy. Guests were expected to turn up anytime between 11 a.m. and 3 a.m. Among the first to arrive that day were Generals Junot and Bernadotte, who had to wait in the drawing room for their hostess to return from morning mass and get changed. The actor Talma gave a reading of a new play – M de Longchamp's *Le seducteur Amoureaux* – for which he asked the literary critic, La Harpe, his opinion. About three o'clock, Fox and his party arrived, including Lord and Lady Holland and Erskine the fellow Whig MP, who had defended the mad would-be regicide Hadfield. Récamier introduced everyone to Fox and after a stroll

---

[1] Churton pp.91-97

[2] Granville p.361

in the gardens, they sat down for lunch. Récamier placed Fox and Moreau, who had also just arrived, either side of her and sat Mr Erskine next to her friend La Harpe. The conversation at the table covered war, politics, literature and the fine arts. Fox talked about Louis XIV with Moreau, who Trotter considered rather dull. Another English guest considered Moreau very simple in manners and appearance, affecting political indifference while at the same time accepting compliments for his role as a symbol of opposition to Bonaparte, whom he complained of treating him and his army badly. Erskine's views on juries and Fox's anti-war speeches in Parliament were discussed, while La Harpe spoke on literature. When coffee was being served, Josephine's son Eugène appeared with a friend. He apologised to Madame Récamier for turning up late and told Fox he hoped to make up for seeing so little of him since he had arrived in Paris. "I am commissioned by my mother to attend you to Malmaison [...] when you can resolve on leaving so many charms as must detain you here. I shall have much pleasure in acting as your guide." After coffee, the company rose and split into groups, Fox opting for a walk with Moreau in the gardens before leaving. Then, after a recitation from Othello and Macbeth by Talma, Fox and his party departed for Malmaison with Eugène.[1]

After Talma left, Récamier entertained the remaining guests and new arrivals by playing the harp and singing. Amongst them were the Duchess of Gordon and her daughter lady Georgiana, who consented to dance a gavotte with the hostess under the instruction of the ballet master Vestris. The ladies then went for a drive in the Bois de Boulogne, returning to find Madame Récamier's husband with more guests. About seven o'clock a Dr Itard arrived with a curious companion. This was a teenage boy called Victor, known as the wild boy of Aveyron, who had been found living like an animal in the woods near the town of that name. He had been brought to the Institute for the Deaf and Dumb in Paris where Dr Itard studied and educated him. Itard had just published a book in March 1802 about the young boy, in which he described his attempts to teach him emotion and language, the two features of humans he believed separated them from animals. Victor only mastered very rudimentary language skills, a failing Itard attributed to his lonely early environment in the woods. In these circumstances, his ear was not an organ "which discriminates the various articulate modifications of the human voice: it was there simply as an instrument of self-preservation, which informed

---

[1] Herriot, Trotter pp.189-190

him of the approach of a dangerous animal, or of the fall of some wild fruit."[1]

Dinner was served and Madame Récamier placed the young boy next to her, perhaps hoping her charms would sooth his bestial nature. He gorged himself and stuffed his pockets with plums. At one point he seemed to be listening to a discussion on atheism, but during a heated discussion on spiders, the guests were startled by loud cries from the garden. The boy had run outside, ripped off his clothes and climbed naked up a horse chestnut tree. Itard tempted him down with a basket of peaches and took him back to Paris. La Harpe wondered aloud – if only Rousseau, the great critic of civilization and advocate of the noble savage – were alive to witness this scene.[2]

More guests arrived, including the Russian and Austrian ambassadors and fruit and ices were served. Noise could be heard across the river. A village wedding was being celebrated and Madame Récamier encouraged them all to attend. On returning from this jaunt further company had turned up, among them Madame de Staël. The rest of the evening was spent reciting proverbs, playing charades and performing amateur theatricals. De Staël let her long hair down, dishevelling it and acted out Hagar in the wilderness while Récamier played an angel. The fun continued until midnight when the remaining guests finally left.

The gathering at Malmaison was unlikely to have been so eventful, but Fox enjoyed the rest of the day there even so. He was charmed by Josephine and the gardens she had cultivated with the help of the English botanists John Kennedy and his son Lewis. John Kennedy supplied Josephine with a large order of exotic florae from his Vineyard nursery in Hammersmith, while his son Lewis supervised their planting. Josephine showed Fox her rare plants and told him of her plans for improvements, asking for his opinion. Fox must have been impressed as he later wrote that he "was enchanted by all he saw and heard".[3]

---

[1] Itard p.78-79

[2] Memoirs of Baroness de Vaudrey cited in Lane, p.108

[3] Memes p.209

The Consequences of Honour

While in Paris, Mr Edgeworth was made an honorary member of the Société d'Encouragement pour l'Industrie Nationale. Another foreign affiliate was the Swedish inventor Mr Edelcrantz. He had been commissioned by the Swedish King to collect information on new industrial processes in Europe, especially alcohol which was an important source of income for the Swedish government. Edelcrantz was also the inventor of the Swedish semaphore telegraph system. When he had been shown the designs of the French telegraph he remarked that "there is nothing in this device I would want to copy." While in Paris, he invented a new lamp, but in late November 1802, what lit up Edelcrantz himself was Mr Edgeworth's daughter, Maria.

One day in early December, while Maria was writing a letter to her aunt, he turned up and offered his heart and his hand in marriage. Edelcrantz was not handsome, but Maria liked his facial expressions, the strength and spirit of his personality and conversation. Her father teased her for finding such an ugly man attractive, but would allow her to make her own decision. She declined his proposal. Although he had "superior understanding and mild manners" she could not return his attachment, knowing him for so short a time and was unwilling to leave friends and family and country to live in Sweden and Edelcrantz would not leave his own. He told her there would be nothing he would not sacrifice for her except his duty and did not fear the ridicule of his fellow countrymen for leaving Sweden to pursue a younger woman, but would despise himself for abandoning his duty for passion. Maria thought it was all very reasonable, but only reasonable for him and anyway she had no feelings except esteem and gratitude.

Edelcrantz was deeply mortified by her refusal, while Maria herself was not unmoved by the affair. Her stepmother believed that she was hiding her true feelings and had more than just esteem and admiration for Edelcrantz. She was exceedingly in love with him and had actually turned him down because she knew how much her parents would have suffered had she accepted. One day, in a Paris shop, Maria sat absorbed in thought while her stepmother and sister Charlotte were buying something. She did not notice her father walk in and stand opposite her. Only when he spoke did she realise he was there, and looking at his tender, anxious face, burst into tears. Attempts to distract herself with French society she found an enormous effort, especially when anybody mentioned Edelcrantz in conversation. Despite this, a story told by a French woman friend inspired her to write so she began spending half an hour a day scribbling on a table by the fire.[1]

---

[1] Hare pp.75-126

28 Jeremy Bentham

Engraving published in the *European Magazine* 1 May 1823 (Look and Learn Collections)

26. English Thought for Paris Table Talk

Yorke saw Thomas Paine often while he was in Paris. He told Paine that he had changed his mind on some of his principles. While in prison, he had become less radical and even supported the war against Revolutionary France. "You certainly have the right to do so," Paine told him, "but you cannot alter the nature of things; the French have alarmed all honest men; but still, truth is truth. Though you may not think that my principles are practicable in England, without bringing on a great deal of misery and confusion, you are, I am sure, convinced of their justice."

Yorke informed Paine that the publication of the *Age of Reason* had lost him many admirers. Paine had written this while he was in prison in France. After finding sanctuary with the French, he had become a member of its Convention, but voting against the King's death made him a suspect counter-revolutionary. He was saved from the guillotine by the intervention of the American Minister in Paris, Mr Monroe, and ultimately by Robespierre's downfall. The *Age of Reason* was an attempt to establish religion on rational grounds rather than revelation. It rejected miracles and the belief that the Bible was divinely inspired, advocating for the existence of a creator God simply from reasoning. By criticising a corrupt Christian Church and its pursuit of political power he upset some radicals as well as conservatives.

Yorke's comment made Paine angry. The *Age of Reason* was intended to "inspire mankind with a more exalted idea of the Supreme Architect of the Universe." He ranted against received opinions: "The Bishop of Landaff may roast me at Smithfield, if he likes, but human torture cannot shake my conviction". This bishop had written *An Apology for the Bible* in defence of Christianity in response to Paine's book. Yorke objected: "The bishop of Landaff is a man too enlightened, tolerant, and humane a disposition, to wish you roasted [...] You cannot say his *Apology* does not breathe tolerance in every page." "Aye," said Paine, "it is an Apology, indeed, for priestcraft; but parsons will meddle and make mischief; – they always hurt their own cause, and make things worse than they were before."

At a dinner party Paine and Yorke attended, there was a religious Catholic lady who had been keen to meet the author of *Rights of Man*.

Yorke implored Paine not to talk on religion and he agreed. Unfortunately somebody else at the dinner mentioned *The Age of Reason*. Paine was immediately prompted to declare that one only had to study the motions of the stars to conclude that Moses was a liar. Yorke tried to steer the conversation elsewhere, by attacking his political principles, but Paine kept returning to religion. Yorke even asked him to sing, which he did, only to resume the sensitive subject when he had finished. The ladies gradually rose from the table and crept out of the room, leaving Paine, Yorke and another man to their debate.

Yorke reprimanded Paine for forgetting his promise. It had not been fair of him to deeply wound the beliefs of the ladies. Paine was unrepentant: "Oh! [...] they'll come again. What a pity it is that people should be so prejudiced!" Yorke pointed out that their prejudices may be virtues. "If so", Paine retorted, "the blossoms may be beautiful to the eye, but the root is weak." Yorke asked him to elaborate and Paine obliged: "There is something exceedingly curious in the constitution and operation of prejudice. It has the singular ability of accommodating itself to all possible varieties of the human mind." He compared prejudices with spiders that live anywhere, even where there is nothing to live on. Prejudices would find homes even in empty minds.

Paine continued to have admirers of his *Rights of Man*, but not among them was his fellow honorary French citizen Jeremy Bentham. Paine had written his pamphlet in response to Burke's *Reflections on the Revolution in France* in 1790, which attacked the French Declaration of the Rights of Man in 1789. When the France issued further claims on the Rights and Duties of Man in 1795, Bentham wrote a pamphlet of his own, criticising this and its predecessor as well as a draft written by Sieyès in 1789. What was at issue was not the notion of rights, but the notion of natural rights, something Bentham regarded as "dangerous nonsense" and "nonsense upon stilts". The concept of natural rights was meaningless, because rights depended for their existence on some positive law. A natural right was "a son that never had a father", "a species of cold heat, a sort of dry moisture, a kind of resplendent darkness". The French Declaration referred to the right to property as sacred and inviolable. This suggestion that nobody could be deprived of it was simply false. The deprivation of property was both physically possible and in some case morally justifiable. Attempts by the declaration to qualify its assertions were so vague as to undermine the whole point of it. Talk of natural rights was simply incompatible with the viability of any plausible political order. Trying to establish absolute standards in political systems was problematic. Attempts to clarify a right would over-generalise it and make it too rigid and would prevent future generations from dealing with changed circumstances. To say that a man had a natural right to something could only mean – if it could mean anything at all – that he could assert an opinion that he ought to have a legal right to it. That is his use of it should be protected and secured by the state: "Reasons for wishing there were such things as rights [...] are not rights."

Bentham never got round to publishing this tract, but wanted Dumont to include it in his book. The Genevan declined to use it from fear of upsetting Sieyès. The book's publication was announced in the *Moniteur* on 15 June 1802 with the title of *Traités de législation civile et pénale* – a treatise on civil and penal codes. It drew mainly on Bentham's writing prior to the Revolution – so was more than ten years old. In his preface Dumont offered Bentham's ideas as a kind of balm to calm a world traumatised by revolution and war. It was not subversive or seditious, but simply sound advice to any ruler wishing to strengthen and stabilise their position. Although Dumont doubted the dogma of the separation of the powers, he insisted that Bentham was indifferent to what constitution a state adopted, the best one simply being the one to which a people were accustomed. The only thing that mattered was the happiness of its citizens, political liberty ultimately being neither necessary nor obstructive to that happiness. No matter how much liberty a people had, they would still be unhappy if they had bad laws. Bentham offered a third way between sceptical conservatism and revolutionary extremism. Conservatives like Burke emphasised tradition as the only guide to law-making, denying the existence of universal principles and therefore recommended laws should be left alone. However, the application to human affairs of the scientific method – experiment and reason – had demonstrated there were universal principles. These were not the imagined abstract principles of radical metaphysicians, principles such as natural rights and natural law, which failed to take account of time and place, seeing only humanity rather than individual humans. Bentham recognised that no such system was worth the happiness lost by the generation paying the price for its imposition.

Laws could only be judged by their consequences and the only way to evaluate their consequences was to consider the pleasure and pain they caused. The only moral rule a legislator should consider was the principle of utility: to maximise the greatest happiness of the greatest number of people. Bentham recognized there were other principles that were used to judge moral actions, but considered that these were either wrong or ultimately derived from the principle of utility. He noted that "it has been customary to speak of virtue in opposition to utility. Virtue is described as the sacrifice of our interest to our duties." No: "Virtue is the sacrifice of a lesser interest to a greater, of a momentary to a durable, of a doubtful to a certain interest."[1] Bentham also rejected the notion that our conscience should be our guide because it was too subjective: "If we judge of everything by feeling, there is no means left to distinguish the dictates of an enlightened conscience from those of a blinded one."[2] As for religion, he was scathing: "ecclesiastical history is an incontestable proof of the frightful evils which have resulted from religious maxims badly understood."[3]

As well as being the ultimate grounds for weighing the moral value of actions, pain and pleasure were also their ultimate motives. What made a crime a crime was the pain it caused, while the motive for the crime was the pleasure the criminal derived from it. Similarly, what made a punishment a punishment was the pain inflicted on the criminal. It was through the manipulation of motives that laws worked, by deterring criminals from crimes by the threat of sanctions against aberrant behaviour.

Although pain and pleasure were the universal motives and measures of value for all humankind, Bentham realised that to compute the relative amounts of pain and pleasure other factors had to be taken into account. The measuring of pains and pleasures depended on their intensity, their duration, the degree of certainty with which they were expected and the length of time that was expected to elapse before they were to be suffered or enjoyed. Individuals differed according to their susceptibility to suffer or enjoy. Such differences were affected by general factors such a person's temperament, health, intelligence or beliefs; and by a person's circumstances – their gender, age, rank, education and race. He acknowledged it was impossible to measure these difference, but the best approach for a legislator was to assume the effect of the same experiences on different people was the same. This may be wrong for any particular circumstance, but as a rule for legislators, obliged to generalise, it was the best option to adopt.

---

[1] Bentham 1871 p.16

[2] Bentham 1871 p.18

[3] Bentham 1871 p.20

Bentham considered that every law was an evil because it was an infraction on freedom: "It is impossible to create rights, to impose obligations, to protect the person, life, reputation, property, subsistence, liberty itself, except at the expense of liberty."[1] It was therefore important that a government made laws that were necessary evils, evils that were not as bad as the alternatives. To discourage wrongdoers, the punishment had to be harsh enough to make the reward of the crime not worth the risk. It was therefore vital that the evil that a law thwarted was a real evil and one that was a greater evil than the law itself. It was therefore unwise to legislate on issues of personal morals, where individuals were harming no-one except themselves. Laws against vices such as drunkenness and fornication produced more harm than good. They unnecessarily complicated the law by multiplying the number of crimes it defined. Because such vices were often difficult to uncover, they obliged penalties to be harsh and wasted public resources that were better employed uncovering real crimes. Bentham also cautioned against false reasoning in establishing what did and did not constituted a crime. Appeals to natural law, tradition, religious authority, supposed dangers of innovation – all these were to be rejected. The greatest happiness principle was the only legitimate way of reasoning about law-making.

Traditional legal opinion divided the law into two distinct areas – civil and penal codes. Civil codes dealt with rights, while penal codes dealt with offences. Bentham realised that these two branches were interlinked, because rights and obligations created offences. The offence of theft was only an offence because the law had already established the right to property. By creating a right for a person, the state had created a corresponding obligation on the part of others not to violate that right, making it an offence to do so. The right to property for one person, created the obligation on others not to use it, the violation of that right and the breech of its corresponding obligation being the offence of theft. The purpose of the state was to maintain laws that optimised the overall degree of happiness of its citizens. It could only do so by curtailing the freedom of people to do things that harmed others. It was not in the business of promoting the joy of its citizens, but only that of protecting them against pain, by creating rights.

Bentham believed that of all the rights a state should consider, the right to security, to person and property, were among the most

---

[1] Bentham 1871 p.94

important. Property rights were justified not by a social contract or by natural or divine rights, but because they established a sense of security, by improving the chances of a person benefiting from hard work. Because wealth offered the most certain opportunity for happiness, property rights had a high priority.

Bentham accepted that economic inequalities seemed to violate the greatest happiness principle, but was sure that an equal society was impossible, simply because "laws are constantly establishing inequalities, since they cannot give rights to one without imposing obligations to the other."[1] "The only equality that can exist [...] is an equality of misery."[2] Even if economic equality were possible, everybody would actually be worse off: "If the lot of the industrious was not better than the lot of the idle, there would be no longer any motive for industry."[3] Equality would remove the incentive of the industrious to work and encourage the idle to remain so.

However, Bentham recognised there were circumstances in which the right to security could be over-ridden. As well as imposing taxes to maintain law and order and defend the country from its enemies, the state should "establish a regular contribution for the wants of indigence". Children, the sick, the elderly and the unemployed ought to be provided for by the state if their savings or charities proved insufficient which they generally were. The poor were too poor to save and those that weren't were often too ignorant to be so prudent and it would be vindictive to allow them to starve from foolishness. The right to subsistence, the right not to starve, did override the rights to property. "For the pain of death, which would presently fall upon the starving poor, would always be a more serious evil than the pain of disappointment which falls upon the rich when a portion of his superfluity is taken from him."[4] The pain of a pauper and their pleasure in being relieved from poverty was much greater than pain suffered by a rich man losing a small portion of their property.

---

[1] Bentham 1871 p.99

[2] Bentham 1871 p.109

[3] Bentham 1871 p.99

[4] Bentham 1871 p.126

Although Bentham recognised that a poor man derived more pleasure from the same amount of wealth than a rich man, he also held that the loss in happiness from losing something was greater than the gain in happiness from acquiring it: "a loss which diminishes a man's fortune by one fourth, will take away more happiness than he could gain by doubling his property".[1] This justified the right of present possession of unearned property. He extended this principle to places and pensions, suggesting that although these were an unwarranted use of public resources, they should only be discontinued after their present benefactors had died. The ruin of a few individuals was far more serious than the minor gains to the public at large. General confiscations of property would threaten the right to security, opening the way to tyranny. Where there was a conflict between the advantages of equality and of security, Bentham advised the legislator to favour the prevailing distribution of property. There were limits to the sacrifice of the vital interest of a minority to the minimal gains to be made by a majority. Nevertheless, he was optimistic that equalities could be diminished. If the economy continued to grow and if the state stopped supporting monopolies and restricted the inheritance of wealth by regulating wills, a fairer distribution of property would gradually emerge.

Governments were a necessary evil, but one way of mitigating the evil was to provide efficient relief and penal institutions. In the third volume of the *Traités*, Dumont included an exposition of Bentham's Panopticon, a plan for the ways such institutions should be designed. The essential part of the scheme was the architecture of the building. An inspection house, like the keep of a medieval castle, would be surrounded by the main circular structure with transparent inside walls, where paupers or prisoners lived and worked to maintain themselves and bear the cost of running the whole institution. The governor of the institution would station himself in the inspection house, but be hidden from the view of the inmates. Not knowing whether they were being watched, the inmates would be obliged to behave and earn their keep with the minimum of supervision.

In early 1802 Bentham had been very impatient to see the book published because, as he disingenuously told the MP Samuel Rommilly, he had "a great curiosity to know what his own opinions are". When he read it, he wrote to Dumont telling him, "whatever parts there may be in it of

---

[1] Bentham 1871 p.108

yours, with very few exceptions I have not been able to distinguish it from my own."[1] At the end of August the *Traités* received a favourable review and Bentham announced to Dumont his intention to go to Paris in September when "everybody" would be there. He also wanted to see a doctor recommend to him, but his main purpose must have been to see for himself the reaction to his ideas. Bentham left London on the 7 September and stayed only three weeks, returning on 2 October. This would have been enough for the hermitic Bentham. Although his trip to Paris was a pleasant event he was uneasy with the many people he was obliged to mingle with.[2] Germaine Garnier, who translated Adam Smith's *Wealth of Nations* into French, complained to Bentham about his unsociability and brief visit: "Your person and your writings are equally attractive to us. Each recommends the other; but you will not let us sufficiently know them. You show yourself for an instant and then disappear."[3] An early critic of Bentham was Andre Morellet the elderly philosophe, who insisted that a man's right to property was prior to any law. Bentham was dismissive: "I read through Morellet's observations on the journey: poor Morellet! – how easy to answer, but to what use?"

---

[1] Bentham to Dumont 28 June 1802. Cited in Blamires p.292

[2] David Chauvet to Dumont 24 October. Dumont MSS 33/I fo.364. Cited in Bentham Correspondence vol. 7

[3] Garnier to Bentham 8 October 1802. Bowring, vol. X pp.398-9 (misdated as 8th February 1802.

27. The Prisoner

An uncelebrated and reluctant visitor to France in the summer of 1802 was Toussaint L'Ouverture. On 6 May 1802 Toussaint had rode into the French held-city of Le Cap on San Domingo and presented himself to General Leclerc. He had agreed to end his insurrection on the understanding that there would be liberty for all on the island. He and his troops were granted an amnesty and his officers would be allowed to maintain their rank and function. Leclerc allowed Toussaint to retire and work on his plantations.

He was not left in peace for long. Leclerc was persuaded by some of Toussaint's former commanders that he would always be a threat to French rule as long as he remained on the island. In early June he and his family were arrested and their property confiscated or destroyed. Leclerc justified the arrest with two letters, supposedly written by Toussaint, implicating him in treason. He and his family were bundled aboard the frigate *Hero* and transported to France. Leclerc urged the Minister of Marine to "have him put in a very strong place situated in the centre of France, so that he may never have any means of escaping and returning to San Domingo, where he has all the influence of the leader of a sect".[1]

On board the *Hero*, Toussaint was confined to a guarded cabin and separated from his wife, his two sons Isaac and Placide, and his niece. After a long voyage the *Hero* arrived at Brest on 9 July, but Toussaint and his family were kept on-board, in quarantine because of some deaths during the voyage. During this time Toussaint wrote to Bonaparte: "Citizen First Consul: I will not conceal my faults from you. I have committed some. What man is exempt?" After being promised these "faults" would be forgotten by General Leclerc, and that he would be protected by the French authorities, he explained he had retired from public affairs and complained that intriguers had poisoned Leclerc's mind against him. He was particularly indignant that his family and wife had been arrested, insisting that "she has no account to render. I alone ought

---

[1] June 11 1802, Leclerc to the Minister of Marine. L'Ouverture Project.

to be responsible for my conduct to the government I have served".[1] He ended by expressing his hope and expectation for justice in France. In another letter he begged the Minister of Marine to use his influence with the First Consul on his and his family's behalf.

When the quarantine ended Placide was put on-board another frigate and sent to Belle-Île. Five days later, a party of local gendarmes came for Toussaint at four o'clock in the morning. He was allowed to say farewell to his family, the first time he had seen them in about a month, and the last time he would see them in his life. Accompanied by his faithful servant Mars Plaisir, he was put on shore at Landernau. There, he and Plaisir were placed in separate carriages and escorted to Paris by two companies of cavalry. On the way, they stopped at Guingamp, where he was recognised by some French officers who had served under him many years ago. Granted permission to salute their old commander, they took turns embracing him inside his carriage.

Arriving in Paris on 17 August, Toussaint was taken to the Temple prison, but remained there only a week before being conveyed to a place of permanent confinement. This was Fort Joux, a castle 3,000 feet above sea level in the Jura Alps, situated on a rocky hill overlooking the river Daub on one side and the road from Besançon to Switzerland on the other.

Stone walls and a stone-arched ceiling enclosed a cell roughly twenty five feet long by twelve feet wide. It could be heated by a large fireplace, aired and lit by a small barred window near the ceiling at one end. Here, accompanied only by his servant Plaisir who was in the next cell, Toussaint still hoped to prove his innocence at a trial he was sure the French authorities would give him. Two weeks later, Plaisir was removed to Nantes.

The immediate responsibility for Toussaint's confinement was with the governor of Fort Joux, Commandant Baille. He reported to General Ménard of 6th Military Division who in turn reported to both the Ministers of War and Marine, Berthier and Decrès. The local civil authorities, the Prefect and Sub-Prefect, were only obliged to provide any necessary support, but the Minister of Police instructed the Prefect to keep him informed if he thought the prisoner was not being held securely.

---

[1] July 12th 1802. Toussaint to the First Consul. L'Ouverture Project.

Toussaint was considered of sufficient importance to require the Commandant to report to the Ministers and Prefects directly twice a month. The Prefect would receive a detailed report of daily precautions taken as well as an update on the physical and mental health of his charge.

In mid-September Toussaint was visited by General Caffarelli, an aide-de-camp to Bonaparte. Bonaparte had told Caffarelli that Toussaint had written to him via the Minister of War and had something important to tell him. Caffarelli was to interrogate the prisoner, asking him especially about the treasure he was reported to have hidden and for any other political intelligence he could render. At their first meeting Caffarelli advised Toussaint to be realistic about his situation and tell the truth. Toussaint spoke at great lengths about events in San Domingo, claiming everything he did was for the good of the colony and out of loyalty to the French Republic. Caffarelli thought Toussaint went on for too long, especially about his own achievements and felt he had learned nothing of any value, suggesting he reflect on what he had advised at the start of the meeting. He would return the next day to find out if the prisoner had anything more useful to tell him.

The next morning, Toussaint was ill and trembling with cold, but the interrogation continued. He handed Caffarelli a memoir, a more detailed account of what he had recounted the day before. Caffarelli returned the memoir to him, telling him coldly that he could not see anything in it of any interest. He wanted something new and more credible than what he had heard or read already. Toussaint asked with vivacity: what was it that was demanded from him? Caffarelli replied that he wanted details about the appointments of military and civil personnel in his service, his treasure, the placing of the whole island in a state of defence, his treaty with the English, and finally, his proclaiming of a new constitution with him as perpetual governor general with the right to nominate a successor. It was on these subjects he wished to be informed.

Toussaint claimed he had only treated with the English twice. Once, after they had been beaten and only to negotiate the terms of their evacuation. Then later he had agreed with General Maitland not to attack Jamaica if the Royal Navy did not interfere with shipping close to their coastline. When the English suggested San Domingo be brought under their protection or trade exclusively with them he had refused. The only things he had received from England were twenty barrels of powder. No cannons, no muskets, no munitions. The agent he had sent to Jamaica was there to negotiate the return of two ships seized by the English in contravention of their treaty. A second agent was ordered to approach the

English government directly if their authorities in Jamaica continued to refuse.

Caffarelli suggested that if Toussaint had sent an agent to London, he must have already established relations with English ministers. Toussaint replied that he had never despatched anyone to London and never written to an English minister. Everything had been done through an American consul in Porte-au-Prince. Neither had he ever received gifts from the British, except for riding equipment, which had only been accepted when General Maitland assured him it was a personal gift from himself and not offered in the name of his government.

As for placing the whole island in a state of defence, Toussaint complained that he had never been notified of the arrival of the French expedition. Had he been informed, he would have received General Leclerc, told him everything he desired to know, and placed himself under his command. Instead he was obliged to defend the island. Caffarelli rejoined with the observation that in publishing the new constitution, Toussaint had formally declared independence, which could only be regarded as an act of rebellion. Toussaint conceded that introducing the constitution had been a mistake, but had only done so because it had seemed necessary to allow the colony to flourish; his intentions had been well-meaning; he had not foreseen any negative consequences at the time and was convinced that it would re-establish peace and stamp out poverty.

Why were French ships not admitted to the colony? asked Caffarelli. Toussaint explained that this was simply the result of General Christophe following standing orders that no vessel be allowed to land until its captain had been seen by Toussaint. When Leclerc forced his entry, Christophe was obliged to resist. Caffarelli was not convinced and claimed that as these orders concerned even French vessels, thereby treating them as the enemy, they could only be considered as hostile towards the motherland. Toussaint understood his point, but pleaded that the measure had been decided in a time of war, and as it had not been revoked, it had to be obeyed.

Caffarelli turned to the subject of money. What funds were held when Leclerc arrived? Toussaint declared that Christophe evacuated 900,000 Francs from Le Cap, while he controlled the rest of the public funds, which he itemised by location. Caffarelli noted that he failed to mention in all this detail his own personal wealth, which he had ordered to be hidden. Toussaint protested: he and his wife had possessed very little. Caffarelli did not believe him and told him that six blacks had been ordered to bury his treasure before the arrival of the French army, and these men had been subsequently murdered. Who had given the order for them to be put to death?

Indignantly, Toussaint insisted that this story was an atrocious calumny, based on a claim, invented by his enemies at the time, that he had ordered the execution of twenty of his guards for burying treasure, and which he had disproved by assembling all of his guards at a roll-call. Caffarelli brought up another claim that he had shot one of his aides-de-camp after his mission of escorting some precious effects in a ship to the United States. Toussaint's reply was that the man was shot for abusing his servants and corruption – and was never sent to the States. Caffarelli continued with more questions. Had he ever placed money in England, Jamaica or the United States? Toussaint denied he held such funds or had any placed any anywhere else. What about his many properties and other assets? These could have been sold. What became of the public cash he controlled? Toussaint claimed he never touched public funds. He admitted he held much land and animals, but very little of his wealth had been in money and was annoyed that his interrogator refused to believe him.

Caffarelli told Toussaint that although he was the first man of colour who had acquired something like military glory and ruled for a long time, he was now broken and unfortunate, with no hope of rising again. However, if Toussaint had the courage to retract his lies and own up to his treacherous ambitions he could rediscover a different form of glory and would be forgiven for his faults. Toussaint was astonished, but after reflecting momentarily, resumed his protests, his claims of devotion to the French Republic and his respect for the First Consul. Caffarelli asked: what about the acts of arson committed by his troops in San Domingo? Toussaint answered that Christophe had burned Le Cap without his authority, for which he was sharply reprimanded. Other places had also been torched, but without his involvement.

When Toussaint pointed out that he had voluntarily surrendered to Leclerc after reflecting on the letter from the First Consul, Caffarelli suggested that it was actually Leclerc declaring him an outlaw that prompted this action. Toussaint assured him that his decision was supported by others, suggesting it could not have been taken from considerations about his personal welfare. When Toussaint asked for news of his family, Caffarelli would only assure him that his parents would receive all respect owing to their age and sex.

In a letter to Bonaparte, which Caffarelli agreed to deliver, Toussaint tried to justify any sins he might have committed. He had not intended any, and would have only done so through too much zeal and pride in what he thought was his duty: "I have had the misfortune to incur your wrath, but as to fidelity and probity, I am strong in my conscience, and I dare affirm, that among all the servants of the state no one is more honest than myself. I was one of your soldiers, and the first servant of the Republic in St. Domingo; but now I am wretched, ruined, dishonoured, a victim of my own services; let your sensibility be moved at my position. You are too great in feeling and too just not to pronounce a judgement as to my destiny."[1]

Another letter in the same vein followed a few days later: "I beg you, in the name of God, in the name of humanity, to cast a favourable eye on my appeal, on my position, and my family". Although he had made mistakes, he had served the Revolution and the French Republic well. "I have asked you for my freedom that I may labour; that I may gain my subsistence and support my unhappy family."

Toussaint's memoir was written in the hope that the details of his life and his dealings with Leclerc would convince Bonaparte of his innocence: "I request that he and I may appear before a tribunal, and that the government bring forward the whole of my correspondence with him. By that means, my innocence and all I have done for the Republic will be seen." He condemned the actions of Leclerc, claiming he had employed against him means he would never have contemplated himself: "Was it necessary", he wrote, "to employ a hundred riflemen to arrest my wife and children in their own home, without regard to their sex, age, and rank; without humanity and without charity?" He argued a great injustice had been perpetrated against him. He had been separated from his wife and children and still had no news of their whereabouts. "General Leclerc has said in the letter to the minister, which I have seen in the newspaper, that I was waiting for his troops to grow sick, in order to make war and take back the command. This is an atrocious and abominable lie: it is a cowardly act on his part." The memoir was sent on 1 October.

---

[1] September 17. Toussaint to First Consul. L'Ouverture Project.

His protests fell on deaf ears. The authorities' main concern was that he did not escape. The Commandant kept all the keys to his cell, checked on the prisoner himself every day and was expected to sleep at the fort every night, only being allowed to leave with the express permission of his superiors. Toussaint was not to be allowed out of his cell and could receive no visitors. The only person he was permitted to speak to was the officer of the guard entrusted with providing for his needs and this officer was under orders not to talk to the prisoner except in relation to his requirements. At night his barred window was closed by studded metal shutters, bolted and padlocked by a guard. He could only shave himself in the presence of a guard using a razor he had to return when completed. He was to be confined as cheaply as possible. When the Sub-Prefect suggested one and a half bundles of firewood per month should be enough, even the Commandant objected this would be insufficient. The Prefect decided two bundles should be provided, but stressed later this was for winter only. He was given one cold meal a day, brought to him in the morning at 9 a.m. by a guard. When he asked for sugar, he was refused. His meals, the repair and laundry of his clothing was provided for by the landlady of a local inn, but after this service was put out to tender it was done by the fort cantinière. As well as security and economy, his captors also strove to humiliate him. The Minister of Interior insisted that "He must not wear the uniform of a general." Arrangements were made to buy clothes from a local merchant.

On 27 October, the Minister of Marine instructed the prison governor that his prisoner had "no right to any consideration other than that demanded by humanity". He was to be searched, and any valuables, including his watch, removed. A large, suitably warm, grey or brown coat and a round hat should be his clothes. Visits by a doctor had to be conducted in the presence of the Commandant. The Minister insisted that the only way he could improve his situation was to stop lying to them and "he can be tranquil concerning the lot of his family; its existence is committed to my care and they want for nothing". Perhaps referring to the memoir, the Minister concluded that when "he brags of having been a general he does nothing but recall his crimes, his hideous conduct, and his tyranny over Europeans. He merits then, nothing but the most profound contempt for his ridiculous pride."[1]

---

[1] Minister of the Marine to the Commandant at Fort de Joux 5 Brumaire Year X (October 27, 1802). L'Ouverture Project.

The Consequences of Honour

On 1 November the commandant carried out his instructions. The prisoner was undressed, his uniform, hat and other items taken from him. He was moved to the next cell while his room and mattress was thoroughly searched. Toussaint was incensed: "You took my watch from me and 15 and seven sols that I had in my pocket, you even took my spur. I warn you that all these objects are mine and the day I am sent to my final agony you are to give them all to my wife and children." He demanded that his gaoler should not "seek to humiliate and vex him without any human feelings and charity, without any consideration for him as a servant of the Republic." He complained that "precautions and machinations were taken against me as if I were a criminal, and I already told you and I repeat again that I am an honest man and if I were without honour I would not have faithfully served my fatherland as I served it and I would not be here either by order of my government."[1]

Commandant Baille, an old man, was feeling the strain of his responsibility. In November he asked his superiors for a junior officer to help him fulfil the functions of concierge and maître d'hôtel as well as prison governor. He also asked for some boards for the corridor outside Toussaint's cell, which was half a foot under water. The least of Baille's concerns seemed to be the health of his prisoner. In October he had written to the Minister of Marine declaring he would not procure a doctor or surgeon unless specifically ordered to do so. The Minister replied that he could send him a health officer who could treat him in his presence, but extra precautions had to be taken. At the end of October Toussaint was in pain, suffering from headaches and fevers. His own remedy for the headaches, which he believed were caused by a past head injury, was to wrap handkerchiefs around his head. When Toussaint had asked for more handkerchiefs, the commandant refused. As well as these aches and pains he complained of the cold. His fireplace was not keeping his cell sufficiently warm. In November, Toussaint had pains throughout his body. Winter was closing in. Toussaint, who had spent all his life in the tropics, would not have had any idea of how cold European winters could be.[2]

---

[1] 1st November. Toussaint to the Commandant of Fort de Joux. (*Toussaint Louverture Fonde la Liberté et l'égalité a Saint Domingue* by General Nemours. Port-au-Prince, 1945)

[2] Nemours, Memoires d'Isaac-Louverture, Metral, pp.227-340

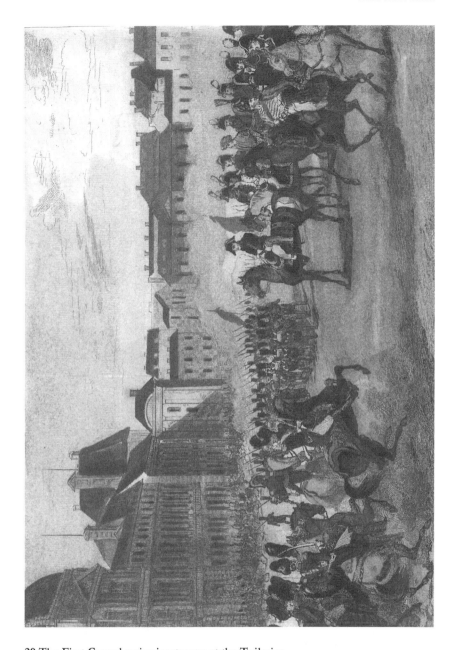

29 The First Consul reviewing troops at the Tuileries

Drawing by Martinet, Engraving by Réville. (Author's private collection)

28. Boney

Despite the prevalence of many police spies in Paris, conversations often turned to the subject of Bonaparte. Thomas Paine told Yorke that when they had met, before becoming First Consul, the General claimed to sleep with a copy of the *Rights of Man* under his pillow and asked advice on plans to invade England. Bonaparte expressed the hope that the English people were ready to rise up against their King, only to be disappointed by Paine's opinion that even if they were able to land, the French would be cut to pieces soon after. He told Bonaparte that the only way to destroy England was to destroy its commerce – and that would depend on a peace. At a dinner before his coup, Bonaparte had stared at Paine in the face while telling another general loudly enough to be overheard that "the English are all alike in every country – they are all rascals." He in turn thought Bonaparte the greatest rascal ever.

Paine, when asked about the peace, thought Britain had lost nothing, but had depleted the resources of France, which were unlikely to be fully restored: "If they should, woe betide you." Why? Yorke asked. Paine replied: "If the French government are intent on the peace, they will set themselves seriously to work on their colonies, and such is the activity of the French that they will soon repair their losses, create a vast commerce, which their local possessions and influence will facilitate, and they will end with a powerful navy." Yorke noted they had already excluded English commerce from France. Paine said that should give him "an idea what a set of fools they are. This false step at the first start, is a convincing proof, that they don't know how to go to work." They should have embraced free trade and been content to catch up with the British gradually. Instead they were in a hurry and had started too many projects at once, all of which they would never finish. Peace could be permanent, but as long as Bonaparte was in power, Paine thought it unlikely. He was the creature of the army whose generals were hungry.

Yorke wondered: was Bonaparte secure? More so than previous governments, thought Paine. The people liked him because he had not guillotined them, "but we have not yet got through the third Act of the Revolution". What would this be? was Yorke's next question. Paine offered two possibilities: either the complete subjugation of Europe or the division of France by civil war, ending in the restoration of the monarchy.[1]

Many visitors would have come to Paris hoping to see the First Consul, of whom they would have heard so much about, and who excited a wide range of passionate opinions. Bonaparte, however, was reclusive. Unless a visitor was distinguished enough to be introduced at the monthly reception of ambassadors at the Tuileries, the opportunities even to see him were rare. A few Englishmen wearing their local militia uniforms could be accosted by the First Consul who was curious to know what regiments they belonged to. He might be glimpsed at the theatre or the opera, but the best place to have seen him would have been at the monthly military reviews held in the Carousel courtyard of the Tuileries Palace.

Admittance to the Palace was by ticket only, but it was still possible to watch the review through the iron railings that flanked it on one side or from the windows of the Louvre, which bordered it on another. Overlooking the courtyard, on the main pavilion of the Tuileries Palace, was a clock divided into ten segments, underneath which was inscribed "République Française".

Once the troops had assembled in the courtyard, their colours were carried inside the Palace and saluted by the guards on duty. The band would strike up the *Marseillaise*, then the flags were carried back out, followed by a man of short stature. The figure would have worn a scarlet velvet coat with leather breeches and riding boots and a little plain cocked hat with a cockade. He would descend to the courtyard and mount a white horse, saluted by his officers.

The troops would then parade past him, their captains saluting him as they passed. The most impressive looking regiments were the Consular Guard and the mounted Guides in red hussar uniforms, led by Bonaparte's son-in-law Eugène. The Consular Guard were all tall veterans, wearing blue coats with white edged facings, red-and-yellow buttons, white waistcoats and breeches. Their height was exaggerated further by a dark fur cap with a gilt plate. The cavalry would approach the First Consul at a gallop and then stop in perfect order in front of him. When he had inspected them all and perhaps exchanged a few comments

---

[1] Yorke vol. II, pp.337-347, pp.360-369

with some, he would ride back to the Palace and retire inside with his officers. The troops would then file out of the courtyard through four gates ornamented with the bronze horses of Venice. One English visitor was so over-awed by Bonaparte that he felt obliged to exclaim: "By God, the man deserves to govern the world."

Fox was keen to meet the First Consul and in early September was formally presented to him by Mr Merry at a levee for the reception of foreigners. "Ah M. Fox, I have heard with pleasure of your arrival," were Bonaparte's first words to him. "I have much wished to see you. I have long admired in you the orator and friend of his country, who, in constantly raising his voice for peace, consulted his country's best interests – those of Europe and Mankind. The two great nations of Europe require peace; they have nothing to fear. They ought to understand and appreciate each other. In you M. Fox, I see with satisfaction that great statesman who recommended peace because there was no just object of war – who saw Europe desolated to no purpose, and who struggled for its relief." Fox was invited to a dinner for 200. In his pocket journal he noted: "Long talk with Bony. He talked mostly."

Fox met Bonaparte again at a levee on 23 September and was again invited to dinner afterwards. Later, he was among a select few to accompany the Bonapartes to their apartments. There, they were able to engage in more informal conversation. Bonaparte began throwing out ideas, asking many questions, but not waiting for answers before asking others.[1] Bonaparte suggested interracial marriage as a means of achieving universal peace and introducing polygamy in the West Indies as a means of speeding up the process of blending black and white. They disagreed over the need for a standing army, with Fox seeing it as a means of oppression. Bonaparte thought the press had too much freedom, particularly in their comments about him. Fox replied that it was a necessary evil and that in England people were not so sensitive about being abused in the papers. It was altogether different in France, was Bonaparte's response. The First Consul then complained about William Windham, who he described as an unfeeling, unprincipled man of mediocre talents. Fox disagreed, but Bonaparte continued with his complaint: "It is easy for you who only know public debate. But for me, I detest him and that Pitt who together have attempted my life."[2]   He

---

[1] Farrington p.31

[2] Granville p.355

would have forgiven open enemies in politics or war, but not cowardly attempts to destroy him such as that involving the infernal machine. Fox assured him that they, like any Englishmen, would be horrified at the idea of secret assassination. "You do not know Pitt," said Bonaparte. "Yes, I do know him," replied Fox, "and well enough to believe him incapable of such an action. I would risk my head in that belief." Bonaparte considered this last remark silently, then walked away. He told his secretary Bourrienne later that he had been pleased with what Fox had said, because he always wanted enemies he could respect.[1] Fox saw Bonaparte one last time on 7 October when they discussed the slave trade. Fox, advocating its abolition, met with Bonaparte's concerns about the difficulties of putting such a policy into practice. His implication was that France could not act without the co-operation of England. Their views were also exchanged on the jury system. Bonaparte considered it gothic, cumbersome and "so inconvenient to a government". Fox pointed out that it was its very inconvenience to government that was its key virtue. Bonaparte was obviously not convinced. On 18 October the jury system in France was suspended in many departments by a senatus-consultum, being replaced by special courts of judges.[2]   Although Bonaparte continued to express to others the deepest respect and admiration for Fox, this feeling was not reciprocated. Fox found the First Consul's conversation limited, saw no great mind or talent at work and was disappointed to find his regime to be nothing more than a court. Bonaparte, he thought, was the greatest imposition upon the world, but was consoled by the belief that he would keep the peace and was doing everything he could to avoid another war.[3]

The English who could not get across the channel to see Boney in person could still gaze upon his likeness in the lower floor of the Lyceum Theatre on the corner of the Strand in London. Here was a life-size and life-like waxwork effigy of the First Consul, part of an exhibition entitled Curtius's Cabinet of Curiosities. The waxworks were the creations of Madame Tussaud who had brought them over from France to join Philipstall's Phantasmagoria magic lantern show at the Lyceum. Bonaparte had sat for Tussaud at 6 a.m. one morning at the Tuileries

[1] Bourrienne p.237, *The Tourist*, p.202, Lefebvre p.129

[2] Trotter pp.42-221

[3] Mitchell p.175,177

Palace in 1801. In 1802 she travelled to England with her best models, including Bonaparte, Josephine and the French royal family, with her four-year old son, leaving her estranged husband, mother, aunt and baby boy in Paris. She also brought her moulds, which she needed as many of the models had to be repaired after the journey. She had agreed to join Philipstall despite his insistence on taking 50% of her profits, because she felt Britain would be a better market for her work.[1]

Other French visitors to England included Madame Récamier and Henri Grégoire. Récamier proved very popular with the English aristocracy. The Duchess of Devonshire and the Prince Regent were both particularly taken with her. When she visited Kensington Gardens wearing a diaphanous veil under her hat which enveloped her entire body, she was pursued by a large crowd of admirers. Grégoire was less popular, even among fellow abolitionists such as Wilberforce, who distrusted his compromising of religion with republicanism. Nevertheless he was shown around London by Sir Joseph Banks and Wilberforce took him to a school for African youth he had established. Grégoire left Britain with 150 books and pamphlets on slavery, some given to him by Wilberforce and others purchased from the abolitionist bookseller Philips. Grégoire considered the English were nice people, but thought that the country "would be enchanting if it had but pleased God to give it sunshine and French cookery".[2]

Trips to France and the continent were shorter for some than others. Bentham only stayed three weeks. On 29 August, after about a month in Calais, William Wordsworth and his sister returned to Dover. On its white cliffs they looked back at the coast of France with melancholic and tender thoughts. Memories of walking with his daughter along the beaches of Calais inspired William to write a sonnet:

> *It is beauteous evening, calm and free;*
> *The Holy time is quiet as a Nun breathless with adoration;*
> *The broad sun is sinking down in its tranquillity;*
> *The gentleness of heaven broods o'er the sea: Listen!*

---

[1] Pilbeam pp.65-72

[2] Alger p.169, Herriot p.77

The mighty being is awake, and doth with his eternal motion make a
sound like thunder – everlastingly.
Dear Child! Dear Girl!
Thou walkest with me here, If thou appear untouched by solemn
thought, Thy nature is therefore not less divine;
Thou liest in Abraham's bosom all the year.
And worshipp'st at the Temple's inner shrine, God being with thee
when we know it not.

On 4 October William and his childhood friend Mary Hutchinson married.[1]

Thomas Paine left France from Le Havre on 1 September, his passage to the States paid for by radical friends in England such as Sir Francis Burdett. The Foxes left Paris on 11 November, arriving at St Anne's Hill on the 17th. Fox wrote: "I have certainly seldom spent time pleasanter than at Paris, but yet I never in my life felt such delight in returning home."[2] Hazlitt was not to return to England until February 1803. After he obtained a certificate endorsed by Denon, the museum director, confirming he had copied ten pictures in the Louvre he set off for Calais. In the carriage taking him there he listened to a conversation between a fellow Englishman and a Frenchman about a man who had finally married his wife after thirteen years of courtship.

"At least he would then have been acquainted with her character," commented the Englishman.

"Mais non, Monsieur, for the very next day she might turn out the very reverse of the character that she had appeared in during all the preceding time!"

****

---

[1] Barker pp.211-212, Legouis pp.1-74

[2] Cited in Russell p.254

While personal relationships between the French and English were being made and renewed, their trade relations were less satisfying. In May 1802 Charles-Etienne Coquebert de Montbret arrived in London to discuss a commercial treaty between France and Britain. Addington had argued that an increase in trade between the two countries was the surest way of consolidating the peace while British merchants had been complaining that it was difficult to export to France. Britain ideally wanted to restore the terms established by the Eden Treaty of 1786. Although this had benefited wine exporters in the south of France, it was not liked by French manufacturers, especially cotton producers. When the British suggested a return to the Treaty while allowing French industry some temporary protection, the French were willing in principle but could not quite agree to anything in practice. The Minister of the Interior Chaptal, to whom Montbret reported, recommended that the English market open itself to French silks and wines on the same basis as port and sherry. The British however, refused to admit French wines because of their agreement with Portugal and French silks because it wanted to shield its own emerging silk industry. Montbret thought the best protection would be to ensure that the value of British imports into France equalled that of French exports to Britain. Chaptal dismissed this as bureaucratic and "absurd" as it would require issuing licences and encourage the emergence of monopolies over foreign trade. Bonaparte wanted an absolute ban on foreign cotton and kept tariffs high. While French exports gradually increased following the peace, British exports dropped by 25 per cent in 1802. If trade was war by other means, it would have certainly seemed to the British that France was winning.

Bonaparte's aspirations for an economically powerful France to rival Britain were also pursued in his colonial projects. The Treaty of Amiens had restored former French colonies, which he was determined to exploit and which the peace, by allowing his Navy access to them, made it possible. He had already sent his brother-in-law Leclerc to restore French authority in San Domingo and despite some initial resistance from Toussaint, this seemed on the verge of being accomplished. His intention was, with the accession of Louisiana from Spain, to make his American and West Indian colonies no longer dependent on U.S. supplies for their own needs. The continuation of slavery in the restored colonies was considered the most efficient economic model, but when in July 1802 Bonaparte ordered Richespanse to restore slavery in Guadeloupe, where it had ceased, news of this found its way to San Domingo, encouraging the blacks to renew their insurrection against the French. By this time, Toussaint had been arrested and conveyed to France, leaving the former slaves to be led by his subordinate, General Dessalines. The French troops, decimated and weakened by yellow fever, failed to stamp out the rebellion. When Leclerc himself died of yellow fever in November 1802 and the bad news reached France in December, a force that was destined for Louisiana was redirected to San Domingo.

Colonial expeditions also allowed Bonaparte to keep his generals and troops busy and hopefully feed the public with news of glorious military victories necessary to sustain his popularity. He realised his hold on power depended on his reputation as a military leader and until his status as a statesman could be secured, he was necessarily obliged to rely on his established credentials for leadership. In June 1802 General Decaen was appointed to command an expedition to the restored Indian colony at Pondicherry. Instructions to General Victor, who was to lead an expedition to Louisiana, were approved by Bonaparte in November.

It was in the Mediterranean that Bonaparte found the means of impressing the French public and all without firing a single shot. The Barbary States in the north coast of Africa, nominally part of the Ottoman Empire, had harboured pirates that had threatened European coasts and ships for many years and were notorious for carrying off Europeans to the slave markets of North Africa. During the negotiations at Amiens, Bonaparte had urged his brother Joseph to persuade the British to join with France in a crusade against this threat. He considered it a great moral issue and letting the Barbary pirates get away with their behaviour for so long shamed the whole of Europe. Such a war would not only have been glorious, but a great act of humanity towards all trading nations. Of course there would also be benefits for nations participating in such a crusade. They would colonise the land, exploiting it to grow sugar, cotton and coffee.[1] The British declined, but Bonaparte did not drop the idea and had plans for an invasion prepared.

In 1802 suitable pretexts for carrying out such a plan arose. A Neapolitan vessel was captured by corsairs, the crew of another boat wrecked off the coast of Africa were kept prisoner, two French ships were stopped and conducted to Algiers and a French officer was mistreated in Tunis by an Algerian official. In July the French questioned the Algerian government on these events. The reply was that France should offer tribute like Spain and the Italian states. In July Bonaparte sent the Dey of Algiers a letter reminding him that he had destroyed the empire of the

[1] Du Casse: Talleyrand to Joseph Bonaparte 18th Feb 1802, Méneval p.162

Mamelukes. Unless French and Italian prisoners were freed and vessels returned and a promise was made to respect French and Italian flags in the future he would send a fleet with troops to invade the North African coast: "God has decided that all those who are unjust towards me shall be punished. I will destroy your city and your port; I will invade your shores myself, if you do not respect France, of which I am chief, and Italy, where I command." To back up the threat, he sent war ships to the area. The Dey released the French and Neapolitan vessels and all his Christian prisoners and promised to respect their flags. The Dey's offer to execute his officials who had abused the French was declined.[1]

Bonaparte's freedom to manoeuvre in his colonies and the Mediterranean ultimately depended on the goodwill of Britain, which was being tested on a regular basis. Through Talleyrand and Otto he complained of the warm reception French Royalty still received at the English court and requested their expulsion. He protested about the émigré and British press, of Peltier and William Cobbett. Hawkesbury told Merry to tell Talleyrand that Britain could only expel the émigrés if they broke English laws or were jeopardising the peace. In response Otto reminded Hawkesbury that Britain could use the Aliens Act to deport non-nationals who were considered a threat to its interests and which it had used to deport Talleyrand during the war. As it could do this, it must also have the power to remove foreigners who were a threat to other nations. Hawkesbury instructed Merry to tell the French that they were not prepared to change the Aliens Act to remove someone who was not a threat to Britain, nor were they prepared to change English law to suppress the newspapers. Freedom of the press was too highly cherished in Britain.

A further strain in Anglo-French relations was the execution of the Amiens Treaty, which was an exasperatingly slow process. The Tsar of Russia would only be a guarantor if the selection of a new Grand Master for the Knights of St John was made according to his procedures as opposed to those outlined in the Treaty. Both Britain and France agreed, but the guarantees took a while to procure. France, Britain and Spain's guarantees were established at the signing of the treaty and Austria accepted in July 1802, but by mid-August, when Britain was supposed to evacuate Malta, both Prussia and Russia had still not given theirs and a new Grand Master had not yet been elected. What seemed to be of more

---

[1] Thiers p.383

concern to the French was the absence of a Neapolitan garrison. On 21 August Otto complained to Hawkesbury that the British Minister in Naples had not authorised the transport of these troops on the grounds that the preliminary conditions for the evacuation of British soldiers had not been satisfied. The Neapolitan troops, Otto reminded the Foreign Secretary, were one of the preliminary conditions. Hawkesbury told Otto that the troops were probably on their way but would instruct them to be sent in any case. What was of more concern to the British was the fact that the French ambassadors in St Petersburg and Berlin had not yet liaised with their British counterparts to formally invite those powers to be guarantors. In September the Pope nominated Ruspoli as the Grand Master, but he seemed in no hurry to accept the post. Meanwhile the strength of the Knights had been considerably weakened by the seizure of its Spanish assets by the King of Spain in April 1802.

The British were also increasingly concerned with events on the continent. In August Spain handed over to France the island of Elba. Piedmont, plagued by bandits and controlled by the military for over a year, was formally annexed by the French in September. French troops still occupied Parma in October while in Germany, Bonaparte's influence was growing.

29. Decline of the Holy Roman Empire

On 16 August 1802, two ambassadors arrived in the Bavarian town of Ratisbon, also known as Regensberg or Radtstadt. They were citizen LaForest from France and Baron de Buhler from Russia, and their joint mission was to present a Franco-Russian plan to the Ratisbon Diet – the legislative assembly of the Holy Roman Empire of the German Nation. This was a loose union of 300 German states that had emerged from medieval times, presided over by an emperor who was elected by the primary body of the Diet known as the Council of Electors. There were only eight Electors, Five of them being the lay rulers of the main German states – Austria, Bavaria, Saxony, Prussia and Hanover. The other three were the archbishops of Mainz, Trier and Cologne. Although in theory they could elect any suitable candidate as emperor, from the mid-15th century the Electors merely confirmed the dynastic succession within the Austrian House of Habsburg. The Diet also comprised two other colleges – a College of Princes consisting of the lay and ecclesiastic princes of Germany, and a less important College of Free Cities.

At the Treaty of Lunéville in 1801 between France and Austria, it had been agreed that the German princes who had lost land on the left bank of the Rhine to Revolutionary France would be compensated with ecclesiastical lands in Germany on the other side. It was also understood that the Regensberg Diet would be responsible for deciding the confiscations and allocations. In October 1801 an eight-member deputation of the Diet was formed for this purpose. Four members were from the College of Electors – Austria, Prussia, Mainz and Saxony. The other four were from the College of Princes and included the representatives from Baden, Bavaria, Württemberg and the Grand Master of the Teutonic Order.

This could never have been a purely German affair as the other powers of Europe could not be disinterested in any re-arrangement at the centre of the continent. The Tsar of Russia's mother was a princess of Württemberg, while his wife was from Baden. George III of England was also the Elector of Hanover. The Prince of Orange and the Dukes of Modena and Tuscany had been promised compensation in the form of German territory for the loss of their Dutch and Italian states. Bonaparte was keen to have the matter settled so that French land on the left bank of the Rhine could no longer be grounds for resentment. The re-arrangement also offered the opportunity of extending French influence further east, inducing many minor German princes to flock to Paris to persuade France to protect their interests from Austrian encroachments.

Bonaparte's strategy to achieve this was explained to Talleyrand in April 1802: "I wish to conduct three negotiations separately: one with Russia [...] to try to discover as much as possible what arrangements will suit her; the second with the court of Berlin, and to agree with this court on the arrangements that relate to it, as well as those of the Prince of Orange, the Elector of Bavaria, and the Elector of Baden; the third with Austria, to agree with that power on arrangements relating to the Grand Duke of Tuscany and to one or, at most, two ecclesiastical electors, and to the Elector of Bavaria." By improving his relations with Prussia and Russia, Austria would become increasingly isolated and less likely to rely on them as allies if it ever tried to reclaim territory lost to France. "In this way, the German Empire will find itself actually divided into two empires" because there would continue to be "various issues between Berlin and Vienna".[1]

The French first sought the agreement of the main German states. In May 1802 France promised to obtain on behalf of Prussia some territory for the Prince of Orange and the bishoprics, abbeys and free cities it coveted for itself in return for their acknowledgement of French acquisitions in Europe and the Prince of Orange's recognition of the Batavian Republic. It also came to a similar agreement with Bavaria.

To keep Russia happy, the French negotiated with the Russian ambassador in Paris, Count Markoff. France promised to back the claims to territory in favour of Baden and Württemberg, but Markoff initially opposed what the French had agreed with Prussia and was inclined to promote Austria's interest. He wrote to Alexander: "In fact Sire, if the plan in question is adopted and executed, Germany will undergo a complete upheaval. The princes who will have gained power through the favour of France will be attached to her forever, and in serving her ambitious views will always think that they are serving their own. The only formidable power, Austria, who could still raise a barrier against the torrent of French ambition, by losing all consideration and all influence, will necessarily lose a great part of her means of sustaining a great struggle

---

[1] Napoleon to Talleyrand 3 April 1802 NBCG 6841 cited in Kagan p.34

already unequal."[1] Alexander replied that he was aware of the issues and did not like the agreement, but it was the only alternative to avoiding involvement in Europe altogether, which was much worse. Without his participation, France would not let Austria have anything.

On 4 June, Markoff eventually accepted Prussia's claims and agreed a definitive plan with Talleyrand, which they intended to present to the Diet at Ratisbon while also offering themselves as mediating powers. Markoff signed this convention on the condition that St Petersburg approved. Hédouville, the French ambassador there, was instructed to tell Russia that France could not wait longer than ten days for a response. If no answer was given, the Russians were to be made to understand that France would offer itself as the sole mediator. However, when the ambassador presented the note later in June, Alexander was visiting King Frederick William of Prussia. The Russian minister asked Hédouville to recall the note, but promised to ask the Tsar to reply as soon as possible on his return. Meanwhile, in Memel, where Frederick was entertaining Alexander, the Prussian monarch received a letter from Bonaparte: "All now depends on the consent of the Emperor of Russia." Although they parted as firm friends, Frederick failed to persuade Alexander to discuss the secularisations. When the Tsar returned to Petersburg he was urged by most of his pro-Austrian cabinet to refuse the French plan, but after receiving letters from Frederick and coming to the conclusion that Austria's demands were unreasonable, he decided to ignore their advice.

The French representative to Ratisbon, LaForest, in conjunction with his Russian counterpart Baron de Buhler, presented a note to the Diet on 18 August, two days after they had arrived. It declared that as the German states had not yet come to an agreement on the reorganisation of Germany, and because the whole of Europe was impatient for the completion of the Treaty of Lunéville regarding this, France and Russia, as disinterested powers, had taken it upon themselves to offer their own plan. The Diet was expected to reach a conclusion within two months. At the same time a note was sent to the Austrians in Vienna, explaining that the delay in the execution of the treaty of Lunéville had obliged the French to devise the plan, which, it was stressed, was not set in stone. This last point was difficult to justify, as Bonaparte had consented to

[1] Markoff to Alexander 23 May/4 June 1802 SIRO vol. 70, doc 169, p.422 cited in Kagan p.35

allow impatient German princes to occupy their allotted territories in advance of any ratification by the Diet, and many of them duly did so.

On the same day, Austrian troops marched into the Bishopric of Passau, a state that it wanted for the Archduke Charles, but which had been promised by France in their plan to Bavaria. The Bishop of Passau, warned that the Bavarians were approaching, had called on the Austrian Emperor for help. The Austrians occupied the city of Passau and its fortresses, declaring that they would remain there until the Diet concluded its deliberations. It would then allow whatever power that became its owner to occupy it. On 22 August, Baron Hügel, the Austrian plenipotentiary at Ratisbon, expressed his Emperor's surprise at the interference of foreign powers in the affairs of the empire and his dissatisfaction with the indemnity allotted to the Grand Duke for his losses in Italy. He therefore claimed in addition ecclesiastical states and cities in Swabia.[1]

Two days later, the eight-member Diet deputation charged with the secularisations presented its initial reaction to the Franco-Russian proposal. Half of them – including inevitably Prussia, Bavaria and Württemberg, were in favour. Baron Albini, representing the archbishopric of Mainz was personally in favour, but was too embarrassed to declare this because Mainz would be one of the few surviving ecclesiastical states. Saxony abstained and the Teutonic Order, whose Grand Master was the Archduke Charles, the Emperor's brother, would only admit the plan as a document to be discussed further. The Austrian deputy, Schraut, complained that for nine months Austria had not received a single reply from France regarding its own proposals for Germany. It had been kept out of the loop of negotiations in Paris and had only known about the proposed mediation the same time as its presentation to the Diet at Ratisbon. Furthermore, the Archduke Ferdinand would not receive indemnities of value promised to him at Lunéville. Austria could not therefore concur in the plan.

In Paris, when Bonaparte heard of the Austrian response he felt obliged to explain his actions. He sent the Diet a note, telling it that Austria's proposals related not to German affairs as a whole, but simply to the extension of Austria at the expense of Bavaria. It was the threatening presentation of these proposals in Munich and the uneasiness the Elector

---

[1] Belsham vol. 8 p.473

of Bavaria expressed to France and Russia that obliged them to act in the interests of the peace of Germany and thereby the whole of Europe.

Bonaparte summoned the Prussian and Bavarian ambassadors and urged them to be firm with Austria. On 5 September they signed a convention with France in which they would agree to unite to secure the indemnities proposed by the French plan if Austria had not evacuated Passau in two months. Bonaparte asked Markoff to send St Petersburg a copy in the hope that the Tsar would join them. By 8 September LaForest had – by threats and the promise of further revenue – induced the representative for the Bishop of Mainz to agree to the French plan, securing a majority of the deputation in its favour. However, Austria still stubbornly refused to give its consent and without Austria's agreement the plan remained nothing more than a piece of paper.[1]

---

[1] Thiers pp.391-417

30 Madame de Staël

Illustration from *The Gallery of Portraits* (Charles Knight, 1836) (Look and Learn Collections)

30. Consolidation

Lucien Bonaparte was at his secret fiancées house, on the Place du Corps Législatif, when his faithful servant Pedro came to tell him that his brother Joseph had arrived at his own residence nearby at the Hotel de Brienne in rue St Dominique. He left his lover and returned home via a secret passage way that connected the two buildings. As he exited the passage, coming out of a fake wall next to a gallery hosting his painting collection, he was noticed by Joseph, who was curious to know what was behind the wall. Lucien was not quite ready to reveal the truth, so he told him he had a little office. The siblings then set off together for Malmaison to meet their brother, the General, as they liked to call him.

When they arrived, Bonaparte's Mameluke servant and bodyguard Roustam showed them to his office, where he was busy writing at the desk, gesturing them to sit down. "Welcome, citizen senators, I am yours," he said, but did not give them his attention immediately, allowing them time to whisper between themselves. When the General rose from his desk they talked mostly of family affairs. After Napoleon asked questions about the theatre and society, he suddenly turned to Joseph and said: "A propos, my dear brother, what has become of your very great and close friend, Madame de Staël? My enemy, they say."[1]

Madame de Staël was the daughter of Louis XVI's finance minister, Necker. She had married a Swedish diplomat posted to Paris, where she attracted enlightened high society to her salons with her conversation and literary reputation. She supported the Revolution, but was obliged to leave France during the Terror, returning in the Directory years. By then, she lived separately from her husband, taking a number of lovers, including Talleyrand and Benjamin Constant, one of Bonaparte's opponents purged from the Tribunate. Fearing a return of the Terror, she, like many other liberal intellectuals, initially welcomed Bonaparte's coup d'état, but was soon disappointed with her new hero. When she had the opportunity to speak to him, she asked him who he thought was the

---

[1] Simonetta pp.120-121, Iung p.214-216

greatest woman in history. The woman who had borne the most children was his reply. In 1801, in her book *On Literature Considered in its relations with Social Institutions*, she suggested that human progress could not be achieved through despotism and deprecated military ambition, declaring its glory as purely frivolous. Military spirit was like religious discipline, both were a barrier to reason and a danger to liberty. She encouraged Constant and others to oppose Bonaparte in the Tribunate and was socially snubbed and temporarily exiled from Paris as a consequence. When Bonaparte purged the Tribunate in January 1802, she described this as skimming off the cream. Despite the growing mutual enmity between her and the First Consul, she continued to meet and correspond with his two brothers.[1]

"My friend, I admit, but my 'close' friend – that's an exaggeration," Joseph replied. "We hardly see each other enough for that to be so; and your enemy, they say, that is a lie."

"Peste! How you do go on! La, la, la, it's a lie? [...] and does Lucien also think she's not my enemy? He should know, as he also associates with Madame de Staël."

Lucien spoke for himself: "I don't know exactly what you mean by 'associate', but the fact is, Citizen Consul, like Joseph, I am honoured by the friendship of this illustrious woman." Lucien added that he would not be her friend if he believed her to be his brother's enemy.

"Very courteous, assuredly. You reduce me to silence. So, nothing more to say?"

Lucien had not finished: "Permit me to add that, if you would only show her a little more goodwill, she would adore instead of simply admire you."

"Ah! That's too much; too much. I don't care for that kind of adoration – she's far too ugly!" The General's mood began to change as they continued to exchange their different views on the famous female writer. Napoleon would not be convinced by his brothers, insisting he knew her too well:

---

[1] Haggard pp.100-108

"Ah! I know her, accustomed to criticising or encouraging the criticism of previous governments. First in the salons of her father, where the trial of Louis XVI was initiated, for you see, it was M. Necker who was the first executioner of that unfortunate king. Then secretly intriguing after Thermidor, then playing her role behind the scenes in the orgies of the Directory, and finally, very recently, bossing the Tribunate, obliging me to purge it of her friends, an act which as you know, she had the impertinence to describe, not as purging, but as 'skimming' the Tribunate."

Joseph and Lucien approved her *bon mot*, prompting their brother to ridicule them for their infatuation with the woman. Joseph reminded Napoleon he had been the first to admire her use of the word.

"Admire!" Napoleon exclaimed, "No, it made me laugh because it annoyed the remaining members of the Tribunate."

"How gracious," said Lucien.

"Yes, see how good I am. Gentlemen, tell that woman that I am neither a Louis XVI [..] nor a Barras. Advise her not to try and bar the road on which it pleases me to go, otherwise, I shall break her, I shall shatter her. I.... But I am silly to get so worked up. Tell her... tell her just to keep quiet; that's the most prudent course."

Lucien insisted on defending her further, praising her conversation, her writing, her metaphysical ideas and her novels.

The General was not persuaded: "Yes, I know, but first, I haven't read a novel in years, and as for her metaphysical works, I must admit to my shame that, leafing through them here and there, I saw nothing motivating me to continue reading them, for the very good reason, alas, that I couldn't understand anything at all."

Lucien replied that she in turn would not be able to solve a problem in trigonometry. Bonaparte was well aware that Lucien was being ironic: "You mean by that I don't understand metaphysics. Well, you are right, as metaphysicians are my pet hate. I categorise all of them under the heading of ideologues, a category that particularly suits them. Seekers of ideas (shallow ideas mostly); well, it is fitting, in applying this word 'ideologue' to them has made them look more ridiculous than I could have expected. The expression has taken hold, I think because it came from me. There is no harm in that. There will be less ideology, that's the right word – 'Ideology', the science of ideas. All in all – and I have thought about it a lot – these poor scholars don't even understand themselves." How could he agree with such men? "Yes, they have the madness to meddle with my government, the chatterboxes. My aversion verges on horror for these ideologues. I don't care who knows."

Now Joseph re-joined the fight: "Then you should not be surprised that they in turn call you an ideophobe." Napoleon was astonished and indignant. "So that's what they call me, you say? I am glad to hear it, the insolents! They will pay for that!" Joseph explained the word was nothing to be angry about and simply expressed his brother's known aversion to ideology: if a seeker of ideas was an ideologue then someone who had a horror of them was an ideophobe. "Enough! Enough!" shouted Napoleon, berating Joseph for behaving as if he was at school, the inevitable effect of his contact with these intellectuals: "Ideophobe! That's nice. Ah! She wants war!"

"The word did not come from Madame de Staël," said Lucien.

"And from whom then?"

"As it displeases you so much, you surely cannot expect me to name its author?" The word might have been technically correct, but Lucien admitted it was a little vicious. Napoleon agreed it was the appropriate word all right and it was for that reason he attributed it to Madame de Staël. Lucien assured him in on his honour the word was not hers. After Joseph confirmed this, Lucien added that de Staël, far from being the author of this unfortunate term, had stated her regret when it was used.

"Ideophobe!" exclaimed Napoleon, likening the word to the blast of cannon in response to his musket fire. "Ideophobe! One cannot govern with such people, especially when among their admirers are my own brothers!" Joseph expressed his surprise that Napoleon was so upset by it. "Ideophobe! That's gracious; why not hydrophobe?" asked the First Consul.

"For the reason it is not the same thing," said Lucien. As the conversation continued to display no signs of lightening up, Lucien was glad to hear voices outside, prompting him to say: "Citizen First Consul, it is mid-day and the other Consuls are arriving". Joseph did not say anything, but his demeanour suggested he too was pleased to conclude their meeting. Napoleon, looking at the clock said: "That's true. Mid-day already. How time passes!" What babblers they were. "Adieu messieurs", he said, encouraging them to leave and asking Lucien to visit more often.[1]

When Bonaparte had first come to power, one of the first acts of his regime had been to repeal the edict of the Directory abolishing the freedom of the press. Very quickly newspapers and periodicals sprang up, some of them critical of Bonaparte, who consequently formed a committee to consider their regulation again. He declared that attacks on the government could not be allowed to continue, and when an objection was raised citing the compatibility of a free press and a harmonious state of affairs in England, he dismissed it, insisting that the circumstances of that country were not comparable. On 17 January 1800 a consular decree suppressed sixty out of seventy-three publications in Paris on the grounds suggested by Fouché that they were instruments of the enemies of the Republic. The surviving papers, including the *Decade Philosophique*, the *Journal de Debats* and the *Gazette de France* were forbidden to be disrespectful towards the government , the sovereignty of the people or the army, while the *Moniteur* became the mouthpiece of the state. By the end of 1800, Paris had no more than eight newspapers with 20,000 subscribers and the *Decade* no longer reported political events. Articles on the army, religion and economy were to be prohibited and headline summaries banned. Departments were restricted to a single newspaper, effectively controlled by the Prefect.[2]

Books remained the only means of voicing opposition in print, but this was not wholly immune to state censorship. Madame de Staël encouraged Camille Jordan to write *Vrai sens du vote national sur le Consulat à vie*, which was published anonymously in July 1802. The author recognised Bonaparte's genius, and consented to the consulship for life, but refused to "bind himself to an unknown successor of Bonaparte, who would lead them into insensate wars and spread the darkness of superstition and despotism over the land [...] Ah! One's blood boils at the horrible thought." Jordan called for the restoration of a free press, universal suffrage and independent law courts. The book was immediately impounded, but was clandestinely reprinted and distributed. Then in

---

[1] Iung vol. 2 pp.233-246 (author's translation)

[2] Villefosse p.97

August Madame de Staël's father brought out *Dernières vues de politique et de finance de M Necker*. Necker accepted Bonaparte was indispensable to France, but criticised the consular constitution as un-republican and asked for one that met the demands of both order and liberty. Necker also objected to the idea of a Bonaparte dynasty. Necker sent a copy to Lebrun who presented it to the First Consul, whose response was: "Necker's daughter will never return to Paris."[1]

On 3 August, while Bonaparte was holding a reception at the Tuileries for foreign ambassadors, a deputation from the Senate presented him with results of the plebiscite on his consulship for life. Five days earlier, they had received the registers of votes from the entire country. "The People of France name, and the Senate proclaims Napoleon Bonaparte Consul for Life." Out of an assumed electorate of five million, 3,653,600 had voted yes. Only 8,272 had voted No, suggesting over a million abstentions, but this was considerably less than the 80 per cent abstention rate of half of France in the 1800 plebiscite. Bonaparte declared that since they had placed their confidence in him in perpetuity, he accepted and pledged himself to uphold the laws of the country. This act would secure the equality, liberty and prosperity of France; its citizens, the best of all citizens, dedicated to their country, would become the happiest of all citizens, and their happiness would contribute to the happiness of all Europe.[2]

Among those voting "Non" were Carnot, Henri Grégoire, General Masséna, Fouché and Lafayette. Lafayette had been grateful to Bonaparte for securing his release from Austrian custody as a preliminary to the Campo-Formio deal, but was suspicious of Bonaparte's ambitions early on. After the Peace of Amiens, when Bonaparte offered him a seat in the Senate, he declined, inviting Bonaparte's reproach. Lafayette justified his action: "I live a retired life in the country and avoid all opportunities of speaking publicly, but if ever someone asks me if your regime conforms with my ideas of freedom, I must answer 'No'; after all, General, I want to be prudent but I don't want to be a renegade." When he voted against life consulship, Lafayette felt obliged to deliver a note in person to Bonaparte explaining his decision: "the 18 Brumaire saved France [...] Since then we have seen the consular regime re-establish a

---

[1] Villefosse pp.165-166

[2] Fauriel pp.39-40, Villefosse p.63, Lyons, p.112-113

dictatorship, which under the auspices of your genius has succeeded in many great things, but none so great as the restoration of liberty. [...] The people of France know their rights too well to forget them forever."[1]

Bonaparte, his consular power now extended temporally, lost no time in extending it over the other state institutions. On 4 August a new constitution was approved by the Council of State. The First Consul could now nominate his successor and the Senate was obliged to accept at least one of three candidates he chose. He would now have the authority to makes treaties, grant pardons and alone nominate candidates to the Senate and the Court of Appeal. He could now, though the Senate, define or interpret the constitution, suspend it, dissolve the Tribunate and Legislative bodies and annul court decisions. The List of Notables, to which all key state offices had to belong, was replaced by a new electoral college whose candidates would be nominated by local assemblies and restricted to the 600 most highly taxed citizens in the area. The Tribunate, its debates no longer held in public and already purged of it most difficult members, was now reduced to fifty. The new constitution was effected by a Senatus Consultum despite the protests of Senators Garat, Lanjuinais and Lambrecht and the abstentions of Sieyes, Volney, Cabanis and Destutt de Tracy.[2]

Bonaparte also increased his personal power by contriving to weaken that of his rivals and enemies. Despite his incarceration in the Temple prison, General Simon continued to refuse to implicate anyone else higher up than himself. Without any evidence the prime suspects, Moreau and Bernadotte, despite their connections with the imprisoned officers and the rumours of their plotting, were not arrested. Even if there were evidence, it would have been difficult for Bonaparte to put either of these Generals on trial, popular as they were with the troops. Instead, the plot was hushed up, as Bonaparte had no wish to publicise his unpopularity with a significant portion of the army. He could not contain his anger however and was determined to have it out with them one way or another.

Bonaparte decided to force a public confrontation with Bernadotte and chose the day of a grand levee at the Tuileries to which

---

[1] Villefosse p.163

[2] Lefebvre pp.147-148, Villefosse pp.163-164

the General was expected. On that day, his secretary Bourrienne noticed the First Consul was in a foul mood and asked him if anything was wrong. "I have resolved to have a scene with Bernadotte today," replied Bonaparte, "It is time there should be an end of this." Bourrienne was alarmed and when he found the opportunity to go to the room before the First Consul entered, he found Bernadotte by a window looking onto the Carousel. "General, for heaven's sake, retire! – I have good reasons for advising it." Bernadotte, seeing how anxious Bourrienne was, consented and managed to leave before Bonaparte arrived.

Bernadotte retired to Plombières on the grounds of ill-health, where he urged Bonaparte's aide-de-camp, Colonel Rapp, to talk to the First Consul on his behalf. Rapp promised he would and when he returned to Paris, waited for an opportunity to do so. It arose on the day he was accompanying the First Consul to a party given in his honour by his brother-in-law General Murat. Bonaparte was in a good mood. Rapp confided his intention to a general also making the trip, who tried to dissuade him, mentioning that he had just seen Madame Julie, wife of Joseph Bonaparte and sister of Bernadotte's wife, come out of a meeting in tears after trying the same thing. Rapp refused to be deterred and approached Bonaparte who was mounted and ready to set off. Rapp said that he had seen Bernadotte at Plombières and related how dejected and mortified he was by his disgrace. He had protested that he had never failed in his love and devotion to the First Consul. "Do not speak of him; he deserves to be shot," replied Bonaparte, just before he galloped off.[1]

Meanwhile Moreau's movements were closely watched by Fouché's police, especially his interactions with opposition intellectuals such as Danou. After a hinted warning from Fouché, meetings at Danou's house were transferred to Destut's residence at Auteuil, and to the salons of Mesdames Condorcet and de Staël. Moreau did not publicly attack Bonaparte, but he was indiscreet in expressing his contempt in private gatherings inevitably infested with police spies. When he flippantly described the placard plot as nothing but a conspiracy of butter-crocks, Bonaparte was incensed: "There must be an end of this! It is not right that France should suffer, thus torn between two men! Were I in Moreau's position, and he in mine, I would be his first aide-de-camp [...] If he thinks himself capable of governing France, very well, be it so! Let him be in the Bois de Boulogne tomorrow morning at four o'clock. His sabre and mine

---

[1] Rapp p.18

shall decide it: I shall expect him!" He charged Fouché with the task of conveying the challenge to Moreau. Fouché summoned Moreau to the Ministry of Police, where he advised the General, who had recently failed to attend public levees, to appear at the next one to signal his private submission without the loss of his honour. A police bulletin of October 8 reported Moreau's presence at the reception on that day.

Colonel Pinoteau and Chausseblanche the printer joined Captain Rapatel and General Simon at the Temple prison. All were eventually to be released, although some after many months of confinement on the isle of Oléron. General Simon was about to be shipped to Guiana when he was freed and re-instated on half-pay. Bertrand was condemned to transportation. In August 1802 he was one of thirteen individuals listed to be embarked by order of Bonaparte. However, no Bertrand was mentioned as disembarking in Guiana.

Bonaparte often tolerated frank opinion from others within the state as long as they did not oppose him publicly or clandestinely. His Minister of Police Fouché had been against the Concordat, believing government should merely allow freedom of worship. He suspected Bonaparte was only interested in religion as a means of making himself emperor. As well as objecting to the consulship for life, Fouché told the First Consul that by the recent constitutional change he had just declared himself the head of a life monarchy whose only foundation was his victories and his sword. When on 16 August Bonaparte proceeded in state to preside over an assembly of the Senate at the Luxembourg Palace, the crowds lining the streets from the Tuileries were quieter than previous occasions. In conversation with the First Consul shortly after, Fouché suggested that this silence was a consequence of Parisians suspecting the loss of their liberty and the consolidation of Bonaparte's absolute power. Bonaparte protested that he would not have been able to govern for six weeks during the peace if he had only the image of authority. Fouché dared to advise that he just had to be paternal, affable, strong and fair to regain what he thought he had lost by the peace. Bonaparte observed that public opinion was too capricious and ended their dialogue by turning his back on his minister.

About a month later Bonaparte summoned Fouché, thanking him for his service, promising it would be well rewarded: "It is with regret that I part with a man of your merit," he said, but insisted that it had become indispensable to prove to Europe that he ran France on a peaceful footing and that his power rested on the love rather than the fear of Frenchmen. He was therefore merging the functions of the Ministry of Police with

those of the Ministry of Justice and considered it unfair to expect Fouché
to work under another minister. Although Bonaparte told him not to
listen to gossip suggesting other reasons for his dismissal, Fouché was
sure that this development was the work of his enemies. He believed that
Joseph and Lucien had advised their brother to disband the Ministry of
Police, arguing that it had been originally set up by the Jacobins to counter
royalist conspiracies which were no longer a threat, while Jacobins still
were. As long as the Ministry remained, Jacobins would have some
protection. Fouché thanked Bonaparte, but told him his dismissal came as
no surprise. The next day he submitted to his former master his parting
thoughts on the present state of affairs: it was not a good time to disband
his ministry, as nothing was less certain than the peace.[1]

By September 1802 Bonaparte began to use the former royal
Palace of St Cloud as an official residence. St Cloud was about five miles
out of Paris, overlooking the Seine and had been refurbished with new
fountains, waterfalls and frescoes at considerable public expense. He had
installed himself in a large office with floor-to-ceiling bookshelves and a
desk made to his own design. As in his Tuileries office, there was a green
taffeta settee. In an adjoining drawing room, where he would hold
meetings with Talleyrand, was a portrait of Charles XII, the Swedish King
defeated by the Russian winter, to be replaced by the more successful
Swedish King, Gustaphus Adolphus. In his office, on the mantelpiece,
were busts of the Carthaginian General Hannibal and his nemesis the
Roman General Scipio.[2]

---

[1] Fouché pp.207-250

[2] Méneval p.174

31 General Bernadotte

Illustration from Cassell's *History of England* (special edition, A W Cowan, c 1890) (Look and Learn Collections)

PART III: RUPTURE

31. The Swiss Crisis

On 28 September 1802, Bonaparte instructed General Berthier, the Minister of War, to send orders to General Ney go at once to Geneva, where he was to take command of French forces on the borders of Switzerland. His mission was to play the role of mediator in a civil war that was erupting again amongst the Swiss and, if it became unavoidable, use all necessary force to restore order. To support this contingency Bonaparte ordered the immediate mobilisation of divisions nearest the Swiss frontiers.[1]

In 1798 Switzerland had been a confederation of independent feudal cantons run mostly by oligarchies of aristocrats until a revolution in that year established a centralised state, the Helvetic Republic, with French support. The new order was resisted, notably by Alois Reding from the canton of Schweitz. Despite the help of Austrian and Russian troops, English spies and money, uprisings were suppressed by the French, who annexed Geneva, occupied Switzerland and obliged the Swiss to decide on a new constitution. A Diet was assembled in Berne in September 1801, which created a provisional government of a senate and a ruling executive council headed by Reding, who wanted the return of cantonal sovereignty. He was opposed by unitaires, such as Dolder, who preferred a more centralised state. When Reding was obliged by France to admit unitaires to the provisional government, he was deposed by them in April 1802 and shortly after they drafted and imposed a unitarian constitution.

As Switzerland now seemed to be in friendly hands, and to comply with the Treaty of Lunéville, on 12 July Dolder was informed that French troops would be withdrawn. The Swiss government, not feeling entirely secure in its authority, tried to persuade the French to postpone their exit. A note from Talleyrand insisted the withdrawal would go ahead on 20 July. Once the French troops left, the central Swiss cantons of Uri, Schweitz and Unterwalden rejected the new constitution and proposed to cede from the Helvetic Republic. They sent representatives to the French

---

[1] NBCG III 7188 p.1110, 7193 p.1114

ambassador in Berne to communicate this, but he refused to recognise them. The Helvetic government announced its determination to impose the new constitution throughout Switzerland, declaring the regional assemblies as illegal. The rebel cantons prepared for war, declared their right to self-legislation and encouraged others to do the same.

As more cantons rebelled, the exchange of words turned into that of blows in August. Peasants, often armed only with Stäckli (wooden clubs), confronted poorly motivated and badly equipped government troops. In September Zurich closed its gates to state forces, which then bombarded the city. Rebels expelled republican troops from Baden and marched on Berne. On 18 September the government was obliged to evacuate the capital and retreat to Lausanne near the border with France. By the 20th, all German-speaking cantons had ceded from the Republic and all rebel regions were invited to send deputies to the Diet in Schweitz which met on the 27th, declaring Reding as president of a new federation of independent Swiss states.

The republican government in Lausanne asked the French to intervene, while the new federation sent its own envoys to Paris in the hope of persuading Bonaparte to leave Switzerland alone. Bonaparte refused to see the latter, but assured the former he would not "be neutral and inactive". He would not leave Switzerland in the hands of British and Bourbon mercenaries: "They speak to me of the will of the Swiss people. I cannot see it in the will of 200 aristocratic families." He could not believe that they wished to be under such a yoke. In any case, his main priority was France, so he would declare himself as mediator and send 30,000 French troops to the frontier. If he could not secure an agreement he would annex French-speaking Switzerland and leave the rest to their 14th century institutions and themselves: "either Switzerland the friend of France, or no Switzerland at all."

In Geneva, General Ney considered the military situation. Helvetian troops, threatened in their rear, had retreated from Zurich and been beaten at Morat. The rebels now controlled Zurich, Berne, Baden and Soleure. Their Diet at Schweitz, by promises of good pay, raised an army of over 7,000 men, including at least a thousand veterans. They were well supplied with arms, ammunition and artillery from the arsenals of the captured towns. The French diplomat Verninac provided Ney with an assessment of the rebel leaders, describing Reding as talented, ambitious, obstinate and determined: "It is generally believed that it was he who ordered the massacre of a detachment of French troops, sent in the year VII to Schweitz to restore public tranquillity." What the insurgents lacked was skilled artillery personnel and cavalry. They only had a handful of Helvetian hussars and a few companies of recently levied inexperienced dragoons. Most of these troops were concentrated between Moudon and Payern. There was also a corps attacking Friburg led by Auf-der-Maur, a relation of Reding who, according to Verninac was impetuous, obstinate and courageous, but "deficient in talent". Against the enemy, Ney had at his immediate command only 400 men of the 2nd Light Infantry. With these he marched towards Versoix, sending orders to his reinforcements to hasten to Locarno, Huningen and Besançon.[1]

Bonaparte instructed Talleyrand to tell the rebel representatives from Berne to leave Paris in twelve hours. On 30 September at St Cloud he wrote a letter to the people of Switzerland: "You have been disputing these three years without coming to any understanding. If you are left longer to yourselves you will kill one another for three years more, without coming to any better understanding than before. It is true that I had determined not to interfere in any respect in your affairs. But I neither can, nor ought not to remain insensible of the evils to which you expose yourselves. I retract my determination. I will be the mediator of your differences; but my mediation will be efficacious, such as befits the great nation in whose name I speak." He demanded the cessation of the activities of the rebel government and the dispersal of its armed units. The Swiss senate of the republic should assemble at Berne and send three delegates to Paris which could be joined by deputies from each canton. "On my part, I have a right to expect that no city, no community, no body, will do anything contrary to the dispositions which I make known to you." He gave the letter to Colonel Rapp who was to deliver it to the Swiss and then co-ordinate the movement of French troops on the Swiss border under General Ney.

Rapp arrived in Lausanne just as the Helvetian troops defeated at Morat were taking refuge there. Soon after, he met with a delegation of rebel officers and a representative of their Diet, showing them Bonaparte's proclamation. When the deputy attempted to make demands, insisting that leaders of the insurgents retain their positions, Rapp lost his patience and told him he had only come to get their acceptance, not to negotiate with them. The rebel officers acknowledged that Rapp had no power to modify Bonaparte's demands and that they could only accept or reject them, while the agent of the Diet remarked that such harshness

---

[1] Ney pp.67-83

would drive the Swiss to extreme acts of desperation. "I believe in the marvels you announce", Rapp replied, "You will no doubt fight and die like brave men; but Ney has put his troops in motion. One of his divisions is assembling at Pontarlier, another at Huningen, a third is advancing by Bellinzona, and a fourth is about to debouch from Valais. If these troops advance a single step, and push on towards Aarburg, Estevayer, Villeneuve, or Locarno, you will be annihilated at a single blow; and in the glen, without a second outlet, in which you have imprudently placed yourselves, you will not have even the satisfaction of a glorious death. I offer this to your consideration." The meeting ended with the rebel General Bachman agreeing to a ceasefire and the representative conceding to the dissolution of the Diet. Ney halted his march, but kept his troops ready to move at a moment's notice.[1]

However, the Diet remained assembled and when Rapp summoned its commissioners in Berne to demand its immediate dissolution, he was told they could not do so unless authorised by the Diet itself. On 21 October the Diet declared to him their position: "As deputies we cannot take it upon ourselves to dissolve our own body." They had a duty to their constituents to insist on their right (inherited from their forefathers) to govern their country according to their wishes and bequeath this right to their descendants. They had only taken up arms to defend themselves against the Helvetic Republic but never had any intention to "oppose the armed forces of the French Government."[2]

In the meantime the Swiss rebels looked around for support from other European courts. Only Britain seemed a realistic possibility. On 10 October Hawkesbury told Otto that His Majesty "sees the late exertions of the Swiss Cantons [...] as the lawful efforts of a brave and generous people to recover their ancient laws and government [...] which experience has demonstrated not only to be favourable to the maintenance of their domestic happiness, but to be perfectly consistent with the tranquillity and security of other powers."[3] Hawkesbury sent Francis Moore to Switzerland to tell the rebels that the English government wished them well and had protested to France. Moore was to find out what the

---

[1] Ney pp.83-92

[2] Zschokke pp.353-355

[3] PRDF pp.63-64

314

insurgents intended to do, but not to advise them to resist. However, if they did fight and the French invaded, they were prepared to send money.[1]

The British protest irritated Bonaparte. Talleyrand wrote to Otto, instructing him to tell the British government that the First Consuls' "resolution is irrecoverable. He will not deliver the Alps to 1,500 mercenaries in the pay of England. He will not have Switzerland converted into another Jersey. The First Consul has no desire for war, because he believes that the French people will find in the extension of their commerce as much advantage as in the extension of their territory. But no consideration shall arrest it if the honour or the interests of the Republic demand that he shall take up arms. You will not speak of War, but you will not permit that it shall be spoken of to you. The least menace, however indirect it may be, must be taken with the greatest haughtiness." Otto was to stress the futility of war because no side could expect to gain any advantage. If England blockaded French ports it would find itself blockaded in turn. "The coasts of Hanover, Holland, Portugal, Italy as far as Tarentum, will be occupied by our troops." France would be obliged to annex Holland, Switzerland and northern Italy creating a new "empire of the Gauls, with which Europe will never cease to be affrighted." England would be forced to "live in the fear of an invasion, always possible, and very nearly certain to be accomplished! Can England support a continental war? But where shall she find allies?" Would it be Prussia or Bavaria, who owed to France their recent acquisitions in Germany? "It is not surely in Austria, already worn out by having volunteered to serve the cause of British policy. In any case, if the war on the continent be renewed, it will be England that will have obliged us to conquer Europe. The First Consul is but thirty-three, he has not yet destroyed any states but those of the second order. Who knows what he may be made to do in time, if he is forced, to change anew the face of Europe, and resuscitate the empire of the west!"[2]

Hawkesbury wanted assurances from France that the Swiss deputies in Paris were not going to imitate the Italian representatives at Lyon earlier in the year when they elected Bonaparte president. The Swiss must be given a wise constitution that did not favour one party over the

---

[1] PRDF pp.65-68

[2] Talleyrand to Otto 23rd October 1802. Cited in Thiers p.439

other. At a meeting with Hawkesbury, Otto reminded him of British obligations of the peace with the phrase "all the Treaty of Amiens; nothing but the Treaty of Amiens". Hawkesbury replied with his own mantra: "the state of the continent at the epoch of the Treaty of Amiens, nothing but that state." Addington also met with Otto, insisting it was his sincere desire to conserve and consolidate the peace by all the means within his power. He added that he had no problem with Bonaparte's increase in authority inside France and would even welcome a hereditary system of government. However, he felt obliged to stress that any actions that tended to augment his power outside of France could not fail to draw the attention of the British government.[1]

When Bonaparte heard of Hawkesbury's response he replied sarcastically through Talleyrand: "France is ready to accept the conditions proposed by Lord Hawkesbury. At the time of the signature of the Treaty of Amiens, France had 10,000 men in Piedmont, 40,000 in Italy and 12,000 in Holland – is it desired that all these shall be placed upon the same footing again?" England lost the right to interfere in the Kingdom of Etruria and the Italian and Ligurian Republics when she refused to recognise them at Amiens:

"She knew of the presidency conferred by the Italian Republic upon the First Consul; she was well aware of the design to unite Piedmont to France, seeing that it had been refused when an indemnity was demanded for the King of Sardinia, and in front of all she signed the Treaty of Amiens! Of what then does England complain? She stipulated one single thing, the evacuation of Tarentum in three months, and Tarentum was evacuated in two. Then in regard to Switzerland, it was known that France had laboured to constitute the government there, and was it to be imagined by any one that France would suffer a counter-revolution to be effected in that country? But in any case, even under the view of strict right, what is there to object to it? The Helvetian government has claimed the mediation of France. The little cantons had also claimed the mediation, by demanding, under the auspices of the First consul, the establishment of their relations with the central authority. The citizens of all the parties, even those of the oligarchic party [...] are in Paris conferring with the First Consul. Are the affairs of Germany new to England? Are they not the literal execution of the Treaty of Lunéville, well

---

[1] Talleyrand to Bonaparte 3rd Nov 1802, summary of Otto's despatches from London. Bertrand, p.22

known to the world, having been published before the treaty of Amiens? Wherefore has England signed the arrangements adopted in regard to Germany, if she thought it was a wrong step to secularise that country? Why did the King of Hanover, who is also the King of England – why did he approve of the Germanic negotiations, by accepting the bishopric of Osnabruck?"

Bonaparte asked: why would Hanover have done so well out of the secularisation if France had not considered the interests of England? The British Cabinet had not involved itself in the affairs of the continent for the last six months. Why was it doing so now? How could England be more able to judge the interests of the continent than Prussia, Austria and Russia?

"It is true," continued Bonaparte, "that in the great Germanic negotiations, the name of the King of England has not appeared. There is no question about that, and it may perhaps mortify his people, who desire to hold, and who have a right to hold, a great place in Europe. But whose fault was it, if not that of England herself? The First Consul desired nothing better than that friendship and confidence be exhibited, to resolve in common with England the great questions that he had settled in unison with Russia; still for friendship and confidence shown there must be some return. But he finds shouted in England only cries of hatred towards France. They say that the English constitution is the reason why things are so. So be it; but that constitution does not command that there be suffered to live in London French pamphleteers, the inventors of the infernal machine, or that the reception and treatment of the Bourbon princes should be with all the honours due to the sovereignty of the members of that house. When England shall show better feelings towards the First Consul, he will be brought to exhibit feelings also, and to divide with England that European influence which he has hitherto partaken with Russia."[1]

The British Cabinet decided to immediately suspend the execution of its treaty obligations. On 17 October Lord Hobart sent instructions to the British commanders in the Cape, Malta and India to halt the process of restoring those acquisitions. At the same time they prepared for the possibility of war. Addington declared: "I consider war as a dreadful evil. But dreadful as is that evil, I shall never hesitate between

---

[1] Cited in Thiers pp.440-441

the alternative of the sacrifice of our honour and war."[1] Lord Hobart ordered the Duke of York to prepare for a French invasion and suggested that the British should join any European state that declared war on France.

In Switzerland, Ney had received further directions from Paris. A dispatch from Talleyrand dated 18 October informed him he had been appointed minister plenipotentiary to the Helvetic Republic by the First Consul: "You will therefore proceed to Berne where you will receive further instructions he has directed me to send you, and you will there fulfil the duties of your mission." Talleyrand was under the impression that Bonaparte's proclamation had calmed things down and Ney was to ensure the Swiss continued to heed his advice. The key objectives were to secure the authority of the Senate in Berne, disperse rebel troops and arrange for the sending of delegates to Paris to agree to a final Swiss constitution. Ney should use his influence to advise on the choice of delegates whose key qualification should be prudence. Ideal candidates were to be among the most reluctant to join the insurrection, the most alarmed at the uprising and the most keen to adopt France's mediation. Talleyrand also elaborated on the wider concerns of the Swiss crisis: "The foreign powers are no longer enemies of France; but the present state of peace cannot destroy envy: and all have not, like France, a wish that Switzerland should enjoy tranquillity. It is the policy of some to consider the agitation of Helvetia a means of giving uneasiness to France and the neighbouring states; and this agitation offers, perhaps, to some men hostile to the peace of Europe, a prospect more or less remote of political dissensions, the result of which might be a renewal of war. Thus, the tranquillity of Helvetia is an advantage common to the whole of Europe; and its prudent and calm organisation under the safeguard of France is connected with the most important interests of the general peace; consequently, the accomplishments of this organization appertains to the duty of the government of the Republic, and forms one of its paramount interests." Any Swiss state that was the friend of France would receive the First Consul's approbation "provided it accorded with the feelings of the majority of the Helvetian people". Ney was also to discourage any idea that Bonaparte wanted the presidency of the Republic, "which is as far from the anticipation of the First Consul, as contrary to his firm

---

[1] Parliamentary History 36:986 cited in Fedorak p.116

determination". Finally, as a last piece of advice, Ney was to avoid behaving too martially with the Swiss.[1]

The canton of Soleure had accepted French mediation and although Friburg had been persuaded to surrender to rebel forces, when they left, the city re-joined the Republican side. The Senate and Dolder had returned to Berne, but much of Switzerland was still in arms, the ceasefire Rapp had brokered had broken down and the confidence of the recently restored Helvetian government was undermined while the rebels remained a threat. Near Moudon on the road to Berne, Ney learned of the Diet's insistence to remain assembled. He sent them his own message: disperse or suffer the consequences. Encouraged by Reding and his soldiers, the Diet remained defiant. Europe would consider it dishonourable if they dissolved themselves rather than oblige the French to do so by force. Ney realised that the Diet had no stomach for a fight and just wanted to avoid losing face. He confided his determination to avoid bloodshed to General Seras. If the French simply made a strong show of force, Swiss resistance would crumble.

In the next few days, Seras took Lucerne, Zug and Sarnen and headed for Zurich with seven battalions of infantry, the third chasseurs and a company of light artillery. Enemy forces retreated ahead of him, first from the river Aar, then from the river Limath until they were driven back to Zurich. When a rebel colonel protested against French intervention to Seras under a flag of truce, he was told to shut up and the French General resumed his advance on the city, his military bands playing victory marches. The citizens of Zurich, after a brief moment of panic, welcomed the French with cries of "Long live the First Consul! Vive la France!" releasing republican prisoners. When the residents were told that the French only wanted to restore peace and secure their liberties and independence, soldiers and peasants laid down their arms and returned to their homes, giving up to the French large stores of ammunition, many muskets and forty pieces of artillery. When Seras then marched on Schweitz, the rebel leaders fled and the Diet disbanded, but not before issuing one last indignant declaration: "The members of the Diet return their powers to the hands of their constituents, having been impeded in their proceedings by a foreign armed force, and by the influence of extraordinary circumstances; they do not renounce the rights guaranteed to the different cantons by the Treaty of Lunéville, of giving to

---

[1] Ney pp.92-100

Switzerland a suitable constitution."[1] By the time Francis Moore reached Switzerland it was all over and shortly after Reding was captured and imprisoned.

The entry of French troops into Switzerland alarmed the British even further. Hawkesbury confided to his father: "I am inclined to think there will be war [...] I did not think it probable that Bonaparte would have ventured to march an army into Switzerland and in that case it might not have been difficult to have come to some compromise. But this circumstance attended with the defiance which he had given us not to interfere in any continental concerns renders any accommodation extremely difficult, if not impossible."[2] Addington, who was becoming "extremely warlike", had moved with his family into the White Lodge in Richmond Park, a residence provided by a grateful King George. On Sunday 24 October, Pitt dined and slept there on his way to Bath, and strongly advised him to continue withholding the restitutions required by the Amiens Treaty. A few days after Pitt left, Addington began to adopt a more cautious approach. Asking his brother Hiley to consult with Pitt in Bath he said: "We must however take care, not only to be right, but very right."[3] Addington decided that they should take no military action without the help of other continental powers. It was important that they did not appear to act rashly. The Cabinet agreed, but thought His Majesty should continue to retain the securities he still possessed while the threat of French encroachment persisted. It also declared – in a Cabinet memorandum of 6 November – that it was His Majesty's particular "determination, in conformity to the wishes of the inhabitants, to appropriate the island of Malta as part of his dominions".[4]

In Bath, Pitt was still strongly advocating the policy of withholding restitutions during Hiley's visit. By 11 November, however, he had also changed his mind. To Addington he wrote that because there was very little prospect of support for Switzerland from other continental powers, he doubted very much "the prudence, though not at all the

---

[1] Zschokke p.358, Ney pp.100-126

[2] Hawkesbury to Lord Liverpool 5th Nov 1802. cited in Fedorak p.117

[3] Addington to Hiley 4th Nov 1802 cited in Fedorak p.118

[4] Cabinet Memorandum 6th Nov 1802 Cited in Fedorak p.120

injustice, of risking at all hazards the determination of withholding such of the restitutions as have not yet taken place." Instead they would have to content themselves "with a state of very increased and constant preparation, both naval and military." On 16 November Lord Hobart sent instructions to resume the restitution of the Cape to the Dutch. Malta, however, was still to be retained as a counterpoise to French encroachments.

RIGHT HON. GEORGE CANNING. FROM AN AUTHENTIC PORTRAIT.

32 George Canning

Illustration from John Cassell's *Illustrated History of England* (W Kent, 1857/1858) (Look and Learn Collection)

32. Two Plots

Walmer Castle, a Tudor fortress on the Kent south coast, was the official residence of the Lord Warden of the Cinque Ports. This was a post of medieval origins, created to oversee the defences of five ports on the same stretch of coast. The Castle was built by Henry VIII as one of a series of fortifications to fend off invasions from France or Spain. As the defence of Britain came to depend more on the Royal Navy, the significance of the ports and the importance of the Warden diminished over time. By the 18th century the office had become a sinecure, an honorary position awarded by the King as a reward for faithful service, while the castle became a home. In 1792 the King appointed Pitt as the Lord Warden and it was Walmer Castle that Pitt made his main residence outside the parliamentary season after leaving office in 1801. Here he spent his leisure time riding, sailing and partridge shooting, but also engaged in more productive activities. He rented an adjoining forty acres and acquired a farm, created walks to the shore, planted trees and made modification to the castle. Additional bedrooms were added after connecting the Gunners' Lodgings in one of the turrets to the central keep. Visitors, such as his niece Lady Hester Stanhope and George Canning were entertained in small dining and reception rooms alongside an attractive terrace.[1]

When in October 1802 Canning paid a visit to Walmer, Pitt told his guest that he had resigned not over the Catholic Question, but over the manner in which it had been opposed. He nevertheless felt he could not abandon his duty entirely at a time of war and therefore pledged his personal advice and support to the new government. This pledge he considered was solemn and binding and could only be broken by Mr Addington's express consent. Pitt admitted to Canning that in private he had been upset with the hasty and conceding way peace had been made. He had supported it publicly because he thought as long as Britain did not disarm, Bonaparte would have been discouraged to make any future encroachments on Europe. Canning asked him: did he now think he was wrong to have thought this about Bonaparte and to have trusted

---

[1] Hague p.492, Stanhope pp. 391-394

Addington's government to stand up to him? Pitt answered in the affirmative. Canning posed him another question: did he think that the consequences of Addington's recent policies left Britain with the dilemma of two choices: war or humiliation? Britain either had to fight – or continue to suffer Bonaparte's insults, encouraging him eventually to think they were so weak as to be easily crushed by him? Pitt again answered in the affirmative. Did he therefore think, persisted Canning, that the current policies of the government, if not changed, would leave Britain in a perilous situation? Once more, the former prime minister said "Yes". Canning continued: did Pitt think that the current government had the ability to affect this change to induce Bonaparte to change his plans? No. If Bonaparte was to attack Britain, did Pitt think there should be a change of Minister? Yes. "Is not then the time arrived," said Canning, "when you [...] are called upon [...] by the strongest and most paramount of duties, to come forward and resume your position?"

"I do not deny it," replied Pitt, "I will not affect a childish modesty, but recollect what I have just said – I stand pledged. I make no scruple of owning that I am ambitious, but my ambition is character, not office."

"You nevertheless admit, that at this moment it is a duty for you to resume office?"

"I do."

"And that you are withheld from performing it, solely from the solemn engagements you say you have contracted."

"Yes."

"But you said these engagements could be dissolved, if Mr Addington chose it?"

"Most certainly."

"Does it not then follow that it is also a duty in you to apply to Mr Addington to release you from them?"

"I cannot bring myself to do it." Pitt argued it would look like he was intriguing for personal power. Canning then proposed that if the King or Parliament asked him, would he feel free from this engagement?

Pitt said either of these options would do so as long as he did not approach Addington directly, but he needed assurance of support from Parliament. Grenville may still have been his friend, but Pitt felt that their political differences had widened. Before Canning left, he told Pitt to expect a visit from Grenville, who, when he duly turned up and found that he agreed with Pitt on the main issues, assured him of his and his brother's support.[1]

****

On the evening of 16 November, Thomas Blades, a private soldier in the First Regiment of Foot Guards, walked into the tap room of the Oakley Arms public house in Lambeth and ordered a pint of beer and a pipe of tobacco. He asked the landlord if he knew a man called Broughton. The landlord told an assistant to go up and tell Tom that someone wanted him downstairs. Moments later, Broughton came down, took Blade's pint and led him upstairs, saying to him, "the Colonel is here." After ascending the stairs to the first floor they arrived in a club room with a fireplace and occupied by a group of about thirty men, mostly workers and some off-duty soldiers. Broughton pointed to a man carrying a green silk umbrella with a yellow handle, wearing clothes that marked him out from the rest of the crowd as a gentleman. This was Colonel Despard. "He is a very fine man," said Broughton. Despard presented Blades with rum and water. The men split into two groups. Those that were to do business were to sit by the fire; those that had only come to show their goodwill were to sit at the other end of the room. Blades stayed to hear some of the conversation, but left early.

About 9 p.m. the meeting was interrupted as a group of men burst through the door. One of them walked towards the fireplace and told everyone present not to be alarmed and that they had a search warrant. The intruders were three Southwark constables and a body of Bow Street officers. When some of the men stood up, the officer in charge asked everyone to remain seated and then ordered his men to start

---

[1] Malmesbury pp.75-80

searching them. A document was found on one man. Colonel Despard refused to be examined and demanded to know what authority they had. The officer replied that their search warrant was signed by two magistrates and told one of his men to get it. The warrant was produced and waved in Despard's face. He asked that they read it to him, but was told that was unnecessary. They proceeded to search him, making him angry. He demanded to know what he was being detained for and then shouted "One and all, follow me," as he walked towards the door. His exit was blocked by other officers. When Despard was finally searched, they found nothing of any interest. He and the others were eventually herded downstairs and sent into custody.

The next day Despard was interrogated by Sir Richard Ford the chief magistrate before being transported in chains to Whitehall, where he was examined for several hours by the Privy Council. They continued for six hours the following day after which he was admitted to Newgate prison. He and some of the other men arrested at the Oakley Arms were indicted for High Treason. The *St James's Chronicle* reported their arrest, informing the public that the life of the Sovereign "was to be attempted on Tuesday next by a division of the conspirators, while the remainder were to attack the Tower and other places."[1]

****

Soon after his meeting with Pitt, Canning and a few other hard-core Pittites considered ways of ousting Addington from office and replacing him with their leader.[2] Next to Addington, the most immediate obstacle was the King. He had to be handled carefully for fear of driving him mad. At the end of October Canning had persuaded Lord Malmesbury to join his scheme and approach the King through the Duke of York. On 1 November Malmesbury met the Duke at the Horse Guards. When the Duke moaned about the government's inability to stand up to Bonaparte,

---

[1] Jay p.300, Gurney pp.99-100, Pocock p.85

[2] Stanhope p.407

Malmesbury agreed and told the Duke that Pitt felt the same and was ready to take office again. The Duke thought that the public would recognise this necessity and drive Addington out. Malmesbury suggested this would be too slow and that it would be better if Addington could be persuaded to step down. The Duke thought that Mr Addington was too vain to appreciate the limits of his abilities or the extent of the danger. He added, however, that he had good reason to believe that Lord Hobart and the Duke of Portland would withdraw their support which would frighten him into resigning. Malmesbury commented that this would be a very desirable event, but it might upset the King.

The Duke replied: "You well know we never talk to His Majesty on public affairs, but from the few things I have heard him say I cannot but suppose His Majesty considers the state of them to be very humiliating to this country."

"Perhaps," Malmesbury wondered, "then if His Majesty also knew that Mr Pitt had entirely given up the Catholic question his return to office would be even an agreeable circumstance to him." Malmesbury emphasised that those who wanted to replace Addington with Pitt needed to be assured that the King would be apprised of Pitt's availability and willingness to drop Catholic Emancipation. The Duke concluded the conversation by declaring that he wanted this as much as Malmesbury, but could not promise to tell the King. He would however do so if the occasion presented itself.[1]

With a possible means of approaching the King, the plotters focused on drafting a letter they intended to send to Addington, asking him to resign. The plan was not to seem to displace the current Cabinet, but merge them with new members to strengthen it sufficiently to stand up to Bonaparte. A first draft was written and Malmesbury showed it to the Duke of York at the Horse Guards a few days after their earlier meeting. The Duke thought it was tactfully worded, but was worried that it was unconstitutional and encroached on the King's prerogative to appoint ministers. He suggested a better approach was for someone of high rank to talk to Addington in private. The plotters welcomed this idea and proposed Lord Eldon for the task, but they continued to revise the letter and look for more signatures. A slight hiccup occurred when it was discovered that Grenville and his party would not join a government

---

[1] Malmesbury p.87

while Addington remained part of it. However, they would not oppose such a reformed administration and this was considered a possible advantage as Addington might have been more willing to step down for Pitt alone rather than Pitt and Grenville.

On 14 November Canning sent to Malmesbury a copy of the revised letter they proposed sending to Addington before the opening of Parliament on 23 November: "At a moment of unprecedented embarrassment and public anxiety, it is hoped that the Chancellor of the Exchequer will not consider the communication contained in this paper, as being either in intention or substance, in the smallest degree personally disrespectful to him." The letter explained that the authors had only taken the step of writing it from the most profound of convictions which they believed were shared by the public and therefore felt obliged to relate this to Addington:

"It is but too evident that instead of having derived from the conclusion of the late war those blessings of tranquillity, economy and confidence, which have usually attended the restoration of peace, the country finds itself in a state which necessarily calls for expensive preparation, a state of increasing insecurity and of continual alarm [...] it is the entire persuasion of all those who are parties to this statement, that the only method of tranquilising the apprehensions and anxiety which generally prevail, and of enabling this country to meet, with advantage, the dangers which threaten it, would be by the administration of the government being placed in the hands of Mr Pitt. [...] This would, as they think, afford the best chance of averting war [...] They are unfeignly anxious that Mr Addington, instead of being called upon to the meet the public wish, should have it in his power to anticipate it."

Pitt was in Bath and oblivious to all the plotting being conducted in his interests. Attempts by Lord Bathurst, Bishop Tomline and Rose were made to persuade him not to attend the opening of Parliament. He felt obliged to express his support for Addington's policies because he had been consulted for his opinion. These visitors felt that he would damage his reputation by aligning himself with the government so publicly. By 15 November, Rose had persuaded him not to go. Canning himself visited Pitt in Bath on the 17th and was pleased to find him still critical of the government and still convinced he should return to office. Canning hoped to keep his scheme a secret from Pitt so that he could not be accused of pursuing his self-interest. However, by Sunday 21 November, Pitt had learned of what was going on from Lord Mulgrave.

On that day he called on Lord Malmesbury (who was also in Bath) early in the morning.

"I know you are one in a plot, not quite so desperate as Colonel Despard's," Pitt said to Malmesbury. He asked who else was involved, expressing his concern that they were likely to be too intimately connected with him to give the impression of non-partisan support. When Malmesbury told him, he was not re-assured and was worried that as he now knew about it he was indirectly implicated. It was therefore his wish that no further canvassing of signatures took place and no presentation be made to Addington. If it was the general will that he was reinstated, this would eventually come about more naturally. Besides, he was still was not well enough for office and needed more time to recuperate. Malmesbury disagreed. Nothing like that ever occurred naturally, except in moments of extreme crisis, by which time Pitt would be assuming office at a disadvantage. Pitt was not convinced. He was not prepared to return to government in this manner. It would be perceived as intriguing and plotting in private against a government he was supporting in public. Pitt allowed Malmesbury to continue finding out the King's views as he would never agree to return without the King's blessing. However, the current scheme could not go ahead and Malmesbury agreed that they defer any parliamentary action until after Christmas.[1]

When the King opened Parliament on 23 November he declared his "sincere desire for the maintenance of peace. It is nevertheless impossible for me to lose sight of that established and wise system of policy, by which the interest of other states are connected with our own; and I cannot, therefore, be indifferent to any material change in their condition and strength. My conduct will be invariably regulated by a due consideration of the actual state of Europe, and by a watchful solicitude for the permanent welfare of my people."

Addington was obliged to re-assure the House, concerned with the invasion of Switzerland, the annexation of Piedmont and the continued presence of French troops in Holland, that Britain's forces were sufficient to deal with any sudden rupture in the peace. His aim was to keep revenue sufficient to meet necessary expenditure, not to reduce expenditure to meet revenue. Although since the end of the war it had been reduced from 250,000 to 120,000 troops the Army was still double

---

[1] Malmesbury pp.80-117

what it had been in 1784 and no further reduction of its strength had occurred except the disbanding of some militia, the strength of which was what it had been in 1792. The Navy still employed 46,000 seamen, 207 ships of war and 35 sail of the line, considerably more than when the country was last at peace. For 1803 he expected to maintain an army of 129,000 soldiers, 60,000 of which would be needed for Ireland and 50,000 sailors. Despite these considerable defence resources, in his December budget he claimed that he would reduce spending on the Army and Navy from £25 million to £15 million and estimated that the total savings resulting from the peace would be £25 million per year and that he would only have to borrow £10 million which he intended to raise through Exchequer bills. Many thought Addington was being boastful about his government and insulting to his predecessors, especially in his reference to Lord St Vincent's "economical management of the navy".[1]

As soon as the preliminary peace Treaty had been signed, St Vincent had ordered the decommissioning of ships and trimming of dockyards. In November 1801 he laid off 500 labourers and 300 shipwrights in Deptford, 32 from Woolwich Warren and 150 coopers and yardmen from the victualing office. Over the course of the year 80,000 seamen had been discharged. He also set about reforming the Navy's dockyards, which the American War of Independence had exposed as incompetent and corrupt. Dockyard workers, permitted to use waste wood chips for firewood were instead cutting up good timber. Copper bolts were stolen and substituted with wooden parts causing the loss of at least two ships. Dockyards were charging the Navy for uncompleted work and recording more men on their payroll than were actually working. It was estimated that the government was losing £1 million per year. Contractors were charging top prices for rotten wood, abetted by little competitive tendering amongst suppliers. Where there was bidding, low bids were not considered as binding and contractors were allowed to increase the price after being given the contract. All this was possible because Navy officials were bribed and the Navy Board was complacent.

In 1798, Jeremy Bentham's brother Samuel had been commissioned to carry out reforms, but this was postponed. Lord St Vincent was keen to set up an inquiry to investigate abuses once peace had been concluded, but Addington persuaded him to wait until after the election. On 29 August he badgered Addington, claiming he had found

---

[1] Stanhope vol. III p.412, Pellew vol. II pp.98-105

"abuse to such an extent as would require many months to go thoroughly into, and the absolute necessity of a Commission of Enquiry to expose them appears to the Admiralty Board here in a much stronger light than ever." He had already commenced inspection of the dockyards, which had uncovered the complicity of the Navy Board in covering up the abuses by protecting offenders and refusing to investigate complaints. Although the Admiralty had reprimanded the Board it had no power to remove its members, as they had been appointed by the Crown. St Vincent's hope was that a parliamentary commission would have the authority to compel the Board to provide evidence for the prosecution of offenders and oblige the current members to resign. An exasperated St Vincent finally persuaded the Cabinet and in December 1802, Parliament set up the Commission, an act that alarmed many in the previous government. Canning called it a "flagrant Admiralty job [...] of trumpery spite, originating in Lord St. Vincent's violence, and forced upon Addington's imbecility".[1]

---

[1] Fedorak pp.102-111, Ziegler, p.170

33 Lord Whitworth

Engraving from a painting by Sir Thomas Lawrence. Illustration for the *Life of Napoleon Bonaparte* by William Milligan Sloane (The Century Co, 1896) (Look and Learn Collections)

33. The Ambassadors

On 3 November 1802, the new French ambassador to London, General Antoine-François Andréossy, was escorted to St James Palace by the Master of Ceremonies, where he attended a very crowded King's levee. Although from a noble Italian family, Andréossy had embraced the Revolution and served with Bonaparte in Italy and Egypt. At the time of his appointment to the London embassy he was the garrison commandant of Strasbourg.

News of his arrival had been welcomed in London and many who attended the levee were keen to meet him, including the royal princes who had come up especially from the country. Lord Hawkesbury introduced him to the King, to whom Andréossy made a brief speech. The King replied: "I have always wished for peace and do so still, and I shall remain of the same mind, as long as no attack is made on the dignity of my crown and the interests of my people. Have you always been an officer?"

"Sire, for the last 20 years I have served in the artillery."

"You are an engineer are you not?"

"In France the duties of Engineer and Artillery officer are distinct."

"You are an engineer. We know that you are qualified for either service [...] and are a man of letters."

Andréossy was known to write and had published a book in 1801 called *Histoire du canal du midi*. He modestly replied: "Sire, I have never laid claim to the title, but it has always been a pleasure to me to devote my leisure to study."

"A literary life must entail many pleasures, and besides, makes a man independent."

After an exchange of comments on his journey and the English weather the meeting ended. The Master of Ceremonies escorted

Andréossy to the courtyard outside, where to get to his carriage, he had to wade through a large crowd of enthusiastic spectators which applauded his progress to the top of St James Street.[1]

Andréossy's instructions, prepared for him in June, were to prevent the British from interfering in continental affairs and persuade them to execute their final obligations of the Treaty of Amiens. On commercial relations between Britain and France, he was to confine himself to assurances of the First Consul's desire to end trade restrictions and agree, if not to a treaty of commerce, a series of private arrangements and compensations. He was to keep the English government informed of the true state of affairs in France and to inform Bonaparte of the condition of Britain – especially relating to its Parliament, Navy, harbours, resources and administration. He was to request the deportation of the Bourbons, royalist conspirators and royalist French bishops and ask the British to prohibit the wearing of French ancien régime decorations.

Meanwhile, waiting in Sevenoaks for orders, was the designated British ambassador to France. Lord Charles Whitworth was a tall handsome man, whose last post had been at the court of Tsar Paul at St Petersburg. He had recently married the widowed Duchess of Dorset, who retained her title following her husband's death. Their marriage in April 1801 had been threatened by a jealous Russian Countess, who had divorced her own husband in St Petersburg on an understanding that Lord Whitworth had promised to marry her. When this countess had arrived in London threatening to expose Whitworth's prior obligations of engagement, the Duchess paid her off with £10,000.

Whitworth had been appointed ambassador earlier in the year and been waiting since spring at Sevenoaks for orders to proceed to Paris. He and his new wife had sent much of their luggage ahead, including the Dorset plate, obliging them to borrow from the Duchess of Dorset's mother Lady Liverpool, Lord Hawkesbury's step mother. With news of the arrival of Andréossy came orders from Hawkesbury for Whitworth to depart. Accompanying him were the Duchess and her two daughters, while her son remained at Harrow.

They arrived in France on 14 November and Whitworth was met in Paris by Merry, who introduced him to Talleyrand two days later.

---

[1] Coquelle pp.6-8

Whitworth's instructions from Hawkesbury were comprehensive. As well as gathering intelligence, his general duties were to help British tradesmen and litigants with just claims in the French law courts, and discuss improving commercial relations with France in general. He was to express to the French His Majesty's wish to preserve the peace, but also his determination not to relinquish the right to interfere in Europe if British interests or the interests of Europe were threatened. This was a right based on general principles, but the Treaty also gave the British a special right to counter the increase in French power in particular. As examples of this he was to refer to recent French encroachments in Piedmont and Parma and French interference in Holland and Switzerland. Colonies were restored to the Dutch at Amiens on the understanding they would remain independent. If the French complained about the British and émigré press, he was to repeat what Merry had told them already. Most importantly, Whitworth was to avoid any commitment to relinquish Malta, even if all the Treaty conditions had been satisfied. Britain was entitled to keep it as a counterpoise to the French acquisitions.[1]

Whitworth and the Duchess moved into the same residence she had occupied when her first husband, the Duke of Dorset, had been ambassador to France before the Revolution. The building was not in the best condition and repairs were undertaken which were interpreted as a sign of optimism by Parisians that the peace would endure.[2] The new ambassador initially restricted himself to the more general duties of his instructions, especially intelligence gathering. By the end of the month, he felt confident enough to tell Hawkesbury that he thought Bonaparte was intending to re-invade Egypt: "As long as we have Malta [...] we shall be able to counteract his plans."[3] A few days later he said that if Bonaparte failed in St Domingo "he will use his utmost efforts to reduce the British colonies to the same deplorable conditions".[4]

In the first week of December, Whitworth was officially introduced to Bonaparte by Talleyrand at the reception of foreign

---

[1] Browning pp.1-10

[2] Yonge p.101

[3] Browning p.19

[4] Browning pp.19-20

ambassadors at the Tuileries. Presenting his credentials, Whitworth expressed the King's sincere desire for peace, a sentiment Bonaparte reciprocated, both to the ambassador and again to the latest batch of distinguished English visitors. The First Consul hoped they would all enjoy their stay in Paris, and return to England assured of his respect for the British and the peace. Later, Whitworth was presented to Josephine at her apartments and then joined the consular couple, their family and two hundred and fifty other guests for a dinner which lasted half an hour.[1]

Most of December and January were diplomatically uneventful for Whitworth. The main formal social occasions were the introduction of his wife to Josephine at St Cloud and the regular monthly receptions of ambassadors at the Tuileries. The Duchess managed to offend the consular court by turning up late to a grand dinner after her maid had got drunk and forgotten where she had placed the Duchess's jewels.[2] At the first reception of the New Year, Bonaparte congratulated himself on the improved state of civilization and increased happiness in France and the rest of Europe, but lamented the pernicious system adopted by most countries of maintaining large standing armies. He said it was a pity they could not all agree to reduce them by two-thirds. Whitworth could not restrain himself from suggesting that one good example would have more effect than the best reasoning.[3]

Whitworth continued to gather intelligence on a number of fronts, some of which at first suggested things on the continent were improving. He felt that Bonaparte was going to leave Switzerland independent and that French troops might be withdrawn from Holland. Later, however, he began to think the First Consul had plans to change the Dutch government. He also heard that Bonaparte was contemplating divorcing Josephine and making himself emperor, but had then decided to delay these plans. In early January Whitworth met Talleyrand, who was annoyed at Britain's' indulgence of the Bourbon princes, especially the Count D'Artois. Talleyrand suggested they should retire to Warsaw and if the British could arrange this, the First Consul would consider doing something for them in return. Whitworth said that His Majesty would

---

[1] Browning pp.21-23

[2] Bristow pp.108-109

[3] Yonge p.101

never oblige them to leave England. At another meeting a few weeks later Talleyrand added more complaints. Bonaparte was angry with the British press again. A publication that he found particularly annoying was *The History of the British Expedition to Egypt* by Colonel Wilson, which accused Bonaparte of massacring Turkish prisoners at Jaffa during his campaign there in 1799. Whitworth replied that the British articles were probably provoked by French ones. Furthermore, he pointed out, the French articles had official sanction, while the British government had no control over the press in England. Talleyrand refuted this, giving examples of journals over which ministers had influence. Whitworth told him that the only way they could influence the press was by favouring one with exclusive public statements. Talleyrand moved onto his main concern: what were the British intentions regarding Malta? Another Grand Master was soon to be elected and even if Russia failed to give its guarantee, the conditions for its evacuation should still be considered as satisfied. The time would soon arrive when England would no longer have a pretext for keeping Malta. Whitworth, unmoved by Talleyrand's points, still thought Bonaparte was a threat to peace in the Mediterranean. He suspected the French of wooing Russia in the hope of partitioning the Ottoman Empire between them and to secure an ally against Britain.[1]

At the end of January, Mr Edgeworth called at the embassy. He had just been ordered by the police to quit Paris in twenty-four hours and France in two weeks, but had no idea of what offence against the government he had committed.[2] Whitworth, on learning of Mr Edgeworth's predicament immediately wrote to Talleyrand asking him the reason for his banishment. It turned out that he had been confused with the brother of the royalist priest the Abbé Edgeworth who had attended Louis XVI in his last moments. In the meantime Edgeworth went to Passy with his daughter Maria. After sending a memorial to the First Consul declaring that the Abbé was not a brother, only a cousin and did not share his political views, he was swiftly allowed to return to Paris.

---

[1] Browning pp.35-40, pp.52-56

[2] Browning p.51

The Consequences of Honour

****

In the Netherlands, the Dutch grumbled about the continuing presence of French troops. The Batavian minister in Paris, Smits, had asked Bonaparte about them in April, but the First Consul evaded offering any specific timetable for their withdrawal. In August Smits complained that whenever he raised the matter with Talleyrand, he was fobbed off with explanations of how useful it was to prolong their stay. Talleyrand told him that as the Dutch needed so many troops to defend their restored colonies, they needed French soldiers to defend the Netherlands itself. This would not necessarily have implied defence against external enemies, but also internal ones. The new Batavian constitution had upset many Dutch democrats as it had allowed conservatives to return to power in the provincial authorities. Amongst them were Orangists who had come back to Holland after being amnestied in March 1801 and who were encouraged to accept positions by the Prince of Orange in December of that year. Bonaparte refused to approve another democratic coup and told Smits: "it is recommended that you keep your peace. Europe has need of rest; governments must not be overthrown. On the contrary, those that exist must be consolidated." The Dutch however, feared that keeping the peace would be difficult so long as the French maintained a strangle-hold on their economy, such as their control of the port of Flushing. In the autumn of 1802 Smits moaned that Bonaparte had no intention of settling this issue with any haste. When Schimmelpenninck, just before he left Paris for the Dutch embassy in London, tried to persuade the First Consul to loosen French constraints on Dutch commerce, he was dismissed with a patronising smile: "Ah, you still have so many resources. The industry of the Batavian nation and its calm and wise character will surely enable it to transcend such difficulties."[1]

****

When in September 1802 Bonaparte invited the Swiss cantons to send delegates to Paris to participate with him in the framing of a new Swiss

---

[1] Schama 2005 p.438

constitution, only thirty-six arrived. These were pro-French unionists. When the former rebel federalist cantons refused to nominate delegates, Bonaparte was obliged to appoint them himself. They declined to attend until Talleyrand convinced them they would be allowed equal influence and when fifteen of them arrived in December talks finally began. French mediation was effected by means of a four-member commission made up of two Senators, one being the former Minister of Police Fouché, and two councillors of state. On 10 December the first conference was held, presided by Senator Berthelemi, who commenced proceedings by reading a letter from the First Consul:[1]

"It is necessary to remain as nature designed you, that is to say, in a union of petty confederated states, different in the rule of your internal government as you differ in soil, attached the one to the other by a simple federal lien – a lien which shall be neither onerous nor expensive." Fouché noticed the expressions of surprise spread among the unionist delegates as the speech continued. Bonaparte seemed to be siding with the rebels in favour of a federal state: "I do not imagine for you a uniform and central government like that of France." There was no point, for a small country like Switzerland, to have a centralized government, because that was only necessary for a great power and Switzerland could never hope to compete with France or Austria: "It is your duty to be a neutral people, whose neutrality will be respected by all the world [...] But in wishing to remain independent, do not forget that it is necessary you be the friends of France." Bonaparte would not expect the Swiss to be allies with France, but in turn he would not tolerate a Swiss government allying itself with his enemies. Republican delegates may have been partly placated to hear that although Bonaparte would allow each canton to determine its own local constitution, he insisted on the abolition of feudal privileges, demanding that "the government of the aristocratic citizens must be put an end to [....] These are among the barbarisms of the Middle-Ages, that France [...] cannot tolerate in your laws."[2]

Two days later Bonaparte expressed his views directly to a deputation of five Swiss delegates and the French commission members. Heated arguments among the Swiss protracted the discussions into January with no agreement among them in sight. Bonaparte decided they

---

[1] Fouché p.251

[2] Thiers pp.442-443

had debated long enough and on 24 January he asked the Swiss to nominate five deputies to receive his Act of Mediation on which they would be allowed to offer their final opinions and suggestions for modifications. An eight hour conference was held, after which the ultimate draft of the Act was drawn up and presented to the Swiss on 19 February. Each of the nineteen cantons would have its own constitution, most with a property qualified electorate. Each canton was free to dispose of public land, regulate feudal dues and religious affairs, unless religious liberty had already been established. Equal rights, the prohibition of alliances and the abolition of internal tariffs between cantons would achieve some degree of unity. Swiss citizens would also be allowed to own property throughout the confederation. A central Diet in which cantons had one or two votes would elect a Landamman from one of the six main cantons.[1]

****

On 25 February, the latest plan for the allocation of ecclesiastical principalities among the German states was submitted to the Diet at Ratisbon. Austria's refusal to accept the Franco-Russian proposals and its occupation of Passau in August the previous year had threatened a deadlock. To break it, Talleyrand held talks with the Austrian Minister in Paris, Count Cobenzl, whom he provided with a residence close to his Chateau Neuilly to keep these talks discrete. Austria indicated that it was prepared to accept most of the plan and allow Bavaria to have some of the territories it coveted, as long as Austria was given the banks of the river Inn. It also proposed creating two new Electors – Salzburg (ruled by the former Grand Duke of Tuscany) and The Grand Master of the Teutonic Order. Bonaparte did not think Bavaria would give up its frontiers on the Inn, so other options had to be considered. A new plan submitted to the Diet deputation on 2 October was approved by five out of the eight deputies, but the other three wanted to wait until the discussions in Paris between France and Austria had concluded. By the 21st, one of these, the delegate for Saxony, changed his mind leaving only two opposed. At the end of December, Bonaparte himself met with

---

[1] Lefebvre p.173

Cobenzl. He refused to let Austria take Bavaria's Inn frontier, but would allow Archduke Ferdinand to take a bishopric on the Danube and the creation of two new pro-Austrian Catholic Electors. On 26 December a convention was finally signed between Cobenzl and Joseph Bonaparte.[1]

The final plan considered by the Diet on 25 February was approved by all three colleges. Despite Austria's efforts, power in Germany had shifted to Protestant or French friendly states. Some 112 principalities that made up a large part of the Holy Roman Empire were swallowed up by other states. Although Prussia lost 137,000 people, it acquired 600,000 more and received the bishoprics of Paderborn, Hildesheim, Erfurt and parts of Munster. Baden lost 25,000, but got 237,000 by obtaining the cities of Mannheim and Heidelberg, as well as the right-bank lands of the Rhineland bishoprics of Speir, Strasbourg and Basle. Baden also became an Elector along with Württemberg and Hesse-Cassel, creating a Protestant majority in the Electoral College, mirrored by one in the Diet as a whole. Passau was divided between Austria and Bavaria, which also gained the bishopric of Fresing and a net gain in population of 274,000. Austria was obliged to cede Breisgau and Ortenay to the Duke of Modena, but received the bishoprics of Brixen and Trent, while the Grand Duke of Tuscany took the archbishoprics of Salzburg and Eichstadt. British interests were not neglected. The Prince of Orange finally received compensation and George III, as Elector of Hanover, acquired the bishopric of Osnabruck. The Catholic Church got the worst deal of all. It lost 2.5 million subjects, 18 universities and 21 million florins per year in revenue. The individual who perhaps gained the most personally from the whole affair was the French Foreign Minister, Talleyrand, who was said to have received 10–15 million Francs in bribes from minor German princes desperate not to lose out.[2]

---

[1] Thiers pp.415-417

[2] Lefebvre p.174, Esdaile p.138

34 Mademoiselle Georges

Lithograph by J. Champagne. Illustration from *The Court of Napoleon* by F. B. Goodrich, (Derby and Jackson 1857) (Author's private collection)

34. The Debut

The debut at Versailles of Mademoiselle Duschenois – a moderate success – had been and gone. The next great theatrical event anticipated by Paris was the debut of her rival – Mademoiselle Georges – Mimi. When she was presented to the Comédie-Française at her first rehearsal the troupe gave her a warm reception, treating her as the child of the house. Although she was growing up fast, she still enjoyed juvenile pursuits, playing hide-and-seek with the girls employed by Josephine's couturiere, whose workshop was in the same building as the flat Mimi shared with her mother. On the eve of her debut, as if it was the last day of her childhood, she raced around the rue des Colonnes, knocking and ringing on every door on the way home from her last rehearsal. The next day was 23 November 1802, the day she was to perform as Clytemnestra in *Iphigénie en Aulide*.

By mid-day a large crowd had gathered outside the doors of the theatre. Women were shrieking and men were rudely pushing themselves forward. Guards had to create a passage to let Mademoiselle Raucourt through. She sprained her foot and had to be carried into Mimi's dressing room. In the orchestra pit playing the violin was Mimi's brother and her sister sat in the stalls. They had put on old gloves to makes as much noise as they could when applauding. The First Consul, Josephine and other members of the Bonaparte family were in their boxes. The play by Racine, in five acts, told the mythological tale of Iphigénie, the daughter of King Agamemnon and Queen Clytemnestra. Agamemnon is about to sail against Troy, but is told by an oracle that the only way ensure a calm voyage is to sacrifice his daughter Iphigénie to the Goddess Diana. Iphigénie is betrothed to Achilles (played by Talma) and neither of them, nor Clytemnestra are aware of the sacrifice Agamemnon is contemplating until it is announced in Act III. In Act IV all three, mother, daughter and Achilles confront the King. Iphigénie pleads for her life while Clytemnestra (played by Mimi) furiously harangues her barbarous and inhumane husband, condemning him for being prepared to spill the blood of his innocent daughter. A hearty applause interrupted Mimi on one occasion, but on another, as she delivered one of the queen's lines in this act, it was badly received by some of the audience who began murmuring. Mademoiselle Raucourt called from her box: "Begin again!" and encouraged her to be firm. She repeated the line but the murmuring continued. Then the sound of clapping could be heard from the First Consul's box, soon followed by clapping elsewhere in the audience with cries of "Begin again!" An actor whispered into Mimi's ear, "That's right my child. They want to intimidate you, but don't give way." She spoke the line a third time and the play resumed. Clytemnestra's speech is followed by one from a furious Achilles, delivered powerfully by the veteran Talma. He was himself subjected to hissing from the partisans of the actor Lafont. Agamemnon is about to go through with the sacrifice when news arrives that they are about to kill the wrong Iphigénie. The oracle was in fact referring to Iphigénie the secret daughter of Helen of Troy and Theseus, who had abducted Helen some time before Paris had carried her off. This Iphigénie is revealed to be Eriphile, a scheming jealous girl Achilles had captured in Lesbos, and left in the charge of the Queen and her daughter. Eriphile stabs herself on the altar, and the Goddess Diana then appears in a pyre of flames accompanied by thunder, lightning and raging winds and waves.

In the dressing room, later, Mimi was swamped with congratulations from well-wishers, friends and family. Some of them had torn clothes, the consequence of a fistfight with her detractors. Her own brother's bloodied hands betrayed his part in the fray, and the conductor's clothes were rags. Mimi also received a reasonable review in the *Journal des débats* by Geoffroy the critic. In it he complemented her beauty, suggesting her face united the French graces with Grecian nobility and compared her figure with a sister of Apollo. Although "the ear was not as favourable to her as the eyes" this could have been due to the stress of a first performance. She was the "germ of a great actress" and "seems destined for the part of queens".

Before her debut she was already a minor celebrity, simply on account of her beauty and was being pursued by many admirers. Lucien Bonaparte gave her presents and money, advising her to save for the day when she was no longer popular with the public. One secret admirer asked her to meet him at the catacombs and stand at her window as a signal that she would go. She stood at her window, but declined to turn up at the rendezvous, hoping this would teach her stalker a lesson. Another admirer offered to dress up as a woman to see her, which she found too ridiculous to consider. She allowed one would-be suitor to curl her hair and when he had left, her maid discovered that the curling papers in her hair were banknotes. It was a Polish aristocrat – Prince Sapieha – who provided Mimi with the means to live in a bigger house. When the family moved in they could also afford to keep a carriage and engaged the orphaned son of the housemaid of her aunt as jockey. His duty was to stand behind the carriage when they travelled, but at night he got frightened and begged to be let inside, and the women did not have the heart to refuse him.

One evening, after a performance of *Iphigénie en Aulide*, Mimi found a man waiting for her at home. This was the First Consul's jolly valet Constant, who begged on behalf of his master that Mademoiselle Georges allow herself to be taken to St Cloud the next evening at 8 p.m. The First Consul wished to congratulate her personally on her success. Mimi was unsure what to do, but replied: "Tell the First Consul, monsieur, that I shall have the honour of repairing to St Cloud tomorrow. You can come and fetch me at eight o'clock, but not at home, at the theatre." She had a restless night worrying about what to wear and what the master of France wanted with her.

The next day dragged for Mimi. To pass the time, she went to the Bois de Boulogne, visited a perfumer and milliner and then went to the theatre house, where she met Talma. He asked her what was the matter, as she looked distraught and he had said good day only to be ignored. Was she ill or angry? Mimi snapped back – it was he who was mad to suggest this. "There is nothing the matter with me." When other actors remarked on her mood, she told them she had a headache. She went home to get changed, then returned to the theatre and watched a play from one of the boxes. An actress noticed her all dressed up and asked her where she was going. A ball? A soiree, she replied. Finally her maid told her Constant was outside.

As she was driven to St Cloud, she told Constant she was dying of fear and thought of making an excuse not to go. Constant laughed and reassured her. On seeing how kind the First Consul was, she would soon lose her fear, he told her. When they arrived, they crossed the Orangery and reached a bedroom window looking out onto a terrace. The Consul's Mameluke manservant and bodyguard Roustam was waiting and let them inside a large room with big green silk curtains. After he closed the window, Roustam left, while Constant went to inform his master of her arrival. Mimi looked around. Opposite the window were a large bed and a big sofa before the fireplace. The room was lit by candles in a large candelabra and a chandelier. She sat down in an armchair. A door next to the fireplace leading to a library opened and Bonaparte entered, wearing silk stockings, white satin knee breeches, a green uniform with red facings and collar, and a hat under his arm. Mimi got up. Bonaparte approached with a charming smile, took her by the hand and made her sit with him on the large sofa. He lifted her veil and threw it on the ground. "How your hand trembles!" Bonaparte said. "Are you afraid of me? Do I seem terrible to you? I found you exceedingly beautiful yesterday, Madame, and I wished to compliment you. I am more amiable and polite than you, as you see."

"How is that, monsieur?" asked Mimi.

"How! I sent you a remittance of three thousand francs after seeing you in *Emilie*, as proof of the pleasure you gave me. I hoped you would ask permission to present yourself to thank me. But the beautiful and haughty Emilie did not come."

"But I did not know," Mimi stammered. "I did not dare to take the liberty."

"Oh, a poor excuse! Were you then afraid of me?"

"Yes."

"And Now?"

"Still More."

Bonaparte laughed. "Tell me your name."

"Josephine-Marguerite."

"Josephine pleases me, I like that name; but I would prefer to call you Georgina. Hein! Would you like it? I wish it [...] You do not speak, my dear Georgina. Why?"

"Because all these lights fatigue me. Have them extinguished, I beg you; it seems to me I shall be more at my ease to listen to you and reply."

Bonaparte rang for Roustam who came in and extinguished some of the lights.

"Come, Georgina, tell me all you have done. Be simple and frank, and tell me." She complained that she would bore him, but he insisted so she related her story. "My dear child, you certainly were not rich; but what is your position now? Who gave you this beautiful shawl, veil and other things?" She told him they were gifts from admirers like Prince Sapieha. "That is good; you do not lie. You will come and see me and will be very discreet. Promise me."

"Not today; wait, and I will return, I promise you." They had been talking a long time. Mimi – Georgina – noticed it was the early hours of the morning. "I should like to go."

"You must be tired, dear Georgina. Goodbye til to-morrow, then. You will come?"

"Yes, gladly. You are too kind and gracious for one not to love you, and I love you with all my heart."

Bonaparte put on her shawl and veil, kissing her on the forehead. Mimi burst out laughing: "That's splendid." He had just kissed Prince Sapieha's veil, she told him. Bonaparte then grasped the veil, tore it up, threw her shawl to floor, snatched a ring from her finger and crushed it under his foot.

Mimi, trembling with outrage, said, "It will be some time before you see me again."

"Dear Georgina, you mustn't have anything except what comes from me. Do not sulk with me; that would be wrong, and I should have a poor opinion of your feelings if it were otherwise."

"You are quite right. No, I am not angry, but I shall be cold."

Bonaparte rang for Constant and told him to bring a white cashmere shawl and a large lace veil. Once she was dressed to his satisfaction, he walked with her as far as the Orangery: "Till tomorrow, Georgina, till to-morrow". Mimi left, unsure of whether to meet Napoleon again. He was charming, but violent and she was worried that his kindness and gentleness with her was insincere. She later confided with Talma, telling him everything that had happened. He advised her she was mad to hesitate and was certain he would always be kind. Bonaparte would not abandon an honest girl who had not yet succumbed to the temptations surrounding her. She hesitated because she would be risking that reputation as an honest girl by seeing Napoleon. She would be forever dependent on him and this would be a form of slavery. Talma suggested she should then get married instead. "That's nice advice to give me. I fear slavery, and you wish me to marry!"

She decided to meet Bonaparte again. He was waiting for her when she arrived. "Good-day, Georgina; are we in good humour?" he asked. "Yes; always for you," she replied. Napoleon expressed his hope that she should tell Prince Sapieha to stop visiting her. Georgina confessed she had not thought of doing so, but Napoleon insisted. He would understand: "See, Georgina, let me love you altogether: I want you to have complete confidence. It is true you scarcely know me, but it needs but a minute to love: one feels all at once the electric movement which strikes you at the same time. Tell me, do you love me a little?"

"Certainly I love you, not only a little; I am afraid of loving you too much, and therefore of being very unhappy. You have too much greatness within you for your heart to nurse a lively affection for anything but glory. Poor women are soon taken and very soon forgotten. For you they are a plaything which amuses you a little more or a little less. Although you may be the First Consul, I do not intend to be a plaything."

"But if you are my favourite plaything, you won't complain I hope. No mistrust, Georgina; you would annoy me."

Despite her doubts, Georgina began to warm to Bonaparte and could not help finding his restrained ardour appealing to her sense of modesty. She agreed to come again the next day, but then remembered she was playing in *Cinna*. Napoleon said he would go to the performance and send a carriage to pick her up afterwards. "But I shall be tired," She protested. "Come Georgina, this time I will see you after *Cinna*, and you will yield to my desire, or I will never see you again."

"I will come," she promised, with tears in her eyes.

"You are crying; you see quite well that you love me a little, you silly little thing!" He dried her tears, embraced her and said "Till tomorrow, my dear Georgina."

When Georgina came on stage the following evening and noticed that Bonaparte was not in his box she was indignant and promised herself she would not go to St Cloud. However, she could not stop thinking about him, even while she was delivering her monologue as Emile. Then she heard a noise in the house followed by a frantic applause. He had arrived and suddenly she was overcome with feelings of joy. Cries of "Begin again" came from the audience and she began her speech again. As she said the line "If I seduce Cinna, I will seduce many other" she was suddenly unexpectedly applauded and thought to her horror that the public knew of her visit to the First Consul, who then might blame her for being indiscreet. When the performance was over, she went to St Cloud, and found Napoleon full of praise. "Talma was sublime," he said. "You were very good too Georgina [...] Come and sit beside me. You are a little fatigued. Come, rid yourself of the shawl and the hat, that you may be seen." As they talked, he undressed her, little by little. Georgina yielded to what she considered was his gaiety, grace and decency. As the evening progressed he became more childish, he embraced her and continued to charm with modest and tender words.

In the morning, about seven o'clock, the mess they had made on the couch embarrassed her. She began tidying it and was touched when Napoleon helped her. "Good-bye till tomorrow Georgina," he said as she was about to leave. "No, not to-morrow, if you permit, but the day after tomorrow" she pleaded. "Yes, my dear Georgina, just as you wish; the day after to-morrow. Love me a little, and tell me that you will come gladly."

"I love you with all my soul; I am afraid of loving you too much. You are not made for me, I know, and I shall suffer; that is written – you will see!"

"Bah!" retorted Bonaparte. "You prophesy badly; I shall always be good to you. But we haven't got as far as that. Kiss me and be happy."

Georgina went home feeling sad. She felt she loved Napoleon and confided with Talma again, who called on her the next day. "Well, did he talk to you about the frightful applause at the line – if I have been seduced by Cinna?" Talma asked. "He never said a word about it," she replied, "but he thought you sublime my dear Talma." She told him she agreed and was impressed with Napoleon's comments about the performance. Talma told her she ought to be happy. In his opinion a man would not display such tenderness, care and patience for a passing fancy: "He spoils you; you will find no one like him."

"I only know too well, Talma, that I love him, and you see that is disturbing."

"When do you see him again?"

"Tomorrow. He wanted to see me today, but..." she tried to explain, but Talma interrupted. A lot of women would like to have been in her place, he said. He advised her to be discrete and Georgina noticed him staring at her. "What have you got in your ears?" he said. Two earrings Bonaparte had given him, she replied. "But those gems are superb." Yes, she agreed. The way in which he had given them to her she declared was finer still: "I am mad over him." Before Talma left, he persuaded Georgina to come to the theatre that evening.

When she arrived there later she went to the green room where the actors were made up and waited before going on stage. One of the actresses, Mademoiselle Mars, had just left to perform, prompting a word of advice from a fat comedienne to a younger actress in the room called Mademoiselle Bourgoin. She would do well to imitate Mademoiselle Mars, she said, although she would never replace her. When the comedienne left to go on stage herself, Bourgoin unburdened her indignation: "Dear me, how rude the fat creature is." These old actresses thought too much of themselves. "When I am as old as you, you rude old thing, I shall have as much talent as you, see! She's been flattered so often she fancies herself as Madame de Pompadour." Everybody laughed. Another actress asked Bourgoin why she had not said this to the comedienne. Bourgoin said she would have been fined 100 Francs. Anyway, she would be even with her one day. "I suppose you are afraid of the fat creature, Georges?"

"I afraid?" replied Georgina, "Not at all". Anyway, she admired Mademoiselle Mars so could not agree with what she said. "Besides, I don't care for arguments."

When Mademoiselle Mars returned she sat opposite Georgina and admired her earrings. She had forgotten to remove them and was irritated by Mars' persistent curiosity. She later complained to Talma about Mars' interrogation and repeated her worries about loving Napoleon. She thought women were very spiteful to each other. Men did not have such petty jealousies. Talma suggested that she might be envious of youth when she was old one day. No, she objected. When she was old, she would love youth and enjoy looking at beautiful people. After all, they would grow old as well one day and have to suffer the compliment "Ah you *were* very beautiful."

When Georgina related the inquisition by Mars to Napoleon the next day, insisting she was very discrete, he was sympathetic: "Never mind; let them talk, let them suppose; I shall not blame you for it. Always be good-natured, dear Georgina, that is the best quality a woman can have." Georgina continued to see Napoleon. The nights she spent with him would endure as fond memories. He never used obscene words but charmed her with hints of vulnerability. "Do you love me Georgina? Are you happy to be in my arms? I am going to sleep, too." He slept like a child, breathing softly with his head resting on her bosom. He always awoke with a smile on his lips. When they got up he liked to dress her. He would put on her stockings with garters he had specially made for her because their buckles were easier to handle and she adored the way he pretended to make the bed in the morning.[1]

Bonaparte's increased visits to the theatre fuelled rumours of the affair. Eventually Josephine discovered that Mademoiselle Georges was being smuggled into a backroom at St Cloud. In tears, she confided to her lady-in-waiting Madame Claire de Remusat. Remusat thought she was shedding more tears than a temporary affair warranted, but Josephine's bitterness could not be contained. Napoleon, she said, had no moral principles. He had only kept his shameful passions in check until he felt powerful enough to indulge them. Had he not seduced his own sisters, one after the other? His brothers were always trying to persuade him to leave her. "It is a great misfortune for me [...] that I have not borne a son to Bonaparte. That gives their hatred a weapon they can always use against me."

"But Madame," said Remusat, "it appears to me that your daughter's child almost repairs that misfortune. The First Consul loves him, and will, perhaps, in the end, adopt him."

"Alas, that is the object of my dearest wishes; but the jealous and sullen disposition of Louis Bonaparte leads him to oppose it. His family have maliciously repeated to him the insulting rumours concerning my daughter's conduct and the paternity of her son. Slander has declared the child to be Bonaparte's." Josephine complained that when she remonstrated with Napoleon he simply told her that he was not an ordinary man. The laws of morals and custom were not made for men such as him.[2]

---

[1] Cheramy pp.114-151

[2] Remusat p.58

One evening at the Tuileries palace, Josephine was again complaining to Madame Remusat of her situation. About one o'clock in the morning, Josephine suddenly got up. "I can't stand it any longer. Mlle George is certainly up there, and I am going to surprise them." Remusat unsuccessfully tried to dissuade her. "Follow me," Josephine ordered, "we will go up together." Remusat then tried to excuse herself, but Josephine insisted. Taking a candle in her hand, she reluctantly agreed. They climbed the uncarpeted stairs to Bonaparte's rooms and were half way there when they heard a noise. Josephine, who was in front, turned round and said: "Perhaps it is Roustam, Bonaparte's Mameluke, who is guarding the door. That wretch is capable of throttling both of us." The thought struck Remusat with instant terror and she immediately descended the staircase, leaving Josephine behind in the darkness. When Josephine caught up with Remusat and saw her terrified face she burst into laughter, infecting her companion with the same uncontrollable disposition. Josephine gave up her plan and Remusat left, deciding she had been wise to yield to her fear.[1]

---

[1] Remusat p.61

35. Sébastiani

Whitworth's suspicions regarding Bonaparte's ambitions in Egypt seemed confirmed when he read an article published in the *Moniteur* on 30 January 1803. A Colonel Sébastiani had recently returned to Paris from a mission to the eastern Mediterranean, including a trip to Egypt. His report to Bonaparte, published in the *Moniteur*, noted that the British were still occupying Egypt and were in no hurry to leave. He claimed the Egyptians and Mamelukes would welcome the return of the French, who would only need 6,000 troops to retake the country. He criticised the conduct of the British commander, General Stewart, describing him as a man of "mediocre talents". Claiming that Stewart tried to convince the Turks the French officer's mission was to rouse the Egyptians against their Ottoman overlords, Sébastiani suggested that it was Stewart's intention to persuade the Turks to execute him. Whitworth posted a copy to Hawkesbury the next day and felt obliged to comment that Sébastiani's article "evidently proves the projects of the First Consul" towards Egypt.[1]

Over the next few days, the French tried to mitigate the offence to England this publication provoked. At a dinner attended by Whitworth, Sébastiani recanted everything disrespectful he had said about General Stewart. A few days later Talleyrand assured Whitworth that the object of Sébastiani's mission was purely commercial. The tone of the article was just the zeal of a young officer. It did however express French concern with Britain's extended presence in this part of the Mediterranean. Talleyrand referred to a copy of a letter sent to Andréossy instructing the French ambassador to demand why the British were still in Egypt and Malta. Whitworth told Talleyrand the response to expect: Malta was being retained because the conditions for its evacuation had not yet been satisfied. Alluding to the Sébastiani report, Whitworth said it was important that France took no further action that would suggest an attempt on Egypt if they wanted no further delays to Malta's evacuation. Talleyrand interrupted him, insisting that the First Consul had no intention of interfering in Egypt, that he was in fact heartily tired of Egypt and that his only interest was commercial. He had his word of honour

---

[1] Browning pp.56-58

that this was Bonaparte's only objective. Whitworth was not convinced. Until perfect confidence had been restored, he said, Bonaparte must be prepared for measures of precaution on the part of Great Britain.[1]

The British Cabinet was alarmed by the Sébastiani report. Its effect on Addington was significant. In 1801 he believed that peace had been necessary. England did not have sufficient financial resources to prosecute the war successfully. Peace was his greatest wish, but he did not expect to be accused of preferring it at the expense of risking the interest of the country or suffer the insolence and arrogance of any power, especially France. Yet he felt he had been accused of this, but bore the accusation in silence, convinced that it was underserved. He felt his conduct was now about to be justified and would satisfy all reasonable men. His maxim from when he first took office was to make and maintain peace and resist all clamour for war at home until France had filled the measure of her folly and had put herself completely in the wrong. Not only by repeated and unprovoked acts of insolence and presumption, but also by acts that clearly threatened the interest of Great Britain, violated the Treaty and were a danger to Europe. He had ignored simple acts of insolence and impertinence like a sober man ignored a drunk, waiting until impudence was coupled with hostility before he acted. He had waited while the French had heaped wrong upon wrong, until their hostility was in no doubt. His policy had been to bear and forbear until this hour came, but not a second beyond it. This hour had come with Sébastiani's report: "This has from the moment it was known, occupied our whole attention, and the opinions of the Cabinet have been unanimous on the occasion." They would have ignored the report as just another insult if it were not for the fact that it clearly revealed France's true intentions which they had to take seriously. Bonaparte's views on Egypt were now made manifest: this document betrayed views of hostile aggrandizement towards England and breached principles of peace and amity.[2]

Andréossy was warned by Talleyrand that the English would not fail to display their indignation at the report and advised how to answer any complaint. His reply should be as follows: "A French officer sent to re-establish normal trade relations between France and Egypt could not but have been astonished to see that the English army had not yet

---

[1] Browning pp.59-65

[2] Malmesbury p.212

evacuated the country. Unaccustomed to politics, the officer must have looked on so manifest a violation of such a solemn treaty as a commencement of hostilities, and hence his mind would naturally turn to military calculations and the chances a war might offer; for the retention of Egypt and Malta, despite the stipulations of the Treaty of Amiens, is an act that provokes the renewal of the war." When Lord Hervey from the Foreign Office called at the French Embassy expressing his uneasiness at the report and the bad impression it would make, Andréossy was prepared: the article's intention was only to highlight the fact that Egypt and Malta remained occupied by Britain. The British were waiting for Russia's guarantee, was Hervey's response. That had nothing to do with Egypt, was the Frenchman's reply. Hervey persisted: and the insults to General Stewart?

"You are very sensitive; and yet every day the London papers are filled with disgraceful calumnies, repugnant alike to decency and good taste."

"The French papers may say what they please, but it is a different matter when it is the *Moniteur*, the official organ."[1]

The Cabinet met several times and was determined to notice the Sébastiani report and use it as an opportunity to force Bonaparte's real intentions into the open and express their own in regard to Malta. Hawkesbury wrote back to Whitworth explaining their response to it. As "it purports to be the report to the First Consul of an accredited agent [...] published in the official papers with an official title prefixed to it", it "must be considered as authorised by the French government". British obligations under the Amiens Treaty were dependent on the state of affairs that prevailed at the time. The independence of Switzerland and Holland were respected by the French then, but since the peace had been agreed, France had extended its power in those countries as well as Italy. Because of this change Britain was no longer strictly bound by the terms of the Treaty, only by the principles underpinning them. In the interests of preserving peace, Britain was going to let the recent French encroachments pass and continue restoring its conquests, but the publication of Sébastiani's report had changed things. Whitworth was instructed to tell the French that the British were no longer prepared to discuss Malta until they had received a satisfactory explanation of France's

---

[1] Coquelle pp.28-30

actions.[1] The British were no doubt emboldened in their persistence to hold on to Malta by recent intimations from Russian sources that the Tsar supported this stance. In December 1802 the Russian Foreign Minister Alexander Vorontsov had hinted to the British ambassador to St Petersburg that Britain ought to retain the island and in January 1803 Prince Adam Czartorski had explicitly declared to the ambassador that the Tsar positively desired it.[2]

In a meeting with Hawkesbury, Andréossy attempted to calm the alarmed Foreign Secretary: "Without a very considerable navy we could have no designs on Egypt; the business of St. Domingo is quite sufficient for us, and besides, when such designs are conceived, care is taken not to divulge them." When Hawkesbury complained of Bonaparte's attempts to intimidate Britain, Andréossy admitted that the Sébastiani report was a deplorable error, but asked about Malta. Hawkesbury replied that as the position of Europe, especially France had changed since the Treaty of Amiens, the gains allowed to Britain to compensate for French power at the time were no longer sufficient. Andréossy could only remind him that the French government had in vain requested that the English Cabinet recognise the Ligurian and Italian republics and no clause of the Treaty required the evacuation of Piedmont. After their meeting, Andréossy wrote to Talleyrand, declaring that "Colonel Sébastiani's report is almost forgotten; but it has left traces behind it. The funds have fallen". Despite Hawkesbury's anxiety, he firmly believed that the British Cabinet "cannot wish for war".[3]

Soon after receiving the letter from Hawkesbury, Whitworth called on Talleyrand one morning without an appointment. He pre-empted any discussion on the British press by telling the Foreign Minister he could not add anything further to what he had already said. On other matters, he had nothing new to report, except to confirm his government's position he had related at their last meeting. The principles of the Amiens Treaty gave Britain the right to interfere in Europe against French encroachments such as in Italy and Switzerland. Britain was about to carry out the remaining articles on Malta when the Sébastiani report

---

[1] Browning pp.66-68

[2] Fedorak pp.121-122

[3] Coquelle pp.32-33

was published. This had now made it impossible to discuss the island until they had been given a satisfactory explanation on the subject of the First Consul's intentions. Talleyrand accepted that it was natural that England should be sensitive about Egypt given its possessions in India, but claimed that nothing in the conduct of the French justified its alarm. French interest in Egypt was purely commercial, the First Consul genuinely wanted peace and England must know that France did not have the resources to start another war. What, Talleyrand asked, was the nature and extent of satisfaction that England required? Whitworth said he had no further details, but suggested that they simply needed to be convinced of French sincerity. He accepted that Britain may be financially better off than France, but insisted that His Majesty was not likely to risk war except for the most absolute and unavoidable necessity.[1]

When Talleyrand reported this meeting to Bonaparte, the latter was convinced that Britain wanted to keep Malta. Their complaints were just a pretext. He reasoned that the best way to test their sincerity would be to have a private meeting with Whitworth. If they had genuine fears, he could allay them in person. Whitworth was duly invited to meet with Bonaparte at the Tuileries on 17 February.

When Whitworth arrived, Bonaparte received him cordially, then asked him to sit down at a table, seating himself directly opposite. Bonaparte, placing his elbows on the table, leaned forward and explained that the best way he could demonstrate his sincerity was by a personal meeting. He began this charm offensive by complaining about Britain's continuing occupation of Malta and Egypt and the British and émigré press.

"Every breeze that blows from England brought me nothing but hatred and outrage. Now we are in a situation from which we must absolutely get out. Will you or will you not execute the Treaty of Amiens? I have on my own part executed it with scrupulous fidelity. The Treaty obliged me to evacuate Naples, Tarentum and the Roman States, in three months; and in less than two months the French troops had quitted all these countries. There are ten months passed away since the exchange of ratifications, and the English troops have not yet evacuated Malta and Alexandria. It is useless to endeavour to deceive us in these facts: will you have peace or war? If you will have war, it is only for you to say as much;

---

[1] Browning pp.73-78

we will make it with obstinacy until one nation or the other is ruined. Do you desire peace? Then you must evacuate Alexandria and Malta. Because this rock of Malta, on which so many fortifications have been constructed, has, there is no doubt, a very great maritime importance, but it has in my view a much greater importance than that – it is the interest it has connected with the highest point of French honour; what would the world say if we suffered the violation of a solemn treaty entered into with us? It would cast doubts upon our strength, upon our energy. As to me, my part is taken; I would much sooner see you in possession of the heights of Montmartre than of Malta."

When Whitworth found a moment to speak, he repeated everything he had already told Talleyrand. It was difficult to suppress licentious newspapers under English laws and the reception at court of French royalists was an act of sympathy and English hospitality towards unfortunates. Besides, the press war would eventually die down.

Bonaparte dismissed these excuses as untenable, but was more interested in Britain's position on Malta. Whitworth explained the main delay had been in getting guarantees agreed, and added that they had every intention to quit when unexpected changes in Europe occurred and the Sébastiani report came out.

"Of what changes do you speak?" Bonaparte asked. "Surely not of the Presidency of the Italian Republic which was conferred upon me before the signatures of the Treaty of Amiens? It cannot be the erection of the kingdom of Etruria, which was well known to you before the same Treaty, because it was asked of you, and you gave hopes of your approaching acknowledgement of that kingdom: it cannot be that of which you speak. Is it of Piedmont? Is it of Switzerland? [...] these two incidents have added little to the reality of things." Whitworth heard him refer to them with a coarse expression he was not prepared to commit to writing. Posterity was to be spared this profanity by the phrase "They are bagatelles!"

Bonaparte continued: "But, however, it may be, you have not the right to complain, because as regards Piedmont, even before the Treaty of Amiens I stated before all the world what it was my intention to do, I stated it to Austria, to Russia, to you. I have never consented, when it has been requested of me to promise the re-establishment of the House of Sardinia to its states. I have never even been willing to stipulate in its behalf for a determinate indemnity. You were then well acquainted with my intentions of annexing Piedmont to France; and besides, this arrangement changes nothing in my influence upon Italy, which is absolute: I wish it should be so and so it will remain. In regard to Switzerland you must be well aware that I will never suffer a counter-revolution to take place in that country. But all these allegations can never seriously be intended. My power in Europe, since the Treaty of Amiens, is neither more nor less than it was at that time. I should have called upon you to take a part in the affairs of Germany, if you had exhibited towards me different sentiments."

Bonaparte told the ambassador: "You well know that in all which I have done I have ever wished to complete the fulfilment of treaties and to secure the general peace." He demanded to know: what state was he threatening or contemplating invading? "There is none, you are aware there is none. [...] If you have any suspicions regarding my view upon Egypt, my Lord, I will attempt to remove your apprehensions." He then tried to clarify his position, admitting an interest in Egypt, but only if there was a war which he would do his best to avoid. If the Ottoman Empire collapsed, he merely wanted France to have its share of it. Had he wanted Egypt he could have taken it a month ago, and anyway he was restrained from doing so by both the European powers and the French people, who would not support such unjust aggression. If Britain went to war, it would not find any allies as he would not risk uniting Europe against him by any acts of provocation. All that he had to do in Germany and Italy was done. He did not want to risk losing the power he had in a "desperate contest", but if he was forced to fight he would defeat whatever allies England had on the continent and attempt to invade England itself despite the risk involved. If he were to succeed, England's descendants would "deplore in tears of blood" the resolution their current government would force him to take.

"It will be best for you and me to give the satisfaction prescribed by the Treaty. Let Malta be evacuated, do not suffer those who attempt my assassination to have an asylum in England; let me be libelled if you will by the English newspapers, but not by the miserable emigrants who so dishonour the protection which you have accorded to them, and whom the Alien Bill permits you to expel from England. Act cordially towards me, and I promise you on my part, the most cordial and entire return: I promise you continuous efforts to conciliate our interests wherever they are reconcilable. Consider what a powerful influence we might exercise over the world if we could obtain the nearer approximation of the two nations! You have a navy that in ten years of consecutive efforts, and in employing all my resources, I should not be able to equal; but I have 500,000 men ready to march under my orders, wherever I choose to lead them. If you are masters of the sea, I am master of the land. Think, then, sooner of our becoming united than of making war upon each other, and we may at will regulate the destinies of the world. Everything is possible within the interests of humanity with our double power – France and England in union."

When Bonaparte had finished, Whitworth said it was only a desire for peace that prevented England from renewing the war, not a fear of having no allies. After the ambassador complained that all British claims in French courts were failing, Bonaparte stood up and promised to ask Andréossy to talk to Hawkesbury. In good humour, he then left. Talleyrand later told Whitworth that the First Consul was re-assured by this meeting. Whitworth was not. In his dispatch to Hawkesbury he noted that not once did Bonaparte claim his interest in Egypt was commercial and concluded that "the object of the First Consul was, if he could not persuade us into those measures which must facilitate the accomplishment of his plans, to frighten and to bully."[1]

A few days later, Bonaparte addressed the opening session of the Legislative Assembly: "The government guarantees to the nation the peace of the continent, and it allows itself to hope for the continuation of a maritime peace [...] In order to preserve it, the government will do whatever is compatible with the national honour, essentially connected with the strict execution of the treaties." He claimed there were two parties in England – a peace party and a war party – struggling to influence the government there. If the war party prevailed, France would be ready with 500,000 men and England would be unable to stand up to France alone.

****

The publication of the Sébastiani report and the war of words in the French and British newspapers fuelled a rumour that war was imminent. Some friends advised the Edgeworth's to leave Paris, while others

---

[1] Browning pp.78-85, Thiers pp.452-454

suggested there was nothing to worry about. An ill relative in Edinburgh gave them sufficient reason to depart, but when news of their relation's recovery arrived they decided to stay longer, hoping the talk about war was unfounded. By the end of February, the rumours resurfaced. Mr Edgeworth wrote to his son Lovell, who was in Genoa on his way to Paris, warning him about the situation. One day, a French friend, Monsieur le Breton, told Mr Edgeworth that he would know by the evening if war was coming. Le Breton, however, was a little nervous about being noticed communicating such information to a potential enemy, so rather than visiting or sending him a note, he suggested they meet at a mutual friend's place that evening. To avoid the possibility of being overheard, he would signal what he knew by the use of his hat. If he suddenly put it on, that would mean there would be war. Mr Edgeworth duly went to the agreed rendezvous and there observed his friend place his hat firmly on his head. The next day the Edgeworths said goodbye to their friends in Paris, promising to return if they discovered the rumours of war were unfounded. By 4 March they were in Calais and only bad weather delayed their arrival in Dover on the 6th.[1]

---

[1] Hare pp.130-132

36. Treason Trial

On 5 February 1803, the jurors for the trial of Colonel Despard were sworn in at the Sessions House on Horsemongers Lane, which adjoined the Surrey County Jail where the accused were being held. The jurors were chosen from a pool of 500 men whom were graded according to their political sympathies. Only sixty-five could be found who were considered a "good man and true" while at least thirty-five were designated as "bad", the remainder of those for whom an opinion could be found were marked as "doubtful". After much haggling by Despard's defence team, a jury was chosen comprising eight good men, three bad ones and a single doubtful.

It had been announced a few weeks earlier, at the pre-trial hearing that Despard would be tried first and separately from his twelve confederates. Despard's wife Catherine, Sir Frances Burdett and Horne Took had started a committee run from the latter's home in Wimbledon. They received funds from wealthy sympathisers and enlisted the support of lawyers including William Draper Best, a Whig MP, who was chosen to defend Despard in court. On the day of the preliminaries, when the jury was sworn in, Despard was asked by the Clerk of the court, "How will you be tried?" Despard simply said, "I suppose that has already been decided." Despard was told that the expected traditional response was "By God and my country." He apologised, declaring he meant no offence, but simply found the question "somewhat strange".

Two days later the trial began. The presiding judge was Lord Ellenborough the Lord Chief Justice, who was a determined advocate for stern measures against radical dissent and convinced that "criminal laws could not be too severe". Ellenborough had declared at the preliminaries that he had "no intention of directing the court" or biasing their judgement, but could not withhold his "horror at the mediated consequences" of the plot. The prosecution was headed by Sir Spencer Perceval, who led a team that included William Garrow, a former defence lawyer with a reputation for aggressively cross-examining witnesses and who had been on the team prosecuting Hadfield for his attempt on the King in 1800.

The Consequences of Honour

Perceval began the proceedings by outlining the case for the prosecution. His goal was to implicate Despard in a plot that included the assassination of the King. The specific treasonable offences the defendant had committed were those of inciting insurrection in the ranks, membership of an illegal society and attempted regicide. These felonies followed from Despard's presence in the club room of the Oakley Arms on the night of 16 November. Despard was the only gentleman in a group comprised of the "lowest orders of society" who were "planning a most desperate act of treason to be executed the very next week [...] How is this to be accounted for innocently?" The most plausible reason was that he was "the leader to whom the rest looked for advice". His presence and his status meant he must have been at the centre of the plot. Even if he had been against the plot or was there to dissuade the others, his attendance still implied his guilt. The conspiracy might have seemed incredible to a reasonable person, but not necessarily so to the perpetrators themselves who must have been unreasonable men to consider such a plan. They were deluded and misled by the revolutionary nonsense they mutually inspired in each other.

The prosecution then trotted out their key witnesses, the constables who testified to Despard's presence at the club room and four soldiers arrested at the time but who had turned King's evidence in exchange for immunity from prosecution.

William Francis, a private in the First Battalion of Foot Guards claimed that Despard had tried to administer an oath to him and that the Colonel had called off a previous date for the plot at the last minute in expectation of money and news from France. On the night of 16 November, Francis claimed he was told of a plan to fire the great gun in the park, loaded with four balls of chain and shot, at his Majesty as he returned from the Houses of Parliament. He added he heard Despard say: "If we have the Tower and the Bank, we have everything." From the Tower, they could have burned the town and battered it to pieces.

When cross-examined by Best, Francis admitted he had been previously charged with desertion and obliged to acknowledge that his testimony would also serve to send his own brother, who had been arrested with Despard, to the gallows. Best asked the court if this was the kind of man they would be prepared to trust with their lives? The soldier Thomas Blades, who had been given rum and water by Despard when he arrived at the clubroom, told the court how they discussed when and where to attack the King. The best place, he said, would have been the

Mall and the best time when the King was returning from his levee to Buckingham House.

A star witness for the prosecution was the soldier Thomas Windsor. Prompted by Garrow, he told the court how he had been invited by John Francis to help overthrow the present tyrannical system of government. He was given a card to read and kiss, considered equivalent to swearing an oath, asked to distribute similar cards amongst his troop and invited to attend meetings in pubs where subscriptions would be raised to pay for delegates to go into the country and print more oath cards. At one of these meetings he claimed to have had a private conversation with Despard. The Colonel had said: "I believe this to be the moment [...] The people, particularly in Leeds, in Sheffield, in Birmingham, and in every capital town in England, are ripe. I have walked twenty miles today [...] and the people are ripe everywhere I have been. [...] His Majesty must be put to death, and the people will be at liberty." The mail coaches were to be stopped as a signal to the country that they had revolted in town. Despard asked him to bring more men to another meeting to discuss the best means of taking the Tower and securing its arms. Garrow then asked Windsor: "Do you remember any other remarkable expression to have been used by Colonel Despard?" Yes, he did, Windsor replied. The Colonel had said: "I have weighed the matter well, and my heart is callous."

Windsor had not been arrested on the night of the 16th, but told the court he had volunteered his testimony to a police officer on arriving at the Oakley Arms after Despard and the others had been arrested. It was in fact Windsor who had alerted the authorities to the conspiracy and told them of the meeting at the Oakley Arms. Windsor had wanted to leave the army, but his application for discharge had been refused. He had joined the plotters in May or June 1802, but when he stumbled across Despard, a "name of some consequence", he approached the authorities in the hope this information would improve his own situation.

When Best made his case for the defence he emphasised that the sheer seriousness of the crime, which "freezes the blood", was no evidence of Despard's guilt. On the contrary, it demanded extraordinary proof and loose talk could not constitute treason. He quoted Montesquieu: "nothing renders the crime of high treason more arbitrary than declaring people guilty of it for indiscreet speeches." The prosecution said that the charges would stand or fall on overt acts, but words did not constitute overt acts. Treason must be committed by writing or deed – verbal statements were insufficient under the law. The only overt acts were illegal oaths found on three drinkers. The only connection between them and Despard was the evidence of William Francis, who was even prepared to send his own brother to the gallows to save his own skin. "Fourteen or fifteen persons assemble together at a common tap-house, with no other fire-arms than tobacco pipes, form a conspiracy to overturn a government [...] and supported by the unshaken loyalty of almost as many millions." This was a preposterous plot. "Not an atom of evidence" supported the testimony of William Francis that the plot involved foreign aid or enemy collusion. Whatever the plot was, it was not a threat to the nation. Of course there was a plot by some to lead troops astray from their allegiance to the King, but Despard was not a party to it. There were no reliable testimonies or written confessions that indicated he was an "enthusiast for the cause" or deluded by "wild and visionary beliefs". Despard was "a disappointed man, yet God forbid that disappointment should be supposed to engender treason". He had, unlike some, earned his rank of colonel by serving in a dangerous campaign, relying on traits incompatible with the rash enthusiasm the prosecution was alleging. Of course, Best had to explain what Despard was doing at the Oakley Arms. Why should Despard have allowed himself to be drawn in? Why, because he had been locked up for three years without trial, felt its injustice and wanted to help those who had also been treated unfairly. He was merely attending to listen to their grievances, unaware there were those there under false pretences, ready to break their oaths and prepared to say anything to save themselves.

The defence then produced their witnesses. First to take the stand was the Right Honourable Lord Nelson, who was asked: "How long has your lordship known Colonel Despard?" "It is twenty-three years since I saw him. I became acquainted with him in 1779, at Jamaica. He was at that time, lieutenant in what were called the Liverpool Blues. From his abilities as an engineer, I knew he was expected to be appointed..." Nelson was cut short by the Judge: "I am sorry to be obliged to interrupt your Lordship," said Lord Ellenborough, who asked Nelson to limit his testimony to Despard's "general character". Nelson continued. "We went on the Spanish Main together [...] we slept many nights together in our clothes upon the ground. In all that period of time no man could have shown more zealous attachment to his sovereign and his country than Colonel Despard did." He had "formed the highest opinion of him at that time, as a man and as an officer".

If Nelson had been allowed to relate Despard's early military career, the court may have found it interesting. Despard, from an Anglo-Irish family, was promoted to lieutenant in 1772 after joining the Royal

Navy in 1766. In 1780 he and Nelson took part in a mission to capture the Spanish colony of Nicaragua. The expedition failed, but both Despard and Nelson distinguished themselves in the capture of Fort Immaculada, a Spanish outpost on the San Juan River. Despard was consequently promoted to captain and in 1782 he led a force that recovered the British settlement of Black River on the Mosquito Coast. As superintendent of the Bay of Honduras, where he married his black wife Catherine, he upset the white settlers by giving the rights they enjoyed to freed former slaves as well. The white settlers complained to London and Despard was summoned there to explain his actions. Back in England, in 1790, he was suspended on half-pay by the then Home Secretary Lord Grenville while the charges against him were investigated. Unpaid expenses from the Honduras and mounting lawyers' fees forced him into debt and in 1792 he was thrown into the King's Bench debtors prison where he languished until 1794. On regaining his freedom he joined the London Corresponding Society, immersing himself in radical politics. In 1798 he was arrested on suspicion of involvement in the Irish rebellion. Thanks to the suspension of Habeas Corpus, he was held without trial for three years. In February 1801 the suspension of the Act lapsed and the state was obliged to release its un-convicted prisoners. Despard was freed in April and resumed his association with radical politicians and agitators.

After Nelson had given his brief opinion of Despard's character he was asked by the prosecution to confirm that this was based on his acquaintanceship from 1779 to 1780. "Yes," replied the Admiral.

"Have you had much intercourse with Colonel Despard since that time?"

"I have never seen him since 29th April 1780" he answered.

"Then, as to the loyalty for the last twenty-three years of his life, your Lordship knows nothing."

"Nothing" he concurred.

Despard was not called to testify for himself, but told the judge: "my counsel have acquitted themselves so very ably, and so much to my satisfaction, that I have nothing more to say." In the summing up, Lord Ellenborough felt obliged to remind the jury that none of the defence witnesses had been able to testify to Despard's character in recent years. The jury took twenty-five minutes to deliberate. The verdict: guilty.

The Consequences of Honour

However, the foreman added, "My Lord, we do most earnestly recommend the prisoner to mercy, on account of high testimonials to his former good character and eminent services."

The next day the others were tried. Of the original twelve who had been indicted only one had the charges dropped. Two were acquitted by the jury, the rest being found guilty. Three of these were recommended to mercy, the remaining six condemned to death. Despard was recalled to court to hear their sentencing and was allowed to make a final statement. "I have only to say that the charge brought against me is one which I could not have the most distant idea of [...] I have now nothing further to say than what I said at first: I am not guilty." Lord Ellenborough then told them their fate.

"It only remains for me to pronounce the sad and painful sentence of the law upon the crime of which you have been convicted, and that sentence is, and this court doth adjudge, that you the several prisoners at the bar, be severally taken from hence to the place from whence you came and from thence be severally drawn on an hurdle to the place of execution, and there be severally hanged by the neck, but not until you are dead, but that you be severally taken down again, and that whilst you are yet alive, your bowels be taken out and burnt before your faces, and that afterwards your heads be severed from your bodies, and your bodies be divided each into four quarters, and your heads and quarters to be at the King's disposal. And may God Almighty have mercy on your souls."

Despard addressed the court one last time. "I beg your Lordship will allow me to say one or two words. Your Lordship has imputed to me the character of being the seducer of these men; I do not conceive that anything appeared in the trial or the evidence against me, to prove that I am the seducer of these men." With that the prisoners were returned to their cells in the Surrey Jail.[1]

Despard did not abandon all hope. In the next few days, he busied himself writing letters, including a petition to the King, in which he pleaded for clemency and solemnly declared "that he never directly or indirectly mediated or connived at any plan or attempt on the life of Your Majesty." He was visited by his wife Catherine every day, who took

---

[1] Gurney pp.3-269, Jay pp.302-329

everything he wrote and visited Nelson at the Piccadilly house of his mistress Lady Hamilton. She arrived in great distress, clearly demonstrating that she was still passionately in love with her husband, presenting the Admiral with a letter from Despard. In it, he expressed his gratitude for Nelson's testimony and asked him to write to Addington with a plea for leniency. Nelson obliged and although Addington was moved to weep with his family over the letter during supper, the death sentence could not be commuted. The government did decide to dispense with the medieval disembowelment and burning of entrails. When the warrant for the execution arrived on Saturday 19 February, Catherine, who had been bordering on delirium the day before, was devastated. Despard's papers and possessions were taken away. Wives and relatives of the other prisoners said their goodbyes on the same day. When Catherine left by coach, waving her handkerchief from the window, she went to Sir Richard Ford's office to plea for a stay of execution, but without success.

On Sunday afternoon she was allowed to visit her husband for the last time and left him anxiously pacing his cell. She returned at 5pm and tried to see him again, but was not allowed. Indignant, she declared her adherence to the cause of her husband. An hour later, his jailers, noticing Despard dozing, overheard him muttering to himself "Me – they shall receive no information from me, no not for all the gifts, the gold, and jewels, in the possession of the crown!" Later in the evening he was visited by the prison chaplain, the Reverend Winkworth, who asked him if had thought about the need for religious consolation. Despard told him that he had read a great deal of theology and had made up his mind on religious matters. Winkworth offered him the book *Evidences of Christianity* to read. Despard offered Winkworth the treatise on logic by his bedside in return. Gesturing with his chains, Despard implored the priest not to attempt to put shackles on his mind as well as his body. Intrigued, Winkworth asked him what his beliefs were. Despard admitted he believed in a deity and suggested that outward forms of worship were useful for political purposes, but otherwise thought that the opinions of churchmen, dissenters, Quakers, Methodists, Catholics, savages or atheists were equally indifferent. His bible was Tom Paine's *Rights of Man*. In his report to the Home Office later, Winkworth wrote that Despard was "very polite [...] never profane, nor did he at any point during his confinement speak disrespectfully or contemptuously of anybody".

Long before dawn on Monday 21 February, large crowds had been gathering around the jailhouse which was surrounded by a cordon of constables recruited from outlying boroughs. A detachment of Horseguards cavalry were in Horsemongers lane and all infantry regiments in the city were placed on alert. The Bell of St George's church tolled at 5 a.m. and continued the whole hour. By 6 a.m. 20,000 people were jammed into the carriageway of Horsemongers lane. At dawn seven wooden coffins were brought onto the flat roof of the jailhouse where a scaffold and gallows had been hastily assembled by carpenters the previous day. Two large bags of sawdust and a chopping block lay nearby.

At 7 a.m. Despard was offered the last rites in the chapel, which he refused. His irons were removed and for a brief moment his body was constrained only by his clothes. He was dressed in grey breeches, a cream waistcoat trimmed with gold lace and a blue undercoat with guilt buttons, a strip of scarlet flannel around his waist. Bareheaded, without wig or powder, in a dark greatcoat and boots, his arms were then bound with ropes and he was led out of his cell. Awkwardly, he shook hands with his solicitor and stepped into the prison courtyard. Waiting there was a procession of horses, carts, sheriffs and priests, keepers, constables, and an executioner with a sword. In one cart harnessed to two horses was clean straw. Despard laughed and exclaimed "What nonsensical mummery is this?" The government may have dropped disembowelment and burning of entrails from the sentence, but the ritual of being drawn in a hurdle to the place of execution still stood. They could not draw him through the crowded streets, so after placing him onto the back of a cart between two executioners, they conducted him briefly across the courtyard to the outer lodge.

At 8.30 a.m. the prisoners filed up to the scaffold on the roof, where nearly a hundred officers, dignitaries and guards had assembled. One of the condemned, John MacNamara, an Irishman, exclaimed, "Lord Jesus, have mercy on me!" Despard looked on impassively as a rope was placed around his neck and a cap put on his head. "I am afraid, Colonel, we have got ourselves into a bad situation," remarked MacNamara. "There are many better, and some worse," replied the Colonel. A Catholic priest and an Anglican vicar read rites to the condemned, but Despard obstinately refused absolution. Instead, he asked the Sheriff if he could say a few words. The Sheriff had no objection "provided nothing inflammatory or improper was intended". If so, the platform would be immediately dropped.

"Fellow citizens," Despard began. "I come here as you see [...] after having served my country faithfully, honourably and usefully served it, for 30 years and upwards, to suffer death upon a scaffold for a crime of which I protest I am not guilty. I solemnly declare that I am no more guilty of it than any of you who may now be hearing me. [...] Though His

370

Majesty's ministers know as well as I do that I am not guilty, yet they avail themselves a legal pretext to destroy a man, because he has been a friend to truth, to liberty and to justice, because he has been a friend to the poor and the oppressed." The front of the crowd applauded with a huzzah. "But, Citizens, I hope and trust, notwithstanding my fate, and the fate of those who no doubt will soon follow me, that the principles of freedom, of humanity, and of justice, will finally triumph over falsehood, tyranny and delusion, and, every principle inimical to the interests of the human race." The Sherriff warned him: any more in this vein and the platform would drop. Despard nodded. "I have little more to add [...] except to wish you all health, happiness and freedom, which I have endeavoured, so far as was in my power, to procure for you, and for mankind in general."

John Francis, the soldier betrayed by his brother, was standing next to Despard and remarked, "What an amazing crowd". Despard looked up and said, "'Tis very cold; I think we shall have some rain."

At 8.53 a.m. the signal to drop the platform was given. Despard was first. He clenched his hands in two spasms and then hung perfectly still, prompting the crowd to remove their hats. After the others were killed, the executioner cut down Despard's body and laid it over the chopping block. A surgeon then tried to cut through the neck with a dissecting knife, but had sufficient trouble that the executioner had to help by twisting the head. When it was finally separated, the hangman lifted it up and shouted: "This is the head of a traitor: Edward Marcus Despard." Some of the crowd hissed at him. By 10 a.m. it was all over, and as the crowd began to silently disperse, it began to rain.[1]

---

[1] Jay pp.13-26, pp.329-336, Burke pp.307-348

37. Tirade at the Tuileries

Hawkesbury was pleased with Whitworth's conduct in the meeting, but was not reassured by Bonaparte's. Just before the First Consul's address to the Legislative Assembly, Andréossy, acting on instructions from France, asked that the Bourbons be expelled and sent to Poland, citing the banishment from France of the pretender Charles Stuart by Louis XV as a precedent. Andréossy also requested the evacuation of Egypt and Alexandria, the deportation of royalist conspirators and the cessation of attacks on France and the First Consul by the British press. Hawkesbury was much grieved at hearing these requests and declared "that England, by refusing to evacuate Malta, had hoped that general explanations could have been made and compensation discussed on the basis of the changed status quo". The Foreign Secretary explained that Malta was playing a part far more important than its real value warranted. However, the British government, its support dependent on an electorate, could not avoid deferring to the voice of public opinion, which could not be too openly opposed.

Writing to Whitworth, Hawkesbury could not "avoid noticing, that nothing approaching to explanation or satisfaction" had been offered by Bonaparte in answer to British complaints about the Sébastiani article. Rather, "the language of the First Consul has tended to strengthen our suspicions". The French could be informed that Egypt was being evacuated, but Malta would not be – for the following reasons: Russia's refusal to provide a guarantee unless the Maltese order of Knights was abolished; the lack of guarantee from Berlin; the abolition of the Spanish orders and the requisition of their Spanish properties by Spain; the threatened sequestration of the Portuguese orders by Portugal unless the Spanish restored theirs; and, lastly, the non-election of a Grand Master. Britain also needed additional substantial securities in light of the extension of French power and influence.[1]

The government was also worried about reports of ships and troops in the ports of France and Holland. Although the British were told

---

[1] Browning pp.92-94

these were intended for Louisiana, they might be quickly turned against Britain if the peace ruptured. Furthermore, the British government had intelligence that suggested France was preparing to invade England. Bonaparte had summoned his key generals such as Masséna, and preparations on the coast did not look like those for a colonial expedition. Although there were no craft or vessels on the French shore, there were many in Holland, and it was from there it was believed a landing would be attempted. Andréossy tried to allay Hawkesbury's fears, telling him that if Bonaparte was obliged to invade England and failed, the Jacobins would end up seizing power in France, so Britain and France would both lose either way. The First Consul, the French ambassador insisted, had no sinister intentions. Hawkesbury was unmoved: Bonaparte, he confided to Malmesbury, was a rank Jacobin, with a Jacobin mind, Jacobin principles and Jacobin projects; but he was a Jacobin who had attained his point, got supreme power in his hands, and was exercising it as all Jacobins would in the same situation. Jacobin means and Jacobin ends did not always coincide.[1] Hawkesbury informed Andréossy that Britain wanted to keep a garrison in Malta for six or seven years. Andréossy reported this back to Talleyrand and added his conviction that although Hawkesbury was anxious about Malta, he was making every effort to bring about a reconciliation.

Andréossy must have therefore been surprised when, on 8 March, Hawkesbury summoned him in the morning to inform him of a King's message to be read to Parliament in a few hours' time. On learning of its content, the ambassador remarked it was in bad taste and ridiculous. The message was a request from the King to grant his government the means to prepare for the possibility of war:[2]

"His Majesty thinks it necessary to acquaint the House of Commons, that as very considerable military preparations are carrying on in the ports of France and Holland, he had judged it expedient to adopt additional measures of precaution for the security of his dominions." The message acknowledged these preparations were supposedly for colonial expeditions, but while "discussions of great importance" were taking place between Britain and France, the outcome of which were still uncertain, His Majesty was induced to ask Parliament to enable him "to adopt such

---

[1] Malmesbury p.230

[2] Coquelle pp.39-41

measures as circumstances may appear to require, for supporting the honour of his crown, and the essential interests of his people". The Commons agreed and voted for 10,000 additional seamen and the reformation of the militias.

On 10 March, on instructions from Talleyrand, Andréossy handed Hawkesbury a note. The First Consul required an explanation for the protracted occupation of Malta. It had been ten months since the ratification of the Amiens Treaty and Britain should have left the island seven months ago. The French had evacuated the Neapolitan and Papal states in Italy. The guarantees sought from the other major European powers were not part of the conditions to be satisfied before Britain was obliged to leave, but the First Consul had nevertheless acknowledged Russia's stipulations for accepting the role of guarantor.

Hawkesbury replied with his own note five days later. The Law of Nations, Hawkesbury said, gave England the right to demand further securities if the relative position of the two states had changed since agreeing to the Treaty. It was also a fundamental principle of the Treaty, formally agreed to by France, that Britain could retain some conquests in compensation for European territory gained by France. The English government was going to ignore the previous encroachments by France, until the Sébastiani article had aroused its suspicions. France had done nothing to alleviate them, but rather had aggravated them further. His Majesty "cannot consent that his troops should evacuate the island of Malta, until substantial security has been provided for those objects" which would be endangered by an evacuation. The withdrawal of French forces from southern Italy was not related.[1]

Meanwhile in Paris, when news of the King's Message to Parliament reached Talleyrand he met with Whitworth before briefing Bonaparte. Their last meeting in the first week of March had not gone well when Whitworth had conveyed Britain's latest position, mentioning the First Consul's continued interest in Egypt as being of particular concern. Talleyrand replied that there were no reasons for Britain's apprehensions. Yes, Bonaparte was interested in Egypt, but not enough to go to war for it. Talleyrand again asked: what security did Britain require the First Consul to give? Whitworth could only say that this would be the subject for further negotiation. Now, after the King's message, it seemed

---

[1] Browning pp.121-125

to the French that the British were preparing for war. Whitworth sensed that Talleyrand was agitated and tried to calm him. The measure was precautionary, was not intended to menace, and was only made because of French preparations in France and Holland. Talleyrand objected that they were for the colonies. The First Consul had no intention of threatening Britain unless Britain threatened France first, but added that a refusal to evacuate Malta would be considered as one.

They resumed their conversation after dinner at the Prussian ambassador's residence. The First Consul, said Talleyrand, was very upset by English suspicions. If the British were prepared to talk, then the First Consul would talk, but if they prepared for war, he would do the same. To expand on this last point, Talleyrand handed Whitworth a note and was asked to forward this on to Lord Hawkesbury. As a consequence of English mobilisation, France would take the following actions:

- French troops in Holland that had been about to go the Americas would now remain where they were.
- The French troops in Switzerland, which were about to leave would now stay there.
- A force would be sent to Italy, ready to re-occupy Tarentum.
- If no satisfactory explanation of Britain's mobilisation was offered, a further 20,000 French troops would be sent to Holland to threaten the King's German possession of Hanover, and military camps would be set up at Calais and other places on the French coast.

If Talleyrand had not conveyed how upset Bonaparte was, Whitworth was about to find out for himself a few days later.[1]

Sunday 13 March was the day the First Consul received the foreign diplomatic corps at the Tuileries. About an hour before the reception, Bonaparte was discussing an issue with Talleyrand in a private meeting. They disagreed, causing Bonaparte to lose his temper. After this clash, Bonaparte was in his apartment with Josephine, playing with little Louis-Napoleon, the son of Hortense and Louis, when an official announced that the 200 diplomats and their visiting compatriots had

---

[1] Browning pp.98-114

assembled. Bonaparte left the child, took Josephine by the hand and walked to the drawing room where everyone was waiting, except for Talleyrand, who had not yet arrived. Bonaparte, seeing the tall English ambassador, walked past other diplomats and straight towards him, leaving Josephine to sit down in an armchair. After asking after the health of the cold-stricken Duchess of Dorset, he enquired if there was any news from England. A letter from Lord Hawkesbury two days ago was Whitworth's reply.

"And so you are determined to go to war?" demanded Bonaparte.

"No, we are too sensible of the advantages of peace."

Bonaparte, as if he had not heard or was ignoring the reply, complained that they had already been at war for fifteen years, which Whitworth suggested was already too long. Bonaparte burst out: "but now you mean to force me to fight for fifteen years more." Whitworth pleaded that this was very far from His Majesty's intention. Bonaparte turned to the Spanish and Russian ambassadors, telling them the British could not be trusted and wanted war, before moving on to insult the Swedish envoy and unsettle the other diplomats. A few minutes later he came back to Whitworth, and tried to be more civil. He expressed the hope that the Duchess of Dorset, having suffered the winter in Paris, would still be able to see it in the summer, but could not help adding that this depended on England's actions, not his. He then demanded: why was England arming? Against what threat were the British taking precautions? "How can they dare to say France is arming itself? They have imposed upon the world! There is not a vessel in our ports. All the ships capable of service have been sent to St. Domingo. The sole armament that exists is at this moment in the harbours of Holland, and no one has been ignorant for four months past that it is destined for Louisiana."

All throughout this outburst Whitworth stood impassively looking down at the figure raging and fuming beneath him. At certain moments, Bonaparte's gestures with his cane in one hand seemed to be verging on physical assault, prompting the diplomat to wonder whether he would have to use his sword. Bonaparte was certainly known for his rough treatment of high-ranking subordinates when seized by rages, striking them with his riding crop, grabbing them by the throat, hammering their head against a wall, kicking them in the stomach and the groin, but a physical attack on a foreign dignitary would be a first.[1] Fortunately for them both, Bonaparte continued his harangue without further escalation: "They say there is a difference between France and England. I know of none. I only know that the isle of Malta has not been evacuated within the prescribed time." Bonaparte refused to believe that the English lacked the good faith to refuse to execute a solemn treaty, adding: "I cannot suppose, further, that by your armaments you have any desire to intimidate the French people". If England armed, the French would arm too. If England fought, so would the French: "it is possible to kill them my Lord, but never to frighten them!"

Whitworth replied that England wished for neither, but just wanted to live on good terms with France.

"Then she must respect treaties! Woe to them who do not respect treaties!"

Whitworth decided to remain silent and Bonaparte left the room, repeating his last phrase for all to hear before walking through the double doors without waiting for them to be opened for him. A few minutes later Talleyrand hobbled into the reception room, noticing it was unusually quiet and the expressions on people's faces unusually startled.[2]

After the reception Joseph told his brother, "You had everyone trembling. People will say you are ill-natured." Bonaparte had calmed down by now. "Yes [...] I was in the wrong". He explained he had not been in the mood for attending the reception.[3]

At a Council of State meeting held shortly afterwards, Bonaparte spoke at length on Britain's actions:

"I am unable to conceive the motives of the Kings message. There are two points; first, the armaments; this reduces itself to the expedition to Louisiana, two thousand men detained by the frost, and

---

[1] Memoir of George Douglas 8th Duke of Argyll, cited in Pocock p.76, McLynn pp.263-291

[2] Browning pp.115-117, Thiers pp.456-457

[3] Cronin p.288

three avisos at Dunkirk, which set sail for St. Domingo the very day of the message. The English ministers cannot pretend ignorance of that: it is sufficiently public. Otherwise, if they had demanded explanations, they might have been made easy on that head. Secondly, there are the discussions on the treaty, but I am not aware of any such; there are none. Do they mean to allude to Malta, or to keep it? But treaties must be executed and France cannot recede on that point without receding on all the rest. It would be contrary to honour. A nation ought never do anything contrary to its honour; for in this case it would be lowest of all; it were better to perish. If we gave up this point, they would next demand to have a commissary at Dunkirk. These times are past [...] We will not become the vassals of England. They well-nigh threatened me with war eight or nine months ago, if I did not conclude a treaty of commerce [...] If they mean to speak of Malta and intend to keep it, war is inevitable [...] We ask nothing from her; all that we require is the execution of treaties."

Perhaps, Bonaparte wondered, the King's speech was intended to encourage the French to extradite political refugees who had fled England to France after the execution of Colonel Despard? It was unlike England to be suddenly and so openly belligerent. War would cost her dearly, much more than France.[1]

A few days later, Whitworth complained to Talleyrand about Bonaparte's behaviour. Unless he was re-assured it would not happen again, he said he would no longer attend receptions at the Tuileries. Talleyrand apologised, but suggested Bonaparte's rage had been provoked by charges against him by the British government. The First Consul could not understand why Britain felt threatened by France. There were no significant armaments in the French ports and it was public knowledge that those in Dutch ports were destined for the French colonies. Nevertheless, he assured Whitworth that the incident at the Tuileries would not be repeated. Whitworth insisted that the King's message did not express any mistrust of Bonaparte. Precautions were merely being taken until their differences had been resolved. Britain was retaining Malta as a counterpoise to the conduct of France in Europe and as a consequence of suspicions that Bonaparte would re-invade Egypt. The French forces for the colonies could be easily redirected. Talleyrand sympathised with this view, but insisted on the First Consul's sincere desire for peace, despite his determination to fight if the treaty was not

[1] Hazlitt pp.383-385

observed.[1] Whitworth did not attend the next reception. When Lord Yarmouth, who was visiting France turned up, unaware that his country's minister was not there to present him, Bonaparte said to him, "My Lord, your Ambassador is sick, very sick."[2]

Whitworth began to pursue an alternative strategy to secure the peace and Malta. The day after the Tuileries reception he had sent to Hawkesbury a letter in cipher suggesting that Bonaparte's family might be induced by bribes to persuade him to allow England to retain Malta if they offered him something in return. By 21 March he had received Hawkesbury's approval. They could afford to pay £100,000 and Britain would not object to France keeping Elba and would recognise the King of Tuscany if Britain could keep Malta. However, no commitments should be made at this stage. Whitworth did not think this enough, but pressed on with his plan. To establish unofficial contact with Bonaparte's family, he relied on an English-Swiss resident of Paris, Bartholomew Huber, who was rumoured to be the natural son of Necker.

Huber approached an old acquaintance of his, Victor Pierre Malouet. Malouet had been an intendant of Marine under the old regime and had owned slave plantations in St Domingo. During the early stages of the Revolution he had been a member of the National Assembly. Now he was retired, supported by a pension from the French government. On 22 March Huber called on his old friend and asked him if he knew an honest influential man who was a friend of peace. Malouet said he did and Huber asked if he could be put in touch with him. Malouet enquired why. Huber confided that he was the bearer of a communication from the English ambassador which could not yet be considered official. Malouet suggested Joseph Bonaparte and agreed to ask a friend in the French government to introduce them, but wanted Huber to assure him he was not being involved in "some political intrigue". Huber divulged their plan and Malouet wrote to his contact, asking him to forward a letter to Joseph, who duly did so. In the meantime, Whitworth had decided Talleyrand needed to be sounded.

Huber met the French Foreign Minister and asked if Bonaparte's position on Malta could be changed. Talleyrand said that it was impossible

---

[1] Browning, pp.125-129

[2] Bristow pp.112-113

as the First Consul expected nothing but the execution of the treaty. But when Huber told him that a peace party, involving Lucien, Joseph and probably Madame Bonaparte was ready to act and that considerable pecuniary advantages might be derived from joining them, Talleyrand responded more positively, asking Huber for a few days to consider this and raising no objection to Whitworth meeting Joseph. A few days later Talleyrand asked Whitworth what he thought would be the outcome of the "discussion". Whitworth gloomily replied that it was unlikely to end as they both wished. His Majesty would not back down without satisfaction and there was no evidence that the First Consul would give it.

After agreeing beforehand not to discuss money, Whitworth met Joseph on 30 March, expressing his sincere desire to "avert the calamities of war" and appealed to the "negotiator of Amiens" and "friend of peace" to help solve the current difficulties. Joseph returned the same sentiments, but was not optimistic, unless Britain executed the Maltese article, explaining that his brother felt honour-bound to insist on its evacuation, especially after the King's message. If he forfeited his honour, he would forfeit the confidence of the French people. Whitworth asked Joseph to consider France's financial position and the instability of the Consular regime. Joseph replied that it was his brother's reputation that had brought him to power. He could not give that up without exposing himself to a greater danger than war itself.[1]

The possibility of conflict between England and France alarmed Russia. Count Markoff reported to his court that because of Bonaparte's weakness at sea he would be more likely to strike indirectly against England on the continent – in Naples, Germany and perhaps even the Peloponnese, thereby threatening Russian interests. The Tsar's reaction was to mobilise 60,000 troops on the Baltic coastline on 29 March, adding 12,000 more two weeks later. The Tsar's Foreign Minister, Vorontsov, was not convinced war was imminent. Despite Bonaparte's passionate views and tendency to offend other governments Vorontsov was "not entirely sure that he is as ready as many believe for breaking the peace [...] there is more instability and boasting in that head than systematic views."[2]

---

[1] Lokke pp.55-64

[2] Kagan pp.46-48

35 Maniac Ravings of Little Boney

Maniac-raving's-or-Little Boney in a strong fit. By James Gilray, 1803 (Courtesy of Library of Congress)

38. Friendship and Libel

By the end of November Canning recognized that a letter to Addington asking him to stand aside for Pitt would have "no impression upon him now". Nevertheless, he still felt that the "present system cannot stand [...] The hope is, that Addington, if left to himself, may feel his difficulties, and offer to give way. But I fear, on the other hand, his great vanity, and am confident that nothing but language in Parliament can cure it." His other fear was that Parliament might opt for Fox instead of Pitt, but thought the "present moment favourable to Pitt's return".

Pitt was still in Bath and shared Canning's concerns. The former prime minister was incensed by Fox's speech in support of Addington's apparent pacifism, and when he considered attending Parliament, Malmesbury restrained him, suggesting it was better for the government to become friendlier with Fox as that would make them less appealing to the King. Pitt concurred, adding "and if, on the other case, the country desires to lower itself to Fox, and to the disgraceful level to which Fox is disposed it should sink, he is the only proper man to govern it".

Pitt was still concerned with the growth of French power, but considered that however great France was, Britain had a revenue equal to all Europe, a navy superior to all Europe, an economy as great as Europe's and – as befitted a gentleman – a debt as large as that of Europe. If with those means, Britain acted wisely, with a just mixture of spirit and forbearance, and delay the war for a few years, war would be an evil much less felt.

An increasingly concerned Canning wrote to Malmesbury on 14 December: "Sooner or later he must act or the country is gone." The government was only posing tough towards France to placate Parliament, but "nothing is really at bottom, but concession – concession – concession. Will Pitt be thus satisfied? God forbid!" Pitt, however, now believed that it was not yet time for him to return to Parliament. The government had shown some energy and vigour not previously apparent. Despite his suspicions that this may not be genuine, he felt he could not criticise them on their supposed character and intentions. Only Bonaparte's audacity and the government's resumption of appeasement would provoke him to step forward now.

Malmesbury objected, claiming the present government's actions were clearly a sham. Pitt replied that "if it is only a sham vigour, it can not last; its consequences will soon be manifest, and then my time is come". Malmesbury persisted: would not this sham vigour lead to a worse situation, which his delay in opposing would make it more difficult for him to correct when he eventually took office again? Would he not regret this?

"If I were absolutely to wait for the sort of extreme case to which you allude, I certainly should, but I only mean to wait until there is any departure, on the side of Mr Addington's government, from the system they now affect to have assumed, or any further encroachment on the side of Bonaparte, which may materially affect the security or strength of this country." By security and strength he particularly meant Britain's maritime power relative to France. "I will add, that, if they insist on Malta being evacuated before the strict letter of the 10th article in the Treaty of Amiens is complied with, and Ministers give way, I then, and in that case shall also feel bound to oppose them avowedly. It is enough, and more than enough, that they have suffered to pass by unnoticed, the various unwarrantable encroachments which France has made since the preliminaries; but to allow them or the Treaty (bad as it is) to be violated, is a disgrace the nation must not hear of. To all these cases I will add any insult to our national honour."

Malmesbury argued that these events would inevitably arise – so why risk the possibility of the present government not dealing with them forcibly? The most important question, Pitt said in response, was how to bear and forbear. Britain's priority had to be to rebuild its strength so that when war came it could face it with greater confidence. Nothing should supersede this except a gross national insult or an open act of hostility or an act of aggrandizement that was comprised of both. Pitt's growing reservations with Addington's government were not limited to its dealings with France. The Budget had also disappointed him. He considered it foolish to borrow money to cover military expenses in peacetime and he calculated it had over-estimated state revenue by nearly £3 million.[1] He had also been annoyed by insinuations in government speeches that his previous administration had managed naval resources badly. What particularly incensed Pitt was an article in December in *The Times*, whose editor was closely associated with Hiley Addington. It described Pitt's

---

[1] Fedorak pp.95-96

Cabinet as "incapable" and accused them of "deserting their posts in the hour of danger, upon some frivolous pretext, or for some mysterious intrigue, which they have not the courage to explain, and which could not have operated on men of courage, or men anxious for character."[1]

When Addington learned from some mutual friends that Pitt was now less disinclined to return to office, he told them he would present no obstacle to such a desirable event. Pitt, on returning to London, suggested a meeting to Addington, who invited him to stay at the White Lodge in Richmond Park. The day after Pitt arrived, he left abruptly the following morning, having forgotten he had committed himself to some other business, but met Addington a few days later at Downing Street and at another brief visit to Richmond Park. On one of these visits, Addington and Pitt found themselves together in a carriage ride to London through Hyde Park. Towards the end of the journey, Addington nervously impressed upon Pitt that if Grenville had not suggested Pitt's return to power, he would have proposed it himself. Pitt replied that if the necessity of his return arose, he would consider it carefully and take into account his Majesty's, Addington's and his ministers' views.

****

On the day Despard was hanged, 21 February 1803, another trial was starting at the Court of the King's Bench. A Frenchman, Jean-Gabrielle Peltier, was being charged with the defamation and vilification of Napoleon Bonaparte. In August of 1802 he had published a number of articles in his journal *L'Ambigu*. The British government, under pressure from Bonaparte's constant complaints about attacks against him in the English press, decided there were grounds for prosecution. The articles appeared to incite the indignation of the French towards Bonaparte, taunting them with the suggestion that they had allowed a mere Corsican to enslave them. His wickedness, one passage claimed, increased every day as he augmented his power at the expense of their freedom. Esteeming nothing honourable, only interested in preserving his authority, Bonaparte

---

[1] Stanhope III pp.423-425

had surrounded himself with his Mamelukes – foreign bandits consisting of mutes, cut-throats and hangmen. Meanwhile men were subject to arbitrary arrest, judges were coerced to pass death sentences and punished for acquitting the innocent.[1]

"And now this tiger who dares to call himself the founder and regenerator of France enjoys the fruit of your labours as of spoil taken from the enemy. He is not satisfied with the destruction of the king nor of so many brave men nor of so many princes whom the war has mown down", while the blood of the army had been shed so that Bonaparte's family and generals could enrich themselves. Soldiers were either banished to insipid garrisons or sent to die like flies on colonial expeditions. Real Frenchmen should avenge these wrongs, recover their liberty or perish with glory. "You must act citizens, you must march you must oppose what is passing if you wish that he should not seize upon all that you have." One of the articles, an ode, invoked ancient history, alluding with approval to the assassination of Caesar by Brutus. Bonaparte was compared to Roman Emperors who were deified on their death: "Finally (and Romulus recalls the thing to mind) I wish that on the morrow he may have his apotheosis."

The prosecution was led by Spencer Percival, the Attorney General, who summarised his case against Peltier by referring to his publication as one "which has defamation for its sole object [...] to excite the subjects of that magistrate whom our country recognises, and with whom our country is at peace – to excite the subjects of that country to rebel against their chief magistrate de facto, and farther, to excite them to his assassination and to his murder." He reminded the court that this was not the first time libellers of foreign rulers had been prosecuted under English law, citing the example of Lord George Gordon's libel of the Queen of France. Percival observed the trial had a large audience, many of whom may have thought that Peltier's acquittal would be considered by Bonaparte as a declaration of war. Below the jury box sat two officials from the French embassy. Also among the spectators were runners of stock-jobbers, ready to report the verdict to the market which was expected to lower funds by five per cent if Peltier was found not guilty.

After Garrow had examined witnesses to confirm the articles had been published in peacetime, that Peltier was responsible for their

---

[1] Howell pp.529-619

publication and that the English translation was accurate, the defence attorney, Mackintosh rose to speak.

"Gentleman, the real prosecutor is the master of the greatest empire the civilised world ever saw. The defendant is a defenceless proscribed exile. He is a French royalist, who fled from his country in the autumn of 1792", driven from his home like many others "by the daggers of assassins". Losing everything, Peltier had been obliged to support himself by writing for the last ten years, but since the peace he had refrained from any serious political discussion and had confined himself to the obscure journal now being debated. Peltier was grateful to the British for not deporting him and had no hesitation in risking his freedom with an English jury. Mackintosh argued that his journal was not intended to be read in France because it was banned there. Because it was published in England and in French it was only intended to amuse fellow French émigrés.

Mackintosh asked the jury to consider the wider context of this trial, which he considered as "the first of a long series of conflicts between the greatest power in the world and the only free press remaining in Europe." He trusted that they would consider themselves as "the advanced guard of liberty". No law could specify in all circumstances and for all time which words should be libellous and which were innocent. It was up to the legal officers and above all the jury to interpret and decide. This made it uncertain what was libellous and it therefore took great courage to perform the duty of informing the public. It had to be done boldly if it was to be done effectively.[1] The government had to allow the press to speak freely about aggressive powers on the continent, because history showed that any attempt by one power to dominate Europe had required that power to neutralise if not destroy England. Britain could not without peril silence public discussions that were a means of rousing public indignation against an inevitable enemy: "A King of England, who in such circumstances, should conspire against the free press of this country, would undermine the foundations of his own throne; he would silence the trumpet which is to call his people round his standard." The press played an important role in sustaining the national spirit.

"A jury must be convinced before they find a man guilty of libel that his intention was to libel – not to state facts which he believed to be

---

[1] Howell p.571

true, or reasonings which he thought just." Peltier was not the author, but merely republishing articles that had already been printed in Paris by others. As an historian could not be considered libellous for republishing past slanders nor should Peltier. The Sébastiani article charged General Stewart with writing letters to procure assassination. Why had the English press been allowed to republish this? Because it was not libel to do so. Of course the prosecution could disagree, but the onus was on them to prove that it was not a re-publication of material. Even if one thought that it was Peltier's own work, who was the libel actually against? As Peltier was claiming the original author was Chenier, one should surely conclude that he was libelling Chenier and not Bonaparte. Indeed, the articles themselves were more consistent with the views of a Jacobin rather than a royalist like Peltier. The only thing they had in common was their dislike of the First Consul. Yet there was no exhortation in the article to assassinate Bonaparte, merely a declaration that the author would not shed any tears if such a deed was done. If the allusion to Brutus was inciting to kill, then all previous allusions to Brutus by other writers must be considered as such, and this was clearly unwarranted. The wish for Bonaparte's apotheosis was not necessarily a call for his death. The word "apotheosis" only meant the raising of someone to divine status and many Roman emperors were deified while they were still alive.

Percival, in response, admitted that there had been Roman emperors that were made divine while they lived, but pointed out the example was Romulus, who was only made divine on his death. He also insisted that even if an article was republishing a previous libel, the re-publisher was obliged to clarify that the purpose of the republication was not to propagate it.

The presiding judge, Lord Ellenborough, summed up, siding with the prosecution's contention that the allusion to Romulus could not be mistaken for a mere wish for Bonaparte's deification. "Gentlemen, upon the whole matter, on the best consideration I have been able to give to these different publications, it appears to me that the direct and indirect aim and tendency of them [...] was to degrade and vilify, to render odious and contemptible, the person of the First Consul [...] and likewise to excite his assassination and destruction [...] I cannot, in the correct discharge of my duty, do otherwise than state that these publications [...] are, in point of law, libels." Addressing the jury, he said: "Gentlemen, the matter is with you, and you will give that verdict, which your own conscience sanctions". The jury, without retiring from their box, immediately returned the verdict expected of them: guilty.

****

In March 1803 Dundas (now Lord Melville) was visiting Pitt at Walmer castle. He came with a proposal from Addington. Would Pitt consider joining the government? Addington would relinquish his role at the Treasury in favour of a compromise candidate, but there was no suggestion of who would take the role of first minister. Pitt replied that his uncertain health made him doubt his ability to take up office and would only return if it was considered necessary by and the express wish of those in the highest quarter. Besides, it was also absolutely essential that there should be an avowed and real minister possessing the chief weight in council and the principal place in the confidence in the King. There could be no rivalry or division of power. Authority must rest in the first minister who ought to control the finances and whose opinion had to prevail if there was dissension in the Cabinet. In the meantime, Pitt assured Melville that although he thought his recent budget statements were incorrect, he was willing to support Addington as long as he stuck to the principles of foreign and domestic policy he considered essential. When Melville left Walmer and met with Addington, he recommended that Pitt become Chancellor of the Exchequer while Addington was made Speaker of the Lords. Addington refused.

On 10 and 11 April Pitt and Addington met in Bromley. Pitt emphasised, that before he could commit to a proposal, he first required the King's consent. Addington concurred, but persuaded Pitt to at least declare what he would agree to, given the King's consent, adding his hope that Pitt did not intend to invite Grenville, Lord Spencer and Windham to join a new government. Pitt was not prepared to talk with any commitment about specific members of a new cabinet at this stage, but said that the abilities of these three were necessary and indispensable to a strong and efficient administration. Addington understood Pitt's position as one that insisted on their return to office as a condition of his own and promised to convey this to his colleagues but had no hope of them accepting it.

He presented these conditions to the Cabinet a few days later at Lord Chatam's. Although they all wanted Pitt back, they could not agree to his return if that required the return of persons whose opinions they considered hostile to the interests and peace of their country. Consequently they were not prepared to submit this proposal to the King. On 13 April Addington wrote to inform Pitt of their decision, who replied: "I have received your letter of the 13th. It requires nothing more than a simple acknowledgement." If Addington was stung by such a short letter, he would have been further upset by the one that followed.

On April 15, Pitt wrote: "It should appear from what you have written that you looked upon yourself as authorised, in consequence of what passed between us, to lay before your colleagues a regular and formal proposal, as coming from me, to return to office under certain conditions, and an intention on my part of drawing up a detailed and specific plan for forming an administration: no such authority was given, or intended to be given you by me." He repeated that he would not be constrained by a present administration to choose or prescribe members of a new one. "My motive for writing this, is therefore, I repeat, not to provoke the renewal of a discussion which I consider as finally and decisively closed, but in order to have an exact record of what has passed; and if at any future period this transaction should ever get before the public incorrectly, or be misrepresented, that there should exist an authentic document which could leave no doubt of the truth."

Addington wrote back, explaining that the Cabinet could only agree to its strengthening by Pitt and other colleagues chosen by him who had not opposed their policy. They could not consent to a complete renewal. He also reminded him that it had been Pitt who had brought up the subject of his return to office back in January. On the 20th Addington discussed these events with the King in a common audience after a levee from which the King got the impression that Pitt was using him. This incensed Pitt further. In a letter to Addington dated 21 April he declared that in January he had merely said that his return was out of the question at that time, but would not have ruled it out in the future if a crisis necessitated it. He never had any intention of strengthening the present government and always had the intention of forming a new arrangement in which a large proportion of the present Cabinet would have remained. His suggestions for new members would have depended on their consent, but which he was not prepared to ask for until the King had first approved them. He ended the letter demanding that Addington submit it along with their previous exchanges to the King. Addington did so, but the King refused to read them, remarking: "It is a foolish business from one end to the other, which begun ill, conducted ill, and terminated ill."[1]

---

[1] Pellew vol. II pp.107-130, Malmesbury pp.176-188

39. Malta or War?

At the end of March Andréossy sent Hawkesbury the French response to the King's message to Parliament. It began by insisting that the ships and troops in France and Holland were limited and not menacing England. British intelligence had misled its government. Why had the British not asked France for an explanation of this before deciding to mobilise? French power had not grown since Amiens. The Sébastiani article was relatively lenient in its offence to England compared to the venom of the British and émigré press. As Egypt had now been evacuated, only one Treaty obligation remained: Malta. The First Consul saw no subject for discussion there. Hawkesbury replied to Andréossy the same day. His government regretted that the French had still not offered a satisfactory explanation regarding England's concerns. He was therefore instructing his ambassador in Paris to ask whether the French would continue to withhold it.[1]

Andréossy was so concerned that the French note would only inflame the situation he wrote to Bonaparte directly: "you afford the English Cabinet no means of escape from the unfortunate position in which they have become involved, and however serious the consequences, it is certain that they will take up any challenge they may receive [...] God forbid that I should for a moment think that France ought to forego the least of her advantages [...] but I am morally certain, that by appearing not to exert pressure on England you can easily obtain all which is necessary to secure the safety of the French government and preserve the advantages it derives from the countries under its control." Andréossy remained convinced that Britain only wanted to retain Malta temporarily as they claimed, until relations with France had assumed a peaceful aspect. To Talleyrand he wrote: "Everything depends on the French government: if it is willing to give an explanation, a satisfactory compromise will easily be arrived at between the two powers; if it refuses, war is inevitable, and will be popular in England. If the French government discusses the matter in a generous spirit, Europe will attribute it to the magnanimity of the First Consul and to his desire to preserve

---

[1] Browning pp.148-152

peace among all the powers, for no one will dare to suggest weakness as a motive; in these circumstances peace will be preserved and England will be persuaded to make a free surrender to the First Consul of anything which he is justified in asking of her."

To Bonaparte, Andréossy tried to explain the precarious position of the British Cabinet. It had tried to secure the support of Grey, but he was too attached to Fox, while Pitt was retiring to Bath. "Everybody wants peace; by preserving the peace of Europe, you will crush this country, without appealing to the arbitration of the mailed fist. But I cannot too often repeat my conviction, that any Cabinet which may be in power must be treated with tact, for the Cabinet is responsible to public opinion as expressed in the Houses of Parliament." The King and merchants also needed to be taken into account. This was especially true of the current administration of "mere mediocrities" who lacked powerful family connections. The First Consul was "now in a most favourable position to decide the world's destiny for all time."[1]

On 3 April the members of the British Cabinet met to discuss the latest developments and decide their next course of action. As well as the disgraceful behaviour of the First Consul towards their envoy at the Tuileries, they had continued to receive intelligence confirming their suspicions of his belligerence. His brother-in-law, General Murat, had been despatched to Italy to demand from the King of Naples free passage for a French army bound for Sicily.[2] Troops were being ordered towards Dunkirk and Boulogne, while Bonaparte himself was expected to tour Belgium and visit Antwerp. The expedition to Louisiana had been cancelled, while another to India had set sail from Brest. Intelligence from Bordeaux suggested that Bonaparte had saved forty to sixty million livres to invade Britain. An intercepted letter from the Dutch ambassador in London, Schimmelpenninck, to a colleague, claimed that Andréossy had orders to be evasive to gain time while the Tuileries considered their next step. Schimmelpenninck thought that Bonaparte was afraid of war with the British, so he meant to bamboozle them by false assurances to gain time in the hope that a great power such as Russia would intervene to preserve the peace in his favour. Other secret intelligence suggested that Bonaparte had a plan to attack Portugal by sea from Toulon, while Joseph

---

[1] Coquelle pp.53-58

[2] Browning pp.106-109

would attack Naples to take Tarentum. Moreau would attack Egypt and Masséna would invade England. Masséna and Fouché were said to be against this plan and General Berthier was ready to resign if Bonaparte went to war.[1]

The Cabinet agreed that if Malta could be retained, thereby securing the Levant and Turkish Empire, they would be prepared to recognise the Italian states and accept that the King of Sardinia would not be compensated, which they could not do anything about anyway. French troops should evacuate Holland and Switzerland and if they still objected to England keeping Malta, Bonaparte should propose some equivalent security for British interests that would be exposed by leaving the island. No time should be lost in bringing this to an issue: "If the French government should decline all negotiation, Lord Whitworth should be instructed to leave Paris."[2] The Cabinet's decision was drawn up in a project which Hawkesbury sent to Whitworth the next day, who was again to ask for an explanation. If none was forthcoming and the French stuck to their rigid line on Malta, then he was to declare the impossibility of peace and his obligation to leave Paris. If the French showed an interest in discussing Malta, then he was to present the project.

On 7 April Whitworth handed Talleyrand a note that formally asked again for a satisfactory explanation. Talleyrand read it and then asked: what was it they had repeatedly refused to satisfactorily explain? Whitworth replied that it was useless to repeat what "had so often been urged in vain". Talleyrand should know perfectly well that the explanation required referred to the aggressive conduct of the French government since Amiens and that the satisfaction England wanted was related to the insulting of the British commander and forces in Egypt by Sébastiani. Talleyrand responded that no explanation was ever asked for any particular act by the French government – if it had been an explanation would have been immediately given. As regards the insult to England, one could not compare the language of Sébastiani to that of Major Wilson in his account of the Egyptian campaign. Whitworth remarked there was a difference between the common publication of the latter and official publication of the former. Talleyrand denied that Sébastiani's article was effectively authored by the French government.

[1] Malmesbury p.242

[2] Yonge pp.114-115

Nevertheless, he would communicate his Lordship's point to the First Consul that evening.[1]

The next day Talleyrand again demanded to know precisely what had caused the recent uneasiness and what it was that the French had refused to explain. Whitworth replied that if it was their aim to protract the present state of suspense and uncertainty, then he would be forced to be more specific, but suggested that it would be more profitable if they just agreed to discuss their difference on the principle underlying the Amiens Treaty – that French acquisitions on the continent were to be equated with the retention by Britain of some of its conquests. If France exercised the right to extend itself on the continent, then Britain had an "undoubted right to seek a counterpoise". Talleyrand did not dispute this principle, but said that the First Consul was upset by the expression "satisfaction", as it suggested an air of superiority. Whitworth rebutted that an inferior could demand satisfaction from a superior, and as France and England were equals no insult could be inferred. "But is there no modification, no means of satisfying both parties?" asked Talleyrand, who insisted that Bonaparte wanted peace so badly that there was nothing he would not sacrifice for it except his honour. It was only because of this that he insisted on the full execution of the Treaty, but would consider other ways of providing Britain with further security. Talleyrand suggested a mixed garrison of English, French, Italian and German troops. Whitworth thought this would oblige Britain to take even more precautions than it had already. Whatever Talleyrand suggested, Whitworth warned him it was unlikely to satisfy England. Talleyrand decided to write down his main point – that France would consider anything else except a proposal that threatened the independence of the Knights or which conflicted with the Treaty of Amiens. He then begged Whitworth to forward this to Hawkesbury. Whitworth consented, despite grumbling they were only losing time by doing so.[2]

When Hawkesbury received news of this meeting he was pleased. It suggested that the French seemed to be recognising Britain's right to counter further French aggrandizement. He told Whitworth to present the project now to see if the French would give way on Malta or not. He was to re-iterate the point that the British only remained in Malta because of

---

[1] Browning pp.159-161

[2] Browning pp.162-167

the unfulfilled Treaty conditions and the Knights' limited resources – and that further French acquisitions gave them the right to seek further gains themselves. He also added other options the British would consider. If the French were only concerned about the independence of the Knights, Whitworth suggested that the Knights be the civil government while Britain retained the forts. Alternatively Britain could be allowed to remain in Malta temporarily – for a further ten years at least – and be allowed to buy the smaller island of Lampedusa from the King of Naples.[1]

Before Whitworth received these instructions he felt that if the French would agree to a temporary occupation of Malta by Britain war could be avoided. He met with Joseph Bonaparte again, who asked him what alternatives would satisfy Britain. When Whitworth could not suggest anything Joseph proposed Corfu or Crete, or a Russian garrison for Malta, emphasising that none of these were official offers. The meeting left Whitworth with a sense of hope, so when he received Hawkesbury's proposals he presented these to Joseph to test the French reaction unofficially, warning that their rejection would be immediately followed by an ultimatum from Britain. Joseph objected to Britain keeping Malta forever, so Whitworth suggested Britain remain in the forts while the Knights ran the civil government. Joseph failed to see how this maintained the independence of the Knights. Malta was effectively controlled by whoever controlled the forts. When Whitworth proposed a temporary British occupation of Malta, Joseph appeared more hopeful of obtaining Napoleon's approval. Joseph was asked to present it to his brother as his own idea, rather than a British plan. Afterwards, the ambassador met with Talleyrand who was also optimistic about Bonaparte accepting a temporary occupation.[2]

The following evening Joseph told Whitworth that he would hear from Talleyrand, who would arrange to discuss the number of years Britain would be allowed to occupy Malta. However, in order to gain his brother's consent, Britain would have to offer something else, alluding to the recognition of the Italian states. Whitworth pointed out that these only related to the option of allowing Britain to keep Malta forever. However, if the years offered were considerable and as long as France agreed to the other demands – the evacuation of Holland and Switzerland

---

[1] Browning pp.170-173

[2] Browning pp.176-179

plus compensation for the King of Sardinia – then this might be acceptable. Joseph did not think this would be a problem.[1]

The next day Whitworth did not hear from Talleyrand, and as Joseph was out of town, went to see the Foreign Minister the following day and asked him if he had any response to the Maltese options. Talleyrand answered that had he called on him sooner he would have told him that Bonaparte had refused to allow Britain to keep Malta in perpetuity. Whitworth explained that the reason he had not called was because he had been led to expect that Talleyrand would call on him. He then enquired about the option of keeping Malta for ten years, adding that this was actually a concession, as Britain already possessed the island. Talleyrand said nothing, so Whitworth expected that when they met the next day they would be discussing the number of years Britain would be allowed to stay in Malta.[2]

Talleyrand and Joseph went to Bonaparte and tried to persuade him to allow Britain to keep Malta temporarily. The Knights would still be restored and maintained to confirm it would only be temporary and to preserve the dignity of the French Republic. Bonaparte was not impressed. All this tampering with the question was beneath him. If they went along with such dissimulation it would be much better to give up the island purely and simply as indemnification for France's supposed encroachments since Amiens: "No. Either Malta or nothing. But Malta is the dominion of the Mediterranean. No person can believe that I can consent to give up the dominion of the Mediterranean to the English without it being supposed that I fear to contest it with them. I lose at one time the most important sea in the world in the opinion of Europe."

"But, after all," said Talleyrand, "the English hold Malta, and in breaking with them, you will not take it from them."

"Yes," replied Bonaparte, "but I will not cede it without a contest at an immense advantage, I shall dispute it with arms in my hands, and I hope to bring the English to such a state that they will be forced to give up Malta and more than that; without counting if I arrive at Dover, it is all finished with these tyrants of the seas. Besides, when one must combat,

---

[1] Browning pp.180-182

[2] Browning pp.183-187

sooner or later, with a people to whom the greatness of France is insupportable, very well, it is better worth doing it today than at a later time. The national energy has not been enervated by a long peace: I am young, the English are in the wrong, more in the wrong than they have ever been; I should love better to finish now. Malta or nothing. I am resolved – they shall not have Malta [...] That they should be given a harbour in the Mediterranean, well and good. But I will not consent that they have two Gibraltars in that sea, one at the entrance, and one in the middle."[1]

As the claim for Malta also came with the demand that France evacuate Holland, the British stance was doubly unpalatable to Bonaparte: "By the Treaty of Amiens I have not engaged to evacuate Holland; so I can stay there without violating the letter of this Treaty. It is true that article II of the Treaty of Lunéville and Article II of the Convention of the Hague forces me to evacuate Holland after concluding peace with England; I admit that this peace was concluded a year ago, but the other treaties were not concluded with England; I do not recognise this power has any right to concern herself with the affairs of the continent; and so I refuse to evacuate Holland. On the other hand, I engaged by the Treaty of Amiens to evacuate Tarentum. I have done so. Therefore the English must quit Malta, for by the same agreement they are under an obligation to give up the island."[2]

---

[1] Thiers p.461

[2] Coquelle p.16

36 Evacuation of Malta

Evacuation of Malta. Bonaparte forces Addington to excrete Egypt, Guadeloupe and Malta into a cocked hat. By James Gilray, 9 Feb 1803 (Courtesy of Library of Congress)

40. Louisiana

Commandant Baille's request for a junior officer to help him in his duties guarding the prisoner Toussaint L'Ouverture was answered with the decision to replace him with a younger man. Bonaparte nominated Amiot, who was installed by the New Year. The new commandant promised not to relax any of the controls established by his predecessor, but did make a few changes. He instituted night searches and moved the time of the prisoner's only daily meal, consisting of biscuit, cheese, salted meat and a little wine, from nine to eleven in the morning. Like his predecessor, Amiot remained at the fort the whole time except for two brief leaves of absence. The first occasion he was away, he left Captain Colomier in charge, who was sufficiently sympathetic to provide Toussaint with some of his own coffee. After this Amiot prohibited the Captain from visiting the prisoner again.

Meanwhile, Toussaint's health got progressively worse. By the end of January 1803, his pains and fever continued to trouble him and were accompanied by a dry cough. In February he developed stomach problems and found it difficult to eat. By the 19th of that month he was vomiting and his body had swollen up. In March he was still swollen, coughing and suffering from a bad stomach. His voice had changed and his arm was in a sling, but despite his illness, Amiot had dismissed Dr Tavernier, who he decided "would have been useless to him" because the "construction of negroes" was "totally different to that of Europeans".[1]

On 7 April at eleven-thirty in the morning Toussaint's food was brought into his cell. The prisoner was sitting in his chair by the fire, his head resting against the fireplace, his right arm hanging down his side. He was not moving and did not respond to being addressed, and remained motionless when touched. His death was confirmed by doctors who found no pulse, no breath and no heartbeat. The next day a post-mortem was conducted. A little mucus mixed with blood was in the mouth and lips. The pia-mater – the inner membrane surrounding the brain and spinal cord – was gorged with blood, as was the right lung. Part of the

---

[1] CLR James p.363 (Poyen p.224)

abdominal cavity was emaciated, suggesting a long illness. The surgeon concluded that Toussaint had died of apoplexy, which at the time may have meant nothing more specific than bleeding of internal organs resulting in a sudden loss of consciousness. He also ascribed death to pleura-pneumonia, an inflammation of the lung and its cavity.

Amongst his belongings was found a letter from his son Placide, written on his way to Belle-Île:

> "*My dear father and mother. I am on board the brig* La Naiade. *As yet I am ignorant of my lot. Perhaps I shall never see you again [...] No matter where I am, I entreat you to take courage, and sometimes to think of me. I will send you news of myself if I am not dead. Give me news of yourselves if you have an opportunity [...] Isaac and Saint-Jean, do not forget your brother! I shall always love you. Many kind thoughts to you all; embrace my cousins for me. I embrace you as I love you. Your son, Placide L'Ouverture."*[1]

****

A few days after Toussaint's death, on Easter Sunday, 10 April, Bonaparte summoned two of his councillors of state to a meeting at St Cloud. He needed their advice on what he should do with the vast North American territory of Louisiana, lost by France to Spain in 1763, but which Lucien Bonaparte had persuaded the Spanish court to return to France in October 1800. This was kept secret at the time, while France was at war with England, and was conditional on a Spanish Bourbon being given the throne of Etruria. Soon after the preliminary treaty of peace with England, the cession became public knowledge. In November 1802, Spain gave the go-ahead for the transfer to take place, much to the alarm of the United States and Great Britain. The Spanish governor in New Orleans had already upset the Americans by prohibiting the free import and export of goods there in October. News of the impending cession to France soon after persuaded many of them that this had been demanded by Bonaparte. New Orleans was an important trade outlet for the United

---

[1] L'Ouverture Project

States. The U.S. ambassador in Paris, Robert Livingston, was instructed to buy the city from the French. Livingston was slightly deaf, a disability that caused some embarrassment the first time he was introduced to the First Consul in 1801. Bonaparte tried to complement the U.S. with the remark: "M. Livingston is leaving a very virtuous world for a very corrupt one." Livingston did not understand. "The old world is very corrupt," Bonaparte repeated. When Livingston still failed to comprehend, Bonaparte asked Talleyrand to explain, who assigned the task to one of the ambassador's compatriots.

On 27 February 1803 Livingston wrote to the First Consul, suggesting that he sell New Orleans to the U.S, arguing that France would not benefit from retaining it and only exhaust its finances trying to protect such an exposed colony. In ceding New Orleans, France would "rivet the friendship of the United States" and French West Indian islands would be assured of continuous supplies.[1] Talks with Talleyrand proved unsuccessful, so President Jefferson dispatched James Monroe to Paris with the authority to offer up to $2 million. He set sail from New York on 8 March.

In the same month a French fleet had disembarked a French army in New Orleans, after dropping off troops in San Domingo. Another expedition was assembling in the ports of Holland, closely watched by the Royal Navy. As the possibility of war with England increased, this force remained on the continent. Bonaparte railed against Britain's rule of the waves. By denying the right of other nations to traverse the oceans with the same freedom as a bird flies through the air, Britain was preventing them from introducing civilization into regions that were "a prey to ignorance and barbarism". This is what England would usurp over all other nations. One of his councillors asked him "have not the English as many motives for dreading a continental supremacy and being alarmed at your great influence over all Europe?"

Bonaparte's response was to read a speech from the English House of Commons: "France obliges us to recollect the injury which she did us 25 years since, by forming an alliance with our revolted colonies. Jealous of our commerce, navigation and riches, she wishes to annihilate them. The proceedings of the First Consul, at the end of a peace made with too much facility, compel us to appeal anew to arms. The enemy, by

---

[1] ASP pp.538-539

a dash of the pen, appropriates to himself territories more extensive than all the conquests of France for many centuries. He hastens his preparations; let us not wait until he attacks us, let us attack first."

The First Consul resumed his own thoughts: "Now propose your theories and your abstract propositions, and see if they can resist the efforts of these usurpers and of their sovereignty of the sea. Leave commerce and navigation in the exclusive possession of a single people, and the globe will be subjected to their arms, and by the gold which occupies the place of armies." To emancipate nations from "the commercial tyranny of England, it is necessary to balance her influence by a maritime power that may one day become her rival; that power is the United States. The English aspire to dispose of all the riches of the world. I shall be useful to the whole universe, if I can prevent their ruling America as they rule Asia."

At the Easter Sunday meeting at St Cloud Bonaparte shared his latest thoughts with his two advisors. He told them he appreciated the value of Louisiana, but with a war looming against Britain he feared he would soon have to accept losing it: "But if it escapes from me, it shall one day cost dearer to those who oblige me to strip myself of it than to those to whom I wish to deliver it." Bonaparte believed that the English, who had already "taken from France Canada, Cape Breton, Newfoundland, Nova Scotia, and the richest portions of Asia", were stirring up trouble in San Domingo and were planning to seize Louisiana. It was their hostile reaction to the restoration of this colony to France that convinced him of their hope to possess it, "and it is thus that they will begin the war. They have 20 ships of war in the Gulf of Mexico, they sail over those seas as sovereigns, whilst our affairs in San Domingo have been growing worse every day since the death of Leclerc." As it would be easy for them to conquer, he had "not a moment to lose in putting it out of their reach [...] I think of ceding it to the United States." If he waited until war broke out it would be too late and by handing over the territory to the Unites States now he would acquire a potential ally. "They only ask of me one town in Louisiana, but I already consider the colony as entirely lost, and it appears to me that in the hands of this growing power, it will be more useful to the policy and even the commerce of France, than if I should attempt to keep it."

One of the councillors, François Barbé-Marbois, agreed: "we should not hesitate [...] to make a sacrifice of that which is about to slip from us. War with England is inevitable; shall we be able with very inferior naval forces to defend Louisiana against that power?" The United

States would not help and would probably take advantage of French weakness in the region to seize New Orleans for themselves. France had a pitifully small army to defend the colony had no means of reinforcing it, or restoring or building forts along a long border. England would only let them do so to exhaust their resources and could attack Louisiana in the south from the sea and the north from the Great Lakes, while the United States from the north east. The Louisiana population was in decline, but even if it did prosper, it could eventually demand independence from France.

Marbois did not advocate abandoning all of France's colonies in the Americas. He considered the economic success of the West Indian colonies was the consequence of slave labour and when Bonaparte remarked he was still undecided on whether to abolish slavery, Marbois declared that "an inexcusable imprudence was committed in suddenly granting to the slaves of San Domingo, a liberty for which they had not been prepared." Although that was too late to repair and the colony was currently a burden, he thought it should not be abandoned. Keeping Louisiana however would serve no useful purpose – they could not occupy it without sustaining considerable expense, despite the fact that it was cultivated by slaves who made up half the population. They would also not be able to restrict the colony's trade to France and forcing it to do so would invite the enmity of the United States.

Marbois' colleague disagreed. They were still at peace with England. It was not wise to abandon it for a remote danger. Why deprive themselves out of fear of war? If peace was maintained, they would regret the cession: "There can be no Marine without colonies; no colonies without Marine!" By ceding, Bonaparte would be letting England remain master of the seas, allowing other nations to acquire colonies only at its pleasure. If there was a war, France could take Hanover if England took Louisiana.

The meeting lasted all night. Early next morning Bonaparte summoned Marbois and showed him the latest dispatches from London reporting the acceleration of naval and military preparations. Bonaparte complained that "the English ask of me Lampedusa, which does not belong to me, and at the same time wish to keep Malta for 10 years. This island [...] would be for them another Gibraltar. To leave it to them would be to give up to them the commerce of the Levant, and to rob my southern provinces of it. They wish to keep this possession, and have me immediately evacuate Holland [...] irresolution and deliberation are no longer in season. I renounce Louisiana [...] the whole colony without reservation [...] I renounce it with the greatest regret. To attempt obstinately to retain it would be folly. I direct you to negotiate this affair with the envoys of the United States. Do not even await the arrival of Mr Monroe; have an interview this very day with Mr Livingston; but I require a lot of money for this war [...] Louisiana has always drained France and Spain [.. .] I want 50 million and for less than that sum I will not treat; I would rather make a desperate attempt to keep these fine countries."

Marbois wondered whether the people of Louisiana could be subject to a commercial contract of exchange. Bonaparte dismissed such concerns as ideological and outweighed by realities: "I require money to fight the richest nation of the world," he said. Such ideas might be greatly admired in London, but they were not applied by the English in the finest regions of Asia. The United States may become too powerful for Europe in two or three centuries, but he could not worry about that now. Finally, he asked Marbois to make the offer without any subterfuge, keep himself and Talleyrand informed and ask the Americans to keep the deal a secret.

****

"I've got some news for you," Joseph Bonaparte said to his brother Lucien, adding that it might spoil his evening. Lucien had just arrived in Paris from his country residence in Le Plessis to attend the opening night of a play at the Comédie-Française. He had stopped at his house to change his clothes and found Joseph waiting for him. "You won't believe it – but the general wants to sell off Louisiana," continued Joseph. Lucien was dumbfounded and could hardly believe that his brother would sell colonial interests that he had declared should always be retained as a matter of national dignity. Even if he had changed his mind, he would still require the authorization of the legislature and surely the Americans would not buy it without it.

The next day Lucien went to the Tuileries, finding Napoleon having his bath and in a good mood. He was sorry that he had not met his brothers at the play the previous evening, where Talma had proven "sublime" and he himself felt appreciated by the audience. People so easily forgot things, Lucien said, suggesting that the Seine itself, like the river of forgetfulness of the ancient Greek underworld, induced this amnesia. "Ah!" Napoleon exclaimed. "You are still attracted to poetry! I much approve of this. I would be upset to see you renounce it entirely for politics." They were not mutually exclusive occupations, noted Lucien, citing David, Solomon and Napoleon himself as examples. The two brothers reminisced about their early literary ambitions and Corsica. Napoleon was about to get out of the bath when a scratching sound was heard at the door, as if a cat was clawing at it from the other side. It was Roustam, using a protocol that had recently replaced knocking before entering a room. He announced the arrival of Joseph.

"Let him enter," Napoleon said, deciding to stay in the bath another fifteen minutes. "And so, my brother," he said to Joseph when he entered, "have you not talked to Lucien?"

"About what?" asked Joseph.

"About our Louisiana project, as you know!"

"You mean about your project, my dear brother? You cannot have forgotten that, far from being mine..."

"Oh come on, preacher [...] But I don't need to talk about it with you – you're so pig-headed." Napoleon declared his preference for talking to Lucien about serious matters, despite his tendency to disagree. He told them both he had firmly decided to sell Louisiana to the Americans without seeking legislative approval. He was about to leave the bathtub when he advised them both in a cold tone to put their minds at rest about it: "you, Lucien about the sale itself, and you Joseph, because I will do without the approval of anyone – you understand this?"

Joseph approached the bathtub and warned his brother that if legislative consent was required, he, Joseph, would lead the opposition against the sale himself. Napoleon made a brief, loud, gruff laugh. Joseph was red with rage: "Laugh, laugh, sure, go on laughing! That won't stop me from doing what I say I'll do," he stuttered, threatening to speak to his fellow legislatures.

"You will have no need to stand as speaker of the opposition, because I repeat, this discussion will not take place, since this project which happily does not have your approval, conceived by me, negotiated by me, will be ratified and executed by me alone, do you understand? By me, and I couldn't care less about your opposition." Napoleon sat down in his bath again.

"Well, I tell you, General," replied Joseph using the familiar "tu", "that you, I, we all – if you do what you say, we may as well be prepared ourselves to join those poor innocent devils you so legally, humanely and oh so justly had deported to Sinnamary."

After a brief tense silence, Napoleon rose again from his tub and began to shout at Joseph, but what he said was soon drowned out by the sound of splashing of water as he sat down again with great force. As Joseph had been standing so close, he was drenched from head to toe. Lucien quoted a line from Virgil's *Aeneid*, comparing Napoleon with Neptune unleashing the ocean's waters against the winds. "Your god is quite mad," re-joined Joseph, while Napoleon quietly remarked to Lucien: "Always a poet on occasion." The valet, trying his best to dry Joseph, was overwhelmed by the situation and fainted. Joseph attempted to pick him up, while Lucien rang for help. When Roustam entered Napoleon ordered him to help Joseph. As another valet assisted him out of his bath, Napoleon suggested that Joseph get changed. "Thank you, I'll change at home. Are you coming Lucien?"

"Has he also been splashed?" asked Napoleon. When Lucien said "No," Napoleon invited him to stay as he needed to speak with him further. A little later, Roustam showed Lucien to Napoleon's office, where the latter immediately raged against Joseph: "Well, let me tell you, when something gets to Joseph, he's worse than you when you think you're right." If Napoleon hoped to persuade Lucien to take his side, he was to be disappointed. Lucien considered it more dishonourable to sell Louisiana cheaply than to lose it through warfare. Instead Napoleon should take advantage of the peace to send more troops like he had done for San Domingo. Napoleon reminded him that at the time he, Lucien, had been against the San Domingo expedition. Lucien replied that was because he thought Napoleon should have negotiated with Toussaint. Napoleon acknowledged his San Domingo policy was a mistake but argued that the current threat of war with England made any adventures outside Europe strategically unsound. The French Navy was too weak to rival the English fleets. Lucien was not persuaded. Strategically sensible or not, this was not the point. Ceding Louisiana without legislative sanction would encourage Napoleon to impose his will on anything he liked.

Napoleon sat in an armchair, inviting Lucien to do the same. Lucien tried to assure his brother that he would sacrifice everything for him except his duty. "Except, you mean, anything that you want to except."

"No, my brother." If ceding Louisiana were a matter of private interest, he would not have hesitated to consent. "But it's just too unconstitutional." Napoleon burst into laughter, prompting Lucien to remark how surprised he was that such an important subject should be so mocked.

Napoleon stopped laughing. "Oh please, leave me alone. And in any case, in what way have I violated your constitution? Answer." Because, Lucien explained, as the supreme representative of national sovereignty, he was giving away an annex of the Republic. As he tried to expand he was interrupted by his brother. "Go to hell! Constitution! Unconstitutional! Republic! National Sovereignty! Big words, big phrases! Do you think you are still at your Jacobin club at Saint-Maximin? We're well beyond that. Ah really! You show us a pretty face! Oh that's a good one, unconstitutional! Suits you well, you, mister the knight of the Constitution, to talk to me in that way! You did not show the same respect for the Chambers on 18 Brumaire."

Lucien reminded Napoleon that when he had intervened in the Council of Five Hundred during the coup of that day, it was to rescue his brother from the deputies he had provoked. It was not the act of an accomplice: "no one in Europe disapproved more than I that sacrilegious attack on national representation." Detecting anger in his brother's gaze, Lucien remained calm: "Yes, unconstitutional attack on national sovereignty – ."

"Go on, go on then, it's too beautiful to be brief, Mr Orator of the Clubs; but meanwhile rest assured, you and Joseph, that I shall do exactly as I please; that I loathe, without fearing them, your friends the Jacobins, of which not a single one will be left in France if, as I hope, it continues to be up to me; and finally that I couldn't care less about you and your national representation."

"I do care about you, Citizen Consul," replied Lucien and when asked by his brother what he thought about him he said that after realising how much he despised his own constitution he declared that "if I were not your brother, I would be your enemy."

Napoleon, scoffing at this last remark, lunged at Lucien as if to strike. Disarmed by Lucien's inertia, he merely shouted: "You, my enemy! I would crush you, you see, like this box!" He threw a snuff box onto the carpet, where a miniature portrait of Josephine became detached from it. Lucien picked it up and gave it back to Napoleon, remarking that instead of breaking the original Lucien, he had broken a copy of his wife. As Lucien left, Napoleon picked up the snuff box and tried to insert the damaged portrait back inside.[1]

****

The meeting with the deaf Livingston did not go well. The U.S. ambassador refused to go above thirty million and no agreement was reached. When Monroe arrived in Paris on 12 April, Livingstone suggested that the United States simply take New Orleans and then negotiate. Monroe, however, was made of more moderate stuff. On the 13 April, he and Livingstone met with Marbois together, and was surprised to find that the whole of Louisiana was being offered, not just New Orleans. He did not have any explicit authority to buy the whole territory, but there was no time to confer with his government. War could have broken out at any moment and England would have captured Louisiana soon after.

Marbois offered Louisiana for eighty million Francs, stating this figure was well below the true value and could not be reduced. The Americans were concerned about the debt they would inflict on their fellow citizens, but sensed this was an opportunity they could not fail to take. They agreed to eighty million, but persuaded Marbois to deduct twenty million relating to indemnities owed by France for losses the U.S. had incurred from a minor conflict between them that had ended in 1800. The purchase would be financed by a consortium of the English bank Barings and the Dutch bank Hope and Company. They agreed to lend the United States government $15 million at six per cent interest per year.

---

[1] Iung pp. 124-192, English translation of dialogue reproduced from Simonetta and Arikha (pp.96-105), *Napoleon and the Rebel*, 2011, Palgrave Macmillan, with permission of Palgrave Macmillan.

Much time was spent defining the territory covered by the term "Louisiana", but by 30 April an agreement embracing over a million square miles was reached and signed four days later. Livingston remarked that "we have lived long, but this is the noblest work of our whole lives [...] From this day the United States take their place among the powers of the first rank [...] the United States will re-establish the maritime rights of all the world, which are now usurped by a single nation."[1]

---

[1] Marbois p.263-313

41. Ultimatum

Whitworth was surprised to hear Talleyrand say that the First Consul would not consent to either a permanent or temporary possession of Malta by England. However, Bonaparte would let Britain have Lampedusa or any of the smaller islands between Malta and the coast of North Africa. Whitworth was sorry they had made so little progress. His orders were clear: he could hear of nothing short of what he had proposed, neither could he possibly undertake to convey such a counter-offer to His Majesty. Lampedusa could not be considered equivalent to Malta as a security. Malta was so essential to England's safety that it was prepared to go to war over it. He was duty-bound to carry out his instructions to deliver an ultimatum that would "have one good effect, that of bringing the matter to an issue; and the certainty even of war was preferable to the present state of indecision". Talleyrand replied that the First Consul could not consent to anything that risked his dignity and honour by appearing to yield to threats. Whitworth claimed that Bonaparte, given his alarming actions in Europe, had no right to claim that consenting to give explanation and satisfaction would compromise his honour or dignity. Perhaps he could be offended by demands for satisfaction and explanation from other states, but not from Great Britain, which had every right to make them.

The next day Talleyrand confirmed he had relayed this conversation to the First Consul, but had nothing to add to what he had said earlier. Whitworth regretted that Bonaparte mistakenly found Britain's actions a threat to his dignity. When asked by Talleyrand to transmit the latest French proposals to his government, Whitworth agreed, but would not refrain from carrying out any instructions he received. If directed to present a formal ultimatum, he promised to let Talleyrand know before he did so. The French Foreign Minister warned him that if war broke out, Holland, Naples and other countries would be its first victims. Whitworth suggested this would only tarnish the honour of Bonaparte and reinforce the determination of the English to resist him by inciting their hatred rather than their fear.[1]

---

[1] Browning pp.183-192

The Consequences of Honour

When Bonaparte learned that Whitworth may soon be presenting an ultimatum he told Talleyrand to adopt a cold, high, even haughty air at their next meeting. If the British note contained the word 'ultimatum' he was to tell the ambassador that this implied war and that "such a style of negotiation is that of a superior towards an inferior. If the note does not contain that word, make him put it in [...] we must know clearly and finally what we are about – that we are tired of this state of anxiety." If England delayed the presentation of an ultimatum Talleyrand was to "frighten him on the consequences of postponement". Talleyrand was to end the meeting on a more positive note, suggesting that Bonaparte would be comforted by confirmation of the evacuation of the Cape and Gorée by Britain.[1]

At his next meeting with the British ambassador, Talleyrand asked if the possession of Malta was still insisted on. Whitworth could only answer in the affirmative and relayed his latest instructions from Hawkesbury. Britain was to keep Malta for ten years and acquire Lampedusa while the French were to evacuate Holland. If these demands were not accepted he was to quit Paris. Talleyrand asked for a written expression of this ultimatum. Whitworth refused. He could repeat himself as many times as the Foreign Minister wished and he would be satisfied with a verbal answer, but he was not authorised to offer a written note. Talleyrand, indignant at this "contempt for formalities", resigned himself to communicating this ultimatum to Bonaparte himself as soon as possible, while Whitworth reminded him that he planned to leave Paris in the next few days.[2]

On 29 April Whitworth was visited by a French official who told him that he would receive from Talleyrand a proposal that might be sufficient to induce him to stay. By 4 p.m. Whitworth had not heard from Talleyrand so went to ask him if he had anything positive to communicate, reminding him of his departure date and asking for passports and necessary travel documents be prepared for himself and his family. Talleyrand expressed his disbelief that he would really leave.

---

[1] Bonaparte to Talleyrand. NBCG, 7629, p.127. This letter is undated, but is presumed by the editors to have been written on 10 May rather than 1 May which was the assumption of the editors of the previous edition of correspondence (vol. 8, 6720). I think that this letter probably dates between 23 April and 27 April as it fits better with the discussions between Talleyrand and Whitworth.

[2] Browning pp.192-196, Coquelle p.59

Whitworth simply said he had been recalled to end the present uncertainty, to which Talleyrand declared he still had hopes that peace could be preserved.[1]

The first day of May was the reception of ambassadors at the Tuileries, which Whitworth had no intention of attending. The evening before, he had received a note from a French official suggesting that his absence might unintentionally give offence. He replied that he did not want to risk exposing his own and his King's dignity to the First Consul's temper and would be unable to maintain a sufficiently calm composure himself in the current circumstances. Moreover, even if he could have remained agreeable, this might be misunderstood. He sent Talleyrand a note the next morning apologising in advance for his absence.

At the reception Bonaparte seemed to be indifferent to the notable absence of the tall English ambassador. Later, when he was alone with some senators and councillors of state, he unburdened himself. He complained of the ultimatum, of the English refusal to countenance any compromise solution:

"Since the English force us to leap the ditch, we will leap it. They may take some of our frigates, or our colonies; but I will carry terror into the streets of London, and I give them warning, that they will bewail the end of this war with tears of blood." What, Bonaparte wondered aloud, was the real source of England's quarrel with France? He protested that since Amiens, they had asked nothing of England. They had left her in peace and faithfully observed the conditions of the Treaty. Of all the men in Europe he claimed he was the most surprised at the King of England's speech.

"The Ministers have made the King of England tell a lie in the face of Europe. There were no armaments going on in France; there has been no negotiation. They have not transmitted to me a single note: Lord Whitworth could not help acknowledging it. And yet it is by the aid of such vile insinuations that a government seeks to excite the passions. For the last two months I have endured all sorts of insults from the English government." They had acted "with as much insolence as we have shown reserve and moderation. Did they, finding me so moderate – me, whom they know to be of little endurance – imagine that I would not dare to

---

[1] Browning pp.198-202

make war? That, being forced to conciliate the people, I should not be able to resist? They deceive themselves. Their emissaries and the sums they expend to sow dissensions among us, have hitherto entirely failed of success; they are employing their money very ill."

British ministers had been deceived about the state of France by badly informed spies. They imagined war would be unpopular with the French, that he would not be able to find a single man to support it. "They have been led to believe that I dreaded war, lest it should shake my authority. I will raise two millions of men, if it be necessary. The result of the first war has been to aggrandize France by the addition of Belgium and Piedmont. The result of this will be to consolidate our federative system more firmly." They wanted to renew the troubles of France, to divide the French and to enfeeble a country that had grown strong. Since they wanted war, France would oblige, and it would be terrible.

What disappointed the British most of all, he reasoned, was that the peace had failed to weaken France as they had hoped. They had believed that "our internal divisions would do us more harm than war, and that we have only to be left to ourselves to perish". But it was the restoration of order, the improvements in government and finance that alarmed them more than "our alleged armaments". Nevertheless, Bonaparte remained astonished by the behaviour of the British ministers. "Can we avoid seeing its positive insanity? What! They want to fight us in a second war, and they begin by restoring to us the Cape, Martinique and Elba, and by evacuating Egypt, and then they make difficulties on one single point of the Treaty, Malta; an article guaranteed by the continental powers!" However, their foolishness did not excuse their insolence:

"I have let them fill up the measure of their offences; they have construed that into feebleness and redoubled their presumption to the point of making their ambassador say: Do so and so, or I shall depart in seven days. Is it thus that they address a great nation? He was told to write, and that his notes would be laid before the eyes of government. No was the reply, I have orders only to communicate verbally. Is this not an unheard of form of negotiating? Does it not show a marked determination to shuffle, equivocate, play at fast and loose as they please and leave no proof against themselves?"

What then should be France's response? "Let him go then! We shall have nothing to reproach ourselves with." The independence of states had to come before liberty and economic prosperity. Could they allow the English to execute only those treaty conditions that were not a

416

disadvantage to them? "To accept a modification of the Treaty of Amiens is to accept the first link of a chain which will afterwards lengthen itself out, and will end by our complete subjection" by a treaty of commerce that would subordinate the French economy to English trade.

"Let us cede Malta, and tomorrow our vessels will be insulted, our ships will be forced to salute those of the English, and to endure a disgraceful inspection." One day "they will forbid our navigators to pass beyond such a latitude. Already they even observe with jealousy that we are clearing out our harbours, and re-establishing our marine. They complain of it, they demand guarantees. A short while ago Vice-Admiral Lesseigues touched at Malta. He had two ships with him, he found fifteen English ones there. They wanted him to fire a salute. Lesseigues refused: some words passed. If he had yielded, I would have had him carried in procession on an ass."

Bonaparte also complained of the English demand for Lampedusa, an island that did not belong to France and was not in their power to give them. "Lastly, they demand reparation for disrespectful articles in our newspapers, while every day their own overwhelm us with insult and outrage carried to excess!" England wanted the freedom to insult France without suffering abuse in return. "Wheresoever in Europe there remains a sense of justice, the blame of this war will be thrown on her." After forty five minutes, the angry monologue ended.[1]

Bonaparte did not however reject the British ultimatum outright. A few days later, Whitworth felt obliged to deliver in person to Talleyrand a formal request for passports. Talleyrand read it and appeared startled, saying that so much time had been lost, but enough time remained if Whitworth could negotiate other terms. Whitworth replied that if Bonaparte could not agree to the terms already suggested "nothing could prevent my departure tomorrow night". Talleyrand promised to speak to the First Consul that day and would contact Whitworth in the evening. Whitworth warned him that nothing could induce him to disobey his orders.[2] In the evening he received a note from Talleyrand with the official French response to Britain's demands: "As the island of Lampedusa does not belong to France, it is not for the First Consul to

---

[1] Hazlitt pp.386-388, Remacle p.308, Mileto p.524

[2] Browning pp.203-207

either accede to or to refuse the desire" of Britain to acquire it. French troops would evacuate Holland, but only once the conditions of the Amiens Treaty had been completely fulfilled. Before France could agree to Britain remaining in Malta for ten years, it would need consent from the other guarantors.[1]

Whitworth responded the next day, informing Talleyrand that he saw nothing in the French note that would end the "state of suspense" and had every intention of leaving. The only problem was that his passports never arrived. At midnight he was talking with Huber and others about this delay when a servant came into the room saying that a person wished to speak to Mr Huber. Huber went down and returned a few minutes later, to report that Malouet and his contact in the French government had a message from Joseph Bonaparte. It was a proposal to leave Malta in the hands of the Tsar of Russia. Whitworth said that was unacceptable and this answer was delivered to the two men waiting outside. An hour later, Whitworth received an enclosed note from Talleyrand. He suggested they meet the next day at 4.30 p.m. at the Foreign Office to discuss business of great importance.

Whitworth suspected that this "business of great importance" was the same proposal made by Joseph, but did not want to ignore the possibility of averting war on an assumption. He met Talleyrand at the appointed hour who handed him a note. It expressed surprise that England was making so much fuss over a "miserable rock". The French could only presume that Britain's only problem with Malta was the strength of the Neapolitan garrison. "The First Consul is ready to consent that the island of Malta shall be placed in the hands of one of the three powers who have guaranteed its independence, Austria, Russia or Prussia." The idea was that Britain would be allowed to occupy the island for a few more years, after which it would be handed over to the Tsar. If Britain did not accept this then they will prove that they were never acting in good faith, while this last offer by France proved they had tried every means of avoiding war. Whitworth remarked that the number of years had to be at least ten, but Talleyrand suggested that if Russia was to be the ultimate occupier the British government ought to settle for less. Whitworth did not think there was much hope his government would

---

[1] Browning p.216

accept this latest proposal, but agreed to send it and delay his departure as it would only make a difference of five days.[1]

---

[1] Browning pp.213-215

42. Collision

On 9 May, Bonaparte, Josephine and Cambacérès went for a drive in the park at St Cloud in a six-horse phaeton. Bonaparte, who fancied driving himself, had the two leading horses unharnessed and mounted the coach box, while Caesar the coachman took position behind. The horses set off at a gallop and Bonaparte immediately began having difficulties controlling them. Caesar barked out instructions, "Keep in middle!" but the horses became more ungovernable. Cambacérès, as white as a sheet, could be heard shouting "Stop! Stop!" as Caesar gave more instructions Bonaparte was unable to execute. "To the left! To the left!" he cried. As the carriage approached a gateway, the road became narrower and Bonaparte was unable to avoid crashing into a pillar, upsetting the carriage and hurling him into the air. The First Consul landed on the ground ten paces ahead. As Cambacérès and Josephine emerged from the carriage, slightly bruised but greatly frightened, they noticed Bonaparte lying face down on the ground, badly bruised and unconscious.[1]

Meanwhile, in Paris, Whitworth had been waiting for Hawkesbury's response to the latest French proposals. He was looking out of a window when he spied his courier Sylvester arrive in the courtyard. When the embassy physician Dr McLaurin learned that he had travelled from London to Paris in less than thirty-one hours, he advised Sylvester to take a hot bath immediately.[2] Whitworth had other concerns. In his dispatch, Hawkesbury told him that only Russia would be acceptable to Britain as one of the powers the French would allow to hold Malta, but doubted that the Russians would accept. He could propose to Talleyrand that the period of a temporary occupation of Malta – which had to be at least ten years – could be made in a secret treaty to save French honour. However, he was to assure them that they were sticking to their ultimatum and if no agreement was reached he was "on no account" to "remain in Paris more than thirty-six hours after the receipt

---

[1] Constant vol. I p.161. Constant must have the dates wrong, as the description of the accident is too similar to that described by Lord Whitworth in his dispatches to Hawkesbury 9 May 1803, Browning, p.229.

[2] Bristow p.117

of this dispatch".[1] He sent someone to request a meeting with Talleyrand, but learned that the Foreign Minister was at St Cloud. Later that day he discovered that Talleyrand had gone to check on Bonaparte, who had been hurt in an accident, but the injuries were not serious. He wrote back to Hawkesbury reporting that he hoped to see Talleyrand the next morning and would plan to leave thirty-six hours after making official communication rather from the receipt of his instructions.[2] The next morning Talleyrand was still not available so he sent the latest English terms in a written note to the Ministry of Foreign Affairs so it would be waiting for Talleyrand when he returned. He also left a personal note for the Foreign Minister, referring to his government's proposal: "I hope to God that they may be of a nature to ensure the tranquillity of both countries, and of Europe". By 4.30 p.m. he still had not heard from Talleyrand so he went over to the Ministry himself and was told the Minister was out of town. Whitworth rewrote the proposal and the letter and at 9 p.m. gave them to a secretary of the embassy to deliver it to Talleyrand's residence at Meudon. It turned out that he was not there either and was still at St Cloud and not expected back until late. At 1 a.m. a note from Talleyrand arrived, asking Whitworth to meet him at the Foreign Ministry at mid-day.

The next day Talleyrand apologised for not being able to see Whitworth sooner with the excuse he had been with the First Consul all day. Whitworth wasted no more time and related Hawkesbury's latest offer. When he had finished and Talleyrand had read through the written proposal, Talleyrand asked if he was authorised to offer the French compensation if they agreed to let them keep Malta. No, was Whitworth's reply, as this would make the negotiation a matter of exchange rather than one of a demand of satisfaction and security. Talleyrand argued that if they had Malta they would have their satisfaction and security. To let them have Malta for nothing would be to give in to coercion. He questioned the justification for refusing to consider an option more acceptable to France. Whitworth responded that he had no need in seeking justification as he was just obeying his government's instructions. Talleyrand persisted – surely an option that still gave them what they wanted "could not be refused a fair discussion?" Whitworth would not be drawn into further argument. It was the resolution of the British

---

[1] Browning pp.224-226

[2] Browning p.229

government to avoid anything which protracted the negotiation. Yet he still asked: what would the French want for leaving Malta in English hands? Talleyrand could not suggest anything specific, but promised to send a proposal in the next few hours. By the time Whitworth returned to his residence, an anxious crowd had gathered outside.[1]

When Bonaparte learned of England's latest terms and Whitworth's determination to leave Paris if no reply was received in thirty-six hours, he was furious. He told Talleyrand he should have sent the note he had received from the ambassador straight back to him. By presenting it to the First Consul, Talleyrand had been disrespectful. Nevertheless, he decided to hold a meeting at St Cloud to discuss it. Present were the other two consuls, Cambacérès and Lebrun, the Ministers of War and Marine – Berthier and Decrès, Talleyrand and Joseph. In front of the others, Bonaparte chastised Talleyrand, who pleaded that he was only trying to preserve the peace.[2] Bonaparte would not be placated, but redirected his anger from Talleyrand to the English. He had effectively but reluctantly agreed to consider the temporary occupation of Malta by Britain, given the consent of the other powers and not objected to the British taking possession of Lampedusa. He had promised he would evacuate Holland once the Amiens treaty obligations had been fulfilled, despite his insistence that Holland was a continental matter and of no concern of England's. Yet still for the English this was not enough.[3] A vote was held to decide whether they should insist on the terms of the Treaty. A majority of the council voted in favour. Only Talleyrand and Joseph were against. Orders were issued to forward the ambassador's passports.

The next day, Joseph had not given up hope of persuading his brother to compromise. While the two of them had a heated argument at St Cloud, Whitworth waited all day for his passports and horses, planning and then delaying his departure every two hours. When the documents were finally delivered at 6 p.m. there was a general groan from the crowd outside, prompting the concern that they might take the horses for his carriage when they arrived. On the suggestion of Dr McLaurin, it was

[1] Browning pp.233-238

[2] Mileto p.532

[3] Cronin, p.290

announced that the ambassador would leave in the morning. At this news, the crowd dispersed. Then, after a brief meeting with Talleyrand, Whitworth and the Duchess departed Paris late in the evening well after 10 p.m. leaving Mr Talbot in charge of the embassy.[1]

The following morning, the Duchess's two daughters, their governor, the young Duke of Dorset and his tutor the Reverend Slade, set off to meet up with their parents at Chantilly. When they arrived, Whitworth had learned of Joseph's row with his brother and had gathered it had failed to change Bonaparte's position. Joseph had still not given up. He went to his brother again and returned from St Cloud with what he thought was good news. He had persuaded the First Consul to allow the British to occupy Malta for ten years if they allowed the French to occupy Otranto and Tarentum in the Kingdom of Naples for the same period. Mr Mandeville was despatched to catch up with the ambassador. When Whitworth received this latest offer on 14 May, he was in Breteuil, nearly half-way to Calais, and immediately forwarded it onto Hawkesbury.

In London, Andréossy had been urged by Talleyrand to reason with the British. The French ambassador enlisted the help of his Dutch counterpart, Schimmelpenninck, to make a two-pronged assault. While Andréossy worked on Hawkesbury, the Dutch ambassador would try to bring Addington round. Both attempts failed. The British refused to hand Malta over to Russia and would only leave the island once the fortifications of Lampedusa were ready. They would recognise the Kingdom of Etruria, the Ligurian and Italian republics if French troops left Holland. Switzerland had to be vacated and the King of Sardinia compensated. The only hint at compromise by the British was the suggestion that they would secretly agree to evacuate Malta as soon as the French abandoned Holland – as long as the French publicly acknowledged they could retain it for ten years. A letter from Talleyrand dated the day Whitworth had asked for his passports, requested Andréossy to use Schimmelpenninck to sound out whether the British Cabinet would allow the French to occupy Otranto and Tarentum for as long as the British retained Malta. "You must realise, General, that if you have the slightest reason to believe that the proposal will not recommend itself to them, you must be careful to leave no trace of it, so that it may always be possible to deny that the French government ever agreed to these terms. The First Consul leaves it to your discretion to decide what

---

[1] Bristow pp.118-119

use you will make of the authorization he now gives you." A further letter the same day sent from St Cloud at midnight urged him to emphasise "the really peaceful character of our dispositions, mentioning the position that has been forced on us and our determination to make war rather than suffer humiliation". Schimmelpenninck agreed to help again, but by the time he saw Hawkesbury the latter told him the proposal was nothing new and was in any case unacceptable.

The formal proposal from the French forwarded on by Whitworth reached Hawkesbury on the morning of Monday 16 May. The Cabinet ministers met the same day to discuss it. They rejected it outright, declaring they could never be a party to the disposal of a town or port belonging to another state. Hawkesbury wrote to Whitworth, now leaving Boulogne for Calais, telling him the proposal was "repugnant" and failed to provide the necessary security. The French were only trying to protract the negotiation. Whitworth was to embark for Dover immediately.[1] Arriving in Calais in the evening, Whitworth had every intention of doing so. The next day, 17 May, he left France. When he arrived in Dover at 11 p.m. Andréossy was there waiting for a direct order allowing his boat to leave. All vessels had been prohibited from sailing and Andréossy had written to Hawkesbury complaining that it would not be seemly for either country for an ambassador to depart as a fugitive. The following morning, Whitworth cordially accompanied Andréossy to his ship, assuring him that he was setting out for London with the intention of recommending his government adopt a conciliatory attitude.[2]

---

[1] Browning p.262

[2] Coquelle pp.64-71

37 Consular Coachmanship

Consular coachmanship!! Print by William Holland 22 May 1803 (Courtesy of Library of Congress)

43. Conflict

On 16 May, the day Andréossy left London, a council was held at the Queen's House. All the key members of the government were present – Addington, Hawkesbury, Chatam, Eldon, Portland, and Castlereagh. They had just rejected the latest French proposal and now drew up instructions for the Navy, ordering it to "seize all ships, vessels and goods belonging to the French Republic".

The same day a King's message was read out in Parliament: "His Majesty thinks it proper to acquaint the House of Commons, that the discussions which he announced to them on 8th March last [...] between His Majesty and the French government [...] have been terminated. That the conduct of the French government has obliged His Majesty to recall his Ambassador from Paris, and that the Ambassador from the French Republic, has left London [...] His Majesty relies with confidence in the zeal and public spirit of his faithful Commons, and on the exertions of his brave and loyal subjects to support him in his determination [...] in opposing the spirit of ambition and encroachment which at present actuates the Councils of France."

On 18 May Addington presented himself in the Commons in his local militia uniform, provoking eruptions of laughter and prompting Sheridan to describe him as "the right honourable gentleman who has appeared this evening in the character of a sheep in wolf's clothing." A declaration from the King was read out, in which His Majesty expressed "the fullest confidence that he shall receive the same support from his Parliament [...] which he has experienced on every occasion when the honour of his Crown has been attacked, or the essential interests of his dominions have been endangered". England was now at war with France, and the King's government expected Parliament's support. The declaration listed Britain's grievances with France, the reasons why it was going to war. It complained of the prohibitions faced by British commerce in France, the seizure of British vessels in French ports and the refusal of justice to English litigants in French courts. There had been no satisfactory answer from France to English complaints. French commercial agents were in British harbours without permission and an intercepted letter from Talleyrand to one of these agents suggested the latter was a spy. The more serious grievances were the presence of the

French army in Holland, the invasion of Switzerland, the annexations of Elba, Piedmont, Piacenza and Parma without compensating the King of Sardinia for being deprived of these territories. When Britain complained of these encroachments, France asserted that Britain had no right to interfere with French actions that did not violate the Treaty of Amiens. Then there were the hostile intentions of France towards Egypt, as demonstrated by the Sébastiani report, Bonaparte's provocative address to his Legislative Assembly, his conduct and language towards the British ambassador, not to mention a libellous article against His Majesty published in Hamburg with the complicity of the French minister there.

The Commons debated on 23 May, after it had received all the necessary documents relating to the peace and the rupture. It was during a speech by Hawkesbury, inviting the House to support His Majesty in the new war against France, that Pitt entered the chamber. Admirers shouted out his name, interrupting the Foreign Secretary, whose motion he had come to support. When Hawkesbury had finished, Grey asked the House to consider an amendment, requesting the King's ministers to do everything in their power to restore the peace before resigning themselves and the country to war.

When Pitt himself rose to speak at 7.40 p.m, shouts of "Mr Pitt! Mr Pitt!" would have woken any dozing members. He did not look well. His voice had not lost its depth and harmony, but his lungs were obviously labouring when emphasising a key point. After listening to preceding speeches in favour of the amendment he suggested their arguments were pointless as they seemed to admit there were sufficient reasons for going to war. Two grounds stood out: the Sébastiani Report and Bonaparte's private conference with Whitworth. Both confirmed Bonaparte's intentions against Egypt. Given his brazen admission of it, did Britain not have the right to take some action to prevent it? And was not the retention of Malta the best action they could take? This alone proved that the war was both just and necessary. Yet there were other grounds that warranted war: the French annexation of Piedmont, their interference in German indemnities, the invasion of Switzerland and the retention of their troops in Holland. Only the lack of a suitable continental ally excused Britain from waging war on these issues.

There were also the specific insults to Britain: demands to suppress British publications and expel émigrés. The activities of French commercial agents in British ports for which in a time of war they would be hanged as spies. He lamented that the government had not expelled them rather than lamely requesting their departure. The seizure of British vessels in French ports. Bonaparte's warlike address to his legislature and the language he used to speak to Lord Whitworth. Never had there been a time when Parliament's duty to support a war had been so clear. This duty was not limited merely to consent, but to provide the means of fighting it. It would be a very different war. It would require a more vigorous and effective system for their defence. They had to prepare for a conflict at least as long as the previous one. Its cost would be so great, the revenue for financing it had to be arranged with the greatest urgency. For an hour and twenty minutes, Pitt railed against Bonaparte, who was "absorbing the whole power of France" and warned of the "liquid fire of Jacobinical principles desolating the whole word". At 9 p.m. he sat down, receiving a drawn out applause and loud cheers of "Hear him! Hear Him!"

At 10 p.m. Fox rose to speak, explaining that he would not trouble the House had he not thought it was his duty to save themselves from great danger and certain misery. He criticised the suggestions from previous speakers that the issue was on the justice of the war and not about the conduct of His Majesty's ministers. They were not separable issues. The behaviour of the French can partly be explained as a response to actions of the British and there had been a great deal of shuffling and hypocrisy on both sides.

Fox did not deny that Bonaparte wanted to govern all Europe or that he should be resisted for doing so. However, it was a blunder to quarrel with France over insults and injuries to England that were not entirely unjustified. Furthermore, acts against one country – Switzerland for example – could not be considered as proof of hostility towards another – such as Great Britain. He agreed that one should not be bound by a specific treaty in deciding whether it was right to interfere when one country threatened another. Of course they had the right to intervene, not only if they were indirectly threatened, but they also had the right as a large power to protect the weaker ones. But this had to be regulated by the prospect of success and the confidence that the vulnerable power would not end up worse off or be harmed as a result of their action. This right was not prohibited by Amiens, even though the Treaty gave Britain limited security in other ways.

Fox agreed that the government was right to reject Bonaparte's demands regarding the press and the émigrés, which displayed a profound ignorance of their laws and deserved only contempt and ridicule. He had no respect for Bourbons, but he would have been prepared to go to war before complying with a demand to withdraw the hospitality they had been promised. However, his respect for the government stopped there.

He lamented that they had not used the opportunity of peace to abolish the slave trade in conjunction with France and criticised their former timidity and silence. If they had made Britain's views clearer earlier, Bonaparte would not have been encouraged to provoke Britain further.

Of course France was wrong in regard to the German indemnities, "a system of common rapine", but it was no worse than Russia, Austria and Prussia. As for Piedmont, it was already a part of France when the Treaty of Amiens was signed and could be considered as much a part of France as Gibraltar was a part of Britain. The invasion of Switzerland was a terrible act. "But what was there to do? Was it right to go to war about it? [...] No! [...] we could not make such a war with any effect." Holland had suffered terribly and to turn that country "into a depot for French troops, for the mere purpose, I sincerely believe, of making the Dutch pay the expense of maintaining them, was an act no less despicable for its meanness than hateful for its atrocity." But Britain should have protested clearly and publicly about this – not privately, not couched in peevish language. He could not be sure of success, but it was his belief that if "Great Britain had only presented a remonstrance, and had done so without any menace of declaring war in case of refusal, such an endeavour would have had a favourable effect on the affairs of Holland in the general opinion of Europe, and on the subsequent conduct of France herself". Instead, Britain waited for the Sébastiani report before it took any action. Although this publication insulted a British general, it was ultimately harmless and should have been dismissed as absurd and certainly not considered as grounds for war. Too much had been made of this report and Whitworth's subsequent private conference with the First Consul, especially the language used by the latter. The idea that Bonaparte was stupid enough to tell the British ambassador of his plans for Egypt was ridiculous. Bonaparte certainly had a desire, but no firm plan was declared. Knowledge of a mere desire could not be grounds for war, otherwise Britain would never have been at peace with the House of Bourbon. British ministers, having found a desire, inferred a plan and Whitworth demanded an explanation. For what? asked the French Minister. "Oh, I can tell nothing about it, Sir!" was the reply. Then an explanation was no longer satisfactory, and they wanted security instead. Security for relinquishing Malta – in perpetuity! Plus Malta itself for another ten years! And what justified adding one provocation to the other? The insults they should have complained about earlier.

Instead they stalled over Malta. The Treaty obliged Britain to surrender Malta when the Grand Master had been appointed, the Neapolitan garrison installed and the guarantees of the major powers supplied. "These conditions have been fulfilled [...] What then, is the result of all this?" Instead of attempting to protect Holland and rousing "all the indignant sympathies of Europe [...] you rest the whole quarrel with France on a point of sheer naked British interest – on your possession and occupation of Malta – a point on which no other European state ever feels an interest or entertains a wish in common with yourselves [...] You have deprived yourselves of every advantage you would have had from the admiration and from the good will of mankind, and you have sent your cause into the world stripped of every motive to union of other nations derived either from their interests or their virtues." Fox advised that they should ask for Russia's mediation. At least then if France were demonstrated to be the aggressor they could have had an ally. Now they would have to fight another war alone and as Pitt had pointed out – at enormous cost. "And all this for what? Why, for Malta!"

Fox sat down after three hours. The House divided at 3 a.m. By 398 votes to 67, what was to be England's last great conflict with France would not be delayed.[1]

---

[1] Russell pp.284-297, Cobbett's Annual Register vol. iii 1803 pp.1676-1685, pp.1701-1707

38 General Junot

Illustration from John Cassell's Illustrated History of England (W Kent, 1857/1858) (Look and Learn Collections)

44. Captives

At five o'clock in the morning, General Junot was summoned to Malmaison. He had worked late the night before and had only one hour's sleep. When he presented himself to the First Consul, the latter was in a bad mood: "Junot, may I reckon you as my friend? Yes or No – no evasion."

"Yes General."

"Well then, you must instantly take measures for arresting all the English, without exception, in an hour's time. The Temple, Montaigu, Laforce, the Abbeye, there will be room in the prisons, and they must all be confined." Their government must be taught, he said, that if it breaks treaties it can still be punished through the subjects it has committed to the guardianship of its enemy. "That perfidious Cabinet refuses to surrender Malta! And gives for a reason ..." Bonaparte choked and paused to regain his breath: "They give for reason that Lucien has by my order influenced the court of Spain to dissolve the Spanish priories, and that by the terms of the Treaty, the island is to be given up only on the entire reconstruction of the order." Britain's excuse in evading the Treaty was to claim that its stipulations depended on the state of affairs prevailing at the time it was signed.

Bonaparte waited for a reply, but Junot was dumbfounded and said nothing. "The measure must be executed by seven o'clock this evening." He did not want an Englishmen seen in the lowest theatres or restaurants. Finally, Junot found the words to express his reaction: "General, you are aware of my devoted attachment to your person and to your interests. It is this very devotedness which makes me hesitate to obey, without supplicating you, General, to take some hours for reflection upon the measure you wish me to execute." The action he was ordering would be injurious to his interest and his glory.

Bonaparte listened with bent brow, but with limited patience: "Again! What, is the scene of the other day to be renewed? Lannes and you take strange liberties. Even Duroc, with his very tranquil air, thinks himself licensed to preach to me." He would show them he would not tolerate it. "Lannes has found it out already, and I suspect is not much delighted with eating oranges at Lisbon. For yourself Junot, do not trust so much to my friendship. The day when I doubt yours, will destroy mine".

Junot was deeply hurt. The First Consul was being unjust in talking to him like that, especially as he was only giving him the greatest proof of his attachment: "Ask for my blood [...] ask for my life. You are master of all that is mine. But to command a thing which must..." Bonaparte interjected – he was only answering the insults heaped upon him by an untrustworthy government – what was wrong with that? Junot could not say if his conduct was wrong, but if it was, it was because he had been influenced by bad advisors.

"Who are you speaking of?"

Junot did not want to mention anyone, but Bonaparte insisted, so Junot listed those he considered untrustworthy. He included Fouché and advised his General to listen to Duroc. Bonaparte insisted they were all devoted servants. One of them had expressed that he would kill his own father if the First Consul had commanded it. Junot remarked that such expressions were not proof of loyalty and reminded Bonaparte that solemn assurances had been given to the English that remained in Paris after Whitworth's departure. "There are old men and women, and children amongst them, my general, and many whom morning and night pray for your welfare! These are chiefly merchants, for the upper classes have nearly all left Paris. The injury which confinement may do them is immense and irremediable." Surely, Junot continued, Bonaparte was too noble to conflate a generous people with a perfidious cabinet: should they be considered the same thing?

At this point, Bonaparte restrained himself from acting on an urge to embrace his old comrade-in-arms: "Perhaps they should be, but I am neither wicked nor headstrong. However..." He went to his desk and after reading a paper handed it to Junot, "Read this report, and answer on your head, as you affect to say, answer me on your head, that persons holding such opinions can, without danger to myself, be suffered to remain at large in Paris." The report told of a Colonel Green from England who had got drunk at a dinner and insulted the First Consul, talking of a change of government that would necessarily arise from the death of a single person. Junot told Bonaparte that he knew Colonel Green and knew him to be one of the First Consul's admirers and instantly doubted the veracity of the report.

Bonaparte replied that he, Junot, was persuasive, but his words confirmed that he and Madame Junot "have a mania for associating with persons who hate me". Junot insisted the report was wrong. It stated that the incident occurred only the day before yesterday, but he knew for a fact that Colonel Green had left Paris on 17 April. Bonaparte looked at Junot in astonishment: "He is not in Paris?"

"He is not General, and have the goodness to remark that it is not a mistake of name, or accident attributable to carelessness, it is an error, and an intentional one." Raging with indignation, Junot declared that the only detail this story lacked was to place himself at the dinner at which the Colonel had made these statements. Bonaparte calmed him down, taking his hands and pressing them between his own. He would still imprison the English, but Junot persuaded him not to incarcerate them in the Parisian prisons like common criminals and traitors. Instead, when Cambacérès had joined them, they decided that the English would be confined in selected towns as long as they were peaceable. Bonaparte justified this by claiming they were prisoners of war. Seeing Junot astonished at this last remark, the First Consul elaborated: "Yes, Prisoners of War; do they not form a portion of the English militia?" Junot did not argue the point, having already achieved some degree of leniency.[1]

In the early hours of 23 May, the English in Paris were rudely awoken at their hotels by the police and told to report to the Commandant of Paris, General Junot. There, they would be given a number. The next day they would be given a pass associated with their number, allowing them to proceed to Fontainebleau, where they were to be detained. Many made their way to the embassy in great distress, some fearing they would be guillotined. They hoped they could be protected there, but nothing could be done for them. Most of the remaining staff were about to leave. All they could do was to accept some of their papers and wills for safekeeping. A Mrs Dundas – a relative of Henry Dundas (now Lord Melville) – threw her arms around the neck of Dr McLaurin's wife, pleading with her to take her and her daughters with them. She had left her other children in Britain and was worried she would never see them again. Lady Yarmouth, whose husband was in England, also wanted to accompany the embassy staff, but Mr Talbot said if they tried they would not be given the horses to leave. A decree clarifying the order was issued by the Senate that all English males enrolled in militia, army or

---

[1] D'Abrantes vol. II pp.29-33

navy would be detained. This was later extended to all males between eighteen and sixty (including clergymen). On 24 May Mr Talbot wrote to Talleyrand to protest. Talleyrand replied the same day, acknowledging his letter, but refusing to recognise Mr Talbot as anyone who held a public office in Paris. Talbot left Paris the same day.

After a restless night for Mrs McLaurin, she and Dr McLaurin, their son and the Reverend Hodgson set off for Calais. Hodgson took a box with a secret compartment containing letters from the English they were leaving behind. At St Denis they were arrested by soldiers who told them they also had Mr Talbot in custody, whose passport and documents had been seized and sent to Paris to confirm his diplomatic status. When they were returned he was allowed on his way, while the Doctor's party had to wait and suffer the same inconvenience. Eventually their passports arrived and they proceeded to Chantilly where they were arrested again. On being released, Mrs McLaurin was so overjoyed she saluted the soldiers who had just been guarding them and chatting to her son. On their way through Amiens they were serenaded with anti-English ballads praising the First Consul.

At the next town they met Mandeville on his way back to Paris from Calais. He had been informed that as his passport was dated prior to the decree ordering the detention of the English, he was not allowed to leave France. However, he was given permission to return to Paris to clarify his position with Talleyrand. Mandeville warned the Doctor and his party they should expect to be imprisoned in St Omer and to destroy any papers they were carrying other than their passports. Also on his way to Paris with special permission was the unfortunate and badly informed Lord Yarmouth. He had just come back from England unaware of the state of affairs in France and had been arrested on his arrival at Calais, where the ship he had sailed in was seized along with its crew.

When the doctor's party finally got to Calais on 29 May their passports were taken and they were told not to leave the town, the gates of which were shut in the evening. The two vessels sent to pick up the embassy staff, the *Prince of Wales* and the *Nancy* had been seized and their crew imprisoned. At Quillacq's hotel, where they intended to lodge, they were met by a large crowd of English ladies and gentlemen – all hoping to be released when the embassy staff arrived. Among them was Colonel Abercrombie, the son of General Abercrombie, who had died defeating the French in Egypt. At a Tuileries reception he had recently attended, Bonaparte had praised his father. When he had heard of Lord Whitworth's departure, the Colonel had been in the South of France and

436

immediately decided it was time to leave. He had managed to get all the way to Calais, only to be arrested there. Mr Talbot, who had arrived at Calais on the 27th, argued with the local authorities that the ladies – who had had no change of clothing for several days – should be allowed to go. There had been much confusion about the fate of the English. Four times in one day, it was reported they were to be released, only for their hopes to be dashed by reports of their continued detention. It was finally clarified that those males under eighteen and over sixty and all women were to be liberated. The other men were to be given passes to proceed to Valenciennes, where they would be interned. A number of Englishmen, who had limited financial resources, were obliged to set off on foot with knapsacks on their backs.

Many women, like Mrs McLaurin, refused to be parted from their husbands. Dr McLaurin tried to persuade his wife to leave with their son. Mr Talbot encouraged this idea, insisting that the French would look after him and adding that the Doctor would bear his confinement better in the knowledge that his wife was safe in England. Talbot also advised that they destroy any papers they were carrying for others. This they did do, but not before noting on a list the sender and recipient details so that they could at least convey something to worried friends and relatives. The Reverend Hodgson opened the letters, calling out names to Dr McLaurin, before destroying them, while Mrs McLaurin kept watch for suspicious French guards. They saved a few letters addressed to persons of importance, including one to Lord Melville. Mrs McLaurin's maid hid some in her stockings. Finally, Talbot had procured a vessel. Mrs McLaurin was selecting her cabin when soldiers told her not to be in such haste: new orders had arrived and they were not to go.

On 29 May, Hawkesbury wrote to Talleyrand, expressing His Majesty's surprise and astonishment at this "extraordinary and unexampled proceeding", while Britain had allowed all the French in England to leave unmolested. "His Majesty expects that the French government will give immediate orders for the liberation of all British subjects now detained in France". If not, then "His Majesty would feel justified in retaliating upon the person and property of all the French citizens who may be within his power."[1]

---

[1] Browning pp.279-280

Meanwhile, Mandeville had arrived in Paris on the evening of the 28th. It was Saturday and the next day he may not have been able to see Talleyrand who he expected to be at St Cloud. He therefore went immediately to Talleyrand's residence at Meudon, arriving there at midnight. The Foreign Minister received him, listening to how he and his colleagues at the embassy had been arrested on their journeys. This was an error by the police and marine authorities, apologised the Foreign Minister. He would report this to the First Consul the next day and was sure he would also be very sorry for what had happened. A new passport would be issued for him on Monday. Mandeville asked him about two packet boats that had been seized. They had been sent to collect the British mission and should also be considered as part of the embassy and released. Talleyrand agreed. The next day, Sunday, Mandeville received a note from Talleyrand confirming what he had said the previous evening. On Monday Mandeville collected his passport at 5 p.m. finding one for Talbot as well. He also asked for new passports for Doctor McLaurin and Reverend Hodgson. When these arrived on Wednesday, he set off and arrived in Calais on 3 June to find that Talbot and the Doctor's party were halfway to Dover. When their ship reached the English coast, it was challenged by the sound of a ship's horns, obliging the crew to run up the British flag. They were asked if they were the suite of the English ambassador. Their confirmation was re-joined by a great cheer. Mandeville followed them a few days later.[1] Left behind in France were hundreds if not thousands of English men and women, many of them remaining captive in walled French cities until 1814. Among them was Edgeworth's son Lovell, arrested on his way to Paris from Genoa.

[1] Bristow pp.119-134, Browning pp.282-284

EPILOGUE

Twelve years later, on the morning of Sunday 18 June 1815, the Emperor Napoleon surveyed the British army and its allies positioned about a mile from where he stood outside the inn of La Belle Alliance. He had been worried that Wellington would have continued his retreat towards Brussels during the night and was relieved to find him still rooted on the ridge of Mont St Jean: "There is no longer time for them to retreat. Wellington has gambled and lost. He has made his defeat certain." Napoleon was also pleased to notice that the heavy rainfall that had continued all night had stopped: "Ah! Now I've got them, those English!" He allowed himself some time to admire the enemy: "How splendidly they form. See those grey horses! What splendid horsemen! Those are fine troops but I shall cut them to pieces in half an hour." Earlier that morning he had Soult issue orders for the army to be ready to attack at 9 a.m.

The Duke of Wellington, who commanded the force facing Napoleon, had risen early that morning in the village of Waterloo. After writing some letters, he mounted his horse Copenhagen outside the Bodenghien inn, dressed in white breeches and white cravat, a dark-blue coat and a cloak. Four cockades, representing the four countries in which he held the rank of Field Marshal, adorned his cocked hat. The Duke headed south to join his troops at Mont St Jean, accompanied by a cavalcade of dignitaries and staff officers. Among them was the Spanish ambassador to the Netherlands, Major General Don Miguel de Alava, a former midshipman in the Spanish navy at Trafalgar, but now nervous with anticipation. The Duke re-assured him with the casual question: "Were you at Lady Charlotte Greville's last evening?" before confidently confiding: "The French are going to get the devil of a surprise when they see how I defend a position." The officers riding with Wellington reflected his confidence, giving one onlooker the impression that the group of horsemen were off on a fox-hunt rather than preparing for battle.

When Wellington reached the troops, they were all in motion, taking up their positions. Most of them had spent the night freezing, soaked in wet, dirty and uncomfortable clothes, waking up shivering and blue with cold, sporting beards now three days old. Officers of the Scots Greys, the cavalry regiment Napoleon had admired though his looking glass, were covered in mud and the dye of their red jackets had run over their white belts like blood. Soldiers roused themselves soon after dawn broke in a heavily clouded sky. The torrents of rain gave way to drizzling showers that gradually ceased. Troops began fetching wood and straw, lighting fires, warming and drying themselves, and if they were lucky, sipping soup and nibbling biscuits. Meat was distributed to some regiments and most troops received a ration of spirits. As infantrymen cleaned their muskets, the occasional popping sound of discharging weapons could be heard all along the line.

As his army took up their positions, ankle-deep in mud and trampling down the head-high grasses of grain, Wellington reviewed them starting with his right wing. Some nervous German troops began leaving their positions at the first sight of French divisions massing closely in front of them. Wellington tried to rally his allies, only to be shot at for his efforts. Shrugging this off, the Duke inspected the troops at the Chateau of Hougoumont to see how well they were carrying out his instructions. The Prussian officer Müffling thought this was the weakest position, but the Duke assured him the chateau had been turned into a fortress and was commanded by Macdonnell, a large Scotsman in whom he had the greatest confidence. Wellington then rode along the front to his left wing, examining the ground and instructing his senior officers, before returning to the centre. Here, near the farm of La Haye Sainte he helped himself to a cup of tea from a huge camp-kettle brewed by his green-jacketed riflemen.

By 9 a.m. the Allied army, about 68,000 men, were in place: artillery and skirmishers at the front, the infantry behind them on the reserves slopes, with the cavalry in reserve. Wellington dismounted at an Elm tree at the cross-roads behind La Haye Sainte farmhouse and looked through his telescope at the French. As he told his second-in-command, Lord Uxbridge, he had no plan, other than to hold his position until Blücher's Prussians could join him. What he did until then would depend entirely on the French.

An hour earlier, Napoleon was having breakfast on silver plate with his marshals and generals in the small room next to his bedroom in the farmhouse of Le Caillou. The table was then cleared and covered with maps. Napoleon was still optimistic: "We have ninety chances in our favour and not ten against us." His generals, who had faced Wellington in Portugal and Spain, were less positive. Soult advised him again to recall some of Grouchy's troops, who were pursuing the Prussians further to the east. Two days earlier, Napoleon had inflicted what he thought was a crushing blow against the Prussians at the battle of Ligny. Napoleon told his generals that they overrated Wellington's general-ship and the quality of the British army: "Because you have been beaten by Wellington you consider him a great general. And now I tell you that Wellington is a bad general, that the English are bad troops, and that this affair is nothing more serious than eating one's breakfast."

When General Reille arrived with the Emperor's brother Jérôme, Napoleon asked the former how he thought the day would go. Reille was just as pessimistic as the others: "In the kind of position which Wellington is so good at choosing, I regard the English infantry as impregnable because of their quiet steadiness and the superiority of their fire discipline. We shall lose half our assault force before we can get at them with the bayonet. On the other hand they are more ponderous, less flexible than we are. They may not be susceptible to frontal attack but we could beat them by manoeuvring."

Napoleon shrugged and turned away, but could not avoid hearing further disquieting comment from his own brother. Jérôme recounted a remark made by an English officer overheard by a waiter and passed onto Jérôme when he had dined at Genappe the night before. The English officer had said that the Duke of Wellington and Blucher had agreed to join forces at Mont St Jean and that the Prussians would approach from Wavre. Napoleon dismissed the story as nonsense: "After a battle like the one at Ligny, the joining up of the British and the Prussians is impossible. If my orders are carried out, we will sleep in Brussels tonight."

The only advice Napoleon was prepared to take was from his artillery expert, who persuaded him to delay his attack to wait for the ground to dry out, as it was too wet and muddy for cannon and cavalry to move. Another concern was the readiness of the soldiers, many of whom had only just reached the field. Napoleon left the farmhouse, mounted his white mare and headed for the Inn of La Belle Alliance where he started to review his troops. The drums beat and the bands played *La Marseillaise*, the *Chant du Depart* and *Veillons au salut de l'Empire*. Napoleon rode along the line of his two forward corps. A soldier deep in the ranks recalled hearing a sudden tempest of shouts of "Vive l'Empereur!" getting closer and closer. He and his comrades stood on tiptoe and craned forward to watch a cloud of generals gallop past. As they rode so fast and as so many troops hoisted their shakos on the tip of their bayonets, only the curve of the grey overcoat on Napoleon's back could be glimpsed through a fast moving forest of embroidered uniforms. The captain just had time to shout "Shoulder arms! Present arms!"

About a mile to the north the Allied troops watched and listened. A slight mist lay on the shallow valley that separated the two armies, giving the impression to a corporal in the Scots Greys that the French were further away. He could make out massive columns of infantry, squadrons of cuirassiers, red dragoons, hussars, and green lancers with swallow tail flags at end of their lances. A regiment of cuirassiers dashed at full gallop, the sun shining on their steel breastplates. As Napoleon displayed his army of 74,000 to his enemy, British soldiers might have been comforted by the fact that he had only a slight majority in men. However, half of Wellington's troops were German auxiliaries and Dutch contingents, who did not inspire confidence in their British allies. To some they were no better than "raw militia". Wellington knew that everything depended on the arrival of the Prussians. Soon after 11 a.m. a messenger reported they were close. An officer on Wellington's staff suggested Napoleon was unlikely to attack that day. "Nonsense", replied the Duke, "The columns are already forming, and I think I have discerned where the weight of the attack will be made. I shall be attacked within the hour and I shall soon want every man."

After Napoleon reviewed his troops, he told his brother Jérôme: "It is now ten o'clock. I am going to sleep until eleven. I'm sure to awake, but just in case I don't, you are to call me." Napoleon went to the farm at Rossome, where he gave some further instructions before taking a rest. Seated at a table in the open air, he composed a dispatch for Marshal Grouchy: "You will direct your movements upon Wavre, so as to approach us, act in concert with us, driving before you the Prussian army which has taken route, and which may have halted at Wavre, where you must arrive as soon as possible." To the commander of his right wing, d'Erlon, he ordered that Colonel Marbot should set up positions further east beyond Fischermont – at Coutures, Mousty and Ottignies. If the Prussians were intending to join Wellington, he would at least find out before they arrived on the field.

At 11 a.m. Napoleon issued his final plans: "[...] at approximately 1 p.m, the moment the Emperor gives the order to Marshal Ney, the attack will be launched to seize the village of Mont-Saint-Jean. To this end, the 12-pounder batteries of the 1st, 2nd and 6th Corps (24 guns) will fire at the troops in Mont-Saint-Jean, and Count d'Erlon will launch the attack by taking forward the division on the left and supporting it, according to the circumstances, with the other divisions of the 1st Corps. The 2nd Corps will advance proportionately to remain level with Count d'Erlon." A pencilled note signed by Marshal Ney added: "Count d'Erlon will understand that it is on the left instead of the right that the attack will begin. Pass on the information concerning this new arrangement to General Reille." This attack on the left by Reille's troops was intended to draw troops away from Wellington's centre, where the main French assault was to take place. To the right of La Belle-Alliance, eighty guns had been dragged through the mud and massed on the forward ridge. About 11.20 a.m. the bombardment of Hougoumont commenced, initiating the last battle of the Napoleonic Wars.[1]

Waterloo secured the settlement reached by its victors and allies in Paris and Vienna. Despite the best efforts of Talleyrand, the First Treaty of Paris in 1814 and the Congress of Vienna in 1815 more than reversed the advantages France had gained from Lunéville and Amiens. In 1814, having fallen out with Napoleon, Talleyrand was instrumental in restoring the Bourbons to power. Under Napoleon's empire Talleyrand had become Prince of Benevento in 1806, but in 1807 resigned as Foreign Minister. He no longer agreed with the path Napoleon's foreign policy was taking France and as he had less influence over its direction, he worked to undermine it. In 1808 at the Congress of Erfurt, when Napoleon asked him to persuade Tsar Alexander to join France against Austria, Talleyrand did the exact opposite. He began to sell secrets to Austria and Russia and intrigued behind Napoleon's back. When Napoleon discovered that Talleyrand had been covertly discussing the issue of succession, Napoleon called him a shit in silk stockings, inviting Talleyrand's lament that such a great man should have been so badly brought up. Talleyrand continued to annoy Napoleon by opposing his Spanish policy from 1808, his harsh treatment of Austria in 1809 and the invasion of Russia in 1812.

At the Congress of Vienna, to which Talleyrand had been appointed as France's chief negotiator by Louis XVIII, he could not prevent Britain from taking the French West Indian islands of Tobago and St Lucia and the East Indian Island of Mauritius in addition to its keeping the Amiens cessions of Ceylon and Trinidad. Britain, represented by Castlereagh, also acquired the Cape from Holland, and in the Mediterranean was permitted to keep the island of Malta. Austria was allowed to keep Venice and re-acquired Lombardy. From France's ally Bavaria, Austria re-gained Salzburg and the Tyrol. France's natural frontiers were dismantled by the merging of Belgium with Holland and the transfer of Nice to the re-instated Kingdom of Piedmont, which also

---

[1] Lachouque pp.124-133, Herold pp.109-113, Pericoli pp.38-43, Naylor pp.107-122

acquired Genoa. Half of San Domingo was returned to Spain. Saxony, an ally of Napoleon, lost territory to Prussia which also acquired France's other German ally Westphalia, along with the pro-French Rhineland states. In addition, Prussia took part of Pomerania from Sweden and Posen in Poland from the Duchy of Warsaw. The rest of this unfortunate Duchy was enveloped by Russia, which was confirmed in its possession of Finland (acquired from Sweden in 1808) and Bessarabia (taken from the Ottoman Empire). In compensation for its loss of Finland and part of Pomerania, and as a reward for joining the coalition in 1813, Sweden was allowed to keep Norway.

Although the settlement at Vienna is credited with keeping Europe from a major war until 1914, it by no means resolved the tensions between liberalism, conservatism, nationalism and imperialism that prevailed before Napoleon seized power in 1799. In 1815, while he was exiled to the island of St Helena in the middle of the Atlantic Ocean, in France, the Bourbons were restored with a constitution of two parliaments similar to those in Britain. The new King Louis XVIII did not restore feudalism and respected Napoleon's laws, including the Civil Code that Bonaparte tried to introduce in 1802 which became law in 1804 and four other codes enacted between 1806 and 1810 with the help of Cambacérès.

After Waterloo, Louis' government shot some 7,000 Bonapartists and purged many others from government and military posts during a brief period known as the White Terror. Fouché, who had also fallen out with Napoleon, proved useful to Louis for this unpleasant task. Napoleon had re-appointed Fouché Minister of Police in 1804 and made him the Duke of Otranto in 1808, but dismissed him in 1810 after learning of his premature talks with the British which had upset his own peace plans. Among the victims of the White Terror was Marshal Ney who had promised to deliver Napoleon in an iron cage after his escape from Elba, only to desert to his former Emperor's side. After Waterloo Ney was arrested and shot by firing squad. Cambacérès was exiled until 1818, when he returned to France. After the Congress of Vienna, Talleyrand took a backseat in French politics until he was appointed ambassador to London in 1830. Napoleon's brother Joseph, who had been made King of Naples in 1806 and King of Spain in 1808, left Europe in 1817 for the United States, remaining there until 1832. Lucien's more difficult relationship with Napoleon had obliged him to live in southern Italy in 1804. Under pressure from Napoleon to divorce his wife, Lucien attempted to flee further from his brother's influence by sailing to the United States, but was captured by the British who kept him under house arrest in England until 1814. He rallied to Napoleon's side after the escape from Elba, but was unwelcome in France after Waterloo. Both brothers eventually settled in Italy. After 1816, Fouché's services were no longer required by Louis XVIII.

Josephine never bore Napoleon a son and was divorced by him in 1810 so that he could marry Princess Marie-Louise of Austria. Josephine was allowed to keep Malmaison where she died in 1814 soon after Napoleon's abdication in that year. Her daughter Hortense became a queen when Napoleon made his brother Louis King of Holland in 1806. The unhappy couple had three sons, the third of which would become the future Emperor Napoleon III. Like Lucien, Hortense also supported Napoleon's return from Elba, an act that obliged her to live in Switzerland when the Bourbons returned. She died there in 1837. Mademoiselle Georges' affair with Napoleon continued until 1804. She had a successful acting career and slept with Napoleon's nemesis the Duke of Wellington, whom she considered the more vigorous lover.

General Junot fought in Spain and Portugal from 1807. He and his wife Laure became the Duke and Duchess D'Abrantès. Badly wounded in Spain in 1810, Junot was still able to fight in Russia. In 1813, after increasing mental instability, he committed suicide. His widow Laure welcomed the Bourbon restoration and from 1828 became the lover of Balzac who encouraged her to write her memoirs. Despite their commercial success, she fell into poverty and died in a nursing home in 1838.

General Moreau was banished from France by Napoleon after being found guilty of involvement in a royalist conspiracy. He lived in the United States until 1812 when he returned to Europe to advise the coalition against France, only to be mortally wounded at the battle of Dresden in 1813. General Bernadotte served as a marshal under Napoleon until 1810, when he was bizarrely elected the heir presumptive to the throne of Sweden. The Swedish king's illness gave him effective control of the government and in 1813 he joined Sweden to the coalition against France. This provided the opportunity of seizing Norway from Denmark. In 1818 Bernadotte became King of Sweden and Norway, remaining in power until his death in 1844.

After the White Terror, France experienced a brief era of liberalism, the achievements of which were reversed by a series of reactionary administrations from 1821 that ended in a revolution in 1830. This brought the more moderate Duke of Orleans onto the throne. The year 1830 also saw a revolt in Belgium, securing its independence from Holland. In 1848 revolutions occurred throughout Europe, which in France brought down the Orleans monarchy and introduced the brief Second Republic. A coup in 1852 saw the return of Bonapartism with the Second Empire under Napoleon III.

Domestic politics in Britain were less violent, but no less dramatic. Soon after the war resumed in 1803, Addington's ministry faced opposition from Pitt, Grenville and Fox, eventually resulting in Pitt's return to power in 1804. After the battles of Trafalgar and Austerlitz in 1805, Pitt's ministry ended with his death in 1806. Lord Grenville assumed power and formed a "Ministry of All the Talents" including Addington as Lord Privy Seal and Fox at the Foreign Office. Fox tried to negotiate a peace with Napoleon, but found him much more difficult to deal with than expected. Fox's efforts were finally frustrated by his death at the end of 1806. Before he died, he had prepared the groundwork for a bill to abolish the slave trade that was approved by Parliament the following year. Elizabeth Fox was granted a pension and was able to remain at their beloved St Anne's Hill until her death in 1842 at the age of ninety-two. When Grenville refused to promise the King he would not pursue Catholic Emancipation, his ministry was replaced by that of Lord Portland's in 1807. Canning as Minister of War and Castlereagh at the Foreign Office initiated a more vigorous prosecution of the war against Napoleon, but the bitter personal rivalry of the two ministers contributed to Portland's downfall. Portland was succeeded by his Chancellor of Exchequer and Colonel Despard's prosecutor, Spencer Percival, in 1809. In 1810, after the death of his favourite daughter Amelia, King George III fell ill. As he descended into permanent madness, the Prince of Wales became Regent in 1811, becoming King George IV in 1820 on the death of his father.

When Spencer Percival was assassinated by a madman in 1812, Lord Hawkesbury, who had become Lord Liverpool, formed the Tory government that saw through the final defeat of Napoleon. In 1813 he appointed Lord Whitworth as Lord Lieutenant of Ireland. Whitworth ruled Ireland until 1817 and two years later visited Paris with the Duchess of Dorset before retiring to Knole Park in England in 1820. Liverpool would remain in office until 1827 and along with Addington (now Lord Sidmouth) at the Home Office, presided over a period of repression for five years after Waterloo. To protect the interests of landowners, their administration introduced the Corn Laws of 1815 which prohibited the import of cheap grains. Taxes were increased to pay off the enormous national debt. Habeas Corpus was suspended again and limits to free speech and demonstrations imposed. In Manchester in 1819, cavalry charged a crowd gathered to hear radical speakers, an event that became known as the Peterloo Massacre.

William Cobbett, after reading in 1803 a tract by Thomas Paine on government finance, turned from a reactionary Tory to a radical firebrand. In 1810 he was imprisoned for libel and on his release in 1812 published a cheaper version of his *Political Register* to reach a wider readership. In 1817 he was obliged to flee Lord Liverpool's Britain to the United States from fear of persecution for sedition. He returned to Britain in 1819 and amongst other populist causes campaigned for parliamentary reform. In 1830 he published his famous *Rural Rides*, an observation and commentary of English country life. When Parliament was reformed in 1832, he became MP for Oldham. Among the radical contributors to Cobbett's *Political Register* was William Hazlitt, who abandoned painting as a profession when he found writing more rewarding. He became a popular essayist, covering philosophy, aesthetics, theatre, poetry and politics. Subjecting politicians and artists alike to the harshest criticism, Hazlitt particularly targeted the increasingly conservative poet William Wordsworth for abandoning his youthful revolutionary ideals. Hazlitt was vehemently opposed to the war against Napoleon and was bitterly disappointed by his hero's defeat at Waterloo. Between 1828 and 1830, in response to a negative biography of Napoleon by Walter Scott, Hazlitt wrote his own book on Bonaparte.

Maria Edgeworth never married but continued to write. Her novel *Belinda* would inspire Jane Austen and may have influenced the development of the characters in Austen's own novels. During the Irish Potato Famine of 1845–52, Edgeworth supported struggling tenant farmers, but favoured those that paid their rents and shared her politics.

Another like Cobbett who became increasingly radicalised in his later years was Jeremy Bentham, whose ideas, thanks to Dumont's book, would become increasingly better known and more easily understood. Bentham, convinced that Parliament was influenced by "sinister interests", advocated greater democracy through his *Westminster Review*, founded in 1823. He died in 1832, leaving an intellectual legacy that had a profound influence on Victorian legislators and political philosophers.

After Castlereagh committed suicide, Lord Liverpool reshuffled his Cabinet in 1822, introducing a period of mild liberal legislation at the instigation of "liberal Tories" such as Canning. Liverpool resigned in 1827, handing over the reins of government to the Duke of Wellington,

The Consequences of Honour

who brought Catholic Emancipation in 1829 and by doing so divided the Tories. In 1830 King George IV died, triggering an election that increased the power of the Whigs, who formed a government led by Fox's ally, Charles Grey, now Earl Grey, and whose favourite blend of tea bears his name. Grey's government passed the Great Reform Act of 1832. Although the Act did not introduce universal suffrage, it saw the end of a system of rotten boroughs that allowed powerful aristocrats too much influence in the House of Commons. Calls for further reform would continue throughout the Victorian age, most notably by the Chartists, a successor to the working class movements of the United Britons and Corresponding Societies.

Was Napoleon responsible for the rupture at Amiens and for the wars that were named after him? The question has divided historians for two hundred years. Although most recognise that it was Britain that initiated the conflict and was in breach of the Treaty, many think this did not make it responsible. By delaying the evacuation of Malta and then issuing an ultimatum, Britain was only confronting the ambitions of Bonaparte to extend his power beyond what he already controlled when the Peace of Amiens was signed.

Napoleon's ambitions would have been partly shaped by the historical context of the long-standing rivalry between Britain and France and the French Revolutionary Wars. Some historians see the Napoleonic Wars as the last of seven conflicts between Britain and France that started in 1689 and which François Crouzet has called the second Hundred Years War. The expansionist outlook of Louis XIV was supplemented by the French Revolutionary aspiration for natural frontiers and sister republics. As well as inheriting the Revolution's disposition to impose itself on the continent, Napoleon reprised the ancien regime's colonial ambitions, resuming its challenge to Britain. These ambitions clashed with Britain's perennial goal to maintain a balance of power in Europe and protect its empire. According to Felix Markham, Britain was not prepared to accept French hegemony on the continent that would allow it access to sufficient ship-building resources to challenge Britain at sea.[1] For George Lefebvre, Britain did not extend the principle of a balance of power to the sea, because "God created the ocean for the English." Lefebvre's view is that the "conflict between Bonaparte and England was in reality a clash

---

[1] Markham pp.98-99

between two imperialisms".[1] Both Jean-Pierre Chaline and Jean Tulard emphasise the imperial rivalry as a key cause of the war. Chaline notes that despite mutually recognizing their respective strengths and weaknesses on the continent and at sea, Britain and France were not willing to allow each other the freedom to operate in their zones of influence. Tulard reminds us that the peace and its rupture not only affected Europe, but also its colonial empires, making the Revolutionary and Napoleonic conflict the first real world war.[2] Of the two imperial rivals, Cronin considers Britain the villain because peace gave her no means of curbing French power, while war provided her with continental allies.

Yet many historians insist that Napoleon's ambition surpassed traditional French expansionism – Brendan Simms regards his ambitions as "limitless"[3] – and that his personality drove France to pursue them. Paul Schroeder goes as far to call Napoleon's foreign policy a "criminal enterprise" and the man himself no better than a mercenary.[4] While Philip Dwyer thinks such language is unhelpful, he does think that Napoleon was the "primary cause of all wars fought after 1803". The fundamental flaws in Napoleon's character – an aversion to independent buffer states, treating allies as enemies, an indifference to human life, a desire for victory and conquest and a propensity for short term solutions while disregarding long-term consequences – these all made war much more likely. Dwyer believes these flaws were the result of three key character traits motivating Napoleon's "drive for glory": an idealised self-image, an unbounded imagination, and a vindictive triumphalism. The self-image of a saviour-warrior-hero obliged him to conform to an impossible ideal and constantly prove his military prowess. An unshakable belief in destiny and his own invincibility encouraged him to take risks, the outcomes of which would reinforce and perpetuate this self-image. An imagination unconstrained by realities led him to consider the wildest and riskiest of schemes, such as his invasions of Egypt and Russia. A need to vindictively subjugate and humiliate others, such as his angry outbursts to Lord

---

[1] Lefebvre p.179

[2] Jean-Pierre Chaline *Une paix non-viable?*, pp.257-264, Jean Tulard pp.273-274 (Chaline)

[3] Brendan Simms *Britain and Napoleon* in Dwyer (2001) p.189.

[4] Paul W. Schroeder, *The Transformation of European Politics, 1763-1848*, cited in Dwyer (2001) p.120

Whitworth, would always put others on their guard and lose the trust that was vital for any foreign policy that was trying to avoid war.[1]

While Dwyer's analysis suggests that Napoleon had no explicit expansionist goal, and that his aggrandizing ambitions came from unconscious processes, emerging when opportunities arose, Grainger does seem to detect more premeditation in Napoleon's behaviour in 1803 and proposes that Napoleon's next step could have been in Germany, Spain or Portugal. Evidence for these ambitions are to be found by the continued presence of French troops in Holland, the invasion of Switzerland and the expedition to India.[2]

It is clear to Grainger that the peace would never have worked while good faith was lacking from the French side. If Napoleon was serious about preserving the peace, he should have withdrawn his troops from Holland and patiently waited for the preconditions for Malta's evacuation to be satisfied. Charles Esdaile, in *Napoleon's Wars*, agrees that Napoleon could have made concessions, but adds that to have done so would have undermined his prestige, the only basis of his power. Instead, Napoleon never ceased risking war. Esdaile quotes Laure Junot who said: "Without any doubt Napoleon was set on the rupture with England. Who would think of denying it?" Rather than respect the balance of power secured by Lunéville and Amiens, Esdaile claims Napoleon continued to ruthlessly expand French influence, which destabilised the Addington government, obliging it to demand concessions from Napoleon which his pride could never concede. Napoleon could not accept any curbs on his freedom of action. The last minute efforts to avoid rupture were made either to buy time or discredit Britain. The proof that Napoleon was resigned to war by May 1803 was his sale of Louisiana.[3] Martyn Lyons also thinks Napoleon was reluctant to meet his own treaty obligations, highlighting the delayed evacuation of Holland and the "cavalier attitude" towards peace terms demonstrated by his invasion of Switzerland.[4] Pieter Geyl, in his classic 1949 review of Napoleonic commentators *Napoleon:*

---

[1] Philip G. Dwyer, *Napoleon and the Drive for Glory* in Dwyer(2001) p.118-135

[2] Grainger p.210-211

[3] Esdaile pp.150-153

[4] Lyons p.205

For and Against, considers that Napoleon's actions in discriminating against British trade, the publication of the Sébastiani article and the tone of his various protests to the British suggests he went out of his way to provoke war.[1]

One common argument that blames Napoleon for war is the idea that the survival of his regime depended on it. Tulard suggests that war served Napoleon's ends because continued peace would have encouraged the radical bourgeoisie to reclaim political rights while their business interests would be threatened by competition from a peacetime British economy.[2] Other historians suggest the necessity of war for other reasons: the demobilization of troops in peacetime would have increased the pressure of a growing population and decreased wages. Markham thinks whatever economic problems peace brought, they would not have been insurmountable. Lefebvre offers a quote by Napoleon insisting that war was "indispensable" to maintain himself in power, and Esdaile makes the point that Napoleon depended on glory and military success.

Esdaile also suggests the common perception that the Peace of Amiens was never anything but a breathing space with the implication that war would inevitably be resumed once the antagonists were suitably refreshed. That Napoleon did not consider Amiens a lasting peace himself is supported by a quote by him offered by Markham:

"Between old monarchies and a young republic the spirit of hostility must always exist. In the existing situation every treaty of peace means to me no more than a brief armistice: and I believe that while I fill my present office, my destiny is to be fighting continually."[3]

However, an alternative interpretation of this quote suggests that rather than resigning himself to war, Napoleon's point might have been that he might avoid the hostility of ancient monarchies by founding a new one. It is generally agreed that the Treaty did not really settle the underlying tensions between Britain and France. Grainger points out the conditions surrounding the evacuation of Malta were impractical and

---

[1] Geyl pp.251-254

[2] Tulard p.134

[3] Cited in Markham p.99

bound to cause trouble later, but even he allows the possibility that Napoleon was willing to give peace a chance as long as it allowed him the freedom to expand his power. Tulard notes the omissions of any reference to Belgium and insufficient terms about India while Chaline highlights the absence of any agreement on commercial relations. However, it would be wrong to see these omissions as deliberately avoided because of a belief the peace would be temporary and there is no reason to suppose such issues could not have been dealt with successfully later. Chaline reminds us that despite reservations by politicians, most people welcomed the peace with enthusiasm and optimism. The flaws in Napoleon's treaties have often been attributed to the difficulties in negotiating with Napoleon, but Tulard suggests such criticism overlooks the problems Napoleon faced in uniting a France divided by civil war with his fragile hold on power, which obliged him to rush the treaties with Austria and Russia.

In exile Napoleon made the case for his own defence:

"At Amiens I imagined in all good faith that I had settled France's destiny and my own [...] I was planning to devote myself exclusively to the administration of France, and I believe that I could have worked wonders [...] I might have achieved the moral conquest of Europe, just as I had been on the verge of accomplishing it by arms."

The sincerity of this statement is doubted by Geyl and Markham and although Vandal thinks Napoleon's genius was certainly capable of achievements in peace as well as war, he admits his character would have held him back. Nevertheless, Vandal is one of those historians who believe Napoleon's key foreign policy objective was world peace and particularly a genuine peace with England. As Napoleon was obliged to fight England instead, he sought an ally on the continent to allow him to devote resources to a maritime conflict. It was the treachery of the European powers that dragged him into a continental war. Geyl considers Vandal as simply regurgitating Napoleon's own propaganda and motivated by a "narrow nationalism". Napoleon always blamed England for the war and singled out Pitt for particular criticism. Some historians have agreed with Napoleon that England was irreconcilably hostile. Armand Lefebvre takes this view, but thinks Napoleon could have made a genuine ally out of Austria had he been more lenient at Lunéville. Only by having such an ally could Napoleon have defeated Britain. Arthur Levy also thinks the war was caused by England's unrelenting rivalry and that Napoleon's sole aim was to achieve a just and lasting peace to secure for France the "status to which she is entitled". However, Levy also considers the other European powers just as hostile and aggressive as Britain while Napoleon's treatment of them far too tolerant. He should have utterly destroyed the monarchies he defeated, rather than counting on their future allegiance.[1]

Sorel suggests that peace was impossible as long as France persisted in its claims to its natural frontiers, claims that Napoleon only inherited from the Revolution. He thinks that Britain was never really prepared to leave France in possession of Belgium, claiming that Pitt supported the peace because he expected the inevitable disappointment it would bring would restart the war once Britain had sufficient time to recuperate. Sorel insists that Napoleon was only interested in consolidating his power in Europe, not extending it. His dreams for France's future lay in trade and the colonies. His efforts to realise this is what provoked England while the other European powers were never going to let France keep her gains from the Revolution. Geyl refutes this interpretation by referring to the invasion of Switzerland and pointing out that the annexation of Piedmont was an extension outside France's natural frontiers. For Geyl, Sorel is blinded by his anti-British French nationalism and historical fatalism. Markham considers that the Treaty of Amiens is sufficient proof that Britain was prepared to accept France's natural frontiers as long as they were not extended.[2]

Michel Franchesci and Ben Weider, in their recent book *The Wars Against Napoleon: Debunking the Myth of the Napoleonic Wars*, resurrect the argument that Napoleon, faced with the implacable hostility of old Europe, bent over backwards to avoid a conflict that was beyond his powers to prevent and point out that Napoleon never declared war. In *Napoleon's Wars*, Esdaile offers no response, but seems confident readers can "judge for themselves whether its authors succeed in their self-proclaimed aim of portraying Napoleon Bonaparte as a man of peace".

As one can see from the preceding pages, the causes of the Napoleonic wars continue to be contested as fiercely as the issues that triggered them. In an Afterword to a 2010 edition of Felix Markham's *Napoleon*, Steven England recounts a ferocious debate between the French and English-speaking scholars he had invited to dinner in 2002. The

---

[1] Geyl pp.215-231

[2] Geyl pp.232-254

The Consequences of Honour

English speakers, insisting Napoleon was wholly responsible, were countered by the French experts who argued that other European leaders shared a considerable portion of the blame. Englund reflects that the passion of the contemporary protagonists seems just as strong as that expressed by their precursors two hundred years ago. It would be ironic if this difference in opinion about the responsibility of an individual for a war is the result of the same socio-economic forces that fuelled Anglo-French rivalry at the root of the original conflict.

And what is my conclusion? The reader might infer from the title of this book I am suggesting that the war was nothing more than a matter of honour. Certainly the antagonists expressed their inflexible positions as being motivated by honour and honour is a theme threading through many of the sub-plots flowing alongside the stream of diplomatic dramas. Yet, I do not see honour as an ultimate cause, but merely the emotional articulation and ethical justification of the struggle for power and security. Addington felt his tolerance towards France was threatening his honour and that of His Majesty and saw the Sébastiani article as a pretext to regain it by demanding satisfaction in terms of the evacuation of French troops from Holland and Switzerland and the right to remain in Malta. Napoleon felt he could not let Britain keep Malta without losing the respect of the French for his regime and the respect of Europe for France. Napoleon was being expected to reduce his own power and allow that of Britain's to be extended. Britain was expected to allow Napoleon to continue lording it over European territories that former treaties had supposedly rendered independent. It may have suited Napoleon's personal ambitions to retain his grip on surrounding countries, but as long as peace with the other powers of Europe remained precarious, Napoleon's policies would quite likely have been pursued by any other French leader. There is no doubt that Napoleon was ambitious for himself and France, but it is quite possible that without war these impulses could have been channelled into more peaceful pursuits, at least as far as Europe was concerned. War gave him the opportunity, which he undoubtedly saw as a right, to expand his power at the expense of others. It was his over-reaction to confrontation that ensured its escalation.

One thing I hope this narrative demonstrates, is that although historians can judge the significance of events with the benefit of hindsight, it is more difficult for contemporaries to judge things as they happen at the time. By immersing the reader into the perspectives of the protagonists, I hope that I have shown how much more complicated and uncertain their situation seems. I have tried hard to think objectively about this, but I recognise that my leaning towards Napoleon's side of the argument might be the result of the formative years of my youthful admiration. Perhaps because of this, and despite his cynical attitude to slavery and democracy, it is difficult for me to find in Napoleon the fiend that terrorised Europe for over ten years.

Bibliography

Published Documents and Speeches

ASP *American State Papers 3 March 1789–3 March 1815, vol. II.* Gales & Seaton 1832.

CCNBJ *Confidential Correspondence of Napoleon Bonaparte with his brother Joseph VoII*, D. Appleton and Company 1856.

NBCG *Napoleon Bonaparte. Correspondance Generale, Tomes III et IV.* Fayard 2006.

OPRP *Official Papers, relative to the Preliminaries of London and the Treaty of Amiens*, A.Wilson 1803.

PRCNP *Papers Relative to the commencement of negotiations for peace with France.* A. Strahan. 1800.

PRDF *Papers Relative to the Discussion with France in 1802 and 1803.* A. Strahan. 1803.

SFOX *Speeches of the Right Honourable Charles James Fox in the House of Commons*, Aylott & Co, 1853.

SPITT *Speeches of the Right Honourable William Pitt in the House of Commons, vol. IV*, Longman. 1806.

Books.

Abbot, John S.C. *History of Joseph Bonaparte.* Harper and Brothers. 1869.

Adams & Mackintosh. *The Trial of John Peltier.* Peltier 1803.

Alger, John Goldworth. *Napoleon's British Visitors and Captives 1801–1815.* Archibald Constable 1904.

Arnold, Catherine. *Bedlam. London and its Mad.* Simon & Schuster 2009.

Ashton, John. *Dawn of the 19th Century in England.* T. Fisher Unwin 1906.

Asprey, Robert. *The Rise and Fall of Napoleon Bonaparte. vol. I.* Abacus 2001.

Augustin-Thierry, Gilbert. *The Plot of the Placards.* Smith, Elder & co 1903.

Ayling, Stanley. *The Life of Charles James Fox.* John Murray 1991.

Barker, Juliet. *Wordsworth, A life.* Penguin 2001.

Beard, John R. *Toussaint L'Ouverture.* James Redpath 1863.

Belsham, William. *Memoirs of the Reign of Georg III vol. 8\History of Great Britain vol. 12.* Richard Phillips 1805.

Bentham, Jeremy. *The Collected Works of Jeremy Bentham: Correspondence vol. 7.* Clarendon Press 1988.

Bentham, Jeremy; Dumont Etienne; Hildreth Richard. *The Theory of Legislation.* Trübner & Co. 1871.

Bertrand, Pierre. *Lettres Inédites de Talleyrand à Napoleon 1800–1809*. Perrin et cie. 1889.

Blamires, Cyprian. *The French Revolution and the Creation of Benthamism.* Palgrave Macmillan 2008.

Botta, Carlo. *Italy During the Consulate and Empire of Napoleon Bonaparte.* Tower & Hogan 1829.

Bourrienne, L.A.F. *Private Memoirs of Napoleon Bonaparte vol. I.* Carey & Lea 1831.

Bowring, John. *The Works of Jeremy Bentham vol. X.* William Tait 1843.

Bristow, Amelia. *Emma de Lisau vol. II Chapter IX (pp.104-141).* T. Gardiner and Son 1828.

Browning, Oscar. *England and Napoleon in 1803 – Despatches of Lord Whitworth.* Longmans, Green and Co. 1887.

Bryant, Arthur. *The Years of Endurance 1793–1802.* Collins 1952.

Bryant, Arthur. *Years of Victory 1802–1812.* Collins 1944.

Burke, Peter. *Celebrated Naval and Military Trials.* Wm. H. Allen & Co. 1866.

Carnot, M.H. *Mémoires de Grégoire, Ancien Evêque de Blois.* E. Legrand et Descauriet 1837.

Chaline, Nadine-Josette (Ed). *La Paix d'Amiens.* Encrage 2005.

Chandler, David G. *The Campaigns of Napoleon.* Weidendfeld & Nicolson 1978.

Cheramy, Paul (Ed). *Memoirs of Mademoiselle George.* Eveleigh Nash 1909

Churton, Edward. *Life of Prince Talleyrand. vol. III.* Schulze & Co. 1836.

Cobbett, William. *Annual Register. vol. III. January to June 1803.* Cox and Baylis. 1803.

Cobbett, William. *Crisis of the Sugar Colonies.* J. Hatchard 1802

Cobbett, William. *Letters to Addington.* 1802.

Cobbett, William. *Annual Register for the Year 1802.* R. Wilks. 1803

Cochin, Augustin. *The Results of Emancipation.* Walker, Wise and Company 1863

Constant. *Memoirs of Constant vol. I.* The Century Co, 1907.

Cookson, J.E. *The Friends of Peace. Anti-War Liberalism in England 1793–1815.* Cambridge University Press 1982.

Coquelle, P. *Napoleon and England.* George Bell and Sons 1904.

Cronin, Vincent. *Napoleon.* Pelican 1976.

D'Abrantes, Duchess. *Memoirs of Napoleon vol. I.* Richard Bentley 1836.

Davis, I.M. *The Harlot and the Statesman.* The Kensal Press 1986.

Derry, John. *W. Politics in the Age of Fox, Pitt and Liverpool. Palgrave 2001*

Du Casse, A *Histoire des Négociations Diplomatiques. Tome III* Adolph Delahays 1857

Du Casse, A. *Mémoires et Correspondence Politique et Militaire du Roi Joseph.* Perrotin. 1855.

Duff, Eamon. *Saints and Sinners. A History of the Popes.* Yale University Press. 2002.

Dwyer, Philip G. *Talleyrand.* Pearson Education 2002.

Dwyer, Philip G. (Editor) *Napoleon and Europe.* Pearson Education 2001.

Erickson, Carolly. *Josephine. A Life of the Empress.* Robson Books 2004.

Esdaile, Charles. *Napoleon's Wars.* Penguin 2008

Farrington, Joseph. *The Farrington Diary vols. I & II.* Hutchinson & Co 1923.

Fauriel, Claude Charles. *The Last Days of the Consulate.* Samson Lowe, Marston, Searle & Rivington. 1885

Fedorak, Charles John. *Henry Addington. Prime Minister, 1801–1804.* University of Akron Press 2002.

Foreman, Amanda. *Georgiana Duchess of Devonshire.* Harper Collins 1999.

Fouché, Joseph. *Memoirs. vol. I.* Charles Knight 1875

Fraser, Flora. *Venus of Empire. The Life of Pauline Bonaparte.* John Murray 2010.

Gattrell, Vic. *City of Laughter, Atlantic Books, 2007*

Geyl, Pieter. *Napoleon: For and Against.* Penguin 1976.

Gifford, C.H. *History of the Wars occasioned by the French Revolution vol. I.* W. Lewis 1817.

Grainger, John D. *The Amiens Truce.* Boydell Press 2004.

Granville, Lord Leveson-Gower. *Private Correspondence 1781–1821 vol. I.* John Murray 1916.

Gurney, Joseph; Gurney, William Brodie. *The Trial of Edward Marcus Despard.* M. Gurney 1803.

Haggard, Lieut.-Col. C.P. Andrew. *Madame de Staël Her Trials and Triumphs.* Hutchison & Co. 1922

Hague, William. *William Pitt the Younger.* Harper Collins 2004.

Hall, Henry Foljambe. *Napoleon's letters to Josephine 1796-1812.* J.M.Dent & Co 1901.

Hare, Augustus J.C. *The Life and Letters of Maria Edgeworth vol. I.* Houghton, Mifflin & Company 1895.

Hazlitt, William. *Miscellaneous Works vol. I.* Derby & Jackson 1859.

Hazlitt, William. *The Eloquence of the British Senate, vol. II.* Prior and Dunning, 1810

Hazlitt, William. *The Life of Napoleon Bonaparte.* Illustrated London Library 1852.

Herold, J. Christopher. *The Battle of Waterloo.* Cassell. 1967

Herriot, Edouard. *Madame Récamier vol I.* G.P. Putnam's Sons. 1906.

Hibbert, Christopher. *George III.* Penguin 1999.

Hibbert, Christopher. *Napoleon. His wives and women.* Harper Collins 2002.

Hortense, Queen. *Memoirs of Queen Hortense.*

Howell, Thomas Jones. *The Complete Collection of State Trials vol. XXVIII* T.C. Hansard 1820.

Hugo, Victor. *Les Miserables.* Wildside Press. 2007

Ingrams, Richard. *William Cobbett.* Harper Perennial 2006.

Itard, Jean Marc Gaspard. *An Historical Account of the Discovery and Education of a Savage Man.* Richard Phillips 1802.

Iung, T.H. *Lucien Bonaparte et ses Memoires. Tome II.* G. Charpentier 1882.

Ivison, Duncan. *Rights.* Acumen 2008.

Jackson, George. *Diaries and Letters, vol. I.* Richard Bentley and Son. 1872.

James, C.L.R. *The Black Jacobins.* Allison and Busby 1980.

Jay, Mike. *The Unfortunate Colonel Despard.* Bantam 2005.

Jennings, Lawrence C. *French Anti-Slavery. The Movement for the Abolition of Slavery in France 1802–1848.* Cambridge University Press 2000.

Jesse, John Heneage. *Memoirs of King George III.* L.C.Page 1902 (?)

Kagan, Frederick W. *The End of the Old Order.* First Da Capo 2008.

Kopans, Dana Gliserman. *The English Malady: Engendering Insanity in the Eighteenth Century.* Phd Thesis 2006 (from ProQuest).

Lane, Harlan. *The Wild boy of Aveyron.* 1976.

Lawday, David. *Napoleon's Master.* Pimlico 2007.

Leeds, C.A. *European History 1789–1914*. Macdonald & Evans 1979.

Lefebvre, George. *Napoleon From 18 Brumaire to Tilsit 1799–1807*. Routledge & Kegan Paul 1969.

Legouis, Emile. *William Wordsworth and Annette Vallon*. J.M.Dent & Sons 1922.

Lemaistre, J.G. *A Rough Sketch of Modern Paris*. J. Johnson 1803.

Liverpool. *Memoirs of the public Life and administration of the Right Honourable the Earl of Liverpool*. Saunders and Otley 1827.

Lokke, Carl Ludwig. *Secret Negotiations to Maintain the Peace of Amiens*, article in American Historical Review, vol. 49 No 1 Oct 1943.

Lyons, Martyn. *Napoleon Bonaparte and the Legacy of the French Revolution*. Palgrave 1994.

Malmesbury, Lord. *Diaries and Correspondence vol. IV*. Richard Bentley 1844.

Marbois, Barbé-. *The History of Louisiana*. Carely & Lea 1830.

Markham, Felix. *Napoleon*. Signet Classics 2010.

McLynn, Frank. *Napoleon*. Pimlico 1998

Melito, Count Miot de. *Memoirs Vol. I*. Sampson Lowe, Marston, Searle & Rivington. 1881.

Memes, John S. *Memoirs of the Empress Josephine*. Constable & Co. 1831

Méneval, Baron C.F. de. *Memoirs of Napoleon Bonaparte*. P.F. Collier & Son 1910.

Merrick, Jeffrey; Ragan, Bryant. *Homosexuality in Modern France*. Oxford University Press. 1996.

Metral, Antoine. *Histoire de l'expedition des Francais a Saint-Domingue*. Fanjat Aine 1825.

Miller, S.T. *British Political History 1784-1939*. Macdonald and Evans. 1977.

Miller, S.T. *Society and the State*. Macdonald and Evans. 1979.

Mitchell, L.G. *Charles James Fox,* Penguin 1992.

Morin, Michel. *Portlis v Bentham*. Essay for 1999 Legal Dimensions Competition.

Muhlbach, L. *The Empress Josephine*. D. Appleton and Company 1867.

Naylor, John. *Waterloo*. Pan Books 1968

Necheles, Ruth F. *The Abbé Grégoire*. Greenwood Publishing 1971.

Nemours, Colonel. *Histoire de la Captivite et de la Mort de Toussaint-Louverture*. Berger-Levrault 1929.

Ney. *Memoirs of Marshal Ney Volume II*. Published by his Family. Bull and Churton 1833.

Packenham, Thomas. *The Year of Liberty*. Abacus 2000.

Patterson, M.W. *Sir Francis Burdett and his times vol. I*. Macmillian & Co. 1931

Pellew, George. *The Life and Correspondence of the Right Hon. Henry Addington vols. I and II*. John Murray 1847.

Pocock, Tom. *The Terror before Trafalgar*. John Murray 2003.

Price, Munro. *The Perilous Crown*. Pan Macmillan 2008.

Rapp, Jean. *Memoirs of General Count Rapp*. Henry Colburn & Co. 1823.

Remacle, Count. L. *Bonaparte et les Bourbons. Relations secretes des agents de Louis XVIII a Paris sous le Consulat*. E. Plon, Nourrit et Cie 1899.

Rémusat, Madame de. *Memoirs 1802–1808*. D.Appleton and Company 1880.

Ross, Charles. *Correspondence of Charles, First Marquis of Cornwallis, vol. III*. John Murray 1859.

Rupp, Leila J. *Sapphistries: A Global History of Love between Women*. New York University Press 2009

Russell, Earl. *Life and Times of Charles James Fox, vol. III, Richard Bentley 1866*

Russell, Earl. *Memorials and Correspondence of Charles James Fox. vols III & IV.* Richard Bentley 1854, 1857.

Schama, Simon. *Citizens.* Penguin 2004

Schama, Simon. *Patriots and Liberators.* Harper Perennial 2005.

Schofield, Philip. *Bentham. A Guide for the Perplexed.* Continuum 2009.

Schofield, Philip. *Utility and Democracy. The Political Thought of Jeremy Bentham.* Oxford University Press 2009.

Simonetta & Arikha. *Napoleon and the Rebel.* Palgrave Macmillan 2011.

Sloane, W.M. *Napoleon's Plans for a Colonial System.* The American Historical Review, Vol. 4, No. 3 (Apr., 1899), pp. 439-455.

Stael-Holstein, Baroness. *Ten Year's Exile.* Collins & Co. 1821.

Stanhope, Earl. *Life of Pitt volume III, John Murray 1862*

Stuart, Andrea. *The Rose of Martinique. A Life of Napoleon's Josephine.* Grove Press 2004.

Talleyrand, Prince de. *Mémoires.* Calman Lévy. 1891.

Thiers, M.A. *The History of the Consulate and the Empire vol. I* Henry G. Bone 1850.

Thomas, Hugh. *The Slave Trade.* Picador 1997

Trotter, John Bernard. *Memoirs of the Latter Years of the Right Honourable Charles James Fox.* Samuel R. Fisher 1812.

Tulard, Jean. *Napoleon. The Myth of the Saviour.* Methuen 1985.

Villefosse, Louis de; Bouissounouse, Janine. *The Scourge of the Eagle.* Sidgwick and Jackson 1973.

Walsh, Robert. *Select Speeches of the Right Honourable William Windham.* Edward C. Biddle 1837.

Warren, Dawson. *The Journal of a British Chaplain in Paris during the Peace Negitiations of 1801–2.* Chapman & Hall. 1913.

Wells, Roger. *Insurrection.* Alan Sutton 1986.

Williams, Raymond. *Cobbett.* Oxford University Press 1983.

Windham, William. *The Windham Papers.* Herbert Jenkins Ltd. 1913

Winegarten, Renee. *Germaine de Staël & Benjamin Constant.* Yale University Press 2008.

Wraxall, Sir N.W. *Historical and Posthumous Memoirs.* H.B. Wheatley, 1884

Wu, Duncan. *William Hazlitt.* Oxford University Press 2010.

Yonge, Charles Duke. *The Life and Administration of Robert Banks, Second Earl of Liverpool.* MacMillan and Co 1868.

Yorke, Henry Redhead. *Letters from France in 1802 volumes I and II.* H.D. Symonds 1804.

Zamoyski, Adam. *Rites of Peace.* Harper Perennial 2008.

Zschokke, Henry. *The History of the Invasion of Switzerland by the French.* T.N. Longman 1803.

The Consequences of Honour

Websites.

Holmberg, Tom   http://www.napoleon-series.org/research/government/code/c_code2.html
Louverture Project http://thelouvertureproject.org/index.php?title=Main_Page

Journals

The Tourist. John Crisp 1833.

The Annual Register For the Year 1806. London 1808.

Archives

National Archives, Kew

FO 27/55	Otto and Captain George	Aug-Nov 1800
FO 27/59	Cornwallis	Oct 1801 - Feb 1802
FO 27/60	Cornwallis	Feb-Mar 1802
FO 27/61	Jackson	Nov 1801 – May 1802
FO 27/62-64	Merry	May – Nov 1802
FO 27/66	Otto, Andréossy	
FO 27/67	Whitworth	Sept 1802 – Mar 1803
FO 27/68	Whitworth	Apr-Dec 1803
PRO 30/11/266	Cornwallis	
PRO 30/11/267	Hawkesbury, Addington	

British Library, Additional Mss.

51455	Fitzpatrick	1802 Journal
51475	Fox	1802 Journal

Archive du Ministère des Affaires Etrangères, Paris. Correspondence
Politique, Angleterre. *microfiche

595	Otto	Apr-Sept 1801
596 (11773)*	Otto	Sept 1801 – Sept 1802
597	Otto	Sept 1801 – Sept 1802
598 (11774)*	Joseph Bonaparte	Sept 1801 – Jan 1802
599 (11774)*	Joseph Bonaparte	Jan – Jul 1802
600	Otto, Andréossy	Sept 1802 – Sept 1803

Notes on Sources

The point of this book is to relate the story of how the Napoleonic wars began. There is no attempt to provide an analysis of its causes, or pinpoint the blame on one side or the other. This issue remains an area of fierce debate among historians of which an overview is offered in the epilogue. I am not lacking any curiosity about this and have my own ideas, but have tried to keep my opinions out of the narrative. This is of course an impossible task, because my opinion will be implicit in the facts I chose to mention and the sources I use to provide them.

In the interest of objectivity, I think it is important to expose my thoughts on Napoleon and his wars, and say something about the sources I use. I don't do this because I think my views are particularly important, but because I think the reader deserves to know a little bit about the opinions of the person presenting them with facts, especially as I am not a recognised expert on the subject. I will be brief about my views, as my intention here is not to justify them, but to make the reader more conscious of them, so that they may take them into account when reading the narrative and guard against any bias that I have allowed to creep in.

Napoleon has fascinated me since I was a teenager. I am embarrassed to confess that I initially saw him as a heroic role model rather than an anti-democratic dictator. I denied that he was a warmonger and blamed the Napoleonic Wars entirely on the oligarchs of Great Britain and the absolute monarchs of Europe. It was only when I read *The Black Jacobins*, that I acknowledged his darker side. So as I read more, my views of Napoleon and the causes of the Napoleonic Wars changed, becoming less firm and more ambivalent.

Napoleon was certainly ambitious and ruthless, but it is not clear to me how far this ruthlessness extended. He was prepared to sacrifice others for what he considered to be for the benefit of France and even to satisfy his personal ambition in so far as he thought that coincided with the interests of state. He did not lack sympathy, but was prepared to ignore his conscience if greater issues were at stake. He undoubtedly enjoyed the thrill of war and the pride of conquest, but it is doubtful that he let these motives determine his political decisions. These may have been swayed more by a quick temper, fostered by an enormous ego that fortune had coddled, although he could never have had such good luck without taking the boldest of risks. His sense of destiny and enormous self-confidence indulged his belief that the interests of France were entwined with those of his own. Despite realising he had tremendous flaws of character, and some reactionary political opinions, I find it difficult to dislike Napoleon in the same way I dislike Hitler or Stalin.

As far as the rupture of Amiens is concerned, Napoleon shares responsibility with the British. I am inclined to think the latter are more culpable, simply because they brought issues to a head that were actually quite weak grounds for war and refused to consider Napoleon's last-minute compromises. They certainly had grounds to mistrust him and fear his swelling power-base, but he was justified in holding the same sentiments about them in return. I also find it difficult to believe that Napoleon wanted war, mainly because I do not see any specific political goal that would have been satisfied by one. It is quite possible, given Napoleon's colonial ambitions, tensions between Britain and France would have eventually been tested, but this would have not necessarily been Napoleon's fault any more than Britain's. Once the war started, Napoleon can certainly be blamed more for escalating it by occupying northern Germany and expecting Europe to close its ports to British trade, but the reactionary hostility of the major European powers is not to be discounted in aggravating this tension. The extension of the French Empire on the continent at their expense was not part of any pre-meditated plan to conquer Europe, but the piece-meal fruits of a chain of victories and a predisposition in Napoleon's character to punish harshly those who crossed him.

As for the sources, much of the information for the key diplomatic events is provided by the correspondence of foreign ministers, conference delegates and ambassadors (Hawkesbury, Talleyrand, Cornwallis, Joseph Bonaparte, and Lord Whitworth). These dispatches are probably the most reliable of sources and I do not see any need to comment further on these.

The most controversial sources are memoirs about Napoleon and it is important for the reader to consider how long after the events described they were written, the context in which they were published and the attitude of the writer. For example, Laure Junot published her memoirs in 1835, over thirty years since the events she writes of. In 1835 the Bourbons ruled France and were keen to suppress positive memories of Bonaparte. Laure, who was eventually exiled from Paris by Napoleon and welcomed the restoration of the monarchy, was able to oblige, by portraying Bonaparte's personal character in an unflattering light. Vincent Cronin, in his biography of Napoleon, considered Laure's memoirs as "more fantasy than fact", written by an opium addict that would do anything for money. He thought that her descriptions of long intimate conversations with Napoleon were ridiculous because he was unlikely to have been so forthright, even with a man, but especially with a woman. Of course Cronin's insistence of Napoleon's reserve itself must depend on the testimony of others. Cronin also claims that the publication of her "lurid" private journals in 1927 reduces her credibility further, but it is not clear to me why their luridity should do so, while the fact that she kept a journal actually suggests her memoirs were not entirely based on old unreliable memories. There is certainly a lot of hearsay gossip in Laure's memoirs, but I do not feel there is any good reason to dismiss her accounts of private conversations with Napoleon as mere fantasy. Having said this, it is important that the reader is aware of opinions like Cronin's. Other historians who are wary of her include Markham, who regards her as "lively but unreliable".

Another key memoir I rely on is Lucien Bonaparte's. The French historian Tulard says this should be "consulted with caution". His memoirs were published by Theodore Iung in 1883, who candidly confessed his aim to demonstrate that Lucien was an "enemy of truth, like his brothers". However, in their recent biography of Lucien, *Napoleon and the Rebel*, Simonetta and Arikha point out that Iung had left out half of Lucien's material, which they discovered in the archives of the French Ministry of Foreign Affairs plus some fragments of his memoirs among the archives of his heirs, the Faina family of Milan. They noticed that Lucien used a form of shorthand to write down his recollections of conversations with his brother. Simonetta and Arikha consider these dialogues as important regardless of their veracity because of their precious fly-on-the-wall quality. They were also prepared to give Lucien the benefit of the doubt, unless they had positive proof of his inaccuracy, an approach I see no reason to dispute.

Hortense wrote her memoirs between 1816 and 1820 to counter inaccurate memoirs hostile to Napoleon and Cronin considers them reliable. Cronin also thinks Joseph's memoirs are "trustworthy", but Tulard calls them "unreliable" and "occasionally inaccurate". Bourrienne was Napoleon's private secretary for the early consulate until he was dismissed for embezzlement. Bourrienne employed a ghost-writer to write his memoirs and was encouraged to publish them to pay off his debts. When they were published in 1829, Comte Boulay de La Meurthe felt obliged to address its errors with a 720-page book. Bourrienne's memoirs are considered "unreliable" by both Cronin and Markham, of "dubious accuracy" by Chandler, but providing "useful information" by Tulard "despite his prejudice".

Napoleon's valet Constant's memoirs were also ghost-written. Chandler calls them "suspect", Markham "unreliable", and Tulard wonders to what extent the publishers had embellished them. One incident Constant describes that I use in my book is Napoleon's crashing of the coach. Constant is actually relating the story second-hand from Caesar, the often drunk coachman, and in his memoirs dates the incident to after Napoleon's trip to Antwerp. The dating is wrong because the incident is referred to as happening in May 1803 by Whitworth's dispatches. However, as most of the details of Whitworth's account match Constant's, I feel no reason to dismiss the additional details supplied by the valet with the proviso that there may be some exaggeration in the story-telling. However, Méneval in his mémoires, which are considered reliable, recalls that it was Hortense and not Cambacérès in the coach with Napoleon and Josephine, so it is possible I bet on the wrong horse in my reconstruction.

Fouché's memoirs, compiled from his notes and papers, are considered by Tulard as "very suspect". Claire de Remusat, Josephine's lady-in-waiting, was (according to Cronin) encouraged by Talleyrand to write her memoirs to avoid any suspicion of Bonapartism after the Bourbon restoration. Cronin and Markham consider her "unreliable". Talleyrand's memoirs were ostensibly written between 1811 and 1816 to find favour with a post-Napoleonic France, but not published until 1891 and it is unclear how much this publication is grounded on the original manuscript by Talleyrand, most of which has disappeared. According to Cronin, a portion that was later found differs considerably to the published version. Tulard considers these memoirs as "very suspect".

To add minor details to Whitworth's time in Paris and the plight of arrested English travellers, I use a letter from Mrs McLaurin published in the novel *Emma de Lisau* by Amelia Bristow. This letter does not form part of the novel and is declared to be a genuine account. As there was a Dr and Mrs McLaurin attached to Whitworth's embassy, I see no reason to doubt this.

Index